Allied
HEALTH
Services

Avoiding Crises

Committee to
Study the Role of Allied Health Personnel

INSTITUTE OF MEDICINE

NATIONAL ACADEMY PRESS
Washington, D.C.   1989

NATIONAL ACADEMY PRESS • 2101 Constitution Avenue, NW • Washington, DC 20418

NOTICE: The project that is the subject of this report was approved by the Governing Board of the National Research Council, whose members are drawn from the councils of the National Academy of Sciences, the National Academy of Engineering, and the Institute of Medicine. The members of the committee responsible for the report were chosen for their special competencies and with regard for appropriate balance.

This report has been reviewed by a group other than the authors according to procedures approved by a Report Review Committee consisting of members of the National Academy of Sciences, the National Academy of Engineering, and the Institute of Medicine.

The Institute of Medicine was chartered in 1970 by the National Academy of Sciences to enlist distinguished members of the appropriate professions in the examination of policy matters pertaining to the health of the public. In this, the Institute acts under both the Academy's 1863 congressional charter responsibility to be an advisor to the federal government and its own initiative in identifying issues of medical care, research, and education.

This project was supported by the Health Resources and Services Administration, HRSA Contract No. 240-86-0066.

Library of Congress Cataloging-in-Publication Data
Allied health services: avoiding crises / Committee to Study the Role
    of Allied Health Personnel, Institute of Medicine.
        p.   cm.
    Bibliography: p.
    Includes index.
    ISBN 0-309-03929-0. —ISBN 0-309-03896-0 (pbk.)
        1. Medical policy—United States. 2. Allied health personnel—
    Government policy—United States. 3. Paramedical education—
    Government policy—United States. I. Institute of Medicine
    (U.S.). Committee to Study the Role of Allied Health Personnel.
    RA395.A3A479   1988   88-37922
    362.1'7—dc19   CIP

Printed in the United States of America

COMMITTEE TO STUDY THE ROLE OF ALLIED HEALTH PERSONNEL

WILLIAM RICHARDSON,* *Chairman*, Executive Vice President and Provost, Pennsylvania State University

JOHN E. AFFELDT,* Medical Advisor, Beverly Enterprises, Pasadena, California

STANLEY BAUM,* Professor and Chairman, Department of Radiology, Hospital of the University of Pennsylvania

FLORENCE S. CROMWELL,* Consultant in Program Development, and Editor, Occupational Therapy in Health Care, Pasadena, California

E. HARVEY ESTES,* Director, Family Medicine Division, Department of Community & Family Medicine, Duke University Medical School

GARY L. FILERMAN, President, Association of University Programs in Health Administration, Arlington, Virginia

POLLY FITZ, Professor, School of Allied Health Professions, University of Connecticut

ALGEANIA FREEMAN, Dean, School of Public and Allied Health, East Tennessee State University

SISTER ARLENE McGOWAN, Vice President for Operations, Providence Hospital, Cincinnati, Ohio

ROBERT E. PARILLA, President, Montgomery Community College

EDYTHE H. SCHOENRICH, Director, Continuing Studies, Johns Hopkins School of Public Health

C. EDWARD SCHWARTZ, Executive Director and Vice President for Medical Center Hospital of the University of Pennsylvania

FRANK SLOAN,* Chairman, Department of Economics, and Director, Health Policy Center, Vanderbilt Institute for Public Policy Studies, Vanderbilt University

PAUL M. STARNES, Assistant Superintendent, Hamilton County Department of Education, and Member, Tennessee House of Representatives, Chattanooga

REED STRINGHAM, Dean, School of Allied Health, Weber State College

MYRA STROBER, Professor of Economics, School of Education, Stanford University

RHEBA DE TORNYAY,* Professor, School of Nursing, Director, RWJ Clinical Nurse Scholars Program, University of Washington

NANCY WATTS, Professor of Physical Therapy, Massachusetts General Hospital Institute of Health Professions, Boston

---

*Member, Institute of Medicine

iii

Study Staff

KARL D. YORDY, *Director*, Division of Health Care Services
MICHAEL L. MILLMAN, *Study Director*
SUNNY G. YODER, *Associate Director*
JESSICA TOWNSEND, *Research Associate*
MARYANNE P. KEENAN, *Research Associate*
CAROL C. McKETTY, *Research Associate*
DELORES H. SUTTON, *Secretary*
WALLACE K. WATERFALL, *Editor*, Institute of Medicine

Consultants

NAOMI BOOKER
RUTH BROWN
EUGENIA CARPENTER
NURIT ERGER
HAROLD GOLDSTEIN
OLIVE M. KIMBALL
EDMUND J. McTERNAN
RICHARD MORRISON
BILL WALTON

iv

Preface

THIS REPORT IS THE RESULT of an 18-month study by the Committee to Study the Role of Allied Health Personnel of the Institute of Medicine to explore policy issues that surround the roles of allied health personnel. It was prompted by a congressional mandate contained in Public Law 99-129, the Health Professions Training Act of 1985 (Appendix A) and implemented through a contract with the Health Resources and Services Administration of the Department of Health and Human Services. The study is the first major independent examination of the diverse set of health care occupations that often fall under the umbrella term *allied health*.

STUDY BACKGROUND

Although some allied health fields such as dietetics date back to the nineteenth century, it was the federal health professions legislation of the 1960s that gave life to the concept of a collectivity now known as allied health personnel.

Despite the withdrawal of most direct federal support for allied health education in the early 1980s, allied health leaders convinced Congress that such a large part of the health care work force (estimated at from 1 to almost 4 million people) should not continue to go unmonitored and unstudied, especially when so much about the health care system is undergoing sweeping change. Some factors in this reshaping include increasing pressure from both the public and private sectors to curtail costs; the introduction of new, sophisticated health technologies; growing numbers of elderly patients; increasing attention to individuals with chronic disa-

v

bilities; and drastic developments in disease, such as the acquired immune deficiency syndrome (AIDS) epidemic.

How the health care system adapts to these pressures depends in large part on whether workers with the requisite education are available at the right place and time. Consequently, a careful assessment of future personnel needs has never been more important than it is now. Making sound policy decisions about education, regulation, and other matters that affect the demand for and supply of allied health personnel is difficult, however, in part because allied health personnel have been among the least studied elements of the health care system. In response to this deficiency, Congress in 1985 mandated this national study.

INTERPRETATION OF THE CONGRESSIONAL CHARGE

Congress posed five tasks for the study:

1. Assess the role of allied health personnel in health care delivery.

2. Identify projected needs, availability, and requirements of various types of health care delivery systems for each type of allied health personnel.

3. Investigate current practices under which each type of allied health personnel obtains licenses, credentials, and accreditation.

4. Assess changes in programs and curricula for the education of allied health personnel and in the delivery of services by such personnel that are necessary to meet the needs and requirements identified pursuant to item 2.

5. Assess the role of federal, state, and local governments, educational institutions, and health care facilities in meeting the needs and requirements identified pursuant to item 2.

These inquiries were not raised in the specific context of existing or proposed federal legislation but rather from a broader concern that a large body of health care workers had received insufficient attention in relation to their importance in future health care. In effect, Congress asked for information about this major component of the health work force to determine whether corrective action was needed, and if so, where responsibility for such action rested.

The study committee was directed to assess the role of allied health personnel in the delivery of health care. It has interpreted this charge as a request for better information about the ways in which allied health practitioners are deployed, their functions, their relationships with other health care practitioners, and the settings in which they work. In addition, the committee has interpreted the charge as a need to elucidate the various factors and forces—education and training, employer requirements, third-party payer policies, and the regulatory apparatus, to name several of importance—that shape that role.

The second item in the congressional charge, in effect, asks the committee to provide its best judgment as to whether the needed future services of allied health practitioners will be available. This task in turn raises questions about the way the allied health labor market operates and whether market adjustments can be expected to take place (for instance, salary increases, if the demand for personnel should outpace supply) before service dislocation or quality erosion occurs. Although much of the report addresses the likely future market demand for allied health workers, the committee has not overlooked the fact that there may be some important service needs that are not being met now. Long-term care is a current example of the way a lack of good jobs and reimbursement can undermine the nation's ability to supply certain basic services.

In the charge's third item, Congress requests an examination of licensure and other forms of credentialing in allied health fields. The committee believes this request expresses concern about the imbalance between the costs and inefficiencies of regulation on one hand and the need to protect consumers from poor quality care on the other. To make the desired adjustments, we need a better understanding of the current situation, the contribution of regulation to quality, and the diverse costs of regulation.

The fourth item of the congressional charge—an examination of education programs and curricula—arises from concerns about whether allied health education is now and can remain in step with the changing nature of health services. The committee also interpreted this segment of the charge to include a consideration of whether allied health education programs are likely to be able to compete for higher education resources and for students interested in pursuing technically oriented careers.

The final congressional request is for an assessment of the abilities of major legislative, educational, and health care entities to make the necessary adjustments that will ensure that allied health personnel can fulfill their potential in the health care delivery system of the future. Some of the questions for which the committee sought answers in this regard included the following: If intervention is needed, who has the final responsibility and leverage to act, and how can they know when and how to intervene?

STUDY APPROACH

To address the questions posed by Congress, the committee and study staff solicited information from a broad array of organizations, including the allied health professional associations, state regulatory agencies, and higher education coordinating bodies, and federal agencies such as the

Bureau of Health Professions and the Bureau of Labor Statistics. In addition, the committee held two workshops with invited experts and a public meeting on the regulation of allied health personnel. The first of the two workshops concerned the future demand for allied health workers; the second concerned education and the supply of workers. (Appendix B is a list of the participants at each of these meetings.) Study staff and committee members also visited health care provider institutions, including several long-term care facilities, health maintenance organizations, and a multihospital system.

The committee has not collected primary data but instead has used existing data from a variety of sources to focus on important issues. These issues were explored primarily through an examination of 10 allied health fields. Individually, these fields reflect different facets of allied health occupations; collectively, they reveal some common threads in the way all allied health fields can respond to the challenge of a changing health care system.

This study is a first step toward addressing a neglected topic in health care policy. The committee did not have the benefits of either large-scale sample surveys or an extensive body of empirical literature. Recognizing that a rich data base may not be in the immediate future for allied health, the committee has suggested strategies for enhancing existing data to improve the grounds on which decision makers act.

Allied health is an ill-defined term. Because there is no consensus about which occupations constitute allied health, and because the more comprehensive definitions encompass so many fields that study is impracticable, the committee settled on a set of fields that exclude some occupations that readers might expect to find. Among those excluded are nurses, nurse practitioners, midwives, physician assistants, pharmacists, and social workers and mental health counselors. Guiding the committee's selection of study fields was the federal health professions legislation and the need to cast light on large but relatively unstudied occupations.

MAJOR STUDY THEMES

The following report is intended for a wide audience: allied health professional organizations, administrators at educational institutions, state regulatory and licensing bodies, employers of allied health personnel, and policymakers at both the state and federal levels. Although the study's findings are most often based on national data and trends, the analysis is intended for use by all "actors" in the field who are looking to the future, including those at the local level—the college administrator considering whether to offer allied health programs, the legislator voting on a licensure law, the home care agency administrator setting salary levels for employees, and the therapist considering whether to establish an independent practice.

The reader may wish to be alert for several themes that have guided the committee in determining areas for its recommendations. These themes, which were derived from the study activities and are interwoven throughout the report, include the following:

- allied health personnel as an under-recognized but important human resource;
- the need for data and research to provide the basis for more effective use of allied health personnel;
- the need for health care and educational institutions to assist each other in adjusting to new realities in the way services will be delivered in the future;
- the fragility of some of the education programs that provide new entrants into the allied health fields;
- the importance of competitive levels of compensation in a labor market in which individuals with technical- and service-oriented skills will be at a premium; and
- the need to balance quality concerns with those of cost, flexibility, and employment opportunity in the regulatory policy arena.

ORGANIZATION OF THE REPORT

Chapter 1 introduces the subject of the study, allied health occupations, and briefly traces the evolution of 10 fields. Chapter 2 examines various data sources and discusses ways to forecast the demand for and supply of allied health personnel. Chapter 3 looks at such forces as demography, disease patterns, the structure of the health care delivery system, and women's study choices, all of which affect allied health personnel demand and supply. Chapter 4 reviews national projections of the demand for allied health workers through the year 2000 and presents the committee's assessment of that demand and its own assumptions and projections of supply.

In Chapter 5 the committee addresses the contribution of educational output to future supply. Recommendations are offered to increase the recruitment of students, including minority students, into allied health education programs and to improve the capacity of educational institutions to support such programs. Chapter 5 also discusses the levels and content of education needed to prepare practitioners for the future work force.

In presenting the employer's perspective in Chapter 6 the committee reviews some of the available options for correcting and adapting to personnel supply imbalances and charts a role for health care administrators in enhancing the size and effectiveness of the allied health work force.

Chapter 7 describes the various mechanisms of control of allied health personnel, focusing principally on the problems state legislators face in making decisions about licensure and other forms of occupational regulation. The chapter emphasizes the need for flexibility in the functions of allied health personnel. Finally, Chapter 8 takes up long-term care and the needs it poses for allied health personnel.

WILLIAM RICHARDSON
Chairman

Acknowledgments

T HE COMMITTEE GRATEFULLY acknowledges the contributions of many people and organizations who provided assistance and information to this study. Chief among the organizations are the allied health professional associations themselves. Despite apprehensions from time to time about what conclusions and recommendations the committee might produce, these organizations generously rose to the challenge of providing the information the committee requested. The committee solicited input from a wide-ranging set of allied health associations and wishes to thank each of them. Special acknowledgments, however, are in order for those associations representing the 10 fields studied in-depth, as well as the American Society of Allied Health Professions and the National Society of Allied Health Professions. The committee was also aided by Dr. Gerry Kaminski, Dean of Cincinnati Technical College, who provided us with information from the organization of two-year college allied health deans on allied health programs in community colleges.

Several government agencies provided critical assistance in the use of federal data systems. Our deepest thanks go to Ann Kahl and her staff, Sandy Gamliel, Steven Tise, and William Austin, who spent considerable time with the staff discussing the Bureau of Labor Statistics (BLS) methodology and their work on specific allied health fields. Alan Eck, also of the BLS, generously offered his expertise in the areas of supply and occupational mobility. Debra Gerald of the U.S. Department of Education was extremely helpful in providing the committee with higher education projections. Numerous individuals in the central office and facilities of the Veterans Administration were willing to describe their experiences in recruiting, retaining, and educating allied health staff. Above all, we wish to thank our sponsors, the Bureau of Health Professions, Health Resources and Services Administration. Tullio Albertini, the study project officer, and other staff members were eager to meet the committee's needs for guidance and information throughout the study.

We also wish to acknowledge a number of institutions who welcomed committee members and staff, allowing us to tour their facilities and speak to allied health personnel in the workplace. These institutions include the Sisters of Mercy Health Corporation, Harvard Community Health Plan, Rancho Los Amigos Medical Center, Beverly Manor Convalescent Hospital, On Lok Senior Health Services, Garden Sullivan Hospital, VA Medical Center Palo Alto, Durham County General Hospital, Beverly Health Care Center, Tarboro, N.C., and the Berry Hill Nursing Home.

Our thanks also go to J. Warren Perry, Alexander McMahon, and John DiBiaggio for attending committee workshops and providing advice to committee and staff.

Finally, we wish to thank all those individuals (listed in Appendix B) who participated in our public hearings and workshops.

WILLIAM RICHARDSON
Chairman

Contents

Allied
HEALTH
Services

Executive Summary

THIS REPORT IS THE RESULT of the first large, national study of the enterprise known as allied health. It identifies the major functions of allied health practitioners, a group that has been relatively unrecognized by health policymakers. A major consequence of this low profile has been that policymakers are often unaware of the impact of their decisions on allied health services.

Allied health personnel constitute a majority of the health care work force. They work in all types of care—primary, acute, tertiary, and chronic—and in all health care settings—physicians' and dentists' offices, health maintenance organizations, laboratories, freestanding facilities offering special services, ambulances, home care, and hospitals. The levels of training of allied health personnel are as varied as the care they provide and the settings in which they work. These personnel include both highly educated persons and others with only on-the-job training. They work with widely varying degrees of autonomy, dependence on technology, and regulation.

Yet there is a paucity of information about them. There is not even a consensus on what the term *allied health* means. Compared with nurses, physicians, and dentists, the allied health work force as a whole has been little studied. Prompted by a congressional mandate and funded by the Health Resources and Services Administration of the U.S. Department of Health and Human Services, this study by the Institute of Medicine was intended to answer the following questions: First, what roles do allied health workers perform and how will these roles fit into a changing health care delivery system over the next 15 years? Second, what will be the future demand for allied health personnel and how can public and private poli-

1

cymakers ensure that that demand is met? Third, should these occupations be regulated and, if so, how? Fourth, what sorts of actions should educators take to prepare allied health practitioners for the workplace of the future?

The committee's recommendations are based on what existing evidence tells about vital characteristics of the allied health labor market:

• the composition of the labor force—namely, the predominance of technically competent women with a service orientation;

• highly regulated professions and work environments;

• education programs that are unable to compete effectively with other academic programs for limited resources and sufficient numbers of students; and

• employers whose organizations are undergoing sweeping changes in their financial incentives and who must make hiring, compensation, and work force allocation decisions in the absence of good information.

Throughout the study a major challenge for the committee has been to capture the diversity of allied health occupations and at the same time devise specific yet encompassing recommendations for those who must make policy decisions that affect allied health personnel. Toward this end the committee chose to focus on 10 allied health fields. It used the following criteria in their selection: (1) each of the 10 must be large and well known; (2) collectively, they must span the spectrum of autonomy; and (3) collectively, their practitioners must work in a wide variety of health care settings.

The occupations that were selected include clinical laboratory technologists and technicians, dental hygienists, dietitians, emergency medical personnel, medical record administrators and technicians, occupational therapists, physical therapists, radiologic technologists and technicians, respiratory therapists, and speech–language pathologists and audiologists.

It is the committee's hope that this report is only the beginning of a process that will clarify the place of all allied health occupations in the health care delivery system.

ALLIED HEALTH PERSONNEL: WHO ARE THEY AND WHAT DO THEY DO?

There have been many attempts to define allied health and to categorize the occupations that should be covered by this umbrella definition. Lacking a satisfactory definition of allied health, however, efforts to classify occupations have focused on specific aspects of work and education (e.g., patient-oriented groups versus laboratory-oriented groups) or on the level of education needed. The results of these attempts have not been enthusiastically embraced by allied health practitioners. The committee chose not to join in the search for a definition. The benefits of making the term more precise are less clear than the benefits of continued evolution. The changing nature of health care makes some practices and practitioners obsolete at the same time it opens up opportunities for the formation of new groups. It is more important that pragmatism continue to prevail and that old and new groups draw what benefits they can from belonging to "allied health" than that a description of common characteristics defines the group.

Rather than define allied health, the committee thus chose to examine policy-related characteristics of occupations that help explain how the fields are variously affected by changes in the health care environment. These characteristics include the amount of autonomy in the workplace, the occupation's dependence on technology, the substitution of one level and type of personnel for another, flexibility in the location of employment, degree of regulation, and inclusion in accreditation standards for facilities.

ESTIMATING SUPPLY AND DEMAND

To respond to the congressional charge "to identify projected needs, availability, and requirements of various types of health care delivery systems for each type of allied health personnel," the committee had to resolve issues of scope and approach. Given its limited funds and time the committee concluded that its greatest contribution would be to try to clarify the future outlook for allied health personnel—which is crucial to strategic planning and policy—rather than to systematically assess the current situation.

Data Limitations

The committee's ability to fulfill its charge was severely hampered by a lack of data, the result of a relatively low interest and small investments of public resources in learning about the allied health work force. The committee had to rely on data sources that included some information about allied health, however incomplete and unreliable those sources might be. It assessed the existing data and conducted hearings, site visits, and workshops to round out its own expertise and enhance its understanding of the forces that will shape the future of allied health occupations. The committee could not make quantitative predictions of personnel shortages and surpluses because of the usual uncertainties of occupational projections and the absence of necessary data elements. Yet if employers, higher education planners, federal and state officials, and others had soundly based projections, decision making might be improved.

The federal government in its role as monitor of the nation's economic activity has a responsibility to monitor the health care work force and to inform participants in the health care labor market and public policymakers of trends and developments. The work of the Bureau of Health Professions, the Bureau of Labor Statistics, and the Center for Education Statistics is to be commended and should be built upon. To improve the data on allied health fields, **the committee recommends that the secretary of health and human services convene an interagency task force composed of representatives from the Bureau of Labor Statistics, the Center for Education Statistics, and other agencies that collect relevant data on the allied health work force. This task force should work toward increasing the amount and improving the quality of data needed to inform public policy decision makers, health care managers, unions, prospective students, and academic institutions about the allied health occupations.**

To help implement this recommendation and others that require federal action, **the committee recommends that the Department of Health and Human Services maintain an organizational focal point on allied health personnel to implement the grant programs recommended in this report, to coordinate the recommended work of the interagency data task force, and to facilitate communication among state legislative committees and the federal government.**

Factors That Affect the Demand for and Supply of Allied Health Personnel

A first step in understanding or projecting the future of the allied health occupations, either as a group or for individual fields, is to understand the ways in which certain forces operate in the environment to drive demand and supply. Early action in response to these forces can forestall the need for more radical corrections at a later date.

THE CURRENT EMPLOYMENT SITUATION

Available data did not enable the committee to develop a reliable estimate of whether the supply of practitioners in the various allied health fields was in reasonable balance with demand. However, during the course of the study, the committee was in contact with people who observe various portions of the allied health labor market. These educators and employers expressed increasing concern about the availability of students and practitioners. Educators generally reported that their graduates found jobs easily; employers, on the other hand, reported increasing difficulties in filling vacancies. There are, of course, variations among fields and localities. The committee heard reports of shortage most frequently for physical therapists. For other fields there were reports of less severe shortages or of hiring difficulties that were related to local conditions, to changes in licensure, or to a particular employer's problems. The volatility of the labor market could be easily seen: at the beginning of the study, some educators were concerned about an oversupply of clinical laboratory personnel; 18 months later concerns centered on employers' growing difficulties in hiring trained clinical laboratory personnel.

It is clear that changes in the health care system have caused and are still causing shifts in employment patterns. Prospective payment and other efforts to control hospital utilization caused initial reductions in hospital employment for some allied health fields. For other fields the rate of increase in hospital employment slowed; still others showed a substantial increase. The growth of out-of-hospital care has accelerated, creating new sites for the employment of allied health personnel. Whether in the long run these changes translate into a substantial number of additional jobs or merely a shift in the location of employment is an important question— not only for projecting allied health personnel demand but also for the way personnel are educated to practice in new settings. Moreover, allied health practitioners working in these new settings also raise issues for regulators who are concerned with the quality of care and for traditional employers who must now compete for personnel with employers who can sometimes offer more attractive salaries and working conditions.

The committee used the best data available to make assessments of how the forces that drive demand and supply will affect allied health labor markets. Its intention is to alert decision makers to the kinds and magnitudes of market adjustments that they should expect and encourage to sustain a long-term balance between allied health personnel demand and supply.

Markets eventually adjust to change. Projected imbalances in demand and supply do not necessarily mean that shortages or surpluses will occur. Rather, they signal that employers and potential employees must and probably will make adjustments. Only rarely do markets fail to accommodate changes in demand and supply. Yet there are inherent time lags and inefficiencies in the process that can be lessened by public and private interventions.

THE FUTURE EMPLOYMENT SITUATION

Barring major economic or health care financing contractions, the growth in the number of jobs for allied health workers will substantially exceed the nation's average rate of growth for all jobs. Unless some existing trends are moderated, the flow of practitioners into the work force through graduation from education programs will be, at best, stable.

For some fields, such as physical therapy, radiologic technology, medical record services, and occupational therapy, the committee foresees a need for decision makers to improve the working of the market so that severe imbalances in demand and supply may be prevented. Employers are already concerned about difficulties in hiring in some of these fields, and there are signs that health care providers are beginning to search for ways to accommodate new realities. Because some of the accommodations are expensive and difficult to accomplish, the committee is concerned that inaction may cause crises that could be avoided—health care services could be disrupted because providers of care are not available.

For some other fields, such as clinical laboratory technology and dental hygiene, there are factors that could cause instability in both demand and supply. For these fields the market is more likely to make the needed adjustments, and serious disruptions are less likely to occur. Yet, in both of these fields, there are unresolved issues concerning the level of personnel that will be allowed to perform certain jobs. The way these issues are resolved could determine whether major demand and supply imbalances will occur.

Demand and supply for speech–language pathologists, audiologists, respiratory therapists, and dietitians are expected to be sufficiently well balanced for the labor market to make smooth adjustments. The kinds of incremental adjustments that make careers attractive and the ways in which personnel are deployed appear likely to maintain a state of equilibrium over time. Nevertheless, for these and other allied health occupations, changes in a number of factors that affect the health care environment could cause disequilibrium. These factors include health care financing policies, technology change, decisions about education programs, and regulatory policies. Those concerned with respiratory therapy, for example, must closely monitor an educational capacity that has proved volatile, as well as changes in home care reimbursement policy.

Our conclusions about the future outlook for allied health personnel refer to the long term and are national in scope. For all fields, there are likely to be periods of greater and lesser imbalance between now and the year 2000, as well as local variations in demand and supply. The objective of policy is to make the process of adjustment less painful and costly. A decline in the quality of care, interruptions or reductions of service, and the curtailment of investment in new technologies and organizational forms (e.g., home or outpatient care) that might improve the efficiency of health care delivery are all possible by-products of personnel shortages. The decision to intervene in the labor market is made through the political process and reflects society's willingness—or unwillingness—to tolerate painful dislocations. In many industries, such dislocations are viewed as normal and acceptable. Yet public policy actions have demonstrated that health care is viewed differently. The committee investigated how educators, employers, regulators, and government can facilitate the smooth working of the market.

EDUCATION

The function of the education sector in determining the size and composition of the work force is clear. Unless educators, in league with employers and professional associations, are successful at fostering an interest in allied health careers among qualified prospective students, both the education programs and the allied health work force will be weakened.

Demographic studies show that the proportion of the U.S. population 18 to 23 years old has been declining since the beginning of this decade and will continue to decline through the mid-1990s. This shrinkage of the college-age population will make it increasingly difficult for allied health programs to attract qualified applicants. In addition, other attractive opportunities compete for that population's attention. This competition suggests that greater attention will have to be paid to maintaining allied health's share of the traditional pool of students and that less traditional sources of students (e.g., minorities, older persons, and career changers) should be tapped.

Academic allied health programs must overcome the perception, and to some extent, the reality, that they are excessively costly and that their faculty do not make sufficient scholarly contributions to their institutions. Modest but strategic actions by the federal government can help education programs deal with these problems and compete more effectively for academia's limited resources. The committee recommends federal actions that would provide a signal to those who carry most of the responsibility for allied health education—states, education administrators, and employers—that these programs must not be undervalued.

The problems of allied health educators can be analyzed in terms of the recruitment of students, the financing of programs, and the supply of qualified faculty.

Faced with increased competition for students, educational institutions must become creative in their approaches to recruitment. Alliances must be forged with organizations that are also interested in recruiting allied health personnel. **The committee therefore recommends that educational institutions, in close collaboration with employers and professional associations, organize for the recruitment of students. Students should be sought in less traditional applicant pools—among minorities, older students, career changers, those already employed in health care, men (for fields in which they are underrepresented), and individuals with handicapping conditions.**

One way to create access to a larger pool of students is to allow entry into education through multiple routes.

Alternative pathways to entry-level practice should be encouraged whenever feasible. State higher education coordinating authorities and

legislative committees should insist that educational institutions facilitate mobility between community college and baccalaureate programs.

The recruitment of minority students is a particular concern for several reasons: minorities represent a relatively untapped source of manpower; their representation in the population as a whole is increasing; and minority professionals are more likely to serve underserved populations.

There have been a number of attempts to recruit and retain minorities in the health professions. The lessons from successful models suggest that interventions must occur early in a student's life and continue through the academic career. The major source of support from the federal government has come from the Health Careers Opportunity Program.

The committee recommends that minority recruitment efforts begin before high school. Academic institutions must offer academic support services for the retention of students and seek to promote educational mobility. To succeed over the long term, these efforts must be made integral to the mission of educational institutions.

The committee endorses the objectives of the Health Careers Opportunity Program and believes that funding levels must be maintained at least at current levels.

Allied health programs are vulnerable to closure because they appear to lag behind other programs in contributing to the academic standing and financial health of the institution in which they are located. The committee made a number of recommendations directed toward several aspects of this problem. The overall strategy it recommends is to put allied health programs on a more equal footing with other academic programs.

To enhance the stability of allied health education, national organizations such as the American Society of Allied Health Professions should investigate models in which academic institutions have succeeded in broadening their financial base through such mechanisms as faculty practice plans, extension courses, and industry relationships. These national organizations should also hold workshops to help institutions implement the models and disseminate information.

Until credible alternative approaches are developed, the federal government and other third-party payers should maintain current reimbursement levels and mechanisms of support for clinical education.

The committee found that in some fields, shortages were inhibiting the expansion of educational capacity despite strong student and employer demand. More generally, deans believe that allied health faculty are becoming disassociated from clinical practice to the detriment of students' preparation for the workplace. This is due in part to the academic reward system, which does not place a high value on patient care. Attention to faculty skills, however, should not come at the expense of progress in solidifying the research underpinnings that guide everyday practice.

The federal government and the states should fund faculty development grants in allied health fields, especially when faculty availability and lack of clinical expertise inhibit the production of entry-level workers.

A cadre of researchers and academic leaders is needed to advance the scientific base of allied health practice. To accomplish this goal, institutions with strong research commitments should consider developing programs that identify and nurture talented individuals. The committee recommends the development of a federal research fellowship program to support these activities.

Private foundations should support centers for allied health studies and policy development. These university-based centers would provide a critical mass of researchers and resources to advance technology assessment, health services research, and human resource utilization.

Institutions offering allied health academic programs should reward and encourage faculty clinical competence. Clinical practice that sustains this competence should be made a requirement and a criterion for promotion.

HEALTH CARE INSTITUTIONS

Health care employers directly generate demand for allied health workers and indirectly affect supply by the conditions of employment they offer.

The committee reviewed the available literature to determine the sorts of activities that employers could undertake to enhance the supply of allied health workers by making a career in an allied health field more attractive to people choosing an occupation and by increasing retention rates. Few studies of allied health were found. Most of the relevant work is from nursing, where intermittent shortages have focused interest on what it takes to reduce nurse turnover. The literature makes it clear that employers are able to affect work force entrance and exit rates. Even a small increase in tenure has a significant impact on the size of the work force.

The committee recommends that employers strive to increase the supply of allied health practitioners by attracting people into allied health occupations and prolonging their attachment to their fields. Some ways to do this include increasing compensation and developing mechanisms for retention. Employers should also look to new labor pools that include men, minorities, career changers, and individuals with handicapping conditions.

Despite the reluctance of employers to raise pay in a cost-contained environment, if shortages occur, compensation will increase as administrators are compelled to try to attract new entrants into allied health professions. This increased compensation will make allied health personnel a more costly resource.

The committee found little evidence of the strategic planning and research that could help employers effectively use allied health practitioners and at the same time preserve the quality of care, working within regulatory constraints and avoiding professional resistance. Nowhere is there a substantial body of research to improve the effectiveness of allied health practitioners' activities.

Available data indicate that in many allied health occupations entry-level pay is currently competitive with other comparable occupations, but allied health salaries over the life of a career are so compressed that there is no incentive to remain in the occupation. The effective use of human resources will necessitate compensation incentives to increase tenure; it will also require that work be organized in a way that uses the greater experience of the more expensive members of the work force.

The committee recommends that health care providers and administrators seek innovative ways to channel limited allied health resources toward activities of proven benefit to consumers. Agencies such as the National Center for Health Services Research and the Health Care Financing Administration should sponsor research and technology assessment to ensure that allied health services are effective and that they are organized efficiently. Associations of employers, unions, accrediting agencies, and professional associations should assist in disseminating research findings and providing technical assistance in their implementation.

Health care managers will not succeed if they must act alone in these efforts. Educational institutions and the professional associations, which provide the basis for practitioners' goals and aspirations as well as technical knowledge and skills, must also participate. Educators, employers, and professional associations must engage in a regular exchange of ideas and experimentation.

Chief executive officers, human resource directors, and other health care administrators must develop methods for the effective utilization of the existing supply of allied health personnel. Such methods must grow cut of experimentation with new ways of organizing work efficiently and the distribution of labor among skill levels, always ensuring that the quality of care is not compromised.

Employers and educators must forge a relationship to ensure that graduates are not frustrated by unrealistic expectations about what their work will entail and employers do not ignore the need for career paths and professional stimulation. To be successful, this effort requires that employers and educators try to understand each other's concerns and constraints and the pressures exerted by a changing environment.

Health care administrators and academic administrators must engage in constructive exchanges to improve the congruence of employment and education. These exchanges, which should take place at the state and local levels, will be enhanced by the participation of educators who are also leaders of the professional associations.

To facilitate this interaction, the committee recommends that state legislatures establish special bodies whose primary purpose would be to address state and local issues in the education and employment of allied health personnel.

LICENSURE, CERTIFICATION, AND ACCREDITATION

The committee took a broad view of the charge from Congress and examined the full spectrum of allied health personnel regulation, including state licensure of individuals and health facilities, certification of individuals by private organizations, the imposition of standards by third-party payers, and voluntary accreditation of education programs.

Collectively, these regulatory measures affect the size and characteristics of the allied health work force. They affect the functioning of the labor market for allied health workers by defining who may enter the various fields, by determining who has what degree of control over health care services and dollars, and by constraining the range of staffing options available to employers. They provide identity and legitimacy to newly emerging occupations and their members.

Occupational licensure is of particular concern to the committee on several grounds. As the most restrictive type of regulation, it grants exclusive control over some health services to one type of worker. The committee concluded that licensure is costly and cumbersome and that its effectiveness in protecting the public has not been conclusively demonstrated. The efforts being made in a number of states to reform the regulatory process are encouraging, particularly the evolution of "sunrise" criteria to evaluate the need for regulating new occupations, which the committee endorses. Increasing the public's participation in the regulatory process is also a positive development. The committee recommends that states strengthen the accountability and broaden the public base of their regulatory statutes and procedures. In the near term, **the committee suggests that licensing boards draw at least half of their membership from outside the licensed occupation; members should be drawn from the public as well as from a variety of areas of expertise such as health administration, economics, consumer affairs, education, and health services research.**

Flexibility in licensure statutes should be maintained to the greatest extent possible without undue risk of harm to the public. This may mean,

for instance, allowing multiple paths to licensure or overlapping scopes of practice for some licensed occupations.

In light of concerns about the future availability of adequate numbers of allied health personnel and in light of the rapid changes in health care delivery, licensure appears to be inconsistent with the flexibility that will be needed in the years to come. The committee believes that states should try to find alternatives to licensure. Professional groups should work toward strong title certification, devoting their efforts to convincing the public and the industry of the credential's value—much as certified public accountants have done in their sphere.

The committee recommends statutory certification for fields in which the state determines there is a need for regulation because this form of regulation offers most of the benefits of licensure with fewer of its costs. Medicare and other third-party payers should accept state title certification as a prerequisite for reimbursement eligibility. Such certification can and should be based on examinations and any other eligibility criteria the states may establish.

The committee was concerned that jurisdictional struggles among health occupations over scopes of practice and over referral and supervision requirements were conducted without a body of research literature or the informed judgments of knowledgeable, disinterested parties to guide those decisions. Without such information, there is considerable risk that decisions will be made on purely political and economic grounds. It was the committee's view that the federal government should take an active part in developing the necessary evidence for use by authorities responsible for these decisions.

The Bureau of Health Professions (or other future focal points for allied health personnel in the Department of Health and Human Services) should sponsor a body with members drawn from allied health and other health professions and from the health and social science research communities to assess objectively the evidence bearing on "turf" issues. This body, in consultation with other experts and interested parties, should consider issues of risk, cost, quality, and access. It should draw on available scientific evidence and identify topics on which research is needed.

LONG-TERM CARE

The committee chose to devote special attention to long-term care for a number of reasons. The aging of the population and the need for long-term care for the elderly are major forces in future demand for allied health services. Despite broad concern about the needs of the elderly, there is no certainty that the current financing systems will enable providers to satisfy those needs. Furthermore, because long-term care requires both therapeutic and social support services, it affords an opportunity to examine the issues that surround the interaction of allied health practitioners with other professionals such as nurses, as well as with workers having relatively minimal formal education—an important group of workers on which the committee wished to focus attention.

Allied health practitioners relate differently to their clients and to other health care providers in each of the three long-term settings that were studied—nursing homes, home care, and rehabilitation facilities. In nursing homes, minimally trained nurse's aides are often the primary care givers with the most frequent patient contact. Recent congressional and Health Care Financing Administration actions to increase aide training are a step in the right direction. Yet, in the future, aides will require an even higher level of training to link them more effectively to nursing and allied health personnel in the delivery of hands-on care.

In recognition of the fact that the greatest amount of direct patient contact and care in long-term care settings and programs is provided by personnel at the aide level, the federal government and other responsible governmental agencies should require education and training to increase the knowledge and skills of these personnel. Demonstration projects should be funded to encourage joint efforts by educators and employers in creating career paths for aides.

Some types of organizations that provide long-term care, such as home health agencies and nursing homes, must coordinate a wide array of services that are needed by fragile clients with multiple disorders. If this coordination is mishandled, the result may be fragmented care, sometimes duplicative efforts, and often less than optimal use of each service. Collaborative team work by the care providers can improve the quality of care by helping team members better understand each other's roles; it also helps to ensure appropriate, coordinated care and might even reduce staff turnover by increasing each team member's involvement in the job.

Therefore, **the committee recommends that, because the problems associated with chronic illness do not fall within the boundaries of any single discipline, administrators and care coordinators in long-term care settings develop effective means to ensure that all personnel involved in patient care work closely together to meet patient needs**.

More generally, allied health workers in all long-term care settings need special preparation to care for patients with chronic illness, to understand the psychological aspects of aging, and to confront disability, death, and dying. Therefore, **the committee recommends that all allied health education and training programs include substantive content and practical clinical experience in the care of the chronically ill and aged.**

COLLABORATIVE ACTION

Taken as a whole, the committee's recommendations are designed not merely to advance the role of allied health occupations but also to preserve the ability of the health care system to confront the problems of the next decade. In drafting its recommendations the committee was cognizant that no one entity in the public or private sector now has the power or responsibility to determine whether allied health education and practice will adequately respond to the challenge of changing patterns of illness and care requirements. Ultimately, collaborative action will be required. None of the committee's recommendations is self-implementing. Each requires a principal party to convince others to join in their efforts or to accede to alterations in traditional ways of operating, whether in educating students, delivering services, or supporting professional interests.

1

What Does "Allied Health" Mean?

A COMPUTERIZED SEARCH of the nation's newspapers for October 1987 found the term *allied health* in two stories. During the same time, there were 443 references to nursing and more than 500 references to physicians. The individual fields that normally fall under the heading of allied health fared only somewhat better. Physical therapists were mentioned in 21 articles, occupational therapists in 8, dental hygienists in 7, and medical technologists in 3. The scarcity of such references reflects a lack of public awareness of what allied health practitioners do and the fact that the term means little or nothing to the public at large. Even in the health care community there is considerable confusion about which fields fall under the rubric of allied health. Many of the people who deliver allied health services or educate its practitioners have long been dissatisfied with the term. Yet this dissatisfaction has led neither to a replacement nor to a commonly accepted definition. The only consensus is a distaste for the predecessor term *paramedical.* Appendix C includes a sample list of job titles and allied health fields that might be included in the broadest definitions of allied health.

In the late 1970s, a National Commission on Allied Health Education, supported by a grant from the W. K. Kellogg Foundation to the American Society of Allied Health Professionals, tried to formulate a consensus definition. The commission's struggle with the concept is reflected in its definition, which follows a six-page discussion: ". . . all health personnel working toward the common goal of providing the best possible service in patient care and health promotion" (National Commission on Allied Health Education, 1980). This definition does not draw boundaries that exclude

15

groups of health care providers, nor does it describe commonalities of task or education that define the fields to be included. Rather, the commission chose to focus thematically on "alliances that need to be built" and "the collaborative approach to providing health services" as part of a team—an approach that has value when the overall purpose of the definition is to bind together a disparate group of practitioners.

The definition offered by the American Medical Association's Committee on Allied Health Education and Accreditation (CAHEA), a body that accredits nearly 3,000 educational programs, suggests the sensitivities involved in designating the fields that allied health comprises. CAHEA (1987) defines allied health practitioners as:

. . . a large cluster of health care related professions and personnel whose functions include assisting, facilitating, or complementing the work of physicians and other specialists in the health care system, and who choose to be identified as allied health personnel.

Definitions of allied health vary due to its changing nature and to the differing perspectives of those who attempt its definition and because certain medically related but traditionally parallel or independent occupations prefer identities independent of allied health: nursing, podiatry, pharmacy, clinical psychology, etc. Other occupations may or may not regard themselves as allied health, depending upon their varying circumstances, e.g., nutritionists, speech–language pathologists, audiologists, public health specialists, licensed practical nurses, medical research assistants, etc.

CAHEA's discussion emphasizes that there are two approaches to defining allied health: the first describes groups or characteristics of groups that fall within certain ill-defined boundaries; the second relies on excluding groups.

In its 1979 *A Report on Allied Health Personnel* (U.S. Department of Health, Education, and Welfare), the federal government adopted the latter view. It attempted to winnow out from 3.5 million health care workers those in fields that came under the federal purview of allied health. Its criteria excluded health care workers who (1) were treated separately by legislation other than the allied health authorization; (2) had general (rather than health-specific) expertise that could be applicable to other industries; and (3) performed functions that required little or no formal training in health care subject matter.

Thus, in addition to physicians, nurses, dentists, optometrists, podiatrists, pharmacists, veterinarians, and other independent health practitioners, the authors of the report excluded

- professional public health personnel;
- biomedical research personnel;
- natural and social scientists working in the health field;

- nursing auxiliaries; and
- occupations requiring no formal training (U.S. Department of Health, Education, and Welfare, 1979).

Despite the continuing debate about definition and boundaries, some groups of practitioners have come together and unequivocally call themselves allied health personnel. The federal programs that supported allied health education provided the impetus for the aggregation of such groups as occupational therapists, clinical laboratory technologists, and dental hygienists. The groups coalesced in three major spheres: (1) academic institutions under schools of allied health, to benefit from multidisciplinary interaction and educational efficiency; (2) health services settings, for reasons of personnel administration; and (3) the professional associations, to attempt to influence policy, collect information, and publish scholarly papers on issues of interest across the fields.

This coalescing is by no means complete; there are many academic programs that lie outside allied health schools, numerous health facilities that, operationally, do not recognize allied health as a useful grouping of occupational categories, and strong allied health professional associations that act independently of each other in the policy arena. Nevertheless, the reasons for the diverse groups to come together under the umbrella rubric *allied health* remain valid.

This committee chose not to engage in the search for a definition. The benefits of making the term *allied health* more precise are less clear than the benefits of continued evolution. The changing nature of health care makes some practices and practitioners obsolete at the same time it opens up opportunities to form new groups. It is more important for pragmatism to continue to prevail and for old and new groups to draw what benefits they can from belonging to *allied health* than it is to have an accurate description of common characteristics that define the group.

Lacking a satisfying definition of allied health, many groups have tried to impose order with a variety of classification schemes. They have been classified according to their departmental affiliation into such categories as dental, dietary, emergency, diagnostic, and therapeutic. One study emphasized certain features that cut across different types of work. It recommended classification according to patient, laboratory, administration, and community-oriented groupings (Bureau of Health Manpower, 1967). A poll of professional associations arrived at three "clusters" according to job function: (1) primary care workers (including medical, dental, and nursing personnel); (2) health promotion, rehabilitation, and administration personnel; (3) and test-oriented workers (National Commission on Allied Health Education, 1980). Clearly, there is no "correct" taxonomy: different classification schemes emphasize different aspects of allied health jobs and personnel. The different emphases can be used to serve different purposes. Rather than rely on a single definition or scheme throughout the study, the committee preferred to emphasize the following characteristics of allied health fields. Each paragraph highlights important policy-related characteristics and helps to explain how the fields are affected in different ways by changes in the health care environment.

1. *Level of autonomy*   Some allied health fields have a history of practice without direct supervision; others are struggling for a measure of independence. Individuals in many fields can work only as employees in supervised settings. Practitioners who can attract their own patients can reap the financial rewards of the public's interest in and willingness to pay for their services. However, independent autonomous practice is not possible unless health care payers are willing to reimburse allied health practitioners for their services and unless the practitioners are free of regulation that requires onsite supervision by a physician.

2. *Dependence on technology*   In a health care system that frequently adopts new machines or techniques, individuals who work with only one machine may lose their jobs as new technologies are developed and brought into use. Those workers who become broadly involved in one or more technologies are less vulnerable to obsolescence. Those involved with technological innovations that are coming into widespread use should benefit from a strong demand for their services.

3. *Substitutability of personnel*   Allied health occupations vary as to whether their "turf" is well marked and protected. If workers from two occupations or two levels of the same occupation can perform the same functions, the workers who are paid more or who are more specialized may be displaced. If more highly trained workers are willing to work for the same wage as those with less education, the lower level practitioner may be displaced. For employers, the ability to substitute one type or level of personnel for another may be helpful when the supply of one type of worker is limited.

4. *Flexibility in location of employment*   Those who can work in a variety of settings are less vulnerable in a job market that responds to altered financing incentives by shifting the location of care or by limiting the amount of care provided in some settings.

5. *Degree of regulation*   If a field is highly regulated (i.e., its practitioners are licensed by the state, required to register with a government agency, or their titles are protected by certification), employers are constrained from hiring anyone but workers from that field to perform a function. These workers are protected from substitution by other personnel. The supply of workers is likely to decrease if the requirements for entry into the field are raised.

6. *Inclusion in facility accreditation or certification standards*   To receive accreditation or certification, a health care facility may be required to employ

practitioners in certain fields. If so, the demand for these workers will respond to changes in the number of these facilities.

Throughout this study a major challenge for the committee was both to capture the diversity of allied health occupations and to devise specific yet encompassing recommendations for those who must make policy decisions affecting the role of allied health practitioners in the health care system. Toward this end the committee chose to focus on 10 allied health fields. It used the following criteria in selecting the fields: (1) each field should be large and well known; (2) collectively, they should span the spectrum of autonomy; and (3) collectively, they should include practitioners who work in a variety of health care settings. However, wherever it has appeared suitable for this report, the committee also chose to draw on information about other allied health occupations that was provided to it.

The fields the committee chose to focus on are clinical laboratory technology, dental hygiene, dietetic services, emergency medical services, medical record services, occupational therapy, physical therapy, radiologic technology, respiratory therapy, and speech–language pathology and audiology.

The final chapter of this report includes an examination of the role of nursing aides in long-term care. Nursing aides often are not included among categorizations of allied health personnel. They are highlighted here, however, because of the crucial role they play in patient care in many long-term care facilities, a role that makes their relationship with allied health personnel very important.

In addition, the discussion of aides in the final chapter focuses attention on some groups that are discussed less thoroughly in the remainder of the report than the committee might have preferred. These lower level practitioners, often called technicians or aides, are frequently trained on the job or educated in short vocational programs or 1-year certificate programs. Analysis of the present and future supply of allied health practitioners depends heavily on data from educational institutions that are not available for lower level personnel. Moreover, the jobs and tasks of lower level personnel generally are not clearly delineated, and even their job titles can be confusing. The committee therefore was unable to evaluate trends in demand or the forces that determine the demand for and supply of lower level practitioners.

The observations made by a commission assembled by the American Dietetic Association (ADA) (1985) to examine their profession help explain why studies of lower level personnel are difficult to conduct. During World War II, high school vocational programs, adult education programs, and hospital education programs began to train dietetic support personnel called food service supervisors. To this array of training sites were added correspondence courses developed by ADA in the late 1950s. When it became apparent that a more highly educated support person was needed, the dietetic technician position was created; these personnel were trained in food service management, nutrition care, or as generalists. The food supervisor title was subsequently changed to that of dietetic assistant. Although in 1972 ADA published program essentials for both categories and began the formal review and approval of educational programs, in the same year a study commission determined that the tasks of the two fields needed definition (American Dietetic Assocation, 1972). A decade later an attempt to determine the numbers of dietetic support personnel failed (American Dietetic Association, 1985). During that attempt, many problems were found. For example, workers identified as dietetic technicians were actually graduates of dietetic assistant or other programs. At the same time, the title dietetic assistant was deemed to be inappropriate because often these practitioners did not assist but rather managed. In 1983 their title was changed to that of dietary manager. In the same year, partly because it could no longer differentiate the roles of the two types of support personnel, ADA withdrew from the review and approval program of dietetic assistants' education. A membership association of dietetic technicians and assistant managers took over this function.

In sum, dietary support personnel are both formally and informally trained, their roles are ill-defined, and their titles are in a continually evolving state. Moreover, ADA also notes that dieticians often use support personnel for clerical rather than dietary tasks.

The committee is aware that aides, technicians, and assistants play an important, if sometimes ill-defined, role in the nation's health care system. By focusing on nursing aides in the final chapter of this report, we hope to give the reader an impression of the vital nature of their work.

This chapter briefly introduces each of the 10 allied health fields covered in the report and outlines their evolution.* It also traces the development of two fields—perfusion and cardiovascular technology—to see whether developing fields tend to follow the same general pathways as the established occupations. Appendix D offers the committee's best estimates of the number of workers currently in each of the 10 fields.

CLINICAL LABORATORY TECHNOLOGY

Clinical laboratory personnel perform a wide array of tests that are used to help physicians prevent, detect, diagnose, and treat diseases. The generalist medical technologist is the most widely recognized practitioner in

---

*The description of the allied health fields was drawn in large part from a paper prepared for the committee by Edmund T. McTernan (1987). Where appropriate, other sources are referenced. For McTernan's bibliography, see Appendix H.

this field and the one on which this report focuses, but there are many specialities within the field including blood bank technology (the preparation of blood for transfusion), cytotechnology (the study of body cells), hematology (the study of blood cells), histology (the study of human tissues), microbiology (the study of microorganisms), and clinical chemistry (the analysis of body fluids).

Practitioners fall into two broad categories: (1) baccalaureate-prepared technologists and (2) associate degree- and certificate-prepared technicians. Technologists perform complex analyses, make fine-line discriminations, and correct errors. They are able to recognize the interdependency of tests and have some knowledge of physiological conditions that could affect test results. They use this knowledge to confirm those results and develop data that aid physicians in determining the presence, extent, and, as far as possible, causes of disease (CAHEA, 1987). Technicians perform routine tests under the supervision or direction of pathologists or other physicians, scientists, or experienced medical technologists. Associate degree-prepared technicians may discriminate between similar items, correct errors by using preset strategies, and monitor quality control programs within predetermined parameters.

The first clinical laboratory in the United States was established in 1875 at the University of Michigan hospital. Soon thereafter, laboratories were established at other hospitals. Physicians specializing in pathology were responsible for these laboratories, but because the work was often routine, they soon hired nonphysician assistants. By 1900 there were approximately 100 technicians in laboratories around the country. The demand for laboratory personnel greatly increased with the expansion of the health care system during World War I. By 1920 there were 3,500 laboratory technicians in the United States, half of whom were women. A census taken 2 years later revealed that 3,035 hospitals had established clinical laboratories.

All early laboratory technicians were trained for their role by the pathologists for whom they worked. In 1922 a training program was established at the University of Minnesota. Today, a bachelor's degree with a major in medical technology, biology, or chemistry is the standard prerequisite for an entry-level job as a medical technologist. Medical technology programs (offered by colleges, universities, and hospitals) are based on considerable course work in the physical sciences and mathematics—often closely resembling the premedical curriculum—and at least 1 year of clinical training. Hospital programs are usually affiliated with universities that grant the academic degree. Technologists can also become recognized as such through a federal certifying exam. In 1972 the federal government established its own testing program to certify laboratory workers and make them eligible to provide reimbursable services in Medicare and Medicaid programs. Successful candidates are recognized for Medicare and Medicaid purposes as clinical laboratory technologists. Medical technicians may be graduates of 2-year programs in community or junior colleges or of 4-year colleges that offer associate degrees; alternatively, they may be graduates of a 1-year certificate program sponsored by a hospital or vocational school.

Five states require that medical technologists or technicians be licensed. Other states require that the practitioner register with the designated legal authority. Although professional association certification is voluntary, it is frequently a prerequisite for clinical laboratory jobs and often necessary for professional advancement. Agencies that certify personnel include the Board of Registry of the American Society of Clinical Pathologists, the American Medical Technologists, and the National Certification Agency for Medical Laboratory Personnel and the International Society of Clinical Laboratory Technologists.

Concerns over the quality of laboratory testing have surfaced recently, and during its public hearing, the committee heard a number of suggested approaches to address these concerns. One approach proposed by some leaders in the field is the introduction of licensure to ensure that laboratory personnel have received the requisite training. They also support efforts to define the scope of practice for each level of personnel. Others in the field do not believe that licensure ensures quality, nor do they wish educational credentials to be the primary tool for differentiating competencies.

According to the American Society of Clinical Pathologists (1987), there were 172,214 technologists and 37,271 technicians registered as of February 1987. The U.S. Bureau of Labor Statistics (BLS) estimates that there were approximately 239,000 jobs in 1986, of which 63 percent were in hospitals. It should be kept in mind that not all people doing work described as that of a clinical laboratory technologist or technician are certified. Individuals with expertise in a science field, as well as persons without a health-related or science-based education, are often hired and given on-the-job training to perform clinical laboratory functions. This is particularly true in settings that are not regulated by the federal government—for example, physician office laboratories.

Clinical laboratory technologists and technicians are most often women; only about 25 percent of the work force are men. The more highly trained practitioners, graduates of 4-year colleges, are a little older than the graduates of 2-year colleges. Of the group of 4-year college graduates, 37 percent are under 35 years old; 53 percent of the 2-year college graduate group fall into that age bracket (Bureau of Health Professions, 1984).

DENTAL HYGIENISTS

Dental hygienists, working under the supervision of dentists, remove stains and deposits from patients' teeth, take and develop x-ray films, apply fluoride, and make impressions of teeth for study models. They also instruct patients in oral hygiene. In states with less restrictive practice acts, dental hygienists also apply sealants to teeth, perform periodontal therapy, and administer local anesthesia. Most hygienists work in private dental offices, although other employment sites include public health agencies, school systems, hospitals, and business firms. Hygienists should not be confused with dental assistants, who work with the dentist handing instruments, preparing for procedures, and performing other tasks that assist the dentist's work.

Dentists first began expressing interest in prophylactic care as an adjunct to restorative dentistry in the mid-1800s. By the turn of the century, many had developed protocols for preventive care and were delivering it to their patients. However, these services were time-consuming for the dentist and hence costly for the patient. In 1910 the Ohio College of Dental Surgery instituted a training course for the "dental nurse and assistant." The 1-year program graduated a single class before a coalition of Ohio dentists succeeded in closing it down.

Three years later, a Connecticut dentist, Dr. Alfred Fones, convinced his local school board to fund a program to train dental hygienists who would work in the school system giving prophylactic care to children. Fones envisioned dental hygienists working in private dental offices as well, but he placed greater emphasis on the public schools.

The profession first gained legal status in Connecticut, which amended its dental practice act in 1915 to permit hygienists to practice under a dentist's supervision. The following year a court ruling in New York held that no existing New York law prevented dental hygienists from practicing. Subsequently, the American Dental Association endorsed dental hygiene legislation, and by 1951 hygienists were licensed throughout the United States.

It was not until 1947 that the American Dental Association and the American Dental Hygienists' Association developed the approved requirements for accreditation of dental hygiene programs. These requirements have been modified several times; to receive approval today, a program must have both liberal arts and science content, and didactic and clinical instruction. Most programs grant an associate degree but often require more than 2 academic years to complete. A smaller number of programs take 4 years and culminate in a baccalaureate. The dental hygiene field reflects some of the ambivalence about education seen in the nursing profession: although 4-year programs undoubtedly have more academic content and presumably prepare graduates for additional career roles, there is only one level of dental hygiene license. All licensed hygienists, regardless of the degrees they hold, are permitted to perform the same range of dental services.

Of the issues facing dental hygienists today, autonomy is the most pressing. Licensure is effectively in the hands of dentists rather than dental hygienists: in all states, hygienists are licensed by a licensing board that is composed primarily of dentists. At present, there is a strong movement within the profession to gain greater self-determination. One goal is to abolish state laws requiring that licensed hygienists work exclusively under dental supervision. In Colorado, hygienists have already won the right to practice independently, although the move has not been made without controversy. The American Dental Association filed suit against the state demanding the reinstitution of the requirement that patients be referred to hygienists only by licensed dentists. The suit was dismissed, but the association is currently appealing the decision.

Dental hygienists are generally young women: only 1 percent of the work force are men, and only 10 percent are more than 44 years old. In 1984 only 13 percent earned more than $25,000 per year (American Dental Hygienists' Association, 1987).

DIETETIC SERVICES

According to the ADA's 1972 study commission, a dietician is a "translator of the science of nutrition into the skill of furnishing optimal nutrition to people." Although all dietitians share a common interest in the science of food and its effect on the body, they work in many different roles—as administrators, educators, researchers, and clinicians. Some supervise large-scale meal planning at companies and school cafeterias; others assess the nutritional needs of hospitalized patients and implement specialized diets; still others advise individuals and groups on sound dietary practices. Dieticians are also involved in hyperalimentation and the clinical frontiers of parenteral and enteral nutrition.

The term *dietician* was first coined at the 1899 Lake Placid Conference on Home Economics, but the roots of the profession extend back two decades earlier to cooking schools in Boston, New York, and Philadelphia. One early practitioner, Sarah Tyson Rorer, held classes on nutrition for physicians and nurses before the turn of the century; she later edited a section of an American Medical Association publication called "The Dietetic Gazette."

Like many other allied health professions, dietetics expanded during World War I. In England, 40 percent of the 2.5 million men screened for military service were found to be physically unfit, most for nutritional reasons. Good nutrition and food conservation for the public and better health care for the troops, especially those who were sick and wounded, were of great concern at the time, both in the United States and in England. Biomedical advances also helped to stimulate the fledgling profession.

From its inception in 1918, ADA was active in accreditation, listing hospitals that offered reputable dietary internships. By 1927 the association had adopted a standard course for dieticians, the first of several steps toward ADA-sponsored accreditation of educational programs. In 1969 the association established a registry of dietitians. To qualify for registration today requires graduation from an accredited college or university, completion of certain course and experiential components, and passing a national registration exam. In addition, dieticians must fulfill continuing education requirements to maintain certification. The term *nutritionist*, which was previously reserved for people working in research, is gaining popularity with clinical practitioners. It has been proposed that "nutrition" be added to ADA's name, but this change has not been approved by the membership. As of the summer of 1987, ADA members continued to call themselves dietitians.

There are several issues of major concern to dieticians today. First, the profession is seeking to extend and strengthen state licensure. Currently, 14 states license dieticians, and a number of others are considering such laws. Second, because there is a slow but steady trend in the field toward private practice, dieticians are interested in obtaining third-party reimbursement for their services. Finally, ADA is exploring how the field might be divided into subfields. Like several other allied health professions, the sum total of knowledge in the field has grown to the point where specialization seems inevitable. Those dieticians who today consider themselves to be specialists have most often become so through concentrated work in specific health care settings. Thus, it is generally on-the-job training rather than formal education that makes them specialists. At present, an ADA committee is developing speciality boards and defining speciality areas.

The best estimate of the size of the dietetics work force comes from ADA which reported 44,570 active members at the end of 1987 (American Dietetic Association, 1987). BLS estimates that there were approximately 40,000 dieticians' jobs in 1986, 37 percent of which were in hospitals (Bureau of Labor Statistics, 1987).

The 1984 Study Commission on Dietetics described the "typical" ADA member as a young, college-educated white woman. According to the Commission, slightly more than 63 percent of ADA members were under 40 years old, 99 percent had a bachelor's degree, 97 percent were women, and 87 percent were white (American Dietetic Association, 1985). Little has changed since then. In 1986 fewer than 1 in 10 ADA members was a man. Eighty-six percent of technicians were white, compared with 88 percent of active dieticians. Sixty-three percent of active dietician members were under 41 years old, while technicians were a little younger (71 percent under 41). Forty percent of active dietician members have advanced degrees, and another 10 percent are working toward such degrees. For 70 percent of technicians the associate degree was the highest degree earned (Bryk, 1987).

EMERGENCY MEDICAL SERVICES

Emergency medical technicians (EMTs), formerly called ambulance attendants, care for people at the scene of emergencies and transport them to hospitals or other health care institutions. EMTs (basic, intermediate, and paramedic) determine the nature and extent of victims' medical and trauma-related emergencies and provide limited care. Depending on their level of training and on state regulations, EMTs may provide such care as opening and maintaining airways, controlling bleeding, immobilizing fractures, and administering certain drugs.

The first ambulance service was started during the Civil War in an effort to decrease mortality rates on the battlefield. By the late 1800s, several hospital-based ambulance services were operating in urban areas such as New York City and Cincinnati; smaller communities began introducing volunteer services in the mid-1940s. The main function of these early operations was transport. Ambulance personnel, who were often morticians and volunteers, were not trained in the delivery of emergency care.

Early in 1960 the U.S. Department of Health, Education, and Welfare (DHEW; now the Department of Health and Human Services) established an emergency medical services program. The program was moved to the Department of Transportation (DOT) with the passage of the Highway Safety Act in 1966, which required states that were receiving federal highway construction funds to develop emergency services or lose 10 percent of those funds. The act recommended that ambulances be equipped with specific lifesaving equipment and be managed by at least two people trained in emergency care.

A 1966 report by the National Research Council summarized practices and deficiencies of various levels of emergency care and gave specific recommendations for a national effort to improve emergency services. The report was the first to identify the need to develop the EMT as an occupational category with formal education. A common basic training course was the first step to increase the professionalism of ambulance personnel. The most widely used training course was developed by DOT in 1969. In 1970 the National Registry of EMTs was organized to unify EMT education, examinations, and certification nationally.

In September 1970, under a contract funded jointly by DHEW and DOT, the National Academy of Sciences Subcommittee on Ambulance Service developed guidelines for an advanced training program to train basic-level EMTs (known as EMT-As) to become EMT-paramedics (EMT-Ps). This development marked the beginning of the paramedic role in the EMS system. EMT-Ps are qualified to carry out advanced procedures (e.g., starting intravenous infusions, tracheal intubation, and defibrillation) under remote medical supervision.

EMTs who did not fit into either of the two previously mentioned categories—that is, those who were more advanced than EMT-As but not as highly trained as EMT-Ps—were not recognized by certification, although their numbers increased steadily. In 1980 the National Registry and DOT determined that a standardized educational program and certification of intermediate-level personnel (EMT-Is) were needed and in 1981 began testing and providing certification for these technicians. EMT-Is receive the basic EMT training and portions of the EMT-P curriculum.

Today, the 110-hour national EMT basic training course is offered by police, fire, and health departments and as a nondegree course in medical schools, colleges, and universities. Since 1982 paramedic training programs have been eligible for voluntary accreditation by CAHEA. All 50 states have some kind of certification procedure. In 24 states, registration with the National Registry is required at some or all levels of certification. Fifteen other states offer a choice of their own certification examination or the National Registry examination. All states require EMT-Ps to be certified by an agency of the state.

Career (paid) EMTs are employed by private ambulance services, hospitals, and municipal police and fire departments. Volunteer EMTs typically work for volunteer rescue squads and fire departments.

Emergency medical services continue to be dominated by volunteer personnel (although they are becoming increasingly difficult to recruit) who are not always able to devote time to attaining and maintaining the training for advanced certification. Volunteer EMTs are overwhelmingly EMT-As. The mix of levels of training varies by locality, however. In rural areas, for example, where the EMT work force typically is composed of volunteers, any EMT-Ps are likely to be volunteers. On the other hand, in many urban localities, emergency medical services are entirely staffed by career personnel.

EMT-Ps are being used increasingly in hospital emergency departments to provide emergency medical service and to supplement nursing staff. EMT-As are sometimes hired but typically perform only limited roles. In at least two states, Pennsylvania and Kansas, nursing groups have formally protested the practice of using EMTs to perform nursing functions in emergency departments. In Maryland, nursing leaders have called for the development of a job description for emergency department EMTs.

MEDICAL RECORD SERVICES

Medical record personnel develop, implement, and manage medical information systems. They are responsible for keeping track of the records of an institution's patients, compiling statistics required by federal and state agencies, and assisting the medical staff in evaluating patient care. In addition, medical record personnel work closely with the institution's finance department to monitor spending patterns. Some medical record personnel code information, evaluate record completeness and accuracy, and enter information into computers. Three out of four jobs in this field are located in hospitals; other major employment sites include health maintenance organizations (HMOs), nursing homes, and medical group practices. Insurance, accounting, and law firms that specialize in health matters also employ medical record personnel, as do companies that develop and market medical record information systems.

The first medical record administrator, Grace Whiting Meyers, was appointed by Massachusetts General Hospital in 1897 to organize the patient care records that had been accumulating for 80 years. Other hospitals in the Boston area and elsewhere soon followed suit, hiring medical record personnel or librarians, as they came to be called. By 1912 a group had organized to share information and ideas. Four years later the group adopted a name—the Club of Record Clerks. Over the next 50 years, the club evolved into a national organization now known as the American Medical Record Association (AMRA).

The American Association of Medical Record Librarians, AMRA's precursor, did not establish official standards for training programs until 1934. In 1942, at the group's request, the American Medical Association assumed the responsibility of approving educational programs for medical record personnel. Yet the number of approved schools grew slowly. To increase the pool of qualified persons in the field and provide recognition to those workers who could not qualify as registered librarians, standards were promulgated in 1953 for programs to train a lower level worker, the medical record technician.

At first, most training programs for both librarians and technicians were based in hospitals. But by the 1960s the field's leaders were convinced that professional record librarians needed a broad liberal arts education. By 1970 all approved programs for medical record librarians granted a bachelor's degree and were based in colleges and universities. Technician programs were also shifted: today, medical record technicians generally hold an associate degree from a junior college.

As health care institutions have grown in size, the role of a medical record librarian has evolved from that of a clerk to that of an information systems manager. Today, the head of a medical record team often organizes a large-scale information service, trains and supervises staff, and devises means of evaluating patient care. Reflecting this shift in responsibilities, the medical record librarian title was changed in 1970 to medical record administrator. Medical record education programs have gradually adopted course work in areas such as business management and data processing. In addition, administrators may now specialize in subfields that include quality assurance, information management, computerization of information, and tumor registry. To become a registered medical record administrator, candidates must have graduated from an accredited baccalaureate program and pass a registry examination.

Because registration in this field is voluntary and because medical record departments use on-the-job trained personnel for some lower level jobs, it is hard to determine the size and composition of the current medical record work force. In 1987 AMRA reported 8,240 registered medical record administrators and 14,690 accredited record technicians. BLS estimated that there were nearly 40,000 technician jobs existed in 1986. AMRA estimates that 98 percent of its membership are women, and approximately 95 percent are white (R. Finnegan, American Medical Association, personal communication, 1987).

OCCUPATIONAL THERAPY

Occupational therapists direct their patients in activities that are designed to help them learn the skills necessary to perform daily tasks, diminish or correct pathology, and promote and maintain health. Therapists work in many different settings including rehabilitative and psychiatric hospitals, school systems, nursing homes, and home health agencies. The nature of their work varies according to the setting. Therapists working in mental hospitals, for instance, typically provide activities that help mentally ill and retarded people learn to cope with daily stresses and manage their work and leisure time more efficiently. In rehabilitative hospitals, therapists may orient patients to the use of equipment (e.g., wheelchairs and splints) or custom-design special equipment; they may also recommend changes in patients' work or home environments to facilitate their functioning. Because the field is so extensive, occupational therapists tend to work with specific age groups or disabilities. The profession can be most readily divided into those who work with mentally disabled people and those who work with physically disabled people. Three out of five therapists work with people with physical disabilities—some work only with the elderly, whereas others work exclusively with children.

The roots of occupational therapy (OT) go back at least 200 years to French physician Philippe Pinel, who found that mental patients given menial tasks to perform improved more quickly than those patients who were idle. In the United States at the end of the eighteenth century, physician Benjamin Rush also advocated work as a treatment for his mentally ill patients at Philadelphia's Pennsylvania Hospital. In 1906 the first training course for occupational therapists was established in Boston.

World War I spurred the growth of OT and expanded its scope of practice to include physical as well as mental rehabilitation. Initially, four OT reconstruction aides were recruited for service in European-based American army hospitals. In 1917, it was decided that 200 others were needed to "furnish forms of occupations to convalescents in long illnesses and to give the patients the therapeutic benefit of activity." Three crash programs were subsequently established that by 1921 had trained hundreds of OT aides.

The National Society for the Promotion of Occupational Therapy was established in 1917; the association changed its name 3 years later to the American Occupational Therapy Association (AOTA), the name it bears today. In 1923, the field received a major boost when the Federal Industrial Rehabilitation Act required that every general hospital treating victims of industrial accidents provide occupational therapy. In addition, during that year, AOTA first established minimum standards for training programs: these called for a 12-month professional training program open to high school graduates. Ten years later, AOTA and the American Medical Association began collaborating on accreditation for OT programs.

Since then, the field's body of knowledge has expanded considerably, and educational requirements have been strengthened. Today, there are two levels of education in the field—technical and professional—and there is no upward mobility through experience alone. Occupational therapy education programs receive accreditation through CAHEA. Technical education programs grant an associate degree and prepare individuals for certification as an occupational therapy assistant (COTA). Professional programs are offered at three levels—baccalaureate, postbaccalaureate certificate, and master's degree—and prepare a person to become credentialed as a registered occupational therapist (OTR). In addition to such training, occupational therapists now specialize in one of several subfields: gerontology, developmental disabilities, training in activities of daily living, prosthetics training and construction of splints, and the rehabilitation of people with spinal cord injuries and neurological disorders.

As of 1987, 34 states plus the District of Columbia and Puerto Rico had OT licensure laws. All of the laws specify that the AOTA certification exam be used as the licensing exam. Licensure also requires a degree or certificate from an accredited educational program.

Although the roots of occupational and physical therapy are similar, autonomy for occupational therapists has been slower to develop than autonomy for physical therapists. Reimbursement for OT inpatient services is covered by third-party payers; until recent changes in Medicare, reimbursement for outpatient and in-home services has been more erratic. Still, a growing number of therapists are in private practice. Some work in consulting firms or multispeciality group practices, while others are solo practitioners. Typically, their patients are referred by physicians or other health professionals.

To leaders in the field, a major concern continues to be OT's difficulty in meeting the demand for qualified practitioners. Demand has grown considerably over the past several decades, but experts also attribute the shortage of practitioners to the profession's failure to attract sufficient numbers of students. One recruitment impediment may be the unwillingness of many people to make their careers in psychiatric settings. In addition, laymen often confuse OT with physical therapy (PT), and the more visible and autonomous PT may be more attractive to potential students.

The best estimate of the size of the occupational therapy work force is AOTA's list of registered active members, who numbered 27,300 at the end of 1987. Occupational therapists are most often women (95 percent) with a median age of 32. Most work full time (70 percent), and 20 percent are self-employed. Twelve percent have master's degrees (a bachelor's degree is the minimum educational requirement). The mean income reported in 1986 was approximately $26,500 (AOTA, 1986).

In 1986 AOTA also counted 7,909 COTAs (certified occupational therapy assistants) among its members. Their characteristics in some ways were similar to those of the therapists. Their median age and the proportions that were women and worked full time were almost identical to those of the therapists. However, their education and earnings differed. Among the COTAs, 74 percent had associate degrees, and 29 percent had diplomas or certificates; their average earnings were $16,182 (AOTA, 1986).

PHYSICAL THERAPY

Physical therapists plan and administer treatment to relieve pain, improve functional mobility, maintain cardiopulmonary functioning, and limit the disability of people suffering from a disabling injury or disease. Therapeutic activities include exercises for improving endurance, strength, coordination, and range of motion; electrical stimulation to activate paralyzed muscles; instruction in the use of aids such as crutches or canes; and massage and electrotherapy to alleviate pain and promote healing in soft tissues.

Physical therapists work in a variety of employment settings. In 1986 one-third of the available jobs were in hospitals. Other major employers include rehabilitation facilities, home health agencies, nursing homes, HMOs, school systems, and clinics. In addition, almost 20 percent of physical therapists are in private practice. Some work alone or in a group practice; others provide care on a contract basis to an institution (e.g., a hospital or nursing home).

Modern physical therapy was born during World War I when the country was suddenly faced with the need to rehabilitate large numbers of wounded soldiers. In 1917 the surgeon general of the army initiated an intensive, short-term program that trained 800 "reconstruction aides" (all women) in physical therapy. Reconstruction aides were civilian employees of the U.S. Army Medical Corps and typically worked in army hospitals. As soldiers were discharged after the war, the need for reconstruction aides grew in the civilian sector. In addition, the army continued to employ aides to work with hospitalized veterans.

In 1920 the American Women's Physical Therapeutic Association was formed by reconstruction aides who had served in the war. Reconstruction aides were considered charter members; membership requirements for others seeking to join the association included graduation from "recognized schools of massage and therapeutic exercise with some knowledge of either electrotherapy or hydrotherapy." By the end of 1921, the new association had 245 members. It became the current American Physical Therapy Association (APTA).

World War II brought a sudden increase in the demand for therapists to treat injured servicemen, a demand that was met largely through the rapid establishment of federally funded, accelerated programs to prepare college graduates from fields such as physical education for practice as therapists. These accelerated programs were often operated in parallel with existing 4-year university degree or certificate programs. They were discontinued at the end of the war, but the many graduates they supplied were generally regarded as highly competent, and this temporary system provided impressive evidence of the ability of educational programs to respond to a sudden change in demand for personnel. During the 1940s and early 1950s a series of severe poliomyelitis epidemics created another rapid rise in demand for therapists. This time, however, both demand and supply were strongly influenced by the private sector. Massive donations to the National Foundation for Infantile Paralysis (the March of Dimes) were used to employ therapists, set up treatment centers, and subsidize therapy for a large number of patients. Concurrently, the foundation invested heavily in the education of therapists by (1) underwriting salaries for many new faculty positions to permit existing schools to expand enrollments, (2) funding an intensive student recruitment and scholarship program that drew many new people into the field, and (3) supporting the development of graduate programs for faculty training.

The dramatic reduction in the number of new polio patients following development of the Salk and Sabin vaccines in the early 1950s had only a brief dampening effect on the demand for physical therapists. Growing interest in the vocational rehabilitation of young adults and the expansion of rehabilitation services to previously underserved groups of patients with a wide variety of movement disorders soon absorbed the personnel previously needed for the care of acute polio patients.

Today, all states require that practicing physical therapists be licensed, and applicants must hold a degree from an APTA-accredited program prior to taking the licensing exam. (APTA directly accredits educational programs independent of CAHEA.) Since 1960 there have been three educational avenues to entry-level jobs as physical therapists: (1) baccalaureate programs, (2) certificate programs for people who already hold a bachelor's degree in another field, and (3) 2-year master's programs. In 1979 APTA announced its intention to elevate the entry-level requirement for the field to a master's degree—a mandate that encountered vigorous opposition, especially from the American Hospital Association, deans of allied health programs, and certain higher education associations. As a result, the mandate has been softened to encourage rather than require a general movement toward the master's degree as the entry-level credential.

In 1967 an assistant-level position was created so that physical therapists could delegate more routine tasks and treat greater numbers of patients. Currently, there are approximately 17,000 practicing physical therapy assistants.

Physical therapists have more autonomy than most allied health practitioners. Many are in private practice, and some states allow patients direct access to physical therapy services, which eases the way into independent practice for therapists. Thirty-eight states now permit physical therapists to evaluate patients without medical referral; 11 of these states also permit the treatment of patients so evaluated. Legislation on direct access is pending in about a dozen other states.

As the scope of practice in physical therapy has expanded to include services as diverse as pulmonary therapy for critically ill patients in intensive care units, developmental assessment of high-risk newborn infants, home care for elderly stroke and arthritis patients, and industrial consulting to reduce low back injuries, specialization has become a feature of the careers of many therapists. In 1978 APTA established a board for certification of advanced clinical competence that currently oversees the examination and certification of clinical specialists by speciality boards in six fields: cardiopulmonary, clinical electrophysiology, neurological, orthopedic, pediatric, and sports physical therapy. Thirty universities now offer postprofessional graduate programs (including nine doctoral-level programs) for advanced professional study by experienced therapists.

APTA estimates that the number of licensed physical therapists in 1986 was nearly 66,000. Physical therapists are most often women; in 1987 men constituted 25.4 percent of the work force, a little down from 28.8 percent in 1978. On average, women therapists are slightly younger (35 years old) than men (38 years old). The proportion of minority therapists remained between 4 and 5 percent in the past decade. The 15 percent of the work force who worked full time for themselves were the highest earners, grossing nearly $73,000 on average in 1986, compared with approximately $32,000 for the 67 percent who were full-time salaried employees. The educational attainments of physical therapists have increased during the past 10 years. The percentage with master's degrees has increased from 15.2 percent to 21.5 percent since 1978. The percentage with a doctoral degree increased slightly from 1.1 percent to 1.4 percent (APTA, 1987).

RADIOLOGIC TECHNOLOGY

Radiologic services as an allied health field began with the diagnostic use of x rays and the applications of these and other types of ionizing radiation for therapeutic purposes. Originally, radiologic services were provided almost exclusively by radiologists (physicians) and their technical assistants or x-ray technicians (now called radiographers); in recent decades, however, radiologic services have expanded considerably. New professions have emerged with medical and technological advances. New applications of radioactive tracers led to the birth of nuclear medicine technology; the invention of therapeutic x-ray equipment for treating cancer resulted in the field of radiation therapy technology; and the development of ultrasound imaging systems has created a new category of radiologic personnel, the diagnostic medical sonographer.

Radiologic technologists and technicians (including radiographers, radiation therapy technologists, nuclear medicine technologists, and diagnostic medical sonographers) held approximately 125,000 jobs in 1986. About two of every three jobs were located in hospitals. Other employment sites included clinics, laboratories, and doctors' offices.

Twenty-five years after the discovery of x rays in 1895 by Wilhelm Roentgen, 13 x-ray technicians gathered in Chicago and formed the American Association of Radiological Technicians (now called the American Society of Radiologic Technologists). In 1920 a committee of physicians was appointed by the Radiological Society of North America to consider standards for the training of x-ray technicians. Two years later the Radiological Society of North America and the American Roentgen Ray Society organized the American Registry of X-ray Technicians (now called the American Registry of Radiologic Technologists). The registry was controlled by physicians until 1961 when the composition of the registry board was changed to include technologists. Initially, all training in radiologic technology was done on the job. Gradually, however, hospitals organized schools for technicians, and a program evolved that comprised a year of classwork followed by a year of clinical training. In 1933 the first three programs were recognized by the registry. Today, CAHEA accredits more than 1,000 formal training programs in the field.

Radiologic technology education changed after World War II, partly as a result of the G.I. Bill. Large numbers of returning veterans were interested in careers in the expanding health care field and, at the same time, wished to pursue formal education under the G.I. Bill. Many administrators of 2-year colleges recognized this new market and established 2-year radiologic technology programs that granted an associate degree. This development came on the heels of a growing movement within the field to extend the duration of training programs.

At present, there are formal training programs in radiography, sonography, radiation therapy technology, and nuclear medicine technology. They range from 1 to 4 years and grant a certificate, an associate degree, or a baccalaureate. Two-year programs are the most common. Some 1-year programs attract health care professionals who are interested in changing fields—most often, respiratory therapists, registered nurses, and medical technologists. Certificate programs also attract radiographers who want to specialize in ultrasound, radiation therapy, or nuclear medicine. Currently, 4-year programs are designed primarily for people interested in teaching or supervisory positions.

There appears to be a trend in the field toward programs of longer duration based in institutions of higher education. Because some educators feel that advances in technology have made it difficult to train students adequately in 2 years, a number of associate degree programs are experimenting with a third year. Some leaders in the field feel that the slight difference between a 3-year associate degree program and a 4-year bachelor's program will push the field toward making the baccalaureate degree the educational standard for entry-level jobs.

As of summer 1987, only five states—New York, New Jersey, Florida, California, and Kentucky—had licensure laws for radiologic technologists. In 1984 Congress passed the Jennings Randolph Bill requiring states either to establish minimal educational standards for radiologic technologists or adopt extant federal requirements, which call for voluntary compliance. Almost all states have opted for voluntary compliance.

The radiologic technology work force is one of the largest among the allied health fields. The Bureau of Health Professions estimates that there were 143,000 radiologic health service workers in 1986, of which approximately two-thirds were women and half were under 30 years of age (Bureau of Health Professions, 1988).

RESPIRATORY THERAPY

Respiratory therapists provide an array of services that ranges from emergency care for stroke, drowning, heart failure, and shock to providing temporary relief to patients with emphysema or asthma. They often treat patients who have undergone surgery because anesthesia depresses breathing and respiratory therapy may be prescribed to prevent the development of respiratory illnesses. The majority of respiratory therapists works in hospital settings, although increasing numbers are being employed by nursing facilities and home health agencies.

Since the 1800s, doctors have prescribed oxygen therapy for individuals with cardiopulmonary problems, and until recently the task of actually administering treatment fell to attending nurses. After World War II, however, much of the equipment for administering oxygen became so sophisticated and expensive that administrators began assigning respiratory care tasks to orderlies who became known as oxygen orderlies. These first respiratory therapists, although usually employees of nursing departments, frequently developed direct relationships with physicians and often came to know more about gas therapy than their immediate supervisors.

The field's first professional organization, the Inhalational Therapy Association, was formed in Chicago in 1946. Now, several decades later, the organization is national in scope and is known as the American Association for Respiratory Care (AARC).

As the field and its body of medical knowledge evolved, the range of tasks performed by respiratory therapists widened to include both the mundane and the highly complex. As a result, in the late 1960s, leaders in the field promoted the idea of developing an entry-level position so that respiratory therapists could be relieved of their more routine tasks. In 1969 the first inhalation therapy technicians were certified.

Today, training is offered at the postsecondary level in colleges and universities, medical schools, trade schools, and hospitals. To be accredited by CAHEA, programs for respiratory therapists must be of at least 2 years' duration and lead to an associate or baccalaureate degree. Technician programs usually last 1 year. Certification is voluntary and available through the National Board for Respiratory Care. As of June 1987, respiratory care personnel were licensed in 18 states, and licensure bills had been introduced in 10 others.

Members of the field currently are concerned about issues relating to competition with other health care workers. They are alarmed by incursions into the field that have been made by other health care workers, especially nurses, who in the early years performed the functions (or the precursors of the functions) that are usually handled by respiratory therapists today. To halt these incursions and protect the quality of respiratory services, therapists are seeking licensure in all 50 states. It should be noted that AARC, unlike many other allied health organizations, is not currently striving to achieve greater independence from physicians for its membership. The AARC leadership anticipates that respiratory personnel will continue to work under the direction of physicians.

BLS estimates that there were more than 56,000 respiratory therapy jobs in 1986, the majority of them in hospitals. AARC suggests, however, that administrative positions were excluded in the BLS count. Two-thirds of respiratory therapists are under 30 years of age, and—unusual for an allied health field—almost 40 percent are men.

SPEECH–LANGUAGE PATHOLOGY
AND AUDIOLOGY SERVICES

Audiologists and speech–language pathologists held approximately 45,000 jobs in 1986. Slightly more than half of these positions were in elementary and secondary schools, universities, and colleges. Hospitals, nursing homes, speech–language and hearing centers, and private physicians provided most of the remaining jobs. Unlike most other allied health professions, the speech–language–hearing profession does not function exclusively or even principally in the medical world. Moreover, the care provided by these professionals was not previously supplied by physicians. The development of these fields took place in the educational sector. Early in this century, educators became interested in introducing speech correction services into the public schools. The Chicago school system was the first to offer these services, hiring 10 speech correction teachers in 1910. Within 6 years, Detroit, Boston, New York, and San Francisco had followed Chicago's lead and were also employing speech correctionists. University education of individuals interested in speech correction was initiated in the United States around 1915 at the University of Wisconsin.

Most early speech correctionists saw themselves as specialized teachers of elocution and belonged to a large organization known as the National Association of Teachers of Speech (NATS). In 1925 a group of speech correctionists decided to form a semiautonomous organization under the auspices of NATS to serve their professional interests, and the American Academy of Speech Correction (AASC) was born. Among the goals of the fledgling organization was raising "existing standards of practice among workers in the field of speech correction" and securing "public recognition of the practice of speech correction as an organized profession" (Paden, 1970).

During the next several years, the academy grew, but with growth came dissatisfaction over its close connection with NATS. The traditional dates of the annual NATS meeting apparently were not convenient for a number of AASC members, many of whom felt that AASC should be affiliated with groups in the medical world rather than with NATS. After 25 years, AASC separated from NATS; today, the organization is known as the American Speech–Language–Hearing Association (ASHA).

A master's degree in speech–language pathology or audiology is the basic credential in this profession, although there are numerous programs in communications sciences and disorders at the baccalaureate level. Of the approximately 235 colleges and universities offering master's degree or doctoral programs in speech–language pathology and audiology, about two-thirds are accredited by ASHA. Course work at accredited schools includes basic communication processes, the study of speech–language pathology or hearing disorders or both, and related areas such as the psychological aspects of communication. Most persons with a master's degree pursue the Certificate of Clinical Competence (CCC), which is offered by ASHA in either speech–language pathology or audiology. To earn the CCC, the individual must hold a master's degree or its equivalent, complete a supervised clinical fellowship year, and pass ASHA's written exam.

Thirty-six states require that individuals providing speech–language pathology and audiology services hold licenses if they practice privately in clinics or in other nonschool settings. Medicare, Medicaid, and other third-party payers pay for the services of licensed practitioners. In states that do not have licensure laws, Medicare and Medicaid require that speech–language pathologists and audiologists meet the educational and clinical experience requirements for the CCC or be in the process of accumulating the necessary clinical experience.

Increasing numbers of individuals within the field are becoming independent private practitioners. This trend, while fairly new, is rapidly growing. Like the leaders of other increasingly autonomous allied health professions, authorities in speech–language pathology and audiology are seeking to ensure that standards of practice remain high.

ASHA estimates that approximately 86,700 speech–language pathologists and audiologists are active in the work force (Shewan, 1988). Approximately 15 percent of the practitioners certified by ASHA are audiologists, and most of the remainder are speech–language pathologists; about 2 percent of speech–language–hearing practitioners are certified in both speech–language pathology and audiology (ASHA, 1986). In 1987 audiologists earned slightly more than speech–language pathologists. The median annual salary in 1987 for ASHA member audiologists was $28,000 compared with $25,000 for speech–language pathologists (ASHA, 1988). The speech–language pathology work force is overwhelmingly white and female (approximately 95 percent and 89 percent, respectively, in 1988).

NEW ALLIED HEALTH FIELDS

The committee recognizes that the 10 fields selected for this study represent established, traditional allied health professions. Yet the changing pattern of health care delivery has tended to spawn new allied health fields—fields that develop as changes occur in the health care system and as technology develops or expands. The committee looked briefly at two fields —perfusion and cardiovascular technology—that recently have come to be recognized as allied health occupations to see if developing fields tend to follow the same general pathways as those of the established occupations. These two fields developed from core elements they once shared with respiratory therapy. Early academic programs covered heart and lung procedures; as technologies developed, practitioners specialized in one or another area, and separate fields and occupations evolved.

Perfusion

Perfusionists began in the mid-1950s as pump technicians for heart–lung machines—equipment that was designed to withdraw blood from a patient's body, cleanse and oxygenate it, and pump it back into the body. These technicians moved with the equipment from experimental laboratories into clinical settings as assistants to surgeons and anesthesiologists. Trainees were often drawn from other disciplines, including nursing and respiratory therapy, and were trained on the job until the mid-1970s.

By the mid-1960s, perfusionists saw the need to develop a system for certifying practitioners and to establish a minimal base of knowledge for the profession. They formed the American Society of Extra-Corporeal Technology (AmSECT) to organize the profession and provide information and professional services to its members; in 1968 AmSECT began a program of certification for perfusionists. The American Board of Cardiovascular Perfusion was established in 1974 to conduct certification as an independent activity. In 1977 CAHEA recognized perfusion as an allied health profession, and the way was paved for establishing accredited schools for training.

In the years following the move to certification for perfusionists and prior to the establishment of accredited training programs, technicians trained on the job were allowed to sit for the certification exam. Since 1981, however, when school programs became available, certification requirements have changed, and no one may sit for the exam without having graduated from an accredited program.

Perfusionists work under the general supervision of a physician. Whereas they used to work only with heart–lung machines, perfusionists now manage highly technical patient monitoring devices in the operating room. In addition, they are no longer limited only to assisting during heart bypass procedures; now, perfusionists also assist during organ transplants. The profession is striving to expand its expertise and not limit its focus to one technology; in pursuit of these goals, it is expanding its scope to include managing patient monitoring devices that have not been claimed by another allied health field. Perfusion thus is taking a course not dissimilar to that of the older, established allied health professions.

Cardiovascular Technology

The field of cardiovascular technology involves the diagnosis and treatment of patients with cardiac and peripheral vascular disease. It is segmented into three distinct areas: (1) invasive cardiology, (2) noninvasive cardiology, and (3) noninvasive peripheral vascular study. As each of these areas developed and as changing technology led to their divergence, technicians in each area were trained to conduct the requisite tests and procedures. The three groups have remained together for the purpose of designing an educational program.

Cardiovascular technology has been recognized by CAHEA as an allied health profession since December 1981. Cardiovascular technologists and technicians specialize in one or more of the three areas. Program accreditation criteria have been developed, but thus far there are no accredited programs for training cardiovascular technicians. Several programs are expected to be available by the fall of 1988.

The range of skills and training required by cardiovascular technologists and technicians is broad. Within the area of noninvasive cardiology, for example, procedures range from electrocardiography (EKG), which may be taught in a few hours, to echocardiography, an ultrasound technique that requires relatively extensive training. EKG technicians are often cross-trained on the job in exercise testing, another noninvasive cardiology procedure.

The associations that represent cardiovascular technicians who do EKGs and exercise tests have established a separate board to test technicians who want to be credentialed; most technicians are not credentialed. Institutions in which these technicians work encourage credentialing but do not require it. Cardiovascular technicians are employed in a variety of settings including physicians' offices, outpatient clinics, and exercise clinics. They work under the supervision of nursing staff or physicians.

Technicians who specialize in echocardiograms are often trained on the job. Only 6 of the 30 schools offering ultrasound training include training in echocardiography, and none of the schools is accredited under CAHEA's new program of essentials for cardiovascular technology. Training in these programs must generally be supplemented by on-the-job training, but not all health care facilities have the capability to train the echocardiography technicians they need. The demand for these technicians is high, and their salaries are rising. They are often drawn from other disciplines, including nursing, physical therapy, and respiratory therapy; few trainees are without a medical background.

The Society of Diagnostic Medical Sonographers represents echocardiographers and other sonographers. Two boards currently provide testing for certification in the field. Generally, individuals need to have several years of experience before they can qualify to take the exam. The majority of echocardiographers are not board certified, but interest in certification is growing—and growing faster than in any of the other cardiovascular technology areas. The American College of Cardiologists is encouraging certification through only one body, which will probably provide increased impetus for such credentialing.

Although echocardiographers have some degree of autonomy, they work closely with physicians. Echocardiography overlaps with radiologic technology, which includes ultrasound technology or sonography. A movement to draft state legislation requiring that ultrasound operators be radiologic technicians is being fought by non-radiologic technicians who work with ultrasound technology.

Invasive cardiovascular technologists, as their title suggests, assist physicians in invasive heart procedures. With the development of bypass surgery the number of catheter labs has risen, and the demand for technologists has grown. Developments in balloon angioplasty and laser technology may have the same effect. Practitioners generally are drawn from other clinical areas, including x-ray technology and nursing, and typically are trained on the job.

Noninvasive peripheral vascular technologists assist in diagnostic studies of the peripheral circulatory system. Ultrasound techniques are used in these studies, and, as in the case of echocardiography, substantial training is required for technicians; in addition, like echocardiographers, noninvasive peripheral vascular technologists who conduct ultrasound tests also face competition from radiologic technologists. Equipment manufacturers have been the primary source of training; they have established educational programs in their own facilities as well as providing onsite, in-service training. In its early days, most of the field's trainees were nurses, but it now draws persons from other disciplines.

CONCLUSION

Allied health practitioners vary greatly in terms of the work they do, the amount of education they require, the types of institutions they attend to obtain that education, and the regulatory control that attends their activities. Yet, the evolution of their professions has followed courses that were common to several if not to all of the fields. The fields developed to meet identified health care needs, often taking over tasks that physicians no longer wanted to undertake. Initially, on-the-job training was the norm, but soon the practitioners of a field formed an organization, defined their roles, and identified minimum qualifications that all practitioners must possess.

The certification of practitioners and the accreditation of educational programs followed. Many allied health fields today use CAHEA to accredit their programs. Others have preferred to keep accreditation within the purview of the field, a decision many groups see as one of the key attributes of a profession. In many of the fields, educational requirements have increased almost inevitably, and licensure often has followed, a development that serves several purposes including the protection of a practitioner's educational investment. In many of the allied health fields, tensions developed between practitioners and the medical or dental speciality from which the field developed. New professions have sought to control their own destinies while the originating professions have sometimes been reluctant to relinquish control, in part because they fear competition from the very groups they initially encouraged in order to relieve themselves of unwanted tasks.

Some allied health fields (e.g., physical therapy) made the transition from hospital training to baccalaureate education in universities and colleges in the first half of the century. With the community college movement in the 1960s, assistant-level programs developed to meet the growing demand for services and the need to make practitioners more productive. For other fields the transition to education and training in academia was made much more slowly. For example, radiography and respiratory therapy are in the midst of evolving toward requiring the baccalaureate degree; consequently, we now see some 1-year programs giving way, primarily to 2-year and baccalaureate programs. Those individuals with advanced degrees tend to gravitate toward administrative roles.

The spectrum of allied health today includes fields at different stages of evolution. This report offers a snapshot of them at one point in time.

REFERENCES

American Dietetic Association. 1972. The Profession of Dietetics: Report of the Study Commission on Dietetics. Chicago: American Dietetic Association.

American Dietetic Association. 1985. A New Look at the Profession of Dietetics: Report of the 1984 Study Commission on Dietetics. Chicago: American Dietetic Association.

American Dietetic Association. 1987. Unpublished data. American Dietetic Association, Chicago.

AOTA (American Occupational Therapy Association). 1986. 1986 Member Data Survey. Rockville, Md.: American Occupational Therapy Association.

APTA (American Physical Therapy Association). 1987. 1987 Active Membership Profile Survey. Alexandria, Va.: American Physical Therapy Association.

American Speech–Language–Hearing Association. 1988. Demographic Profile of the ASHA Membership. Rockville, Md.: American Speech–Language–Hearing Association. March 9.

Bryk, J. A. 1987. Report on the 1986 Census of the American Dietetic Association. Journal of the American Dietetic Association 87(8):1080–1085.

Bureau of Health Manpower. 1967. Education for the Allied Health Professions and Services: Report of the Allied Health Professions Education Subcommittee of the National Advisory Health Council. Washington, D.C.: U.S. Government Printing Office.

Bureau of Health Professions. 1984. An In-Depth Examination of the 1980 Decennial Census Employment Data for Health Occupations, Comprehensive Report. Rockville, Md.: U.S. Department of Health and Human Services, Health Resources and Services Administration.

Bureau of Health Professions. 1988. Report to the President and Congress on the Status of Health Personnel in the United States. Washington, D.C.: U.S. Department of Health and Human Services.

Bureau of Labor Statistics. 1987. Employment by Occupation and Industry, 1986 and Projected 2000 Alternatives. Washington, D.C.: Bureau of Labor Statistics.

Committee on Allied Health Education and Accreditation (CAHEA). 1987. Allied Health Education Directory, 1987. Chicago: American Medical Association.

McTernan, E. J. 1987. Allied health professions in the United States: A summary of the origins, development, and potential futures of a selected sample of allied health fields. Background paper prepared for the Institute of Medicine Committee to Study the Role of Allied Health Personnel.

Paden, E. P. 1970. A History of the American Speech and Hearing Association. Washington, D.C.: American Speech and Hearing Association.

Shewan, C. M. 1987. An update on supply estimates for speech–language–hearing personnel. American Speech–Language–Hearing Association, Rockville, Md.

U.S. Department of Health, Education, and Welfare. 1979. A Report on Allied Health Personnel. Washington, D.C.: U.S. Government Printing Office.

2

Approaches to Measuring Demand and Supply

CONGRESS DIRECTED that this study "identify projected needs, availability, and requirements of various types of health care delivery systems for each type of allied health personnel." Before it could respond to this charge, however, the committee had to resolve several issues of scope and approach.

1. *Current versus future "needs, availability, and requirements"* The committee believes that, given its limited funds and time, it can make a greater contribution by providing its best assessment of future needs and requirements for allied health personnel and its best assessment of the kinds of adjustments that will be needed to meet those needs and requirements. Although it recognizes that there is intense interest in the current situation, the committee believes that most of the study's resources would have been exhausted in performing a systematic assessment of that situation. The future outlook, on the other hand, is crucial to strategic planning and policy; therefore, the committee chose to devote most of its efforts to developing a picture of the future. To the extent that it became aware of perceptions of current imbalances in demand and supply of allied health personnel as the study progressed, those perceptions are noted in the report.

2. *"Each type of allied health personnel"* As the charge implied and the committee clearly recognized, it is neither feasible nor useful to consider the needs and availability of allied health personnel collectively. The allied health rubric comprises occupations with varying labor market characteristics (e.g., paths of entry, levels and types of responsibilities, wages and

44

salaries, labor force entries and exits, and work sites). As a consequence the demand and supply situation must be considered separately for each occupational field. The approach used in this study has been to examine 10 allied health fields in some depth to illustrate the diversity among them. To the extent possible, these fields are used as the basis for several general conclusions about the future employment outlook.

3. *"Needs, availability, and requirements"* Two different approaches are implied by the charge. "Needs," as used in the context of health personnel planning, refers to a normative idea of the number and type of personnel required to provide therapeutic and preventive services to a defined population. Need is usually defined independently of economic constraints. Demand (or effective demand), on the other hand, refers to the number and type of personnel required to fill the available jobs and provide services for which consumers are willing and able to pay.

The committee elected to assess future needs and requirements in terms of the effective demand for allied health personnel. This decision was based on the committee's judgment that this approach is of most use for realistic planning. However, in the case of long-term care (see Chapter 8), the committee chose to take a patient-centered approach in examining the future need for allied health personnel.

4. *Planning horizon* The committee selected the year 2000 for its projections of future demand and supply. Because most of the available base data are for 1986, this decision means, in effect, looking ahead 15 years. The committee recognizes the great uncertainty that goes with so long a horizon. Yet many decisions require some assessment of the future, however rough, and the types of decisions that affect the labor market for allied health practitioners (e.g., starting or modifying educational programs) necessitate long lead times. On balance, then, the committee's decision was to take the long view.

DATA FOR ASSESSING DEMAND AND SUPPLY

The committee was limited to the use of existing data as the basis for its assessment of demand and supply in allied health fields because it was not possible to design, field, and analyze a survey within the available study time, particularly considering the requirement for the Office of Management and Budget's approval of such a survey. The paucity of existing data on allied health fields severely constrained the committee's ability to carry out its charge. Thanks in large part to significant federal investments in developing data bases in medicine, dentistry, and nursing, previous Institute of Medicine (IOM) studies of those fields have been able to draw on large amounts of data and on requirements and supply projections made by the Bureau of Health Professions of the Department of Health and

Human Services based on those data. In the allied health fields, however, data are limited.

Nonetheless, some data do exist. BLS collects information on employment, earnings, and labor force behavior of a number of allied health occupations in its ongoing analysis of the U.S. work force. The decennial censuses and the Current Population Survey offer detailed information by occupation. In addition, allied health associations conduct surveys of their members that provide invaluable data on persons meeting their membership criteria. Associations of hospitals, nursing homes, and home health care agencies also collect data on employment in their constituent institutions.

The committee has examined these and other data sources to inform its assessment of personnel demand and supply. In the sections that follow, we point out problems and weaknesses in the data and offer some suggestions for improvement that, if heeded, will ease the way for future studies.

ASSESSING CURRENT DEMAND AND SUPPLY

How do we know if there is a current shortage of allied health personnel? This is not a straightforward question. First of all, the term *shortage* has a variety of meanings. Sometimes it is defined normatively: a shortage exists if there are fewer respiratory therapists than are needed, according to some definition of need. Economists define a shortage as a situation in which fewer people are employed than employers would like to employ at the current wage. Although they may be cognizant of other factors that influence employers' decisions to employ workers and prospective employees' decisions to seek work, economists traditionally focus on levels of salaries and wages, and sometimes on fringe benefits, as the principal variables that equilibrate employer demand and the labor supply.* According to economic theory, if the labor market were functioning properly, a shortage could exist only temporarily because employers would pay more to attract more workers until all jobs were filled. Thus, economists view any labor shortage as reflecting either a lag in the adjustment of the labor supply to demand or an imperfection in the functioning of the labor market. For example, if the demand for labor grows at a rapid rate over a period of time, a temporary labor shortage may occur. Barriers to adjustment can also result in labor demand and supply not coming into balance. These factors will be described later.

---

*This explanation is somewhat oversimplified, however, because other aspects such as the risk involved in work and working conditions are also considered in economic analyses of labor demand and supply.

A shortage can occur over the short term or the long term, although long-term shortages are unusual unless there is some market imperfection such as a price ceiling that prohibits market adjustments. In the short term, workers must be recruited from the existing pool, and employers must use existing technology. Over the long term, however, new workers can be trained and new technologies employed to change the nature of the work.

Indicators of a Labor Shortage

A number of signals can indicate that labor shortages exist. Such signals include large numbers of job vacancies, rising compensation levels, and low unemployment levels.

Vacancies

The most commonly cited indicator of a labor shortage is job vacancies. A large number of vacant positions or a high ratio of vacancies to total employment is taken as evidence of a shortage. "Large" and "high," of course, are relative to some expected level of vacancies. This expectation may be based on historical vacancy levels for the occupation of interest or on a comparison with current vacancy levels in other occupations.

There are some vacancies in an occupation at all times because of job turnover. Because job mobility is important to a well-functioning labor market, such vacancies can be viewed as a sign of the market's health rather than its pathology. As Hall (1978) has pointed out,

The role of vacancies can only be understood against the background of the ceaseless motion within the labor market. . . . Every month, several million workers change jobs, and hundreds of thousands of others move in and out of the labor force. Much of this turnover is attributable to fluctuations in the labor requirements of individual employers and the rest to the changing circumstances of individual workers.

Vacancy rates are not reliable indicators of job opportunities for several reasons. For one thing, the highest rates occur in occupations with the highest turnover; construction work is an example often cited. Among the health occupations, turnover is much higher for nurses' aides than for highly trained personnel (e.g., medical technologists or physical therapists).

In addition, reported vacancies should be viewed with caution because they do not always represent a shortage. If, through one mechanism or another, wages are kept below the level that would bring demand and supply into equilibrium, employer demand will always exceed the number of allied health personnel who want to work at the going wage. Such excess demand cannot really be characterized as a shortage but rather as an imperfection in the operation of the market.

Sloan (1975), Yett (1975), and others have pointed out in the context of nursing that if the labor market is not competitive and therefore one or several employers have some control over wage levels, the market can be in equilibrium even though there are vacant jobs. In this case, an employer would report vacancies but would not raise wages to fill them. Another possible explanation for market equilibrium in the midst of vacancies is the systematic undervaluation of work in occupations in which female workers predominate. Institutional barriers—long-standing custom, the misperception of market conditions by employers, and inflexible recruitment practices—rather than an insufficient number of qualified persons available to work may account for vacancies.

Compensation Levels

Another signal that is often interpreted as indicating a shortage is rising compensation levels. Wages are the element that is most easily observed, but compensation in this instance means the entire package offered by employers: wages or salaries, benefits, hours, and conditions of work. If employers are unable to attract workers with their current package, presumably, they will improve it. Increases in compensation levels, however, are not in themselves evidence of a shortage. Rather, they may indicate normal and often temporary market adjustments in an environment of rising demand.

Relative changes in compensation levels are better indicators of labor market conditions than are absolute changes. If the earnings of physical therapists are rising much faster than earnings in, for example, medical technology or teaching (fields that require similar educational investments) and if employers are unable to fill vacant physical therapist positions, we might conclude that there is a shortage, or at least that, at present, demand is outstripping supply. If market signals are sufficiently strong—that is, compensation rises, unemployment drops, and so forth—the shortage presumably would be alleviated over time by new entrants to the physical therapy field. The interim may bring painful dislocations, however. Services may have to be curtailed, or substitute workers may have to be employed, with an unacceptable decrement in quality. In some industries, of course, such dislocations are viewed as normal.

Unemployment Levels

Some frictional unemployment (a level of unemployment resulting from the time involved in changing jobs) is characteristic of a dynamic labor market in which people change jobs, often with an interval in between. Unemployment levels will tend to be relatively higher in occupations with high turnover. Very low unemployment levels (virtually everyone seeking employment is finding it) are another signal that may indicate a labor shortage. Low unemployment levels are especially indicative of shortages if vacancy levels remain high.

The employment experience of new graduates is one indicator of conditions in the labor market. If, for instance, most physical therapy graduates find work in the field within a year after graduation, the labor market may be tight. As with the other signals mentioned above, however, caution must be exercised in interpreting such signals. New graduates can be hired at lower wages than experienced therapists, and some employers may prefer to substitute less experienced workers for more experienced ones to keep costs down. In addition, new graduates tend to be more mobile; therefore, their experience may be more favorable than that of other, less mobile workers.

Any one of these signals alone does not indicate a shortage. On the other hand, when a number of them occur together, especially if they persist over time, it becomes ever more likely that there is a real problem. If employers are constrained from making such adjustments as substituting less highly trained employees for more highly trained ones (for example, substituting corrective therapists for physical therapists) or importing workers from abroad, or if the necessary adjustments are unacceptable to society, it would be fair to call the problem a labor shortage.

Data for Assessing Current Vacancies

National data on job vacancies are not available. For both technical and budgetary reasons, BLS does not collect vacancy data. The American Hospital Association collects data on allied health employment but not on vacancies. Qualitative assessments are often made in surveys of local employers by, for example, education administrators. Surveys by professional associations may include questions about their members' perceptions of the labor market in their communities. Anecdotal data are reported in health care journals and newsletters from time to time. In addition, regional or state development bodies such as the state-sponsored Massachusetts Technology Development Corporation sometimes attempt to make assessments.

Data on Salaries and Wages

The BLS Industry Wage Survey program collects and publishes average straight-time hourly wages for selected occupations in hospitals and nursing homes in 23 standard metropolitan statistical areas (SMSAs). Hospital surveys were conducted in 1978, 1981, and 1985; the allied health occupations that were covered included diagnostic medical sonographers, electroencephalographic technicians, electrocardiographic technicians, medical laboratory technicians, medical technologists, nuclear medicine technologists, radiation therapy technologists, radiographers, surgical technologists, dietitians, medical record administrators and technicians, and all of the therapy occupations. The survey excluded such elements of compensation as premium pay for overtime and work on night shifts or holidays and such in-kind compensation such as room and board. Fringe benefits were also excluded. These data are quite useful for examining trends in basic wages in urban hospitals and nursing homes and for comparing wage levels among SMSAs.

Occupational earnings are available from the Census Bureau's Current Population Survey. Data on the earnings of allied health association members are collected through member surveys. In addition, the University of Texas Medical Branch at Galveston annually surveys 33 hospitals, 16 medical schools, and 28 medical centers.

Unemployment statistics are collected monthly by BLS. Although extremely useful in the aggregate, these data have some weaknesses when used to assess market conditions in specific occupations. Unemployed persons are classified by the occupation in which they were last employed. Thus, a person seeking work as an audiologist whose last job was as a teacher would be categorized as an unemployed teacher. Recent graduates seeking their first job are excluded from the unemployment figures by occupation. As with other market indicators, BLS occupational unemployment data must be used carefully and only after being critically examined.

Surveys by allied health professional associations generally elicit information on whether their members are employed and where. Less frequently do they provide information (e.g., whether the respondent is looking for work) that would complement data from the Current Population Survey. CAHEA·has conducted surveys of education program directors about offers to their graduates as a means of assessing the job market; some state education departments conduct similar surveys. In addition, individual educators sometimes survey employers in their community regarding employment opportunities.

How to Improve Data on Current Allied Health
Personnel Demand and Supply

The balance between the current demand for and supply of allied health personnel is of concern to a wide range of organizations, to educators seeking jobs for their students, to facility administrators who are unsure about the availability of needed personnel, and to allied health practitioners and the associations that represent them, all of whom are concerned about jobs, compensation, and career prospects. In functional terms an assessment of current personnel demand and supply is the essential baseline data point from which projections start. Current information about the labor market also enables those in positions to do so to act early to prevent the occurrence of serious imbalances and the need for major corrective action later.

In the previous sections, we have noted the types of data that are needed to estimate current demand and supply. Some of these types of data are available but usually only for certain allied health fields in some localities. Health care institutions are already responding to heavy demands for operating data and are reluctant to add to their burden in the absence of a belief that such data will serve their interests. Additional data collection activities should be undertaken only after a careful consideration of the benefits of such efforts and of ways to minimize the burden of undertaking them. The data to assess current labor market conditions are more readily available for other health care professions—such as physicians and nurses—than for allied health fields. The committee believes that the lack of data about allied health fields, compared with the data available on other types of providers, reflects an underestimation of the role of allied health practitioners in the health care system. Both the large contribution to care made by such practitioners and the high total costs associated with the aggregate use of allied health professionals strongly suggest that data collection strategies that allow the assessment of current personnel demand and supply should be seriously explored.

For example, associations of employers could try to develop simple, inexpensive surveys to learn about problems in recruiting. Survey questions might include the following: What kinds of employees are you finding the most difficult to recruit? Are you using any exceptional recruitment measures? What actions are you taking to cope with vacancies? These surveys might be conducted in a small sample of "sentinel" institutions as frequently as twice a year.

Professional associations should use standard labor statistics terminology to increase the usefulness of their surveys to BLS and vice versa. It is especially important to count people who are not working but who are actively seeking work; these are the people the U.S. Department of Labor categorizes as unemployed. Professional associations should also explore longitudinal studies of a sample of their members; studies of this type could provide better data on members' work histories, labor force participation, earnings, and other characteristics than can be gathered from the cross-sectional surveys that are usually conducted. In addition to technical improvements, associations should look for ways to make their research more relevant to current policy issues. Associations would be well served to strengthen the links between their research and policy functions.

The committee also recommends that the U.S. Department of Health and Human Services' Health Resources and Services Administration (HRSA) reconstitute the Forum on Allied Health Data as a technical assistance endeavor. HRSA should also hold workshops with experts in survey design, statistics, and labor economics to help the allied health associations improve their data collection programs. Other possibilities for improving the information on current labor market conditions for allied health personnel include the following:

• When renewing licenses, state licensing bodies could ask whether applicants are currently employed in their field, employed in another occupation, looking for work, or not looking for work.

• State and regional health planning agencies could make larger investments in education and employment data and planning. They could also operate as an important link between educational institutions and employers.

• Educational institutions could pool information on the job-finding experiences of recent graduates and alumni. Local experience could be aggregated to develop state and national pictures.

ASSESSING FUTURE DEMAND AND SUPPLY

Forecasts of the future are often inaccurate, either because they do not take into account all of the relevant factors or because the factors change in ways that were not or could not have been predicted. Yet decision making is based on assumptions about the future, however crudely they are formed. The committee's task has been to use the limited data available to formulate a "best guess" and to let that projection inform its recommendations. Thus, the committee's recommendations are based on the interpretation of general trends in the work force and in the economy and of specific projections for selected allied health fields.

Several approaches are possible to assess future needs and requirements for allied health personnel. Some of the approaches that have been used for other types of health manpower fields are described below to illustrate the available assessment options, the ways they can be used, and the types of data that are needed for their use.

Needs-based projections usually define the number of personnel required to provide a given set of services to a defined population. The needs approach, which was pioneered by the Committee on the Costs of Medical Care in the 1930s, involves two types of judgment: (1) the quantity and type of health care services judged to be appropriate, and (2) the appropriate division of responsibility for those services among the various types of health care personnel. The projections that finally result depend on who makes these judgments and on their views of what constitutes good health care. Needs-based models represent an unconstrained social ideal: they are norms against which to compare actual performance. They can be used to establish health care program objectives and to assess the probable availability of personnel to meet those objectives.

The Graduate Medical Education National Advisory Committee, which was established by the secretary of health and human services in the late 1970s, used a needs-based approach to project physician requirements for 1990. The committee began with estimates of the incidence of particular illnesses or medical conditions in the population and then made judgments about which conditions required medical care, how many visits would be required, and how many of these visits might be "delegated" to persons other than physicians. The total estimated visits were transformed into physician requirements based on assumptions about productivity (Jacoby, 1981).

A model of requirements for nurses developed by the Western Interstate Commission on Higher Education also had its foundations in judgments of need. Panels of nurses provided professional judgments about desirable changes in health care delivery and about the mix of registered nurses (RNs) and licensed practical nurses (LPNs) needed to provide the desired services (Bauder, 1983).

Another approach to projecting health care human resources requirements is to extrapolate from current levels. Instead of assigning ideal health care services utilization levels (and their corresponding health care personnel requirements) to projected population segments, current utilization levels are projected into the future. Most simply, current health care personnel-to-population ratios are applied to population projections. The Bureau of Health Professions of the Department of Health and Human Services uses this method to project physician requirements by starting with current utilization levels and then adjusting for projected changes in population, trends in health insurance benefits, and other factors that affect utilization such as the cost of health care services. Productivity assumptions are used to translate projected utilization into the number of physicians required. The Division of Nursing also employs a model that projects population, per-capita use of health care services, and the associated required numbers of RNs and LPNs.

The simplest extrapolation models are strictly mechanical; the health care personnel-to-population model is an example. More sophisticated models incorporate "behavioral" components, such as the price elasticity of demand for health care services, and then make independent projections of prices. They may also incorporate changes in production technology—for example, capital–labor substitution or the division of tasks among health care personnel.

As extrapolation models become more sophisticated, they begin to resemble models of economic demand. A demand model is based on the relationship of such independent variables as health status, income, and prices to the demand for health care services. In the case of labor demand, the model is based on such variables as wages, the price of capital, and product prices. Although not strictly a demand model, the BLS projections of employment are made in the context of projected labor force and economic activity.

The committee chose to rely heavily on the BLS employment projections for its assessment of future demand. The principal reasons for this reliance were the following:

• The BLS projections are grounded in projections of the entire economy, which include projections of the work force and levels of economic activity. Health care expenditures and health care industries employment are estimated in the context of growth in other types of expenditures and employment in all other institutions.

• BLS's projections use a consistent methodology across occupations. Not only can the allied health occupations be compared with each other, but they can be viewed in the context of all other occupations for which projections have been made in the same way.

• The BLS projections are widely known and used; they are reviewed regularly and revised biennially.

The committee did not, however, use these projections uncritically. It took several factors into account in using the BLS data:

• Occupational employment projections are subject to considerable error, more so than the projections of total employment by industry.

• BLS staff use their knowledge and judgment to project the number of jobs for each occupation in an industry. For the health care industry, many judgments have to be made about how changes in health care financing and delivery will affect different occupations. Because these judgments by BLS staff are not published, it is difficult to subject the results to a critical assessment.

• The occupational definitions used by BLS are not identical to those of professional associations or educators. Although great improvements have been made in the system of occupational classification, BLS definitions still rely more heavily on functions and less heavily on credentials. In addition, the data are not adequate in some cases to distinguish among different levels within occupations. For instance, BLS combines data for laboratory technologists and technicians. In some instances (e.g., for perfusionists, dialysis technicians, and cardiovascular technologists), no employment projections are made. (See Appendix E for further discussion and evaluation of BLS data.)

HOW BLS MAKES EMPLOYMENT PROJECTIONS

Because the committee relied heavily on BLS for its assessment of future demand, it is important to understand how these projections are made.

BLS projections are made from a base year to a target year. The base for the bureau's most recent projections was 1986; the target year was 2000. Harold Goldstein, in a background paper (1987) prepared for the committee, characterized the BLS approach as follows:

The basic approach followed is to estimate the employment in each occupation that will be generated by economic demand. This goes back to the demand for the goods or services the occupation provides, and this in turn is affected by the total spendable income available to consumers and government and to the changing patterns of what they spend it on. These are influenced by a wide variety of social and economic factors, including changing tastes and styles, scientific discoveries and technological change affecting both what is produced and how it is produced, the growth and changing composition of the population, taxation and government expenditures policies ("guns or butter") and what other countries are buying from and selling to us.

There are several steps in the projection sequence, the first of which is the projection of the labor force. The foundation for this projection is the Census Bureau's population projections by age, sex, and race, which are based on assumptions about birth rates, death rates, and migration in and out of the United States. Labor force participation for each age, sex, and race group is projected by extrapolating from past participation rates. The projected labor force participation rates are applied to the corresponding population projections to arrive at the projected labor force in the target year.

Next, BLS uses a macroeconomic model to develop projections of the gross national product (GNP) and major categories of demand and income. Some of the assumptions that affect the macroeconomic model, such as population projections, are fairly certain; other assumptions, such as net imports, energy prices, and the exchange value of the dollar, are quite uncertain, depending as they do on international political and economic developments. Because assumptions about certain key variables have major impacts on the projections, BLS produces three sets of macroeconomic projections based on differing sets of assumptions. These assumptions involve the levels of expenditures in major components of federal spending, the major components of state and local government spending, the size and composition of the population, and the key variables underlying foreign trade. Low, medium, and high projections of GNP are then produced from differing assumptions for each of these variables (Table 2-1).

The effect of these variations in assumptions can be seen in the figures for GNP and employment. The low, moderate, and high GNP projections that result from these and other assumptions are (in billions of dollars) $4,617, $5,161, and $5,552, respectively. The corresponding projections of total employment (in thousands) are 126,432, 133,030, and 137,533 (Monthly Labor Review, 1987).

TABLE 2-1   Assumptions Used in Making Spending and Labor Force
Projections for the Year 2000

Variable	Low	Moderate	High
Federal defense spending ($ billions)	222.5	251.0	263.0
Federal nondefense spending ($ billions)	97.3	103.4	108.2
State and local spending on education ($ billions)	195.3	223.1	232.5
Size of the civilian labor force (millions)	134.5	138.8	141.1

BLS next estimates the principal GNP components: personal consumption of durable and nondurable goods and services, capital investment,
foreign trade (imports and exports), and government expenditures. These
estimates of final demand are translated into estimated levels of production
for each industry in the economy using an input–output table based on
historical relationships that is compiled by the Department of Commerce.
The input–output table shows what each industry in the economy purchases from every other industry. For example, the automobile industry
purchases raw materials (iron ore), intermediate products (tires and glass),
and services (electrical power and transportation) from other industries to
produce its final product, automobiles (Goldstein, 1987). This step in the
projection process results in estimates of the level of production for every
industry in the target year.

The next-to-last step is the estimation of total employment for each
industry from a regression equation that estimates worker-hours as a function of industry output, the unemployment rate (a measure of capacity
utilization), the relative price of labor, and the ratio of output to capital.
The estimated worker-hours are translated into the number of workers by
dividing worker-hours by the estimated annual hours per worker.

Finally, BLS develops estimates of occupational employment by industry,
using base year data on the distribution of industry employment by occupation. Sources of data for these estimates include the Occupational
Employment Survey conducted periodically by state employment security
agencies under a BLS–state cooperative program (see Appendix E for a
discussion of OES and other data sources), the decennial census, and the
Current Population Survey. In projecting occupational employment in each
industry, adjustments are made in the occupational composition of the
industry.

In the BLS estimates, the health services industry is broken down into
components that reflect the different employment settings (e.g., hospitals,
physicians' offices, nursing homes). The next step of the process takes into
account factors that are not explicitly included in the mathematical model.
BLS analysts with responsibilities for specific occupations consult experts
(e.g., the staff of the professional associations), use the relevant literature,

and make site visits to assess whether staffing patterns are likely to change and if so, how they will change. Because the aggregate employment for each industry provides the parameters of employment, BLS analysts confer with each other to determine how each occupation in each industry will fare relative to one another. For example, the analysts who follow health occupations will meet to discuss hospital staffing patterns, the changes that are expected, and why those changes will occur. Factors that are taken into account include new technologies that are likely to change staffing intensity, changes in insurance coverage, and regulatory policies that may influence the demand for a service or individual occupation.

Table 2-2 shows the BLS low, moderate, and high projections of employment in the allied health fields for the year 2000. The differences among the three projections are attributable to different assumptions about economic growth and aggregate employment. The same assumptions about and adjustments to the occupational distribution of employment are used in all three groups of projections.

TABLE 2-2 Bureau of Labor Statistics Wage and Salary Employment (in thousands) in the Allied Health Fields, Actual for 1986 and Projections for the Year 2000

Occupation	1986 Employment	Projected Employment for the Year 2000		
		Low[a]	Moderate[b]	High[c]
Clinical laboratory technologists and technicians	238	285	296	307
Dental hygienists	87	134	141	145
Dietitians	40	52	54	55
Emergency medical technicians	65	73	75	77
Medical record technicians	40	67	70	72
Nuclear medical technologists	10	12	12	12
Occupational therapists	26	43	45	46
Physical therapists	56	109	115	118
Radiologic technologists and technicians	114	183	190	196
Respiratory therapists	56	74	76	78
Speech–language pathologists/ audiologists	42	58	61	63

[a]The low projection reflects annual growth rates of 1.6 percent in GNP, 1 percent in the civilian labor force, and 0.9 percent in employment.

[b]The moderate projection represents annual growth rates of 2.4 percent in GNP, 1.2 percent in the civilian labor force, and 1.2 percent in employment.

[c]The high projection represents annual growth rates of 3 percent in GNP, 1.3 percent in the civilian labor force, and 1.5 percent in employment.

SOURCE: Silvestri and Lukasiewicz, 1987.

FUTURE SUPPLY

In a dynamic labor market the supply of workers in an occupation is constantly changing. New graduates emerge from education programs. People enter the labor market who have worked in other occupations or who have studied related subjects. Individuals leave the work force and later reenter; some leave permanently.

Projecting the future supply of workers in an occupation requires, first, an estimation of how many people are in the field in a base year and then an estimation of the various inflows and outflows that will occur between the base year and the target year. Which inflows and outflows are important depends on the purpose of the projection.

For example, in the nursing field, there has been concern voiced about the many trained nurses who are outside the nursing work force, either working in other fields or not working at all. Although data on licensed nurses provide a picture of those nurses who keep their licenses active, some have argued that there may be many nurses who have dropped their licenses but who, in some sense, constitute a potential supply. If market conditions warrant, the argument goes, these nurses could be attracted back to work, even if some retraining were necessary. This pool of trained workers can be estimated and projected using data on the number of graduates and applying standard mortality rates to each age group. The supply estimated by this life table approach represents an estimate of all living nursing graduates (Institute of Medicine, 1983). For this purpose, the only inflow is new graduates, and the only outflow is death.

However, if the question is whether there will be enough nurses to fill the jobs that we expect to be available in the future, more information is needed about the likelihood that those who are not in the work force will reenter it. We also need to know about the likelihood that nurses who are in the work force will leave. Variations in the rates of reentry and loss from the labor force and the average time practitioners spend in the labor force produce large differences in the supply projected for the future. For most purposes, it is the "effective" supply of health personnel, trained and wanting to work, that is of greater interest.

The committee, where feasible, has projected the future supply of workers in allied health fields in the year 2000, assuming inflows to and outflows from the labor market remain as they were in 1986 and the number of allied health program graduates remains at the current level. These assumptions are unrealistic, but they are used to indicate the magnitude of change that must take place to meet future demand. The committee used a simple arithmetic equation to arrive at its projections. The work force at the beginning of one year was said to equal the work force at the beginning of the year before, minus those persons leaving the work force for reasons other than unemployment, plus graduates of allied health programs and other additions. These additions include people resuming work and people transferring from other occupations.

The base year for our observations was 1986. To achieve comparability among fields, the BLS estimate of total employment for each occupation was used. An estimated number of unemployed practitioners was added in each case.

For some allied health fields the number of graduates in 1986 was assumed to remain constant through the year 2000. When it was reasonable to do so, the 1986 share of bachelor's degrees granted in a field, relative to all bachelor's degrees granted, was applied to the Center for Education Statistics' projection of bachelor's degrees to be granted each year through 2000.

Labor force accession and separation rates that BLS derives from Current Population Survey data were used to determine additions to and losses from the work force. Because the sample size of most allied health fields in the survey is small and estimates are subject to great sampling variability, we used rates of labor force accession and separation for larger groups. For example, the rates for therapists overall were applied to physical, occupational, and respiratory therapists separately. In approximating additions to the work force, the accession rate for 1983–1984 was applied to the 1984 work force to generate an estimate of the number of persons who joined the work force in 1984. That number was held constant each year.

Chapter 4 brings together the committee's information about the demand for and supply of allied health practitioners. The BLS employment projections for each field to the year 2000 are evaluated in light of expectations about the forces that drive demand. The results of the process to estimate the supply of workers that has been described in this chapter are compared to the expected demand. To this, the committee has added its knowledge of how the fields are faring in current labor markets and the trends in the fields in numbers of graduates and programs to make an assessment of the future balance between demand and supply.

DATA FOR PROJECTING THE FUTURE SUPPLY OF ALLIED HEALTH WORKERS

Current (Base Year) Supply

The BLS Industry–Occupational Employment matrix estimates the number of employed persons in each of 480 occupations. It is not an unduplicated count; wage and salary workers holding two jobs would be counted twice. The most recent data, used as the base for employment projections to the year 2000, were for 1986. The next year for which these data will be available is 1988.

The occupational classifications used in the Occupational Employment Survey, the principal source of data for the matrix, are consistent with the standard occupational classifications used by all federal agencies that collect data. They represent a balance between comprehensive coverage that provides quality data and the ability (and willingness) of employers to respond. (Appendix C gives the current definitions used in hospitals.) These categories and definitions should be continually evaluated and modified, if necessary, to portray the allied health work force accurately.

The other data source for examining the base year supply of workers is membership data from allied health associations. For fields that are well defined and have a single route of entry, and in which the associations represent a very large proportion of the field (e.g., occupational therapy), this source usually provides a good estimate. For many allied health fields, however, association membership data are incomplete or nonexistent. (See Appendix D for a discussion of the different sources of data on the supply of workers for each field.)

New Entrants

For fields in which the bachelor's degree is the entry-level educational requirement, there are two main sources of data. The U.S. Department of Education collects historical data on degrees awarded by field of study. These data include the allied health fields of occupational therapy, physical therapy, dental hygiene, medical record librarianship, medical laboratory technologies, radiologic technologies, and speech pathology and audiology. The Center for Education Statistics periodically makes projections of the total number of bachelor's degrees and the number of awards to men and women. These projections are based on mathematical projections of historical trends in college enrollment by different age groups. As discussed earlier, the committee has projected new entrants from bachelor's degree programs in some fields by assuming that the field's share of bachelor's degrees in the years 1987 through 2000 will remain constant at the 1986 level.

The second principal source of data on new graduates is the bodies that accredit education programs. CAHEA is the largest, representing 24 allied health field occupations in 1987. Others include the American Physical Therapy Association and the American Speech–Language–Hearing Association. Estimates of the number of future new entrants to the various fields can be extrapolated from historical figures on graduates. Individual states can use data from their own higher education institutions.

Other Inflows

The weakest links in projecting the future supply of allied health workers are the data for estimating entrants from outside the labor force, from other occupations, and from abroad (immigration). These inflows (and mirroring outflows) are important short-run labor market adjustment mechanisms. The BLS staff has made some headway by matching Current Populaton Survey data and calculating inflows and outflows for the matched observations (Eck, 1984). Yet for occupations with small numbers of workers (such as many of the allied health fields), these estimates are based on an extremely small number of observations. Estimating inflows and outflows of workers is an area in which the professional associations could do a great deal to improve the data. The Forum on Allied Health Data, with the help of appropriate expert consultants, should give attention to this serious data weakness.

CONCLUSIONS AND RECOMMENDATIONS

The committee found that available data for assessing the current supply of allied health personnel are inadequate, and it suggests that efforts be made to improve these data. The BLS employment (demand) projections are quite valuable and, when used in conjunction with other data, are likely to be the only available demand estimates that are comparable across fields.

The federal government has a responsibility to monitor the health care work force and to inform participants in the health care labor market and public policymakers of trends and developments. The work of the Bureaus of Health Professions and Labor Statistics and the Center for Education Statistics is to be commended and should be built upon. To improve the data on allied health fields, **the committee recommends that the secretary of health and human services convene an interagency task force composed of representatives from BLS, the Center for Education Statistics, and other agencies that collect relevant data on the allied health work force. This task force should work toward increasing the amount and improving the quality of data needed to inform public policy decision makers, health care managers, unions, prospective students, and academic institutions about the allied health occupations.**

Staff for the task force should be provided by the U.S. Public Health Service focal point for allied health personnel that is recommended in Chapter 5.

REFERENCES

Eck, A. 1984. New occupational separation data improve estimates of job replacement needs. Monthly Labor Review 107:3–10.

Goldstein, H. 1987. Projections of demand and supply in occupations. Paper prepared for the Committee to Study the Role of Allied Health Personnel, Institute of Medicine. November.

Hall, R. E. 1978. Job vacancy statistics in the United States. Background paper no. 3. Washington, D.C: National Commission on Employment and Unemployment Statistics. May.

Institute of Medicine. 1983. Nursing and Nursing Education: Public Policies and Private Actions. Appendix 5, Projections of Registered Nurse Supply and Requirements. Washington, D.C.: National Academy Press.

Jacoby, I. 1981. Physician manpower: GMENAC and afterwards. Public Health Reports 96(4):295.

Saunders, N. C. 1987. Projections 2000: Economic projections to the year 2000. Monthly Labor Review 110(9):11–18.

Silvestri, G. T., and Lukasiewicz, J. M. 1987. Monthly Labor Review 110(9):46–63.

Sloan, F. 1975. The Geographic Distribution of Nurses and Public Policy. Washington, D.C.: U.S. Government Printing Office.

3

Forces and Trends in Personnel Demand and Supply

CHAPTER 1 DESCRIBED 10 ALLIED HEALTH FIELDS. People working in these fields have seen their roles evolve in response to such forces as demographic change, disease patterns, financing trends, structural changes in the delivery system, and technological development. This chapter examines these and other forces to establish a context for Chapter 4, which discusses demand and supply in individual allied health fields. Before considering each of the environmental pressures that projections of employment must take into account, the interaction of several forces in one allied health field—respiratory therapy—is illustrated.

RESPIRATORY THERAPY'S MOVE INTO THE HOME: THE ROLE OF INTERACTIVE FORCES

Respiratory therapy's move into the home is an example of how several environmental forces acting together may affect the evolution of a health care service. These forces may bring about a shift in the work site and can affect the independence, earnings, and educational requirements of practitioners.

As with other allied health services, some respiratory therapy services have shifted from hospital-based to home-based delivery. Although respiratory therapists have long provided oxygen to patients at home, only recently have technologically advanced life-support systems (e.g., mechanical ventilators) been widely used there. Several forces operating together may have accelerated the trend toward home delivery of respiratory therapy services. These forces include the following:

1. *Demographic change*   As of 1984 approximately 28 million Americans, or 11.9 percent of the population, were aged 65 or older; the over-75 group is now the fastest growing age segment of the population (Public Health Service, Office of Disease Prevention and Health Promotion, 1987). The aging of the U.S. population can be viewed in terms of its relationship to disease prevalence: as the population ages, chronic diseases grow more prevalent. It is estimated that over 3 million Medicare patients suffer from chronic obstructive pulmonary diseases such as emphysema, chronic bronchitis, and asthma. Almost a quarter of a million others experience breathing difficulties for reasons other than pulmonary disease (e.g., spinal cord injuries). As many of these conditions progress, respiratory therapy becomes necessary.

2. *Technological change*   Several innovations in technology have made home-based respiratory care feasible and more acceptable to patients. For instance, equipment has become smaller. Some microprocessor-controlled ventilators and suction machines are compact enough to be mounted on wheelchairs or specially designed carts, giving people who need the machines a measure of mobility.

3. *Health care financing policies*   Environmental forces are not always expansionary. Health care financing policies, including pressures to cut health care costs, may fuel the move to home care. On the other hand, financing policies may also be used to curtail an expansion of home care that is made possible by new technologies.

Medicare's prospective payment system is stimulating the need for respiratory therapists outside the hospital. PPS gives hospitals a strong incentive to discharge all patients as quickly as possible, thereby reducing hospital costs. Pulmonary patients, although well enough to be discharged, are often in need of care at home. Yet Medicare does not reimburse the home care services of respiratory therapists on a per-visit basis. Rather, the cost of their services may be included as an administrative expense by agencies providing home care services. Only 6 percent of home health agencies retain a respiratory therapist. The rest occasionally consult with therapists, contract with durable medical equipment services, or arrange short-term training courses for their nurses assigned to pulmonary patients. Respiratory therapists employed by suppliers of oxygen and other equipment are reimbursed under Medicare's durable equipment benefit. In a 21-state survey, Gilmartin and Make (1986) found that Medicare and Medicaid were paying more than $270,000 per year for each ventilator-assisted hospital patient. The association estimated that the cost for equivalent care in the home would be $21,000 per year. Furthermore, it was estimated that over 2,000 chronic ventilator-dependent hospital patients were well enough to be cared for at home (Gilmartin and Make, 1986). The Health

Care Financing Administration argues, however, that expanding Medicare coverage to include home-based respiratory care is likely to increase Medicare costs because it would be difficult to limit specialized care to those who truly need it (Health Care Financing Administration, 1986).

In sum, financing policy has provided an impetus for respiratory home care as well as impeded its growth. Improved technology (spurred by the availability of financing) has made respiratory home care feasible, and the increasing number of elderly people in the population has heightened the demand for such a service. The social value placed on independent living has increased the marketability of delivering respiratory therapy services in the home and has placed pressure on policymakers to expand insurance benefits to include home-delivered care.

The remainder of this chapter examines a number of separate forces to determine how each impinges on the demand for and supply of allied health personnel and to emphasize how an understanding of these forces can help local decision makers interpret change in their own environment.

FORCES THAT DRIVE THE DEMAND FOR ALLIED HEALTH PRACTITIONERS

Population Growth and Demographic Trends

Demographic trends provide clues about tomorrow's health care consumers and their health care needs. An analysis of the changes in the composition and growth of the U.S. population shows how these trends translate into changes in health care needs.

Population growth in the United States is slowing. The population increased by 1 percent annually between 1972 and 1986, but the Bureau of the Census projects growth of only 0.8 percent annually to the year 2000. The rate of growth will not be uniform among age, race, or ethnic groups, as shown in Table 3-1, which is based on the moderate projections of the Bureau of the Census (Fullerton, 1987). Minority populations will grow faster than the white population; the number of children and youths (with the exception of high school youths) will decline; the working-age population will grow twice as fast as the total population; and the number of people of retirement age will increase with the greatest rate of growth occurring among people aged 85 or older.

The Elderly

Between 1940 and 1984 the number of people aged 65 and older more than tripled, growing from 9 to 28 million; this group is anticipated to grow to 35 million, or 13 percent of the population, by the year 2000.

TABLE 3-1 U.S. Population (in millions) by Race and Age, 1986 and Projected for the Year 2000

Population	1986	2000	Percentage Change, 1986–2000	Percentage Distribution	
				1986	2000
Total	241.6	268.3	11.1	100.0	100.0
White	204.7	221.5	8.2	84.7	82.6
Black	29.4	35.1	19.4	12.2	13.1
Asian and other	7.5	11.6	54.7	3.1	4.3
Hispanic	18.5	30.3	63.8	7.7	11.3
Age group					
0–4	18.1	16.9	−6.6	7.5	6.3
5–13	34.2	33.5	−2.0	14.2	12.5
14–17	14.8	15.3	3.4	6.1	5.7
18–24	28.0	25.2	−10.0	11.6	9.4
25–64	116.3	142.5	22.5	48.1	53.1
65–84	26.4	30.3	14.8	10.9	11.3
85 and older	2.8	4.6	64.3	1.2	1.7

SOURCE: Fullerton (1987).

While increases in the number and proportion of individuals over 65 have been considerable, a faster rate of growth is evident in the very old segment of the population. In 1950 there were just 600,000 people aged 85 or older; by the year 2000 it is expected that number will have increased nearly eightfold.

As the number of elderly people increases, the demand for allied health practitioners in a variety of fields will rise accordingly. About 17 percent of occupational therapists' total practice in 1982 was service to the elderly in nursing homes and acute care hospitals. Audiologists now spend one-third of their time with older persons (National Institute on Aging, 1987). Using straight-line projections and assuming that the mix and ratio of personnel to patients will be the same in the year 2020 as they are today, the National Institute on Aging estimates that twice as many occupational and physical therapists will be needed in 2020 as are available today. It also estimates that 40 percent more audiologists will be required to maintain service at the current level (National Institute on Aging, 1987).

Children

Between 1980 and 1984 the number of school-age children fell by 2.5 million. During that same period, however, the under-5 population rose 9 percent to 17.8 million, the largest under-5 population since 1968, when it was 17.9 million. The Census Bureau expects that there will be fewer children under 5 (16.9 million) by the year 2000, and the number of children as a whole (under 17 years old) will fall from 67.1 million in 1986 to 65.7 million in 2000 (Fullerton, 1987).

Children and adults use health care services differently. Children have less need of acute care services and have fewer hospital days (National Center for Health Statistics, 1986). A reduction in the number of children in the population does not affect the demand for all allied health practitioners. For those practitioners employed by schools (speech–language pathologists, for example), the number of children in the population has a noticeable impact on demand. For practitioners focused on acute care, the impact, if any, is slight. Children are also major users of disease prevention services, some of which employ allied health practitioners—for example, dental hygienists in dental caries prevention. For practitioners in many allied health fields, children represent only a small portion of their practice.

The implications for allied health practitioners of the predicted drop in the number of children in the population must be balanced against the effect of disease prevention efforts and the vigor with which such efforts are being made.

The demand for those allied health personnel who are most central to child health services (e.g., dental hygienists, speech–language pathologists and audiologists) will depend to a great extent on public investment decisions that are often made at the local level. Local funds are the sole source of support for health education programs in 75 percent of all school districts. About 20 percent of school health education programs receive state funding; only 3 percent receive federal, private, or special funds for such programs (Public Health Service, Office of Disease Prevention and Health Promotion, 1987).

Minorities

One out of five persons in the United States in 1986 was a member of a minority group. Blacks, the largest group at 29.4 million, constituted 12.2 percent of the total population in 1986. By the year 2000, 35.1 million blacks will constitute 13.1 percent of the population. The number of Hispanics is rising even more sharply. Hispanics totaled 9.1 million in 1970 and 18.5 million in 1986; they are expected to total 30.3 million people— more than 11 percent of the population—in the year 2000. The number of Asians and Pacific Islanders in the United States is also growing rapidly. Between 1970 and 1980 this population group grew 120 percent to 3.7 million. By the year 2000 it will total 11.6 million (Fullerton, 1987).

The prevalence of some diseases is higher among minorities than among whites. Diabetes, for example, is far more prevalent among blacks than among whites, and the incidence rate for cancer in 1983 was highest among black males. Among native Americans, cirrhosis, pneumonia, and diabetes are more common than among whites, and the prevalence of diabetes among Mexican Americans is nearly twice that among whites (Public Health Service, Office of Disease Prevention and Health Promotion, 1987).

The changing proportion of the total minority population and the higher prevalence of some diseases among the various groups in that population may affect the demand for services as health care needs change. Factors such as financial and geographic access barriers also influence the demand for health care services, however, and health care needs do not always translate into a demand for services. Minorities are more likely than whites to lack health care insurance, and they consistently report greater difficulty than whites in gaining access to medical care. Twenty-six percent of Hispanics have no medical coverage compared with 9 percent of whites and 18 percent of blacks (Public Health Service, Office of Disease Prevention and Health Promotion, 1987).

These differences between whites and minorities in access to health care are reflected in health care utilization rates. Twenty percent of blacks and 19 percent of Hispanics indicate they have no usual source of medical care, compared with 13 percent of whites. Between 1978 and 1980 the percentage of people 4 to 16 years old who had never received dental care was higher among Mexican Americans (30.7) than among blacks (22.3) or whites (9.7). Similarly, the percentage of individuals with no physician contact was higher among Mexican Americans (33.1) than among other Hispanics (23.9), blacks (23.8), or whites (20.4) (Public Health Service, Office of Disease Prevention and Health Promotion, 1987).

The expected increase in minority population groups by the year 2000 could have an effect on the need for allied health practitioner services. For these needs to translate into effective demand, however, the current barriers to care must be eliminated.

Disease Patterns

There are two changes in disease patterns within the United States that deserve special attention because of their potential impact on allied health personnel. First, there is the growing acquired immune deficiency syndrome (AIDS) epidemic. Second, whereas infectious diseases such as influenza, smallpox, and tuberculosis were the leading causes of death at the turn of the century, today chronic diseases predominate in this area.

Acquired Immune Deficiency Syndrome (AIDS)

AIDS is a notable and unexpected exception to the trend of declining death rates from infectious disease. As of 1987 an estimated 1.5 million Americans were infected with the human immunodeficiency virus, now known to be the cause of AIDS. AIDS cases in the United States rose from 183 in 1981 to nearly 40,000 by the middle of 1987. Over 75 percent of persons diagnosed with AIDS die within 2 years of the diagnosis.

As the disease spreads and the number of cases grows, and particularly if the life expectancy of infected individuals lengthens with the discovery of new treatments, the health care system will be increasingly taxed. In 1985, AIDS was the cause of 23,000 hospitalizations, an increase from the estimated 10,000 of the year before. The average length of stay for an AIDS patient was more than double the overall average of 6.5 days (Trafford, 1987). The federal government estimates that it will spend $1 billion on AIDS in fiscal year 1988, 40 percent of which will go to patient care. The Health Resources and Services Administration (1988) estimated that AIDS will account for $8 billion to $16 billion in direct medical care expenditures in 1991.

Estimating the impact of AIDS on the demand for allied health personnel is fraught with uncertainties. Greater precision in estimating needs and workloads will come from a better understanding of some key determinants of the disease. Epidemiologists can estimate only roughly the number of individuals who are currently infected, as well as those who will develop the full-blown symptoms of the disease.

The disease manifests itself in many forms, and treatment patterns vary. The progression of the disease often resembles the chronic illnesses of old age (e.g., dementia and wasting). AIDS patients therefore need some of the same services as the elderly and may compete for scarce resources (e.g., skilled nursing care and home health services) (Health Resources and Services Administration, 1988). The volume of acute care facility use for AIDS care and treatment relative to that provided in community settings now varies among localities. The introduction of new preventive, diagnostic, and treatment modalities may alter the mix of personnel and settings of care in ways that are now difficult to predict. Methods of financing care may also play a role in determining the type and focus of AIDS care.

Some allied health fields already play a major role in addressing AIDS; the role of others is still emerging. Clinical laboratory personnel are not only conducting the tests used to detect the virus that causes the disease, but they are also facing a heavier workload generated by the secondary infections that AIDS patients often acquire. Occupational therapists are helping AIDS patients learn how to conserve their energy, and respiratory therapists are providing care to patients who develop lung infections. A host of counselors is emerging to assist patients during the various stages of the disease.

The committee noted growing concern about the effect of AIDS on the supply of as well as the demand for allied health practitioners. Some educators fear that potential allied health students may be dissuaded by their perceived increased risk of exposure to the disease. To date, however, there has been nothing beyond anecdotal evidence to indicate that this perception is a serious factor in allied health career choices.

Chronic Diseases

Chronic conditions are the most prevalent health problem for the elderly, and the proportion of elderly people in the U.S. population is increasing. More than four out of five persons who are aged 65 and older have at least one chronic condition, and multiple conditions are commonplace among older persons (U.S. Senate, Special Committee on Aging, 1987).

The demand for allied health practitioners may be influenced both by efforts to curtail the incidence of chronic disease and by medical successes in treating chronic conditions. For example, some allied health fields are directly affected by widespread efforts to reduce the risk factors for cardiovascular disease. Clinical laboratory personnel are conducting more blood tests and dieticians are providing more counseling in an effort to determine and control cholesterol levels. Increased rates of survival in cases of stroke and heart attacks may mean increased demand for health care because the majority of patients do not make a full recovery (Public Health Service, Office of Disease Prevention and Health Promotion, 1987). Of the nearly 2 million stroke patients in the United States, 40 percent require special services and 10 percent require total care. The results from a large, longitudinal study also indicated the need for care: when stroke survivors were examined an average of 7 years after their stroke, 31 percent needed assistance in self-care and 2.7 percent required help in ambulation (Public Health Service, Office of Disease Prevention and Health Promotion, 1987).

Economic Growth

The growth of the economy as a whole dictates how much income will be generated and how this level of income will affect government spending and the income that will be available for families to spend on health care (and other kinds of consumption) and to save.

There are many uncertainties involved in projecting economic changes. They range from the policies that will be adopted regarding taxes, government expenditures, foreign trade, and events such as wars and revolutions, to scientific discoveries that affect technology, and even to the weather, which may kill crops or create disasters. Making a projection entails making assumptions as to how each of these uncertainties will affect economic change. BLS, whose employment projections the committee used, details a long list of such assumptions; from these, it calculates high, low, and moderate projections to illustrate that there is a range of error around any projection and to describe the sensitivity of the projections to these variables.*

Personal income affects all kinds of expenditures, including health care spending, in many ways. For instance, it influences what consumers are willing to spend on health insurance. Consumers are also responsible for about a quarter of total national health care expenditures through direct, out-of-pocket payment for services (Health Care Finanacing Administration, 1987). Under BLS's moderate scenario, real disposable income (i.e., income after taxes and before inflation) is expected to grow by 2.4 percent annually (low projection, 0.7 percent; high projection, 1.9 percent), less than the 2.7 percent average annual growth for the previous 14 years. From this projection are derived the BLS projections of personal consumption expenditures on services (of which health care services are a part). The expenditures on services are expected to grow faster than total personal consumption expenditures, as they have in the past: 3 percent (low projection, 2.2 percent; high projection, 3.3 percent), compared with the 3.2 percent average for 1972–1986.

Government spending is influenced by economic conditions. BLS projects higher levels of federal government spending in their high-growth projection than in their low-growth projection. This factor is important for health care employment because the federal government accounts for nearly 29 percent of national health care expenditures. BLS projects the Medicare portion of federal health care expenditures in constant dollars. The increase from the low projection in 1986 to that of the year 2000 is 30 percent; the increase from the 1986 high projection to that of the year 2000 is 62 percent. Between the 1986 and year 2000 moderate projections, BLS predicts a 43 percent increase in expenditures. These differences could have an effect on those allied health practitioners whose employment is significantly dependent on Medicare spending.

Private health insurance, which pays for more than 30 percent of national health care expenditures, is affected by economic conditions in several ways. For instance, the size of corporate profits can affect the richness of the benefit packages and health insurance that employers offer employees. Furthermore, the number of people covered by private insurance depends in part on the unemployment rate, which in turn depends on economic conditions. Because unemployed people often lack health insurance, in times of high unemployment the demand for nonessential (and some essential) care is reduced. In that case, health care employment will also be reduced.

---

*Data for the discussion of the BLS economic projections that follows are drawn from Saunders (1987).

Structure of the Health Care Industry

The structure and organization of health care services are constantly evolving in response to such forces as the availability of money and human resources, regulation, consumer demand, financial incentives, and technology. Major changes in recent decades include the growth of multihospital systems and investor-owned health care providers, the growth of managed care, and the movement of care from inpatient settings into outpatient departments, physicians' offices, and specialized freestanding centers. Figure 3-1 illustrates the decline in the hospital as the prime employment site for the health care industry. This decline reflects a structural change: the hospital's fall from its position of primacy in health care provision.

Structural changes may or may not affect the delivery of health care services and the demand for health care workers. Changes in the location of a service may represent only a change in work site for allied health personnel without altering the number of persons who are actually employed. For example, hospital admission testing today is often done on an outpatient basis, and unless there is a change in the volume of tests performed, there is no numerical employment significance to the change in the testing site. Although structural changes may not affect demand, they could have an effect on educational requirements and regulation. Practi-

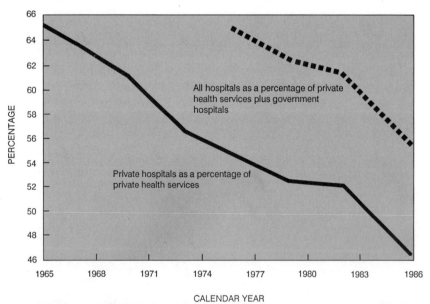

FIGURE 3-1 Hospital employment as a percentage of health care industry employment: calendar years 1965–1986.

tioners may need new levels or arrays of skills in the new settings, and new quality concerns may emerge that could result in changes in regulation.

Other changes in the structure of the health care industry have considerable implications for allied health practitioner demand. For example, as patient lengths of stay in a hospital become shorter, the need for home care increases and more practitioners may be needed. To determine whether a change in the location of care has implications for demand, one must ask whether each allied health field used in the traditional location is likely to be used in the new setting, and whether the volume of service and productivity will change.

The growth of HMOs has had no real impact on allied health employment to date. A 1987 survey of allied health employment in 56 HMOs that included staff, group, and independent practice association models across the country found that employment for most allied health fields was not substantial. For example, 22 HMOs employed a total of 110 medical technologists, 26 HMOs employed 42 nutritionists, and 13 HMOs employed 34 physical therapists. Respondents stated that they did not expect to employ larger numbers of practitioners in the near future (Rudman et al., 1987).

The formation of multihospital systems is important to allied health employment if these systems staff their facilities differently than independent hospitals. Studies that compare staffing in different types of hospitals have often focused on ownership characteristics such as public, private, for-profit, and not-for-profit status (see, for example, Watt et al., 1986; Mullner and Andes, 1985). Little is known about the differences in staffing between independent and multi-institutional facilities.

BLS has projected employment in the health care industry to the year 2000 (Personick, 1987). (See Appendix E for a detailed discussion of these projections.) The projections take into account some of the structural changes discussed in this section. Notably, BLS foresees that hospitals will increase employment despite the shift to outpatient care. This trend is largely due to the expected increase in the proportion of elderly people in the population and to advances in technology. Table 3-2 shows actual employment in 1986 in five health care settings and the BLS projections to the year 2000. Outpatient facilities with an annual growth rate of 4.6 percent are expected to show the highest growth rate and rank as the second fastest growing industry in the economy in terms of employment. But because the private hospital sector is so much larger, its 1 percent annual increase will add almost as many jobs as the 4.6 percent growth of the outpatient setting. The second fastest growing sector—offices of health practitioners—reflects the growth of such activities as physicians' office labs, office surgery, and independent allied health practices. Nursing homes will also experience rapid growth as the aged population grows and early discharge from hos-

TABLE 3-2   Wage and Salary Employment (in thousands) in Health Care Services by Setting, 1986 Actual and Projected for the Year 2000

Setting	Actual, 1986	Projected, 2000	Annual Increase (percentage)
Health care services excluding federal hospitals	7,599	10,844	2.6
Total private health care services	6,551	9,774	2.9
Offices of physicians, dentists, and other health care practititioners	1,672	3,061	4.4
Nursing and personal care facilities	1,250	2,097	3.8
Private hospitals	3,038	3,513	1.0
State and local hospitals	1,048	1,070	0.2
Outpatient facilities and health care services not cited elsewhere	591	1,103	4.6

SOURCE: Personik (1987).

pitals increases the demand for nursing home care. Thus, an additional 800,000 jobs will be generated by nursing and personal care homes by the year 2000.

Health Care Financing

Health care expenditures in the United States are rising. In 1986 Americans spent an average of $1,837 per person on health care for a total of $458 billion. This total constitutes 10.9 percent of the GNP, an increase from 10.3 percent in 1984 and 5.9 percent in 1965. The Health Care Financing Administration projects health care expenditures of $1.5 trillion in the year 2000—the major payers being the federal government, which will pay one-third; private insurance, which will pay 30 percent; and patients, who will pay one-quarter (Health Care Financing Administration, 1987). As health care payers look to the future, the picture is one of increasing costs as the population ages and scientific advances make care ever more complex.

It is difficult to overstate the effect that financing policy has on the demand for allied health personnel. Two types of impact on employment should be highlighted.

First, financing incentives can change the way a health care provider views allied health services. Whereas some services, such as laboratory services, were considered to be revenue producing prior to the recent financing change to prospective pricing, they are now perceived as a cost element in the health care product and thus ripe for management economizing efforts. Alternatively, the way health care services are reimbursed can create incentives for the expansion of a service to which allied health workers contribute. For example, the ability of a hospital to enter the sports medicine market will depend on its ability to attract physical therapists.

Second, financing policy also affects the ability of individual allied health practitioners to prosper in the health care market. At issue in this case are fee-for-service reimbursement and direct access to patients without physician referral. Tied to these issues are a set of regulatory concerns embodied in licensure laws, such as scope of practice and supervision of practitioners by other health professions. Respiratory therapists, for example, are seeking to gain direct Medicare reimbursement for home services so they can move from a consideration of their services as part of home health agency overhead to marketing their own skills in a manner not unlike that of occupational and physical therapists. Likewise, dental hygienists are seeking to gain independence from dentists in their ability to bill for services, a move requiring both licensure and reimbursement accommodation.

Perhaps the most dramatic example of the importance of financing in generating demand for services and personnel is the spread of third-party reimbursement in the 1960s, a trend that generated increased demand for services, an era of hospital building and technology adoption, and rising employment for health care personnel. More recently, the federal government has established a cost containment measure, the prospective payment system (PPS), that shifts the risk of the cost to the provider. Under PPS, hospitals are reimbursed on the basis of a preset per case payment, and the level of payment depends on the diagnosis.

A number of observers have examined PPS's initial impact on hospital operations. Following initiation of the system, length of hospital stay decreased at a faster rate than had been occurring previously (although there was a slight upturn in 1986), and occupancy has averaged only 66.6 percent since 1983, when the phase-in of the program first started. However, the proportion of patients with complex problems has increased (Prospective Payment Assessment Commission, 1987), and staffing has been altered as hospitals adapt to these changes. Hospital employment, which had been increasing at a rate of 4.9 percent per year in the 6 years before prospective payment, decreased in 1984 and 1985 (2.1 percent and 1.8 percent, respectively) and increased only slightly (0.4 percent) in 1986 (Prospective Payment Assessment Commission, 1987). Further analysis of hospital staffing shows that the use of part-time employees has increased and for many allied health fields there was a shift to employees with higher levels of training. It is not clear whether the move to higher skill levels reflects the needs of sicker patients or a perception that a more highly educated employee is a more cost-effective employee. The shift to part-time staffing could be a cost containment effort as well as a way to make flexible staffing easier. For some allied health fields, it may simply reflect the difficulty of hiring full-time staff. Alternatively, it may signal a move to policies that are designed to minimize the cost of employee benefits.

The Bureau of Health Professions (Health Resources and Services Administration, U.S. Department of Health and Human Services) asked the American Hospital Association to report staffing changes since the introduction of PPS. The following general trends were found:

- increased emphasis on productivity;
- heightened demand for employees who can work in more than one functional area and thus decreased interest in professional credentialing that restricts the practitioner's scope of practice;
  - increased use of part-time employees, contract services, and float pools;
  - increased competition among professionals;
  - replacement of personnel by capital;
  - fewer management positions; and
  - increased retraining and cross-training of personnel (American Hospital Association, 1985).

A small study of 13 Philadelphia hospitals in 1985 provides some insight into the personnel strategies of institutions that are adjusting to PPS. Most of the hospitals surveyed had cut their labor force through attrition, primarily in the ranks of less skilled patient care employees (Appelbaum and Granrose, 1986).

More recent studies of PPS's impact on hospitals suggest that the downward trend in staffing has been reversed. A 1987 national survey of laboratories found that after sharp post-PPS staff and budget cuts, testing volume is up, budgets are bigger, and staff reductions are abating. In 1986 only 16 percent of labs reported staff increases; a year later, 31 percent were reporting staff increases (Gore, 1987).

Another aspect of health care financing—mandated benefits—may also influence the utilization of health care services. States mandate insurance coverage to improve access to services. In the past two decades, 645 mandated coverage bills have been passed by the states (Scandlen, 1987). Currently, coverage is mandated for physical therapists in two states and for speech and hearing therapists in four states (Scandlen and Larsen, 1987). Some states mandate the coverage of all licensed health care practitioners.

Technological Change

The direction of technological change and its effect on allied health employment are difficult to predict. Some of the changes in health care financing and the structure of the delivery system suggest likely future directions: health care managers appear to be interested in technologies that will improve productivity and lower costs; technologies that enable providers to establish organizations that fill a special market niche are also likely to be purchased.

Technological change is not only reactive (to such factors as financial incentives) but prospective as well; that is, it drives the type of care provided by delivery systems. For instance, the technology of renal dialysis gave rise to the creation of dialysis centers and to practitioners who specialize in treating patients with end-stage renal disease. Technologies also drive the organization of delivery systems. Electronic telemetry equipment, for example, enables patients to be treated in nontraditional settings such as satellite facilities, homes, and vehicles. How technologies that are as yet underdeveloped will influence allied health employment is, of course, not known. Seymour Perry, professor of medicine at Georgetown University and former director of the National Center for Health Care Technology, described the following advances at the workshop held by the committee in April 1987:

• Automation in clinical laboratories will progress, decreasing the complexity of tasks and increasing productivity. It is anticipated that the only category of lab personnel that may be replaced by computers is that comprising the least skilled. More highly trained individuals may actually be in greater demand as computers are added to the laboratory.

• Computer-based technologies will be used increasingly, especially for clinical decision making, administration, medical recordkeeping, and patient monitoring.

• Genetic and monoclonal antibody technologies will generate new diagnostic tests. Many monoclonal antibody-based diagnostic tests will be self-administered in the future, and new test reagents will replace more labor intensive tests such as culturing. The early diagnosis and monitoring of tumors permitted by these technologies will change treatment modes and prognoses for numerous cancers.

• Advances in technology will permit more health care to be delivered in outpatient settings. The development of less invasive surgical technologies will spur outpatient surgery. As new generations of laboratory and diagnostic imaging equipment become smaller, more diagnostic procedures will be performed in physicians' offices and other nonhospital sites. Other technologies, such as programmable infusion pumps for pain medication or chemotherapy, will shorten hospitalization and allow for home care of patients.

New technologies that emerge from basic science and that represent real advances in diagnosis and treatment are likely to be adopted. Yet initially, the effectiveness of such technologies is not always clear; hence, there is growing interest in technology assessment. In addition, it is not always clear how technological change will affect human resources, especially in the long run.

The development and adoption of new technologies follow various paths and have differing effects on the demand for allied health personnel. Along one path, for example, a new technology initially requires highly skilled personnel and is of low productivity until it becomes a routine procedure that can be performed in high volumes by lower level staff. In the path typically taken by laboratory tests, the test becomes automated. Other technologies may use personnel differently.

The relationship between human resources needs and technological change fluctuates constantly but is seldom explored, making it difficult to assess the future with much certainty. Although we have some understanding of the forces that drive technological change, the effects of such change on allied health practitioners have not been adequately researched.

The Supply of Other Health Practitioners

The supply of other health practitioners—doctors, nurses, dentists—influences the demand for allied health services in several ways. As the supply of physicians continues to grow at a rapid pace (over 50 percent growth is expected between 1980 and the year 2000), allied health practitioners must ask whether physicians whose practices fail to bring the income they desire will seek to take back functions they had delegated to allied health practitioners in earlier periods. Physicians also wonder about this. One surgeon wrote:

To abrogate one's responsibility for postoperative care is retrogressive and tends to return to the period of 200 years ago, when the surgeon was simply a technician. I do not believe that only the respiratory therapists can understand the controls of the MA2 or Bear respirators. I do not believe that the surgeon who operates upon the intestinal tract should need an enterostomal therapist to take care of the problems in a patient with an ileostomy. I do not believe that the surgeon who performs a mastectomy should require a physical therapist to assure that the patient has normal arm motion following this operation. (Jordan, 1985)

Since the Graduate Medical Education National Advisory Committee (GMENAC) made its prediction in the 1970s of a surplus of 70,000 physicians by 1990, there has been considerable debate in the literature about whether these numbers are in excess of an "optimal" level and, if there were, indeed, an excess of physicians by 1990, what that could mean for the health care system. GMENAC concluded that nonphysician providers (that is, physician assistants, nurse practitioners, and nurse-midwives) may substitute for physician services and thus aggravate the physician surplus (GMENAC, 1980). Some allied health leaders have been concerned that this conclusion has been generalized inappropriately to all allied fields.

For physicians to assume what are now considered to be allied health functions, at least three conditions must be satisfied:

1. Physicians must be willing once again to take on tasks that the medical profession had delegated to less highly skilled providers because these tasks were considered repetitive or unchallenging.

2. Physicians must be competent to perform the tasks. While in theory the medical doctor license permits the physician to perform most of the tasks of allied health practitioners, in many cases their training has not prepared them to function effectively or productively in the full range of services of many of the allied health fields.

3. Payers and managers must be willing to recompense the cost of the substitution. The decision to substitute physician time for the time of the allied health practitioner must make economic sense to the physician or the organization that employs the physician. In a physician's office this substitution implies that physician time is so underutilized that it is preferable to use a physician to do the tasks rather than pay an allied health practitioner to do them. In an organization that employs physicians, for example, an HMO, such substitutions mean that physician and allied health personnel salaries are so nearly equal that allied health practitioners are not worth employing because of their more limited scope of practice and sometimes more limited patient appeal.

Competition between physicians and allied health practitioners is most likely to occur when allied health practitioners are increasing their autonomy. For example, although physical therapists, physicians, and chiropractors offer the same service, in some senses they can be viewed as competing for the first contact with patients having musculoskeletal pain symptoms. The American Physical Therapy Association views competition in the following light:

Members of the American Physical Therapy Association are actively seeking legislative removal of the requirement for referral, that is, legislative provision for direct access to their services, and have succeeded to date in 14 states (evaluation with referral is permitted in another 22 states). This is an effort toward independence in practice that does not put the physical therapist in direct competition with the physician, and may, in fact, increase referrals to physicians in appropriate circumstances. This is not to say that competition is lacking between physical therapists and physicians. Such competition as does exist between these two practitioners is competition between their businesses, not between the services that each personally provides to patients. In recent years, physicians have increasingly employed physical therapists in their businesses and compete directly with the businesses of self-employed physical therapists and, in some instances, with the businesses of hospitals which have a variety of out-patient and "outreach" physical therapy units. (American Physical Therapy Association, 1987)

Medical technologists who are attempting to move more forcefully into roles as directors of full-service laboratories are raising issues involving "arbitrary barriers" that are being imposed by facility accreditation standards. Competition may come from physicians who are reportedly seeking a greater involvement in the laboratory business, and, to the extent that physicians' office laboratories substitute for other testing sites, the use of medical assistants and on-the-job trained personnel to run office laboratory equipment may be seen as a form of physician substitution and competition.

Anecdotally, there appears to be growing evidence of competition and "turf" disputes between nurses and allied health personnel. At the committee's public hearing (Washington, D.C., July 1, 1987), the Association of Surgical Technologists spoke about their controversy over the operating room sphere and whether they or nurses will perform certain functions. Future nurse–allied health practitioner confrontations will in part be determined by the supply of nurses and by whether managers will begin to limit the breadth of nursing duties. On the other hand, nursing appears to be moving up the ranks of faculty leadership into higher levels of decision making about whether nurses or others will perform certain roles.

Counterbalancing the possible direct competition to allied health practitioners from growing numbers of physicians is the positive effect of the volume of work that may well be generated by their increased supply. Utilization management techniques are geared to controlling the unnecessary use of services, but it is unclear how effective these tools will be in reducing the volume of ancillary services and how this in turn will affect allied health employment. Moreover, the continuing specter of malpractice militates against vigorous efforts to control testing. A far-reaching response to physicians who protect themselves against liability by practicing defensive medicine does not appear to be imminent.

The net effect of the growing physician supply weighs more heavily on the side of increasing rather than decreasing the services delivered by allied health personnel. That is not to say that turf issues between allied health practitioners and others will lessen, but it appears that demand for allied health personnel will not be unfavorably affected.

FORCES THAT DRIVE THE SUPPLY OF ALLIED HEALTH PRACTITIONERS

The discussion thus far has focused on the factors that drive the demand for allied health practitioners. In this section, we turn to forces that shape the supply of allied health personnel.

The U.S. Labor Force

The future availability of allied health workers cannot be divorced from larger trends in the U.S. labor force. The labor force is growing more slowly than in the past, and the participation rates of various groups within

TABLE 3-3 Projected Changes in the U.S. Labor Force Between 1986 and the Year 2000 by Age, Sex, and Race

Worker Group	Percentage Change 1986–2000	Percentage Distribution 1986	Percentage Distribution 2000
Total workers aged 16 and older	17.8	100.0	100.0
Men			
16 and older	11.8	55.5	52.7
16–24	−6.1	10.4	8.3
25–54	19.4	37.7	38.2
55 and older	−1.8	7.4	6.2
Women			
16 and older	25.2	44.5	47.3
16–24	0.1	9.4	8.0
25–54	35.8	29.8	34.4
55 and older	10.1	5.2	4.9
Race			
Whites aged 16 and older	14.6	86.4	84.1
Blacks aged 16 and older	28.8	10.8	11.8
Asians and other groups aged 16 and older	71.2	2.8	4.1
Ethnicity			
Hispanics aged 16 and older	74.4	6.9	10.2

SOURCE: Fullerton (1987).

it is changing. The labor force is becoming older; it also includes more women and more racial and ethnic minorities than in the past (Table 3-3).*

The number of women in the labor force is projected to increase more than twice as fast as the number of men, and in the year 2000 women will constitute nearly half the labor force. They will also account for 63 percent of the additional workers filling new jobs. Men and women of prime working age—that is, between the ages of 25 and 54—will be the most rapidly increasing group, while the number of younger workers will decline. The proportion of workers of prime working age will increase from 67.5 percent in 1986 to 72.6 percent in the year 2000. The number of black workers will increase twice as fast, Asian workers will increase five times as fast, and Hispanic workers more than five times as fast as the number of white workers. Hispanic workers will make up 29 percent of the workers entering the labor market between 1986 and the year 2000; other minority groups combined will constitute another 29 percent. Thus, by the year 2000 the economy will be more dependent on women workers (who have always been prominent in the allied health professions) and on minority workers.

---

*The discussion of the labor force that follows is based on data in Saunders (1987).

Trends in College Enrollment

In the majority of the allied health occupations, graduation from 4-year or 2-year college programs is the way workers qualify for employment. We must therefore examine trends in higher education enrollments and graduations as a first step in estimating the potential labor supply of allied health personnel.*

The college-age population—those people aged 18 to 24—is declining as a result of a decrease in births two decades ago. After peaking in the 1980–1982 period, this population had dropped 8 percent by 1986; it is expected to continue declining through 1996 when it will be 23 percent below the 1980–1982 peak. The number of college-age people will then begin to rise again, and by the year 2000 it is projected to be 6 percent above the 1996 low point but still 19 percent lower than the 1980 peak and about 12 percent lower than in 1986 (Figure 3-2). The resulting constriction in the flow of new workers into the labor force will affect all occupations. Whether it will affect the professions and other occupations that require college education as much as it affects those occupations that do not require college education depends on whether college attendance declines as much as the size of the population. College enrollments and graduations will maintain their current levels, or increase, only if a higher proportion of youths go on to college.

Workers in the allied health fields are primarily women. There are a few fields—emergency medical services, for example—in which women constitute a small minority; in a few others, such as respiratory therapy, the share of men and women in the work force is roughly equal. For the most part, however, women predominate in the allied health fields. For this reason, we focus on women's college participation rates and on the trends in women's choices of fields of study.

The number of women receiving bachelor's degrees increased steadily between 1970 and 1986, reaching 502,000 in the latter year (47 percent more than in 1970), as a rising proportion of college-age women completed college. The Center for Education Statistics projects a further increase in the number of women earning bachelor's degrees that will peak at 512,000 by 1989, followed by a slow decline through the year 2000 to 470,000 graduates—about 6 percent below the 1986 level. Because the size of the college-age population is expected to be 12 percent smaller than the 1986

---

*The following assessment uses data from the Census Bureau's Current Population Surveys and data developed by the U.S. Department of Education's Center for Education Statistics (National Center for Education Statistics, 1985; Center for Education Statistics, 1970–1987, 1987; D. E. Gerald, U.S. Department of Education, personal communication, 1988).

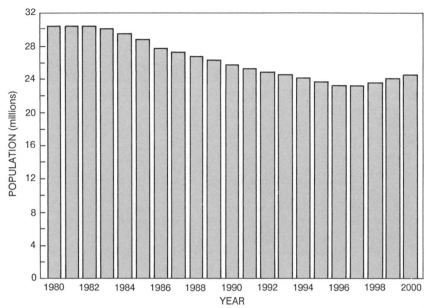

FIGURE 3-2　College-age population (18 to 24 years): Actual, 1980–1982, and projected, 1983–2000.

population by the year 2000, this projection of female graduates assumes that the proportion of women completing college will continue to increase.

Since these projections were made, the Center for Education Statistics has released preliminary data for 1987 (based on a sample of colleges). These data indicate an increase in the number of graduates between 1986 and 1987 instead of the decrease that had been projected. The preliminary estimate of female baccalaureate degree graduates for 1987 was 512,000— 2 percent above the 1986 figure instead of 1 percent below it, as had been projected. This increase may mean that the rising trend in the proportion of women completing college is continuing even more strongly than earlier estimates had assumed.

Graduations from programs that required fewer than 4 years of study increased more rapidly than all other awards granted by institutions of higher education from 1975 to 1985. Associate degrees awarded increased by 26 percent. Whereas the increase in men earning associate degrees was only 6 percent, almost 50 percent more women earned associate degrees in 1985 than had earned them a decade earlier. Other degrees awarded for programs of less than 4 years increased by 45 percent between 1975 and 1985.

There was a decline in the number of associate degrees awarded between 1985 and 1986 that is projected to continue through 1996, when the number of graduates will be about 11 percent fewer than in 1985. The Center for Education Statistics does not make sex-specific projections for associate degrees, but if current trends continue in the relative shares of degrees awarded to men and women, we may expect that the decrease in female associate degree graduates will be less than 11 percent. The number of associate degree graduates is expected to resume its upward climb in 1997, but in the year 2000 it will still be 8 percent below the 1985 level.

The Center for Education Statistics' 1972, 1977, 1982, and preliminary 1986 data show no trend toward increased college enrollment among people aged 25 to 44.

Trends in Women's Choices of Fields of Study

The proportion of female baccalaureate graduates who enter health fields (i.e., allied health, health sciences, and nursing) has increased over the past decade and a half. In 1970 slightly less than 5 percent of female baccalaureate graduates chose these fields. This proportion increased to about 11.5 percent in 1980; in 1986 it was just below 11 percent. Thus, at a time when the number of women bachelor degree graduates was increasing, the health fields nearly doubled their share of that rising total. Together, the fields of business and management, communications and communication technologies, computer sciences, and engineering did even better. Their share of female graduates increased approximately 11-fold— from less than 3 percent in 1970 to more than 32 percent in 1986. Yet the gains in the fields of health, business, and communications were at the expense of education. Education's share of female graduates declined from about 36 percent in 1970 to 13 percent in 1986, indicating a major change in women's career goals. The fields of psychology and the social sciences attracted gradually declining shares of graduates over the 16-year period, falling from 21 to 14 percent (Figure 3-3).

Among women earning associate degrees between 1983 and 1985, business and management was also the top-ranking field, followed by the health sciences. For men, the health sciences were not among the three top-ranking fields during these years.

Trends in the choice of study area within the health fields provide additional information to estimate the potential labor supply of allied health personnel. Nursing still accounts for almost 60 percent of the bachelor's degrees in the health fields that are awarded to women, although this figure has fallen slightly since 1970 (Figure 3-4). Hospital and health care administration, once the domain of men, has become increasingly attractive to women. For physical therapy, occupational therapy, and speech–language pathology and audiology, fields that require at least a bachelor's degree for entry, the number of graduates has grown over the years, but their relative shares of health degree awards have remained constant. Nurs-

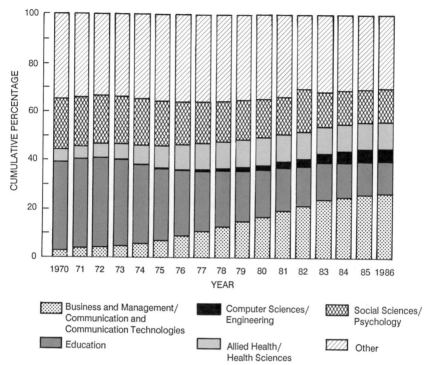

FIGURE 3-3 Women earning bachelor's degrees: Relative shares of selected major fields of study, 1970–1986.

ing also dominates the degree awards for programs that require fewer than 4 years of study, accounting for about 52 percent of these degrees in recent years.

For some fields, colleges are not the primary sponsors of CAHEA-accredited educational programs. Programs in radiography, for example, are based primarily in hospitals rather than in educational institutions. Consequently the Center for Education Statistics data just cited include only degrees and awards granted by institutions of higher education; they do not encompass all allied health program graduates. Nevertheless, the impact of non-college education programs on the validity of the trends portrayed by the data is marginal. Although noncollege sponsors accounted for 40 percent of all CAHEA-accredited programs in 1986, they accounted for only 33 percent of the graduates during the 1985–1986 academic year.

One of the factors influencing career choice is student perception of employment opportunities. The BLS expects the number of jobs in some of the fields that are currently popular with women (teaching, psychology, social work, and, surprisingly, most of the business executive occupations) to grow more slowly than the allied health fields in the coming years.

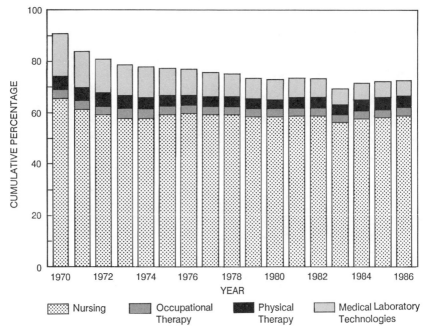

FIGURE 3-4 Relative shares of selected health fields, Women baccalaureates in allied health and health sciences: 1970–1986.

Accounting and nursing are expected to grow at roughly the same rate as the allied health fields. Employment in a few fields, including computer sciences, is projected to grow at a faster rate than employment in the allied health fields. To the extent that these expectations affect students' choices of careers, the allied health fields may be able to hold their own or even gain a larger share of female college graduates. Because the number of female college graduates is projected to remain at close to current levels or to decline only slightly over the next 12 years, the supply of graduates in the allied health fields may remain at close to current levels through the year 2000, despite the decline in the college-age population.

Education Financing

A commonly cited maxim among allied health leaders relates to the position of allied health in the pecking order of health professions education programs: "Allied health fields are the last to be funded in good times, the first to be cut when resources are reduced." This statement reflects the importance of the economic climate in which higher education resource allocation takes place and how decisions about allied health education resources are related to broader financing trends. Education financing, the efficiency of education programs, and higher education's perceived contribution to society all have an impact on the longevity of allied health education programs and future supply of allied health personnel.

Overall, national higher education expenditures in the past 10 years have grown. Between 1973–1974 and 1983–1984 current funds expenditures, adjusted for inflation, increased 23 percent for public institutions and 31 percent for private institutions. Much of that growth came in the mid-1970s. Public college spending in the latter half of the 10-year period grew by only 5 percent; private college spending grew by 13 percent (Center for Education Statistics, 1986).

There were shifts in revenue sources between 1973 and 1983. For public institutions the federal share of total revenue decreased from 12.8 percent to 10.5 percent; the state share remained relatively stable. For private colleges the percentage of total revenue attributable to federal sources rose slightly to 19.4 percent by the middle of the period but dipped to 15.7 percent by 1983–1984. State and local appropriations were relatively low and declined slightly over the 10 years—from 3.2 percent to 2.5 percent. Both public and private institutions that own hospitals have seen revenues from their hospitals increase from 5.1 percent to 7.4 percent for public colleges and from 8.7 percent to 10.1 percent for private schools. Private institutions rely more heavily on tuition than do public schools (39 percent compared with 15 percent), but the contribution of tuition is increasing in both types of schools (Center for Education Statistics, 1987).

Although they fare better than most arts and sciences programs in garnering external funding, allied health programs are nonetheless relative newcomers to academia. As federal support has diminished, allied health program administrators have become pessimistic about their place in higher education institutions relative to traditional departments (e.g., history and mathematics) and professional programs (e.g., engineering, medicine, and business administration).

Federal funds to stimulate allied health education program development peaked in 1974 at nearly $30 million and diminished substantially thereafter. No data are available on aggregate allied health education expenditures, but much of the cost is borne by state and local government expenditures and by tuition support in private institutions. The key driving forces behind allied health education financing are state and local appropriations, student demand, and the availability of clinical facilities and teaching staff. Allied health education programs are vulnerable in each of these areas (see Chapter 5).

Although there is variability among the states in the generosity of their educational funding, cutbacks often mean that allied health programs, because they are perceived to be expensive, are especially vulnerable. For some allied health fields, this vulnerability is compounded by falling student enrollments. Unlike other types of curricula, allied health education is dependent on clinical facilities for teaching resources and is therefore affected by health care financing policy as well as higher education budgets.

State legislators and higher education officials faced with difficult resource allocation decisions are seeking ways to ensure greater accountability from collegiate institutions. For example, a Michigan commission on the future of higher education in that state recommended various measures to attain a "stronger, leaner, more efficient system" and save on capital and operating costs. These measures focused on the review of "non-core" and "low-degree producing" undergraduate programs, health care profession programs, high-cost programs, and programs with excess capacity because of their geographic location (McKinney, 1986).

State officials are also paying close attention to the products of the higher education system and its impact on local economic development. Respondents to a 50-state survey revealed that formal assessment of student and institutional performance is a growing trend and is likely to intensify in the years ahead. Among the broad array of activities evaluated by outcome assessment are graduates' employment experiences, their evaluations of the education they received, employer hiring patterns, and former students' job performance. Counterbalancing this orientation toward jobs is a growing concern that technically trained individuals be creative, have the capacity for civic responsibility, and receive a liberal education. Specialized accrediting bodies for the professions are the continual targets of exhortations to foster curricula that include general education in the humanities, the arts, and the social sciences (Boyer et al., 1987).

Although most allied health programs report good initial job opportunities for their graduates, this advantage in terms of outcome assessment is balanced against the liabilities of unfilled student spaces, the need for expensive equipment and high faculty/student ratios, and an image in some academic circles as lacking in scholarly attributes.

Other Forces Influencing Supply

Unions

We noted earlier that the ability of the allied health fields to attract students depends in part on the attractiveness of allied health occupations relative to other occupations open to women. The ease with which a graduate can find work and the earnings that can be expected for that work are both facets of the perceived attractiveness of an occupation. One factor that affects both an occupation's earnings and the kind of work life it offers is the extent to which unions are present and active.

In many fields, unions help to determine demand and supply. Demand is affected by collective bargaining agreements concerning such issues as the length of the working day, the tasks that may be performed, and compensation. Supply is affected by altered pay, benefits, working hours, job security, and other factors that make an occupation more or less attractive to workers.

In recent years, unions have viewed health care, with its many unorganized workers, as a major opportunity for expansion. In the past the union movement has not had much success with health care workers. Its limited success has been in the public sector and then only in some areas of the nation. This situation has changed recently. Although union activity in the private sector as a whole declined from 23 percent to 18 percent between 1980 and 1985, union membership among health care workers increased by 6 percent to about 20 percent of the health care work force (American Hospital Association, 1986). In general, allied health occupations appear to be covered less frequently by labor–management contracts than are nurses, for example. In private hospitals in 23 metropolitan areas, 26 percent of nurses were covered, compared with 5 to 12 percent of occupational, speech, and physical therapists, medical record administrators, and dieticians. Approximately 20 percent of medical laboratory technicians were covered, as were 16 percent of radiographers (American Hospital Association, 1986).

Unions have not yet become a major factor in many allied health fields, but service workers have become, with some success, the focus of much union activity. The recent swing away from an emphasis on direct economic considerations that nursing unions are exhibiting may provide some clues about the concerns of other health care workers and suggest what may be done to make employment in these fields more attractive.

Malpractice Litigation

The supply of allied health practitioners in some fields is also vulnerable to the impact of malpractice litigation. Since the late 1960s the number of medical malpractice claims and the size of jury awards have soared. By the mid-1970s physicians in several states were having difficulty purchasing malpractice insurance as insurers withdrew from the market; some physicians could not buy insurance at any price. For all physicians the average cost of insurance increased by 81 percent between 1982 and 1985 (Health Care Financing Administration, 1987). Malpractice litigation raises questions about quality, liability, and other issues. The experience of physicians in this regard suggests how the supply of some allied health practitioners potentially could be affected by malpractice litigation and insurance. Twenty-one percent of respondents to a 1984 survey by the American Academy of Family Physicians reported that they had restricted their obstetrics practice because of high premium costs. Thirty-five percent of respondents to a survey by the American College of Obstetricians and Gynecologists said that they had responded to professional liability risks by altering their practice—reducing or eliminating the obstetrical component or eliminating care for high-risk pregnancies (U.S. Department of Health and Human Services, 1987).

The supply of allied health practitioners whose autonomy of practice is limited is unlikely to be affected by malpractice considerations. But for some allied health fields, these considerations could, in the future, become an important issue. The extent of physician supervision of an allied health practitioner's work can determine the practitioner's legal responsibilities. For example, if a physical therapist is the primary manager of a patient, the therapist is responsible for assuming that appropriate informed consent procedures are followed (Banja and Wolf, 1987). A 1982 case brought against an audiologist in the California Supreme Court (*Turpin* v. *Sortini et al.*, 643 P. 2d 954) reveals the vulnerability of practitioners to malpractice litigation even when the possibility of harm seems remote. In this case an audiologist's failure to diagnose deafness in a child was claimed to have damaged a child born subsequently to the parents who, because it had not been diagnosed, were not informed of the inheritability of the defect.

How the physician supply has been affected by malpractice issues can be studied to good effect by those concerned with the future supply of allied health practitioners. If practitioners successfully push toward modes of practice in which supervision diminishes and autonomy increases, malpractice litigation and the cost of insurance could eventually limit the supply of practitioners to those who are willing to endure the stress of litigation threats and who have the resources to pay high premiums.

ALTERNATIVE PATTERNS FOR DEVELOPMENT OF HEALTH CARE SERVICES: THREE SCENARIOS

It is obvious from the discussion thus far that there are many forces that affect health care services delivery and the demand for and supply of allied health personnel. It is virtually impossible to consider all of the elements of these forces in attempts to evaluate the future for any single allied health field. Instead, the committee developed alternative assumptions about the major factors that influence employment in the health industry. It believes that looking at a limited number of broad scenarios is a useful tool for decision makers trying to evaluate the future of specific allied health professions.

BLS's employment projections are based on macroeconomic factors—the trade balance, employment rates, productivity, and overall demand (see Appendix E). Although demand for health care services and allied health practitioners is related to macroeconomic growth, there are other forces at work that may operate independently of these factors and in some cases overwhelm them. Thus, the committee offers three simple scenarios that are driven by the single force most likely to determine the size and direction of change in health care services—health care financing. Unfolding events can be considered in the context of these scenarios; decision makers concerned with balancing demand and supply can apply the scenarios to estimate the demand side of the equation.

The three scenarios are based on health care financing for two reasons. First, financing is the major force shaping technology development and adoption, the structure of the industry, and other determinants of allied health personnel demand. Second, health care financing responds, through public and private policy decisions, to other important influences such as the economy, demographics, disease patterns, and social values. Thus, financing responds to some important determinants of demand and drives others.

Scenario 1: The Mixed Model

The mixed model assumes a continuation of the existing mixture of methods of payment. Selected services, both inpatient and outpatient, would be paid on a prospective basis (using capitation, diagnosis, or some other unit of payment); other services would be charged on a retrospective, fee-for-service basis. Within the fee-for-service sector, some payers would negotiate rates with providers, whereas other payers would pay on the basis of customary and reasonable charges. First-dollar coverage would be less usual than the use of copayments and deductibles as utilization controls.

Other assumptions of the model include an increase in the proportion of the population in managed care systems, which is projected to grow steadily from today's approximately 10 percent. The model also assumes that hospital utilization by younger patients would continue to drop, but upward pressure from the aging population would overwhelm any downward trends and cause overall hospital admissions to rise slowly. The intensity of care would continue to increase, as would selectivity in hospitalizing young people and the number of admissions of older patients with complex problems. Hospitals would continue their vertical integration as they sought to retain their share of the market.

Under this scenario, non-inpatient services would increase, especially in freestanding centers, the home, hospices, hospital outpatient departments, and the like. Some long-term care would take place at home, but modest expansion in the supply of nursing home beds would allow nursing homes to continue as the chief long-term care institutional site. However, efforts would be made to moderate the growth of nursing home beds to contain costs.

Technologies that appeared to be cost-effective would be adopted relatively quickly and diffused throughout the health care system. Technologies that promised to improve patient care outcomes would also be sought, as would advances that allowed procedures to be performed on an outpatient basis.

Scenario 2: Prospective Payment

This scenario assumes that prospective payment would become the dominant payment mechanism, with not only hospital care but also most other sorts of care paid on that basis. Generally, payment would be established at a preset, negotiated level that was determined on a capitated or diagnosis basis. Under this scenario, HMOs and preferred provider organizations (PPOs), owned and run by insurance companies, would gain a substantial share of the market. Indemnity insurance would be expensive and infrequently used. Large organizations of employers would become sophisticated bargainers to successfully control health benefit costs through negotiations with insurance companies and HMOs. Those organizations in turn would bear the risks and thus would be impelled to exercise strict utilization control and case management and become skillful at payment negotiation to ensure their profits. The number of salaried physicians would increase substantially.

Hospital utilization would be affected by the growth of HMOs and other managed care systems that were successful in controlling admissions. Although the upward pressures of the aging population would be felt, under this scenario, those pressures would not be sufficient to prevent a small drop in overall hospital utilization. Because hospitalized patients would be more seriously ill, care would be more complex. Within the hospital, there would be great emphasis on employee productivity and ensuring that unnecessary or ineffective services were eliminated.

Outpatient and other cost-restraining delivery styles would increase rapidly with this scenario. Physicians who were not employed by managed care systems would broaden the scope of their practices, supplying an increasing range of services. All existing outpatient services would burgeon, and new ones would be added as technology and entrepreneurial providers took advantage of opportunities.

Technologies that were seen to be cost effective would be eagerly sought; other technologies would be viewed more skeptically. However, the increased emphasis on ensuring effective care would encourage increased technology assessment. The results of such research would be rapidly adopted.

Scenario 3: Access

Under this scenario, policy decisions would be made that attempt to ensure access to care for all in need, a goal that could be achieved by a number of mechanisms used singly or together. It could be accomplished by a scheme of national health insurance that might incorporate mechanisms of cost control. It could also be achieved by expanding public programs, expanding mandated insurance benefits, ensuring payment to providers who care for unsponsored patients, requiring all employers to provide adequate health insurance benefits, and instituting catastrophic insurance for those with incomplete coverage. Developing an adequate "safety net" would halt the cost shift to other payers, one way in which uncompensated care is supported today. This scenario is not necessarily an alternative to the first two scenarios but could occur in tandem with either.

It is assumed with this scenario that whatever funding arrangements were made, they would encourage individuals who might have postponed elective procedures in the absence of third-party payment to seek care in a timely fashion rather than delay seeking it until they became seriously ill. Thus, the intensity and complexity of inpatient care would decrease marginally. It is also assumed that funding would be made available for health promotion and disease prevention services that are thought to decrease total health care costs.

In Chapter 4 we show how these scenarios would affect the demand for practitioners in each of the 10 allied health fields named in Chapter 1.

CONCLUSION

This chapter described a number of factors—including aspects of population and economic growth and changes in financing and the structure of the health industry—that drive the demand for personnel in the health care fields. It also considered forces that may affect the supply of health care workers—for example, the growth of the U.S. labor force and the college-age population and trends in female students' choices of study field. Finally, the chapter presented three health care financing-driven scenarios that decision makers may find useful in trying to evaluate the future of specific allied health professions.

Educators, employers, and others are faced with difficult investment decisions in planning for future human resource needs. They must make their best guesses about the forces that drive the demand for and supply of workers—guesses about their magnitude, the directions they may take, and their interactions. The answers are not always obvious. There is no certainty, for example, as to how many AIDS patients will require and receive physical therapy services or whether sonograms will be routinely used to screen for cancer. Despite uncertainty, however, it is possible to learn more about how these forces influence allied health employment and the supply of workers in allied health fields. Methods may include tracking disease and treatment patterns and how allied health practitioners are used, or identifying new technologies and determining their likely impact on allied health services. Whatever the methods used, monitoring and investigating the key forces in the demand for and supply of allied health personel provides useful insights into the future and better information for determining policy actions.

REFERENCES

American Hospital Association. 1985. Effects of the Medicare Prospective Pricing System on Hospital Staffing. Final Report. Chicago, Ill.: American Hospital Association. December 31.

American Hospital Association. 1986. Report on union activity in the health care industry. (Unpublished paper.) Department of Human Resources, American Hospital Association, Chicago, Ill. September.

American Physical Therapy Association. 1987. Independent practice? Comments on draft background papers prepared for the American Society of Allied Health Professions' Invitational Conference, June 15–16, Washington, D.C.

Appelbaum, E., and C. S. Granrose. 1986. Hospital employment under revised medicare payment schedules. Monthly Labor Review August: 37–45.

Banja, J. D., and Wolf, S. L. 1987. Malpractice litigation for uninformed consent: Implications for physical therapists. Journal of the American Physical Therapy Association 67(8):1226–1229.

Boyer, C. M., P. T. Ewell, J. E. Finney, and J. R. Mingle. 1987. Assessment and Outcomes Measurement—A View from the States. Highlights of a New ECS Survey. Denver: Education Commission of the States. March.

Center for Education Statistics. 1970–1987. Digest of Education Statistics. Annual Reports. Washington, D.C.: U.S. Government Printing Office.

Center for Education Statistics. 1986. Higher Education Finance Trends, 1970–71 to 1983–84. Department of Education Bulletin OERI, CS 87-303B. Washington, D.C.: Government Printing Office.

Center for Education Statistics. 1987. Less-Than-4-Year Awards in Institutions of Higher Education: 1983–85. Washington, D.C.: Government Printing Office.

Fullerton, H. N., Jr. 1987. Projections 2000. Labor force projections: 1986–2000. Monthly Labor Review 110(9):19–29.

Gilmartin, M. E., and B. J. Make. 1986. Mechanical ventilation in the home: A new mandate. Respiratory Care 31(5):406–411.

GMENAC (Graduate Medical Education National Advisory Committee). 1980. Report of the Graduate Medical Education National Advisory Committee to the Secretary, Department of Health and Human Services. GMENAC Summary Report, vol. 1, no. 3. Washington, D.C.: U.S. Department of Health and Human Services.

Gore, M. T. 1987. The impact of DRGs after year 4: A swing to better times. Medical Laboratory Observer December:27–30.

Health Care Financing Administration. 1986. Report to Congress. Study of Home Respiratory Therapy. Washington, D.C.: U.S. Department of Health and Human Services.

Health Care Financing Administration. 1987. National health expenditures, 1986–2000. Health Care Financing Review 8(4):1–36.

Health Resources and Services Administration. 1988. Report of the Intragovernmental Task Force on AIDS Health Care Delivery. Public Health Service, Department of Health and Human Services. January.

Jordan, G. L., Jr. 1985. Presidential address: The impact of specialization on health care. Annals of Surgery 201(5):537–544.

McKinney, H. T. 1986. State control of higher education in Michigan: A new scenario. In Michigan Higher Education: Meeting the Challenges of the Future. Report from the Michigan Senate Select Committee on Higher Education. Lansing, Mich.

Mullner, R., and S. Andes. 1985. Differences in composition of personnel among government, voluntary, and investor-owned U.S. community hospitals. Executive summary paper. Hospitals and Health Services Administration January/February:72–88.

National Center for Education Statistics. 1985. Projections of Education Statistics to 1992–93: Methodological Report with Detailed Projection Tables. Washington, D.C.: Government Printing Office.

National Center for Health Statistics. 1986. Health United States 1986 and Prevention Profile. Public Health Service Publ. No. 87-1232. Washington, D.C.: Government Printing Office.

National Institute on Aging. 1987. Personnel for health needs of the elderly through year 2020. Unpublished draft. Washington, D.C.

Personik, V. A. 1987. Projections 2000: Industry output and employment through the end of the century. Monthly Labor Review 110(9):45.

Prospective Payment Assessment Commission. 1987. Technical Appendixes to the Report and Recommendations to the Secretary, U.S. Department of Health and Human Services. Washington, D.C.: Prospective Payment Assessment Commission. April 1.

Public Health Service, Office of Disease Prevention and Health Promotion. 1987. Prevention Fact Book. Washington, D.C.: Government Printing Office. April.

Rudman, S. V., J. R. Snyder, and S. L. Wilson. 1987. Allied health professionals and HMOs: A national survey. Paper presented at the annual meeting of the American Society of Allied Health Professions, Las Vegas.

Saunders, N. C. 1987. Projections 2000. Economic projections to the year 2000. Monthly Labor Review 110(9):11–18.

Scandlen, G. 1987. The changing environment for mandated benefits. Blue Cross and Blue Shield Association, Washington, D.C. April.

Scandlen, G., and B. Larson. 1987. Mandated coverage laws enacted through December 1986. Blue Cross and Blue Shield Association, Office of Government Relations, Washington, D.C. February 10.

Trafford, A. 1987. AIDS: The New Phase of Denial. Washington Post Health. July 28:8.

U.S. Department of Health and Human Services. 1987. Report of the Task Force on Medical Liability and Malpractice. Washington, D.C.: U.S. Department of Health and Human Services. August.

U.S. Senate, Special Committee on Aging. 1987. Aging America. Trends and Projections. U.S. Department of Health and Human Services, Washington, D.C.: Government Printing Office.

Watt, J. M., R. A. Derzon, S. C. Renn, and C. J. Schramm. 1986. The comparative economic performance of investor-owned chain and not-for-profit hospitals. New England Journal of Medicine 314(2):89–96.

4

Demand and Supply in 10
Allied Health Fields

MAJOR ECONOMIC, DEMOGRAPHIC, AND SOCIAL FORCES must be taken into account to assess the directions and magnitude of changes in the U.S. health care system and the implications of these changes for allied health employment. This chapter examines how each of 10 allied health fields is affected by these forces and how they will determine the demand for and supply of personnel for each field by the year 2000.

The discussion that follows deals with national trends, even though local decision makers concerned with allied health practitioners may be faced with conditions that differ substantially from the national experience. The committee believes that its national analysis will be helpful to those who must draw conclusions about the future of allied health personnel in their own localities.

The committee based its assessment of the future on several types of information. Bureau of Labor Statistics (BLS) projections of demand are the source of quantified demand information which the reader will find throughout this chapter (Bureau of Labor Statistics, 1987). To draw conclusions about demand the committee incorporated its own judgments about the impact of the many forces that drive demand. Assessments of supply were based on what would happen if the situation remained unchanged with respect to the rates at which individuals leave and enter the allied health work force. To that assumption were added assessments of the likelihood of the situation remaining unchanged. A final element in trying to foresee the future was the application of our limited knowledge of current demand and supply balances. Because decision makers must act even in the absence of complete data, the committee decided to make assessments of future labor markets for allied health practitioners using BLS data. (Chapter 2 described the BLS data collection and projection process.) The committee advises readers to view the projections critically, in light of their inherent limitations. These projections should be interpreted not as a precise prediction of the future but rather as indications of the magnitude of change. The tools can then be used as a basis from which local and federal decisions makers can develop their own best estimates of the labor market. The committee emphasizes the importance of continued data collection to allow more precise projections.

In some allied health fields the committee's assessment showed large discrepancies between demand and supply. The committee is not suggesting, however, that these gaps will necessarily occur. Rather, the market will eventually adjust so that a reasonable balance is achieved over time. If employers are sufficiently hard-pressed, they will raise salaries, which will attract more people to allied health careers. Employers whose ability to pass on costs is increasingly limited by prospective payment will also try to increase productivity and reduce the number of workers they employ as those workers become more expensive.

Yet the committee is concerned that the market response will not be quick or creative enough to avoid some negative consequences—for example, erosion of the quality of care, service disruptions, and constraints on the ability of providers to make timely investments in new modes of service. Because these are serious consequences, the committee believes that it is important to try to anticipate them well enough in advance to forestall them if possible. Later chapters in this report are devoted to examining ways in which health care provider and educational institutions can protect themselves and, ultimately, patients from the costs associated with imperfectly working markets.

The committee's comments about the way the year 2000 will look do not allow for major changes in the ways in which Americans pay for health care. If a major financing change should occur, the future of many allied health fields will be significantly altered. To illustrate the effects of financing changes, the committee applied the scenarios presented in Chapter 3 to each of the 10 allied health fields discussed in this chapter.

In assessing future personnel demand for each of the 10 occupations, we have assumed that the current mix of fees for service and prospective payment (i.e., the mixed model scenario) will prevail for the next 12 years. As health care policy decisions are made at the national and local levels, however, planners must adjust their views of future allied health employment. To assist in this process, the committee has indicated how each profession might be affected by incentives characteristic of the access scenarios (which could include new state Medicaid entitlements or a nationally mandated benefits program) or the prospective payment scenario (which could include a new state hospital rate commission or the extension of PPS to settings other than acute care hospitals).

The committee has also attempted to alert readers to the significant trends in factors influencing supply—most often, the number of graduates and the number of educational programs. Yet labor force behavior is equally important. Unfortunately, there are only crude data on entrance into and exit from the allied health labor force; thus, the committee could make only very rough estimates of future supply. What is known is that even small changes in tenure in the work force can have a substantial effect on the future supply of allied health personnel.

CLINICAL LABORATORY TECHNOLOGISTS AND TECHNICIANS

Demand for Medical Laboratory Technologists and Technicians

BLS predicts that between 1986 and the year 2000 the number of clinical and medical laboratory jobs for technologists and technicians will grow from 239,400 to 296,300, an increase of 24 percent. Although the growth rate is below that forecast for many other allied health occupations, it represents a substantial number (57,000) of new jobs. By comparison, the expected dramatic 87 percent increase in physical therapist employment represents only 54,000 new jobs. It must be remembered that the BLS data are based on employers' responses to questions about the numbers of people performing defined tasks. Respondents are not asked to distinguish licensed or certified personnel from those without such credentials.

Clinical laboratories are in a period of rapid change. Technological changes are allowing the performance of tests in new settings and are also generating new tests. PPS has caused hospital managers to rethink the relative roles of in-house and reference laboratories. Changes in reimbursement have made physicians seek the benefits of providing office laboratory services. New settings for health care, such as ambulatory centers, are encouraging the establishment of laboratories in nontraditional settings.

When analyzing these changes in terms of their impact on the demand for technologists and technicians, it is important to distinguish between changes that reduce demand, changes that increase demand, and changes that make no difference to manpower but only represent a change in location, techniques, or practice style.

Because approximately 63 percent of clinical laboratory technicians and technologists are employed by hospitals (Table 4-1), changes in that setting will greatly influence the demand for those personnel and where they work. Indeed, a number of factors that are currently affecting the hospital laboratory work load may, in turn, affect personnel needs.

TABLE 4-1   Major Places of Wage and Salary Employment for
Medical and Clinical Laboratory Technologists and Technicians, 1986
Actual and Projected for the Year 2000

Employment Setting	Number of Jobs, 1986	Percentage[a]	Number of Jobs, 2000	Percentage[a]
Total employment[b]	239,400		296,300	
Total wage and salary employment	238,400	100.0	295,200	100.0
Hospitals, public and private	149,800	62.8	160,000	54.2
Offices of physicians	30,100	12.6	46,200	15.7
Offices of dentists and other health care practitioners	890	0.4	1,800	0.6
Medical and dental laboratories	28,100	11.8	43,200	14.7
Outpatient care facilities	5,300	2.2	13,000	4.4

[a]These percentages were calculated using unrounded figures and therefore will not be identical to percentages that are calculated using the rounded figures provided in the table.

[b]Total employment = wage and salary employment + self-employment. These figures include 1,000 self-employed workers in 1986 and 1,027 in the year 2000 who are not allocated by place of employment.

SOURCE: Bureau of Labor Statistics (1987); moderate alternative.

The introduction of PPS and the resultant reduction in occupancy rates, as well as the incentives it offers to provide less costly care, all affect hospital laboratories in several ways. Many hospitals have increased their use of reference laboratories for specialized tests, concentrating in-house laboratory work on widely used tests for which economies of scale can be achieved. Simultaneously, much preadmission testing is done on an outpatient basis, and the inpatient test mix has changed as more complex cases are admitted. According to the American Hospital Association, full-time-equivalent (FTE) employment in U.S. registered hospitals fell between 1983 and 1986, with medical technologist employment falling by 2.4 percent. FTE employment of other laboratory personnel fell by 5.3 percent between 1983 and 1985 and rose by 2.1 percent in 1986 (Bureau of Health Professions, 1985; American Hospital Association, 1987). A survey of the early impact of the diagnosis-related group (DRG) system on 122 hospital laboratories noted that 63 percent of hospitals experienced increased test volume in 1983. Increases in test volume occurred in only 32 percent of hospitals in 1984.

The number of hospitals experiencing decreased test volume almost doubled from 24 percent in 1983 to 44 percent in 1984. The effect of the decreases on staffing was observable. Fifty-seven percent of laboratories reduced employment after PPS—only 4 percent increased employment (Medical Laboratory Observer, 1984). These early changes that reduced demand did not continue, however. Current utilization and budgets are growing, and staff reductions have abated (Gore, 1987). Because the hospital census is thought to be a less reliable laboratory work load predictor than the severity of patient illness (Harper, 1984), one must look to the patient mix for explanation. With an aging population, the severity of illness is increasing. Although the number of lab items per discharge fell substantially during the early years of PPS, it rose 19.8 percent in 1985. Possible reasons for the upturn include increased case complexity, fewer opportunities to shift care to outpatient settings, and fewer opportunities to eliminate unnecessary services (Prospective Payment Assessment Commission, 1987).

Medicare is not the only payer that is trying to reduce laboratory work. Other payers are becoming increasingly conscious of laboratory costs. For example, in 1987 Blue Cross and Blue Shield issued diagnostic testing guidelines for the appropriate use of 13 laboratory tests. Some of these tests are routine hospital admission or preoperative tests. While these guidelines were not associated with coverage rules, the recommendations are expected to be adopted by most of the plans and possibly by other insurers (Abramowitz, 1987). Efforts like that of Blue Cross and Blue Shield may herald a move from exhaustive testing to more targeted use of laboratory work.

Technological change affects clinical laboratories in all settings. Today, while there is much discussion of automation in the laboratory—even robotics—that may reduce personnel needs or lower the skill levels required, concomitantly, there are potentially offsetting developments of new and complex labor-intensive, nonautomated tests.

Technological changes, together with financial incentives and patients' desires, have stimulated physicians to make laboratory services available in their offices. Several surveys have been conducted of the extent of this practice. Estimates of the number of physician office laboratories range from approximately 80,000 to more than 250,000 (American Society for Medical Technology, 1986). BLS estimates that there are 30,100 technologist and technician jobs in physicians' offices, a number that is expected to rise to more than 46,200 in the year 2000. Observers close to the scene perceive diminishing enthusiasm for small physician office laboratories, possibly because they are not proving to be cost-effective and possibly because there are rising expectations of increased regulation to control quality.

Two important questions for laboratory personnel demand emerge from the physician office laboratory phenomenon. One is whether physician office tests are additional tests or substitutes for testing at other sites. Another is whether physicians employ clinical laboratory technologists or technicians. No evidence exists to answer the first of these questions. On the question of staffing, a literature review concluded that personnel other than technicians and technologists are more likely to do laboratory work in small or solo practices. Often, nurses are used. The larger the practice, the more likely that trained laboratory personnel are employed. One study found that more than 50 percent of group practices employed medical technologists (Frost and Sullivan, Inc., 1985). However, changes in the staffing of physician office laboratories may be on the way. Under its Omnibus Budget Reconciliation Act of 1987, congress enacted provisions that will require office laboratories that perform more than 5,000 tests on their own patients to conform to the Medicare conditions of participation developed for independent laboratories. This policy is scheduled to become effective in 1990. Technologists in independent practice are finding increasing employment opportunities as consultants to physicians who need help with calibration, quality control, test interpretation, more sophisticated procedures, and management of their office laboratories.

Other new sites for laboratory work include HMOs and ambulatory care centers. Although 5,500 such centers are projected to be in operation by 1990, not all will employ highly trained lab personnel. At small centers now, nurses and x-ray technicians often perform routine tests, with cross-training conducted by the facility owner (Baranowski, 1985).

The development of HMO laboratories is providing employment opportunities in a new setting, but this employment site should not be thought of as increasing the demand for personnel. Indeed, in the long run, as HMOs in competitive environments begin to seek new ways to control costs, it is reasonable to speculate that a reduction in demand for laboratory work may be brought about by curtailing superfluous testing.

Future demand for clinical laboratory personnel has thus far been discussed as if changes will affect technologists and technicians equally. Whether this will actually be the case is unclear. Although incentives to reduce costs might lead one to expect that employers will seek to use less expensive personnel, at times more highly trained staff can be more cost effective. Similarly, although some technological changes, such as increased automation, may allow employers to expand their use of technicians or on-the-job trained personnel, others will require more highly trained staff. The trend in this field appears to be toward the increased use of higher level personnel with demand for lower level staff strengthened by difficulties in hiring more highly skilled workers. A 1987 survey of the American Society for Medical Technology members reports: "Where hiring has occurred in the past two years . . . more technologists with the bachelor degree were hired than were clinical laboratory technicians (CLTs). Though some facilities reported substituting specialists and more advanced personnel for entry-level practitioners, others reported hiring more CLTs and on-the-job trainees (OJTs)—to some extent as a result of a shortage of clinical laboratory scientists (CLS) professionals" (Price, 1988).

In sum, many of the changes occurring in clinical laboratories involve alternatives in the settings in which testing occurs. Some of these changes are spurred by financial considerations; some are driven by changes in the structure of the health care delivery system. Generally, these changes do not affect the demand for trained personnel in a major way because they do not have significant effects on the numbers or types of tests ordered. Although some extra testing is stimulated by the new settings, not all of the work is being done by clinical laboratory technologists or technicians. A concern about laboratory work that has surfaced in the popular press and that has also been voiced by the professional associations relates to quality. Reports of inaccurate PAP smear readings and false-positive AIDS tests have often focused on the laboratory personnel—a focus that could result in increased demand for licensed personnel or in the hiring of more personnel of all kinds to relieve pressures on staff.

For the future, downward pressures on test volume caused by payers' attempts to reduce costs will be offset by upward pressures as new tests are developed and the aging population demands more services. Similarly, technological change will cause as much expansion as reduction in demand for trained personnel of all levels.

Any growth in the demand for medical and clinical lab technologists and technicians will derive from a general expansion of the health care industry, the aging of the population, and an increase in some specific trends such as increased therapeutic drug monitoring, testing for substance abuse, and AIDS screening. Together, these upward pressures should lead to employment growth at a rate that could even exceed BLS's predicted growth of 24 percent to the year 2000. If either AIDS or drug testing becomes widespread, the demand for clinical laboratory technicians and technologists will increase further. This rate of increase could be reduced if, as is likely, tests eventually become more automated.

Factors that would cause demand to change significantly and should therefore be monitored by those attempting to track the employment of clinical laboratory personnel include the following:

- policies concerning AIDS screening;
- policies concerning substance abuse testing;
- technological change;
- payers' attempts to control test volumes;
- quality concerns; and
- trends in state and federal regulation of laboratory settings.

The three scenarios described in Chapter 3—mixed financing, prospective payment, and access—have some straightforward implications for clinical laboratory technologist and technician demand. Under the mixed model, growth in jobs is expected (as described earlier in this chapter)—probably in excess of 24 percent to the year 2000. If prospective payment becomes the dominant model, laboratory testing will come under scrutiny and incentives will ensure that all testing contributes to the clinical management of patients. Technological changes to improve cost-effectiveness and decrease personnel, both in numbers and skill levels, will be adopted. Yet demographic pressures will still exert upward pressures. In sum, demand will grow at a slower pace under the prospective payment model than under the mixed financing scenario. If a policy to expand access to health care occurs, additional individuals receiving care will increase the demand for laboratory personnel in all settings.

Supply of Medical Technologists and Medical Laboratory Technicians

The number of baccalaureate graduates in the field of medical technology has shown a downward trend since the end of the 1970s. In 1986 4,477 medical technologists graduated from accredited programs, a decrease of 28 percent from 1980. The number of accredited programs for medical technologists also decreased—26 percent over the 10-year period ending in 1986. Hospital-based programs closed most frequently, but closures in general occurred because of budget restrictions, the impact of PPS, a lack of qualified applicants, and a decreased need for laboratory personnel in the program's immediate geographic area (CAHEA, 1985b).

During the past 10 years, total certificate medical lab technician programs decreased 69 percent. Yet associate degree medical lab technician programs increased over the 10-year period, and they increased more than four fold—from 38 programs to 214 programs. Between 1985 and 1986, however, there was a 5 percent drop (CAHEA, 1987a).

The trend in certificate and associate degree personnel (technicians) is less clear than that for technologists. Although the 2,747 technician graduates in 1986 represent a 9 percent increase over 1980, graduations peaked at nearly 4,000 in 1984 and show a downward trend since then. There are two routes to becoming a technician. One is graduation from a certificate program. Only 817 medical laboratory technicians graduated from certificate programs in 1986, 24 percent fewer than in 1981. The other route is through associate degree programs, from which the number of graduates (1,930) in 1986 was an increase of 11 percent over those graduating in 1981 (CAHEA, 1987a).

At the start of this study, anecdotal evidence from educators and others pointed to a surplus of clinical laboratory technicians and technologists. But during site visits and discussions with knowledgeable observers toward the middle of 1987, the committee began to hear of managers who were having trouble hiring staff for clinical laboratories. Other reports confirm this change (Meyer, 1988), and other evidence supports the suggestion that the labor market is getting tighter. A recent survey of the directors of accredited education programs shows that between 1981 and 1986 the percentage of directors who considered the job market for laboratory technicians and technologists to be attractive increased substantially (Parks and Hedrik, 1988). An informal survey by the American Society for Medical Technology found 54 percent of constituent societies reporting an undersupply of clinical laboratory technologists. The undersupply figure was 38 percent for technicians (Meyer, 1988). A study commissioned by the Health Resources and Services Administration noted that shortages of medical technologists are occurring in some locales (Mathematica Policy Research, Inc., 1987). Statewide surveys in North Carolina (North Carolina Area Health Education Centers Program, 1987b) showed the vacancy rates for clinical laboratory staff increasing from 4.6 percent in 1981 to 16.5 percent in 1986. However, the salaries of technologists and technicians employed in hospitals between 1981 and 1986 increased 24 and 21 percent, respectively. Yet this increase is small compared with 18 other types of hospital employees—of these employees, only engineering technicians had an increase smaller than 21 percent (University of Texas Medical Branch, 1985, 1987). These figures suggest that the difficulties in hiring noted earlier in this paragraph may not have been evident in 1986.

Conclusion

Making statements about the likelihood of future balances or imbalances between the demand for and supply of clinical laboratory personnel is complicated by the multiple routes of entry into laboratory work. Laboratory workers may have 4 or more years of postsecondary education, or they may qualify for a job through a combination of shorter educational programs plus experience. Baccalaureate-prepared technologists need less supervision than other personnel, and they may hold a variety of higher level positions—for example, laboratory director, manager, consultant, and education coordinator for hospital schools. Technicians may have 2-year associate degrees or combine education and experience to become certified through a professional organization. Other laboratory workers are certified in special areas (e.g., cytotechnology or hematology), and still others may have specialist certification in such disciplines as blood banking or microbiology. Finally, there are large numbers of uncertified workers as indicated by the discrepancy between the BLS job count and the number of certified personnel. These multiple routes of entry into a career in clinical laboratories make it difficult to assess the future supply of laboratory workers.

Taking into account the comparatively modest expected growth in new jobs, and assuming that work force behavior and staffing patterns will not change radically, graduations from clinical laboratory programs should be sufficient to keep demand and supply in reasonable balance to the year 2000 if the rate of graduation is sustained at a minimum at its current level. The recent decline in the number of graduates must be halted, however. If this decline should continue, some improvements in salary and working conditions can be expected to bring supply and demand into balance. A number of factors make prognostications in this area tentative. If the growing numbers of biomedical technology firms become major users of laboratory personnel, thus diverting trained personnel from clinical laboratories, salaries and benefits would improve as employers compete for trained personnel. If personnel trained in such disciplines as chemistry and microbiology are no longer available to medical laboratories, there could be problems because these personnel are used to fill jobs when the labor market is tight. A significant change could come about as a result of employers using personnel differently. (For instance, laboratory managers may choose to substitute one level of personnel for another.)

A great deal of flexibility is possible. Today, there is sometimes little or no differentiation in the way technologists and technicians are used, a situation that could change. If a 4-year degree becomes mandatory for licensure and licensure becomes a more widespread requirement, the demand and supply balance could be severely disrupted. There is increasing debate concerning the advantages and disadvantages of licensure whose purpose is to differentiate jobs according to academic qualifications. The scope of this study did not admit of a conclusion on this matter.

As a final note, the clinical laboratory labor market seems to adapt rapidly to change—for example, changes in health care financing incentives. In the course of this study the reports of graduates having a hard time finding jobs were succeeded by reports of shortages of personnel.

The reasons given for this turnaround are varied. Laboratories may have allowed staffing levels to decline too far in an overresponse to prospective payment. Laboratory volume may have risen faster than the supply. Others say that the level of stress at the work site has increased because of productivity pressures and the increased complexity of care. Fear of AIDS adds to the stress, and salaries are not high enough to compensate for such stress; consequently, people are leaving the field (Meyer, 1988). If these factors do generate an increase in the separation rate of workers from the labor force, it would have a significant negative impact on the supply of clinical laboratory technologists and technicians and necessitate greater market adjustments.

DENTAL HYGIENISTS

Demand for Dental Hygienists

BLS estimates that in 1986 there were 86,700 jobs for dental hygienists. By the year 2000 this number is expected to have increased by 63 percent to 141,000 jobs. Such rapid growth is based on several considerations. First, BLS analysts consider employment growth in dental offices to be the most important element in generating jobs for dental hygienists because the vast majority (97 percent in 1986) is employed in that industry sector (Table 4-2). The BLS projection for dental hygienist employment is hampered by data collection problems that apply only to this sector. The survey on which the BLS data are based was sent to incorporated businesses only. A high proportion of dentists are not incorporated and therefore were not included in the survey.

Dentists' offices provided nearly 460,000 jobs in 1986; this number is projected to reach 706,000 by the year 2000, a 53 percent increase. Contributing to this projected expansion is the BLS expectation that the number of working dentists will substantially increase by the year 2000 (from 151,000 to 196,000, almost 30 percent compared with 19.2 percent for all occupations). Moreover, these dentists are expected to sustain their level of use of dental hygienists. BLS analysts also believe that the entrance into the dental profession of younger dentists, who are taught how to make effective use of hygienists, will cause a slight increase in the ratio of hygienists to total dentist office staff.

Other assumptions on which BLS has based its high-growth prediction include the continued spread of dental insurance, which will generate further demand for dental services; the aging population's need for dental

TABLE 4-2 Major Places of Wage and Salary Employment for Dental Hygienists, 1986 Actual and Projected for the Year 2000

Employment Setting	Number of Jobs, 1986	Percentage[a]	Number of Jobs, 2000	Percentage[a]
Total employment[b]	86,700		141,000	
Total wage and salary employment	86,700	100.0	141,000	100.0
Offices of dentists	84,300	97.3	137,300	97.4

[a]These percentages were calculated using unrounded figures and therefore will not be identical to percentages that are calculated using the rounded figures provided in the table.

[b]Total employment = wage and salary employment + self-employment. Self-employed persons are not allocated by place of employment.

SOURCE: Bureau of Labor Statistics (1987); moderate alternative.

services, part of which comes from the fact that people are now retaining their own teeth longer; and the "baby boom" generation's entry into middle age when periodontal disease becomes more prevalent.

BLS notes that dental hygienists are often hired on a part-time basis. To be fully employed a hygienist will often take two or more part-time jobs. The projection of 141,000 hygienists' jobs by the year 2000 must therefore be substantially decreased to be translated into the number of hygienists employed. BLS analysts suggest that the reduction could be as high as 30 to 40 percent, which would result in an estimated 84,600 to 98,700 employed hygienists in the year 2000. This estimate is supported by data from a 1982 survey of 1,503 dental hygienists. The survey found that 29 percent of the respondents worked in more than one location indicating multiple jobs for most of this group. Six percent worked at three or more locations (Dental Hygiene, 1982).

The demand for hygienists depends on the number of working dentists and the level of activity in their offices. The level of activity in turn depends on the prevalence of dental disease, the extent of dental insurance, and the willingness and ability of uninsured people to pay for dental treatment.

The BLS assumption that the rate of growth of hygienist jobs will be double that of dentists depends on dentists being busy enough to want to employ hygienists. The prevalence of dental insurance has shown rapid growth (rising from 12 million to 81 million insured people between 1970 and 1980), and there is still untapped potential for further growth. But some analysts suggest that the rate of the spread of dental insurance has passed its peak. The "easy pickings" have been accounted for as most large, multistate employers now offer dental benefits (Bishop, 1983). The question remains whether the employment stimulation from increased dental insurance will be sufficient to offset the effect of such dental disease prevention as fluoridation and regular maintenance care. A major factor will be the extent to which dentists can expand the number of restorative treatments they perform.

More than 70 percent of dental costs are paid out-of-pocket, and price is the barrier to dental care most often cited. As a result, only about half of the population visits the dentist each year (Grembowski et al., 1984). HHS's Bureau of Health Professions in a recent report noted the relationship between demand for dental care and national economic growth. The bureau used two different data series for dental expenditures to develop forecasts to 2015 using two scenarios of economic growth. For neither data set and scenario does future growth in dental expenditures reach the rate of growth observed from 1965 to 1985 (Bureau of Health Professions, Division of Associated and Dental Health Professions, 1987). Although the number of employed hygienists per dentist has increased substantially (from 4 per 100 in 1950 to 33.3 per 100 in 1986), the rate of increase since 1981 has been very slow (Bureau of Health Professions, Division of Associated and Dental Health Professions, 1987). Only in the unlikely event that dentists become very busy will the momentum of the 1950s to early 1970s be regained.

There is also reason to question whether the BLS estimate of 196,000 dentists in the year 2000 is too high. The number of graduates from dental schools peaked in 1982–1983 and is expected to continue to decline, reaching the level of the 1950s by the year 2000 (Solomon, 1988). A number of dental schools have closed largely because the perception of an oversupply of dentists has affected students' career decisions. The Bureau of Health Professions thus expects dentists to number 156,000 by the year 2000—40,000 less than the BLS estimate of dentist's jobs.

There is clearly great potential for the increased use of dentistry. Some of this potential will be realized by the expansion of insurance and the growth of real income. Some expansion will stem from increased periodontal disease and other opportunities for intervention that arise from the new types of procedures needed to serve an aging population. Nevertheless, the committee questions whether these increases will be sufficient to allow dentists to employ hygienists at the rate predicted by BLS.

The opportunities for hygienist employment outside dental offices today are limited by regulations that require them to work with dentists on site. Thus, populations such as the elderly in long-term care facilities and physically and mentally retarded people in institutions, whose access to dental care is limited by their lack of mobility, cannot be served by hygienists alone. Many in the dental hygiene profession are fighting the regulations that restrict their independence; yet if independent practice is achieved, it should not be viewed as creating demand unless the regulations are changed.

In sum, although the number of jobs for dental hygienists will continue to grow, it seems unlikely that jobs will expand by over 60 percent by the year 2000—that is, twice the high rate of expansion predicted for dentists.

The major factors that those concerned with future demand for dental hygienists should track include the following:

- number and age of working dentists;
- extent of dental insurance;
- growth of real personal income;
- dental disease patterns;
- changes in the practice of dentistry that influence consumers' attitudes toward dental use (i.e., technological developments that may reduce the pain of dental treatment);
- changes in staffing patterns in solo and group dental offices; and
- progress toward independent practice.

The three scenarios described in Chapter 3 are driven by changes in health care financing. Yet the financing of dental care is often independent of the financing arrangements for other types of health care; therefore,, the differences in demand for dental hygienists that may be caused by the financing-driven scenarios are small. Unless dental care becomes a usual component of the benefit packages in prepaid health plans, the expansion of the types of plans envisioned in the managed care scenario will have little impact on the demand for hygienists' services. Similarly, unless access to dental care is included in policies that increase access to health care generally, the demand for hygienists will be remain unchanged.

Supply of Dental Hygienists

The Council on Dental Education reported that in 1986, 198 accredited dental hygienist programs graduated 4,037 hygienists. The number of graduates declined gradually between 1980 and 1985, with 22.4 percent fewer people graduating in 1985 than in 1980, but showed a slight upturn in 1986 (American Dental Association, Division of Educational Measurements, 1987).

Although most accredited dental hygienist programs require 2 years of study or its equivalent, the number of programs taking 3 or more years to complete has been increasing. In 1985, 33 percent of all programs had this longer requirement. Thus, the time it takes to produce a dental hygienist is increasing. Entry requirements are also being strengthened. In 1970, 80 percent of the programs required only a high school diploma. By 1985, 64 percent of the programs still used the high school diploma as the minimum qualification for acceptance, but 23 percent required some college courses.

Representatives of the American Dental Hygiene Association and anecdotal evidence suggest that in some locations there are acute shortages of hygienists. In one such locality, after a survey confirmed that there were shortages, the dental association was willing to help the community college financially to create a new hygienist program. This collaboration is an example of the sort of adjustments that are often made to rectify labor market imbalances (McMahon, 1986).

Conclusion

Whether the number of dental hygienists available over the next 12 years will be enough to maintain a good balance between demand and supply depends in part on whether the decline in the number of dental hygiene graduates can be halted. If there is no further decline in graduations, there should be no need for major labor market adjustments. To halt the decline, however, some changes must take place; dental hygiene must become more attractive to prospective students. This change will occur if salaries are increased and working conditions improved. The resolution of some of the tensions between dentists and hygienists (which are discussed in Chapter 7) may prove to be a key to improving working conditions. These changes would also decrease the number of workers leaving dental hygiene, and bring back into the work force some of those who have left. Relatively small adjustments now would avoid future dislocations and major adjustments later.

DIETITIANS

Demand for Dietitians

BLS predicts that by the year 2000 there will be 53,800 dietitian jobs—an increase of 13,600 jobs, or 34 percent, since 1986. This employment growth rate is the same as the rate BLS expects for respiratory therapists and speech pathologists but substantially below that expected for some of the other allied health occupations (e.g., physical therapists, dental hygienists, and radiologic technicians).

The BLS data show that nursing homes and hospitals are the major sources of wage and salary jobs in this field (roughly 14 percent and 39 percent, respectively, as shown in Table 4-3). School systems, public health departments, HMOs, and ambulatory facilities also employ small numbers of dietitians, as do retail eating and dining establishments, publishers of nutrition and other magazines, diet counseling services, child care centers, and food manufacturers. BLS data indicate that there were 2,000 self-employed dietitians in 1986; this figure is projected to rise to 2,700 in the

TABLE 4-3 Major Places of Wage and Salary Employment for Dietitians, 1986 Actual and Projected for the Year 2000

Employment Setting	Number of Jobs, 1986	Percentage[a]	Number of Jobs, 2000	Percentage[a]
Total employment[b]	40,200		53,800	
Total wage and salary employment	38,200	100.0	51,100	100.0
Hospitals, public and private	14,800	38.7	16,700	32.6
Nursing and personal care facilities	5,400	14.0	9,000	17.6

[a]These percentages were calculated using unrounded figures and therefore will not be identical to percentages that are calculated using the rounded figures provided in the tables.

[b]Total employment = wage and salary employment + self-employment. These figures include 2,000 self-employed workers in 1986 and 2,682 in the year 2000 who are not allocated by place of employment.

SOURCE: Bureau of Labor Statistics (1987); moderate alternative.

year 2000; these figures constituted 5 percent of jobs in both years. A 1986 survey of members of the American Dietetic Association confirmed that hospital and extended care facilities are the primary employers, employing 54 percent and 10 percent of full-time members, respectively. The survey also noted that although only 3.7 percent of full-time workers were self-employed, more than 33 percent of dietitians who worked part time were self-employed (Bryk, 1987). BLS estimates that about 5 percent of dietitian jobs are filled by self-employed people. Dietitians thus differ from many other allied health occupations in their variety of employment settings and somewhat lesser dependence on hospitals.

Analyzing employment in terms of factors that will either stimulate or depress demand indicates that overall modest growth can be expected, although it will probably be lower than BLS's projections. Factors that tend to restrain employment growth in the field include the slow growth of the hospital industry. Indeed, it is notable that FTE employment in hospitals decreased even before the introduction of PPS and that the decrease accelerated thereafter (Bureau of Health Professions, 1985; American Hospital Association, 1987). However, all of this reduction in hospital employment does not necessarily reflect the reduced use of dietitian services by hospitals. Hospitals can contract for services rather than employ dietitians directly. Similar changes may be taking place in nursing homes.

The move to out-of-hospital services is likely to produce a modest shift of employment to ambulatory clinics but no significant change in the number of dietitians employed. Although prospective payment for hospital care is generating an increased need for home care, the growth of dietitian employment in home care is inhibited by Medicare reimbursement regulations that prohibit dietitians from billing for home visits. Instead, they are included in the administrative expenses of home health agencies. A study charged with making reimbursement recommendations to Congress noted that, although dietary therapy is important and necessary for a wide range of diseases, the present reimbursement approach is adequate (Health Care Financing Administration, 1986a). Another factor that can constrain the growth in demand for dietitians is the extent to which other professionals such as nurses or health educators are thought to provide substitutable services. In the current environment of price competition, except for some specific tasks, dietitian duties could conceivably be eliminated or performed by other personnel. There are currently no data on this phenomenon, however.

On the other hand, there are factors today that are increasing demand. One is the increased use of high-technology nutrition services such as enteral and parenteral nutrition (feeding through tubes and veins) in institutional as well as home settings. (Here, too, however, other professionals such as pharmacists compete with dietitians to provide services.) Furthermore, the aging of the population and the increased hospitalization of patients with complex problems requiring nutritional intervention should stimulate demand. Another important upward pressure on demand is the societal value now being placed on nutrition. For example, the fitness movement includes a consciousness of the importance of good nutrition in health promotion and disease prevention. Grocery stores and magazine publishers employ dietitians to advise on the nutritional content of foods and to develop recipes. Individuals are willing to pay out-of-pocket for nutritional consultation that is available through independent practitioners or as a package with other services. Health care providers who compete with each other to attract consumers are increasingly aware of the importance consumers place on nutritional advice in obesity and cholesterol control. Also associated with disease prevention and the high cost of treating acute conditions is the use of nutrition in preventing coronary disease, diabetes, obesity, hypertension, atherosclerosis, and arthritis. Providers at risk for the cost of care, such as HMOs, can be expected to use nutritionists to reduce the likelihood of acute illness. Public health departments are also concerned with preventing disease and thus provide nutritional services through such programs as the Special Supplemental Food Program for Women, Infants, and Children (WIC). One survey identified 22 state health agency program areas that were expected to use nutrition services and noted expanded nutrition services by both local and state public health agencies (Kaufman et al., 1986). Although public health funding is limited, it appears that a new appreciation of the value of nutrition services is generating an increase in their use.

The aging of the population will drive up the demand for dietitians to care for the complex nutritional needs of nursing home patients. The BLS data reflect this expected increase, projecting 3,600 more jobs in nursing homes in the year 2000, which will increase the proportion of dietitian jobs in that setting from approximately 14 percent of all jobs in 1986 to 17.6 percent in the year 2000 (see Table 4-3).

Overall, employment growth expectations for dietitians are well above the national average but are moderate to modest when compared with some other allied health fields. The hospital sector is not likely to be a major source of new demand. Independent practitioners contracting with hospitals and nursing homes do not represent new opportunities but a different employment pattern. On the positive side, public demand for nutritionists' services should create some new employment. This employment will most likely occur in settings that market such services directly to consumers and in settings in which the dietitian's role in health promotion and disease prevention is valued. However, the increased potential for employment in any of these sites will create only a minor overall increase in demand.

The following is a list of factors that are important determinants of demand for dietitians:

- consumer desire for nutritional advice;
- new places of employment such as the food industry and publishing;
- trends in private practice;
- trends in the substitution of other professionals (nurses, health educators, home economists, pharmacists) for dietitians; and
- interest in and payment for health promotion/disease prevention and perceptions of the importance of nutrition.

The three scenarios that were described in Chapter 3 have different effects on the demand for dietitians, mainly through their role in health promotion and disease prevention.

Scenario 1: The Mixed Model

Moderate growth in the demand for nutritionists' services would occur through the expansion of employment opportunities created by the aging of the population, direct consumer demand for services, and hospital admissions of patients with complex problems.

Scenario 2: Prospective Payment

Although hospital utilization of dietitians would be reduced under this scenario, overall employment would be less affected than in other allied health occupations that are more dependent on hospital employment.

The growth of HMOs and managed care systems that emphasize health promotion and disease prevention, as well as marketing to consumers, would increase the demand for nutritional services. Under this scenario, physicians working outside managed care systems would increase their scope of services and employ or contract for dietetic services in their offices. Consumers would adopt the attitude of health care providers emphasizing wellness and would therefore be eager for nutritional services and information from all sources—food labeling, publications, independent practitioners, and the like.

Scenario 3: Access

Policies that enhance access to care could stimulate dietetic services in several ways. By relieving financial pressures caused by low occupancy rates, hospital demand would revive. Hospitals would then be able to hire staff to provide services that were considered marginal in times of fiscal constraint. In addition, access to services for groups with special nutritional needs, such as migrants and pregnant teenagers, would stimulate the demand for dietitians employed in primary care settings. The increment in demand overall would be only moderate, however, and substantially less than for the occupations more closely tied to acute illness.

Supply of Dietitians

There are three main ways to become a registered dietitian. One is to graduate from a baccalaureate program in an appropriate field of study and complete an internship; the second is to complete a graduate program in dietetics. Because internships are in short supply (only about 900 per year, compared with approximately 3,000 students who need them), some graduates of dietetic programs do not proceed to registry. The third course circumvents the internship requirement: students complete graduate degrees that do not require internships and proceed to registration by that route. Coordinated undergraduate programs combine academic course work with approximately 1,000 hours of clinical experience.

Since 1980 the number of newly registered dietitians has fallen 20 percent from just over 3,000 to just under 2,400 (American Dietetic Association, 1987). The consensus for the past few years is that there has been a surplus of dietetic professionals (American Dietetic Association, 1985). This conclusion should be only tentatively modified by the salary increase of 29 percent between 1981 and 1986 received by dietitians who were employed in hospitals—an increase comparable to that received by pharmacists and staff nurses, who are perceived to be in short supply (University of Texas Medical Branch, 1981, 1986). Because no other evidence of shortage or surplus was found, it is assumed that a reasonable balance exists today.

Conclusion

If the annual number of new registrants is maintained at around the 1986 level of 2,400, or if only a very modest decline occurs, the committee estimates that demand and supply for dietitians will be in balance up to the year 2000.

However, halting the current decline in registrations will require both that academic programs remain viable and that health care employers and educators act aggressively. Employers need to offer jobs that are as attractive as their competitors for dietitians outside the health care industry. In addition, dietetics must be made as attractive as other possible careers. Yet it is not always possible to discern differences between some of the jobs that registered dietitians hold and the jobs held by other types of dietary personnel—for example, nonregistered graduates of dietetic programs and graduates of home economics or food service management programs. It is possible that these latter groups will be used in greater numbers if employers find it difficult to hire registered dietitians.

EMERGENCY MEDICAL TECHNICIANS

Demand for Emergency Medical Technicians

As it does for other fields, BLS estimates the number of paid jobs for emergency medical technicians (EMTs). Because emergency medical technology jobs are often filled by volunteers—by a ratio of 2 to 1 in 1984—the BLS stresses that its estimates cover only paid EMTs.

The bureau estimates that there were 65,200 paid EMTs in 1986, a small number of whom had received the advanced training and field experience required to become an EMT-paramedic (EMT-P). The BLS data exclude volunteers and do not distinguish among the three levels of EMTs. The lower (basic) level EMT-A and the upper level EMT-P have existed since the late 1970s; in 1981 an intermediate level (EMT-I) was added to the available certifications (McKay, 1985). By the year 2000 the number of paid EMTs is expected to increase by 15 percent to 75,000. This growth is substantially below that of the other allied health fields discussed in this chapter and below the expected 19 percent growth in the total U.S. labor force. BLS notes that this slow growth in employment will be shaped by conflicting forces. On one hand, population growth, especially the proportion of the elderly, is expected to spur demand for EMTs. Progress in emergency medicine is also expected to increase demand. On the other hand, the rising cost of training and equipment coupled with the termination of federal start-up funds for community emergency medical services, taxpayer resistance to increased local government expenditures, and the availability of unpaid volunteers are factors that are likely to constrain job growth for paid EMTs (Bureau of Labor Statistics, 1986).

Of the 10,000 new EMT jobs expected by the BLS in the year 2000, state and local government will account for almost 40 percent (Table 4-4). It has been noted anecdotally that the governments of major metropolitan areas throughout the United States have been examining their existing emergency medical services and contrasting the benefits of contractual services versus government-run services. Any decisions to use contractual services will, of course, lessen the expected growth of jobs within government, but overall demand should not be much affected by a change in employer.

There also appears to be movement toward the privatization of emergency medical services. Along with large companies that provide services on a contractual basis, there has been growth in physician-owned ambulance

TABLE 4-4   Major Places of Wage and Salary Employment for
Emergency Medical Technicians, 1986 Actual and Projected for the
Year 2000

Employment Setting	Number of Jobs, 1986	Percentage[a]	Number of Jobs, 2000	Percentage[a]
Total employment[b]	65,200		75,000	
Total wage and salary employment	65,200	100.0	75,000	100.0
Local and interurban transit	25,500	39.2	27,900	37.2
State and local governments[c]	24,500	37.6	29,700	39.6
Hospitals, public and private	14,600	22.4	16,200	21.7

[a]These percentages were calculated using unrounded figures and therefore will not be identical to percentages that are calculated using the rounded figures provided in the table.

[b]Total employment = wage and salary employment + self-employment.

[c]These figures do not include government hospitals and schools.

SOURCE: Bureau of Labor Statistics (1987); moderate alternative.

services and privately run emergency departments that operate their own ambulance services. BLS foresees that 2,400 new EMT jobs—nearly a quarter of all newly created jobs—will be available in privately owned ambulance services.

BLS also predicts that hospital employment of EMTs will increase by 11 percent. This projection is based on a determination that hospitals, expecting emergency medical services to be profitable, will compete with private ambulance services. Yet anecdotal evidence suggests that no trend toward hospital-managed emergency services is developing. Although some hospitals have been entering the market, others have tested it and stepped away. However, there is evidence (also anecdotal) that EMTs are sometimes employed in hospital emergency departments—the nurse shortage being a major factor in decisions to employ EMTs (McKay, 1985).

The BLS projection does not differentiate between jobs for the basic EMT versus those for the more highly trained paramedic; yet the availability of volunteers makes such a differentiation important. Technological developments have virtually transformed ambulances into mobile intensive care units that employ technicians with skills in defibrillation, endotracheal intubation, pharmacology, and other aspects of intensive care. Usually, volunteer technicians are not adequately trained to appropriately assume that level of care (Smith and Bodai, 1985). As the use of advanced life-support techniques becomes more commonplace, the demand for paramedics is likely to increase sharply relative to other levels of EMTs. Volunteer technicians typically have only basic training and so provide little or no competition for jobs requiring advanced skills. However, the lower level basic EMT seeking a job must compete with the volunteer.

Increased demand for the basic EMT can be expected from the non-emergency transportation sector. One consequence of Medicare's PPS has been the early discharge of elderly patients. Patients still in need of nursing care are often transported in ambulances to nursing homes. Basic EMTs are employed to care for the patients in transit.

Supply of Emergency Medical Technicians

EMTs are trained in a variety of settings. Accredited educational programs for EMT-Ps came into being in 1982 and have graduated a total of 2,466 technicians through the 1985–1986 academic year (CAHEA, 1984, 1986, 1987a; Journal of the American Medical Association, 1983, 1984, 1985). A greater number of paramedics are trained in unaccredited programs. According to the National Registry of EMTs, there were 440 EMT-P training programs in 1985, of which only 15 were accredited. The 1985 National Emergency Medical Services Data Summary lists a total of 5,059 EMT-Ps being trained annually; however, only 42 states and the District of Columbia responded to the survey. Three large states—California, New York, and Texas—were not among those reporting figures. Thus, the number of EMT-P graduates is substantially higher than 5,059. The same survey shows a total of 83,650 basic EMTs being trained annually (National Emergency Medical Services Clearing House, 1985).

Observers of the field say that paramedics are in very short supply. The opportunity cost of training and rapid burnout discourages entry into the field. There is also very rapid job turnover among EMTs. The average volunteer is active for only 5 to 6 years (Lucash, 1983). The turnover rate among full-time employed EMTs is said to range between 20 and 40 percent.

The committee was frustrated by the lack of reliable data on the basic characteristics of the EMT work force and on the forces that influence their training and use. These characteristics and forces appear to vary among communities and are also changing rapidly. This field exemplifies the problems of trying to predict the future in the absence of a well-organized professional association that collects or stimulates the collection of manpower information. This also makes it difficult for BLS to make a precise and useful occupational classification.

Lacking data on the numbers and trends in training of EMT-Ps and basic EMTs, it is impossible to make an assessment of future trends in the balance between demand and supply. Anxiety about the quality of emergency services has begun to surface in some cities. Should this anxiety spread, the demand for more highly trained technicians could put pressure on the supply pipelines. Data collection could help clarify the facts that decision makers need to ensure the smooth running of emergency medical services. As recommended in Chapter 2, an interagency task force could work toward a data collection plan.

MEDICAL RECORD ADMINISTRATORS AND TECHNICIANS

Demand for Medical Record Technicians

BLS projects that the number of jobs for medical record technicians will grow by 75 percent from 39,900 in 1986 to 69,800 in the year 2000. This rapid growth exceeds the rate predicted for any of the other allied health fields discussed in this report, except for physical therapy. Unfortunately, BLS does not project employment for medical record administrators. The expectation of rapid growth in jobs for medical record technicians is predicated on the increasing importance of the medical record function in financial control and billing. BLS analysts believe that this high rate of growth is likely because health care payers are requiring more detailed and more accurate medical records for reimbursement purposes in all settings, including outpatient facilities. In the past, many jobs in medical record departments and physician offices were filled by individuals trained on the job to perform coding and transcription tasks. But increasing payer demands have made the work so complex that staff trained on the job are no longer adequate. Thus, a surge in demand for certified technicians is expected.

This analysis can be substantiated to a great extent. Data from the American Hospital Association show that medical record technician employment in U.S. registered community hospitals grew by 6 percent in the 2 years following the introduction of PPS, compared with 2.5 percent in the 2 earlier years (Bureau of Health Professions, 1985; American Hospital Association, 1987). Employment of the more highly qualified medical record administrators expanded by 2.1 percent in both the 2 years before and the 2 years after PPS. The American Medical Record Association (AMRA) studied the impact of PPS on a sample of 775 hospital medical record departments. The study's findings noted that 93 percent of the respondents agreed that prospective payment required greater expertise, and 75 percent noted more stringent hiring standards (Schraffenberger, 1987). Another AMRA study attributes at least some of the observed increases in numbers of employees and salaries to the advent of PPS (Bernstein, 1985). Whether this translates into the hiring of more credentialed practitioners is not stated, but another AMRA survey noted that a "substantial percentage" of hospital record departments filled coding positions exclusively with credentialed professionals (Whitlock and Whitmore, 1987).

Although the impact of PPS is one factor in accelerating the demand for medical record technicians, the role of medical records in utilization review and quality control must also be noted. The complexity of medical record systems that interface with utilization and quality review systems and with physician office linkages raises the required skill standards for staff, in addition to generating an increased demand for personnel.

The automation of medical record departments has been rapid. In 1981, 28.3 percent of hospitals sampled by Shared Data Research had some automation. By 1984 this figure had risen to 48.1 percent (Packer, 1985). Undoubtedly, the close connection between medical records, billing, and cash flow encourages automation to speed payments. The questions of whether—and if so, when—the use of computers will slow down the demand for medical record technicians are not clear. However, retention of the paper medical record appears to be common because computer technology cannot completely substitute for the tangible form. (For example, a paper record is needed if litigation occurs.)

Even official attempts to simplify medical record tasks seem to backfire. The UB-82 form, an attempt to create a form that all payers could use, only increased the work load for coders and resulted in the hiring of additional staff (Burda, 1984).

In 1984 about three-quarters of all medical record technician jobs were in hospitals. The pattern of employment is changing, however, and BLS expects that it will continue to change. By 1986 only 61.5 percent of all jobs were in hospitals. By the year 2000 BLS expects hospital employment to have fallen to about 58 percent and employment in outpatient facilities to have risen from 9 percent in 1986 to almost 13 percent in the year 2000 (Table 4-5). The demand for medical record technicians from nonhospital health care providers is expected to rise for many of the same reasons that demand from hospitals is rising. Payers' documentation requirements are increasing for all settings, and documentation for billing purposes is tied to medical records.

In sum, the demand for qualified medical record personnel is related to the amount and sophistication of required documentation for purposes that include reimbursement of services, malpractice protection, and quality of care considerations. The ongoing changes in reimbursement policies, with payers increasingly concerned with the appropriate use of services, will continue to generate steady increases in the demand for medical record personnel. Yet the rate of increase is likely to slow as record systems become better established. Thus, the greatest increase would occur at the beginning of the period we have been considering. BLS's estimate of a major (75

TABLE 4-5   Major Places of Wage and Salary Employment for
Medical Record Technicians, 1986 Actual and Projected for the
Year 2000

Employment Setting	Number of Jobs, 1986	Percentage[a]	Number of Jobs, 2000	Percentage[a]
Total employment[b]	39,900		69,800	
Total wage and salary employment	39,900	100.0	69,800	100.0
Hospitals, public and private	24,500	61.5	40,800	54.2
Nursing and personal care facilities	4,500	11.2	7,500	10.8
Outpatient care facilities	3,600	9.1	9,000	12.9
Offices of physicians	2,400	6.0	5,800	8.3

[a]These percentages were calculated using unrounded figures and therefore will not be identical to percentages that are calculated using the rounded figures provided in the table.

[b]Total employment = wage and salary employment + self-employment.

SOURCE: Bureau of Labor Statistics (1987); moderate alternative.

percent) overall increase in demand to the year 2000 is supported by the expansionary forces at work.

For those looking to the future, the following are important factors that should be monitored:

- changes in payment systems and regulation;
- growth of new employment opportunities in out-of-hospital settings;
- impact of automation; and
- new uses of the information contained in medical records.

The three financing-driven scenarios described in Chapter 3 have direct and fairly simple implications for the demand for medical record technicians. The spread of prospective payment stimulates demand as the amount and complexity of documentation tied to payment increase and facilities use the medical record to review utilization as a part of cost-control efforts. Under the access scenario, demand increases in proportion to the amount of additional service generated.

Demand for Medical Record Administrators

Because BLS does not project demand for medical record administrators, there is no estimate of employment for the year 2000. The number of persons with a bachelor's degree in medical record administration is relatively small: approximately 9,500 people have graduated with the credential since 1970 (CAHEA, 1979, 1980, 1981, 1982, 1983, 1984, 1985a,

1986, 1987; Journal of the American Medical Association, 1984; Council on Medical Education of the American Medical Association, 1972, 1973, 1974, 1978). It is difficult to determine how employers view the difference between the more highly educated administrator and the technician. Roughly half the directors of medical record departments have the administrator credential, and half are registered technicians (Amatayakul, 1987). In cases in which medical record technicians are department directors, there is no way to determine whether this occurs because administrators were not available or were too expensive, or because technical-level skills are adequate for this work. Given this uncertainty, it is not possible to discuss differences in future demand for medical record administrators and medical record technicians.

Supply of Medical Record Personnel

Although graduations of both medical record administrators and medical record technicians have increased since 1980—20 percent for administrators, 27 percent for technicians—the increase shown by technicians has been steadier. Together, the two types of programs produced almost 2,000 graduates in 1986, of which about 46 percent were at the administrator level. The number of accredited technician programs grew rapidly in the late 1970s. Today, there are 87 programs, but the last 6 years saw the establishment of only 7 percent of them (CAHEA, 1987a). Some schools have closed, in part because of a decline in the applicant pool and in part because of budget problems and accreditation requirements (CAHEA, 1987b).

Graduates of accredited programs do not represent the total supply of workers to fill jobs in medical record departments. Substantial numbers of the employees who "compile and maintain medical records" (the BLS job description) are trained on the job to do transcription and other tasks for which extensive training is not necessary.

Determining whether there is currently a good balance between the demand for and supply of medical record administrators and technicians is complicated by the availability of workers who can be trained, if necessary, to fill the medical record jobs requiring lower level skills. It seems unlikely that widespread reports of job vacancies will occur if employers can concentrate their use of skilled practitioners where needed and fill in with others. Yet the findings of one salary survey suggest that employers may be struggling to fill jobs with qualified practitioners. Between 1981 and 1986 the starting salary for medical record administrators in hospitals increased by 45 percent—a substantially greater increase than occurred for any of 19 other types of hospital employees. Medical record technicians did less well (possibly because they are more available or possibly because they are more vulnerable to substitution). Their gain was 24 percent, an increase exceeded by half the group of hospital employees (University of Texas Medical Branch, 1981, 1986).

Conclusion

If one assumed that graduates from accredited schools were the only source of medical record technicians and that demand would grow at the rapid rate predicted by the BLS to the year 2000, there would not be enough trained technicians to fill the jobs. These assumptions are not realistic, however. They are offered merely as a starting place from which to indicate how the labor market is likely to work. First, workers who have not had the benefit of accredited education do fill jobs in medical record departments and will continue to do so to some extent. Nevertheless, current trends indicate that the knowledge and skill level needed in medical record positions are rising and will continue to rise in the foreseeable future. Therefore, a greater proportion of trained practitioners will be needed to fill current and new jobs. Graduations of administrators and technicians show a rising trend, and the number of accredited programs is growing, albeit slowly. Thus, it is likely that the supply of trained technicians will grow—and not remain constant as in our initial assumption. In sum, to avoid a shortage of medical record personnel from now until the year 2000, the labor market must make major adjustments that will cause medical record technology to be viewed as a more promising career than it is today. One likely change is that the investment in medical record education will be recognized in greater pay, status, and task differentiation—there are indications that this is already happening. As such changes occur, the number of specially trained workers should grow, enabling employers to continue to phase out those with only on-the-job training.

OCCUPATIONAL THERAPISTS

Demand for Occupational Therapists

BLS estimates that jobs for occupational therapists will increase by 52 percent between 1986 and the year 2000, rising from 29,400 to 44,600 jobs. This predicted high growth rate is still lower than that predicted for physical therapists, in part because a greater proportion of occupational therapists are employed in the slow-growing educational sector. In 1986 just over 36 percent of occupational therapist jobs were in hospitals; 13.2 percent were in government employment (excluding educational institutions and hospitals). BLS classified 4.5 percent of jobs as being in "offices of other practitioners"—that is, offices of practitioners other than physicians (including osteopaths) and dentists and including the offices of independent practice occupational therapists (Table 4-6).

TABLE 4-6   Major Places of Wage and Salary Employment for Occupational Therapists, 1986 Actual and Projected for the Year 2000

Employment Setting	Number of Jobs, 1986	Percentage[a]	Number of Jobs, 2000	Percentage[a]
Total employment[b]	29,400		44,600	
Total wage and salary employment	26,300	100.0	40,000	100.0
Hospitals, public and private	9,600	36.3	13,700	34.3
Outpatient care facilities	16,000	6.3	3,400	8.6
Offices of physicians	400	1.5	760	1.9
Offices of other health care practitioners[c]	1,200	4.4	3,100	7.9
Educational institutions, private and public	4,400	16.7	5,100	12.8
Federal, state, and local government institutions[d]	3,500	13.2	4,100	10.2

[a]These percentages were calculated using unrounded figures and therefore will not be identical to percentages that are calculated using the rounded figures provided in the table.

[b]Total employment = wage and salary employment + self-employment. These figures include 3,000 self-employed workers in 1986 and 4,644 in the year 2000 who are not allocated by place of employment.

[c]Offices of health practitioners other than physicians (including osteopaths) and dentists. The figures also include offices of occupational therapists.

[d]These figures do not include government hospitals and schools.

SOURCE: Bureau of Labor Statistics (1987); moderate alternative.

BLS analysts identified a number of factors they expect will drive this predicted strong growth in employment. These factors include the trend of occupational therapists increasing their share of hospital employment; federal legislation involving services for handicapped children, which will increase employment in the area of school services; and increases in private practice opportunities generated by improved reimbursement.

These factors will undoubtedly stimulate the demand for occupational therapists. Hospitals provide more than one-third of the available jobs in the field today, and the growth rate in this sector alone will have an important influence on the demand for occupational therapists. Occupational therapy is one of the few allied health groups that sustained employment growth in the 2 years after the introduction of PPS. FTE employment in U.S. registered hospitals increased by 10.7 percent between 1981 and 1983 and by 22.7 percent between 1983 and 1986 (Bureau of Health Professions, 1985; American Hospital Association, 1987). Some of this growth in hospital employment results from more hospitals offering occupational therapy services. Between 1980 and 1983, 268 hospitals added occupational therapy to their list of services, and a 1984 survey of hospital chief executive officers indicated that 18 percent planned to add or expand their occupational therapy services (American Occupational Therapy Association, 1985). Yet despite this history of strong growth, unless occupational therapy can be established as enhancing the early discharge of patients, the service could be vulnerable to cuts if hospital operating margins continue to be threatened.

The demand for occupational therapists in prolonging the independence of AIDS patients could, in the future, generate demand for more occupational therapists. The role of occupational therapy in caring for the mentally ill in hospitals and in such settings as halfway houses can only be inferred from the BLS data. Psychiatric hospitals and psychiatric units of general hospitals are included in the hospital industry estimates, and occupational therapy services are often provided by contractors to, for example, halfway houses. However, occupational therapy has a long history as part of the team that cares for people with mental illness. Future demand from this sector of the health care system will be determined by mental health insurance coverage, the availability of publicly sponsored programs, and the evolution of treatment modalities for mental illness.

What the data do not show is the extent to which employment growth in the field was sustained by the use of occupational therapists in hospital-based rehabilitation facilities, which have not come under PPS. According to the American Occupational Therapy Association's 1986 member survey, roughly 40 percent of hospital employment was in rehabilitation (American Occupational Therapy Association, 1987). The demand for occupational therapists in rehabilitation care is being stimulated by two factors. One is the discharge of patients from the acute care hospital to rehabilitation facilities to escape the PPS setting. The second, effective July 1987, is the addition of occupational therapy as a Medicare-covered rehabilitation agency service under Part B of the Medicare regulations (Scott, 1987).

Medicare has also made other changes that will stimulate the demand for occupational therapists. Since July 1987 occupational therapy has been covered by Medicare Part B for service in skilled nursing facilities. This provision will allow providers to bill Medicare for occupational therapy services and will offer a new incentive for therapists to establish practices that market services to nursing homes.

Home health care is another area of potential growth in demand for occupational therapists. The number of occupational therapists employed by certified agencies rose from 410 in 1983 to 3,979 in 1985, then dropped to 1,997 in 1986 (National Association for Home Care, 1987). In view of the upward pressures on occupational therapy service demand in the home, it seems likely that some of the decrease is due to increased contracting for services.

In 1986 new federal legislation (Public Law [P.L.] 99-457) was enacted that should increase demand for occupational therapists by the educational sector. This legislation increased federal funds to encourage state departments of education to provide special education and related services to handicapped preschoolers. Under the act, occupational therapy would be available to children who needed it in order to benefit from special education (American Occupational Therapy Association, 1986b).

Other factors that tend to generate a demand for occupational therapists are related to demographic and disease changes. These changes include the increased survival of head trauma victims and low-birth-weight neonates. In 1973 no respondent to a survey by the American Occupational Therapy Association reported head injury as being among the most frequently seen problems. By 1986, 3.3 percent reported head injuries as the problem seen most frequently. Similarly, developmental disabilities (excluding mental retardation) have now become the most frequently seen problem, rising from 5.8 percent in 1978 to 16.5 percent in 1986 (American Occupational Therapy Association, 1985, 1987). In addition, the aging of the population has implications for greater use of occupational therapy in nursing homes, home care, and hospitals. It is estimated that about 17 percent of occupational therapy work is done with elderly patients and that large numbers of nursing home residents would benefit if occupational therapy were available (National Institute on Aging, 1987). Yet significant increases in occupational therapy's role in nursing home care are unlikely unless financing becomes more generous or regulations require them.

Some disease patterns and financing moves should generate downward pressures on the demand for occupational therapists. For example, the incidence of cardiac disease and cerebrovascular accidents (whose sequelae are commonly treated by occupational therapists) is declining—although this will be offset to some extent by increased survival rates. On the financing side, efficiency incentives and competition are expected to continue to force facility managers to seek ways to reduce costs. Occupational therapists may be asked to increase productivity, or they may be vulnerable to reductions in employment by managers seeking to trim staff.

In sum, the upward pressures on occupational therapist demand are expected to exceed and overwhelm downward pressures. Growth in demand will be greater outside the acute care hospital sector and should be of the order of magnitude predicted by BLS. One uncertainty that could substantially decrease demand in the future is the issue of Medicare payment for rehabilitation services. Although the extension of PPS on a diagnosis basis in rehabilitation is unlikely, the introduction of some sort of incentives for economic restraint are slated for implementation.

Factors that should be monitored by those interested in assessing the demand for occupational therapists include the following:

- Medicare payment and regulations for rehabilitation services;
- growth of the hospital sector;
- demographics concerning school-age children and programs for handicapped children;
- participation of home care and other long-term care services; and
- the roles of competing occupations such as recreational therapists.

Our three scenarios, which reflect three different health care funding environments, affect occupational therapist demand mainly through the impact of the scenarios on hospital care.

Scenario 1: The Mixed Model

This scenario foresees the continuation of most of the trends in evidence today. The demand for occupational therapists to work in hospitals and rehabilitation facilities would continue to increase steadily, assuming that the latter remain free of PPS. The demand from skilled nursing facilities and home care agencies would also show modest but steady growth as more older people need services.

Scenario 2: Prospective Payment

The financial incentives incorporated in the prospective payment scenario would create downward pressure on the demand for occupational therapists. Under this scenario, managers in general hospitals would scrutinize cost-effectiveness studies for evidence that occupational therapy decreases the length of hospital stays and is cost-effective. Similarly, large employers would include occupational therapy in benefit packages if it were shown that it speeds the employee's return to work. Lacking such evidence, growth in acute care hospital and outpatient employment would be negligible. Under this scenario, rehabilitation facilities would also work under prospective payment, thus reducing the demand for all types of personnel.

Nursing homes and home care agencies would increase their demands for occupational therapists, but these increases would not offset the drop in demand from the hospital sector. Independent practice would thrive, however, as consumers sought services that were no longer available from institutions striving to reduce costs.

Scenario 3: Access

The general surge in demand for medical care generated by a policy of increased access to care would stimulate a demand for occupational therapists, providing rehabilitation services for newly entitled groups were incorporated into new benefit packages. Orthopedic problems that might have remained untreated for lack of funding would be cared for; in addition, the rehabilitation services needed after the acute phase of trauma or stroke could be provided. Handicapped individuals would have good access to occupational therapy services beyond their school years. If such groups as homeless people also gained access to care and mental health coverage were expanded, the demand for occupational therapists would be increased.

Supply of Occupational Therapists

For the past decade the number of occupational therapy graduates has fluctuated from year to year but has averaged around 2,000 for the last 2 years. After several years of stagnation in the 1980s the number of accredited programs recently jumped from 56 in 1985 to 63 in 1986 (CAHEA, 1987a). This surge appears to have outstripped the availability of full-time faculty, forcing programs to rely increasingly on part-time faculty (American Occupational Therapy Association, 1985). Furthermore, fieldwork placement of students is becoming more difficult. Educational programs reported that 424 facilities canceled placements in 1984–1985. This figure rose to 625 in 1985–1986. The most frequently cited reason for cancellation was the loss of occupational therapy staff (American Occupational Therapy Association, Research Information and Evaluation Division, 1986a).

The committee heard persistent reports of employers' difficulties in recruiting occupational therapists, especially for rehabilitation facilities. These reports are substantiated by the few employer surveys that exist (Veterans Administration, Office of Personnel and Labor Relations, 1987; North Carolina Area Health Education Centers Program, 1987c).

Also supporting the notion that occupational therapists are in short supply is the finding of a survey that starting salaries of occupational therapists in hospitals increased 31 percent between 1981 and 1986. This increase is comparable to those for pharmacists (30 percent) and staff nurses (27 percent), who are generally felt to be in short supply (University of Texas Medical Branch, 1981, 1986). These indicators of a tight labor market appear in the health care sector. Whether employers in other sectors are also having trouble hiring occupational therapists is not known. Nor is it known whether better opportunities for employment outside the health care sector are the cause of the health care employer's hiring problems.

Conclusion

Assuming that through the year 2000 the education sector is unable to respond to an increased demand for occupational therapists because of faculty shortages, the committee expects to see health care employers making some adjustments that use the existing labor force more effectively and that encourage extended tenure and return to the labor force. Such adjustments are likely to include improvements in productivity, eliminating the use of occupational therapy in ways that have the least effect on patient care, and raising salaries. If faculty can be recruited to allow educational programs to expand, employers will have to make adjustments to attract people into careers in occupational therapy. Thus, to maintain a balance in demand and supply will take both salary and working condition improvements to bring in students, as well as expanded educational capacity to prepare the students for the workplace. If for some reason (e.g., health care facilities being unable to afford salary increases) the market fails to adjust sufficiently, a shortage of occupational therapists is likely.

PHYSICAL THERAPISTS AND ASSISTANTS

Demand for Physical Therapists and Assistants

BLS expects the growth in the number of jobs available to physical therapists to exceed growth in all other allied health occupations. Between 1986 and the year 2000, 53,500 new jobs are predicted, representing an increase of more than 87 percent from 61,200 jobs to 114,700 jobs. This prediction is based on an expectation of rapid growth in several settings. In the hospital the push to shorter stays is expected to increase the demand for therapists, as is the move to home care. In addition, the attractions of independent practice are expected to continue to draw therapists.

Although all of the major settings in which physical therapists work are expected to experience substantial increases in demand, it is notable that employment in "offices of other health practitioners" (that is, the offices of health practitioners other than physicians and dentists) will grow nearly threefold (adding over 25,000 jobs). Such offices will become the major employment setting for physical therapists, constituting almost 35 percent of all jobs. By contrast, hospital employment will grow about 43 percent, adding 8,500 jobs, but by the year 2000 will provide only 27 percent of jobs compared with the 35.5 percent share it had in 1986 (Table 4-7). Nevertheless, some of the therapists working in the "offices of other health practitioners" will be supplying services to hospitals and other health care facilities on a contractual basis.

BLS expects the demand for physical therapy assistants to increase by 82 percent between 1986 and the year 2000, rising to 65,000 jobs. The similarity of the rate of growth for this group of practitioners to the predicted growth rate for physical therapists is due to the BLS analysts' de-

TABLE 4-7   Major Places of Wage and Salary Employment for
Physical Therapists, 1986 Actual and Projected for the Year 2000

Employment Setting	Number of Jobs, 1986	Percentage[a]	Number of Jobs, 2000	Percentage[a]
Total employment[b]	61,200		114,700	
Total wage and salary employment	56,200	100.0	105,400	100.0
Hospitals, public and private	19,900	35.5	28,400	26.9
Offices of physicians	3,300	5.8	4,900	4.6
Offices of other health care practitioners[c]	11,500	20.4	36,600	34.7
Outpatient care facilities	3,000	5.3	6,500	6.2

[a]These percentages were calculated using unrounded figures and therefore will not be identical to percentages that are calculated using the rounded figures provided in the table.

[b]Total employment = wage and salary employment + self-employment. These figures include 5,000 self-employed workers in 1986 and 9,300 in the year 2000 who are not allocated by place of employment.

[c]Offices of health practitioners other than physicians (including osteopaths) and dentists. The figures also include offices of physical therapists.

SOURCE: Bureau of Labor Statistics (1987); moderate alternative.

termination that the same factors drive demand for the two groups. Payers can have a significant effect, however, on the use of assistant-level practitioners. Comments made during the committee's site visits to hospital physical therapy departments mentioned that limited use was made of assistants because of Medicare requirements that physical therapists perform the regular evaluations needed to document patient progress. These requirements were felt to limit the usefulness of assistants, resulting in their curtailed employment. Physical therapists themselves have often been reluctant to use assistants.

There is substantial support for the assumptions made by BLS about the growth in demand for physical therapists. Unlike the level of hospital employment of most other allied health occupations, hospital employment of physical therapists was not reduced in the years immediately following the introduction of PPS. Rather, physical therapist employment continued to grow by 5.3 percent between 1983 and 1985 (Bureau of Health Professions, 1985; American Hospital Association, 1987). Other evidence supports the idea that PPS has not reduced the use of physical therapy in hospitals. A study of seven acute care hospitals in one county indicated that referrals of Medicare patients to both inpatient and outpatient physical therapy increased after the introduction of DRGs. The implication to be drawn from this study is that physical therapy is seen as an effective and efficient treatment that can help to rehabilitate patients within time and economic constraints (Dore, 1987). Hospital employment is also being sustained by the expansion of hospital rehabilitation facilities and by the increasing intensity of care needed by inpatients. Because rehabilitation facilities are excluded from PPS requirements, these units are used to facilitate discharges from the PPS environment of the hospital.

The American Physical Therapy Association (1987c) reported that therapists in home health care increased their hours of service and that demand for services in nursing homes increased. In 1983 there were approximately 1,700 physical therapists employed by Medicare-certified home health care agencies. An additional 2,155 provided contract services in the home. By 1985 the number of therapists employed in such agencies had increased to 6,685; employment dropped only slightly—to 6,234—in 1986 (American Health Care Association, 1987).

The movement of patients out of the hospital to home health care, nursing homes, and rehabilitation facilities represents a change in the location of services rather than an increase in employment. Yet some factors are generating an increase in physical therapist employment in all settings. One such factor is physicians' and the public's perceptions of the need for physical therapy. Practitioners note that physician perception of the value of physical therapy services remains favorable, thus sustaining the level of referrals; at the same time, patient demand for therapy, especially for sports-related injuries, is at an all-time high.

This latter reason is one of the factors that enables physical therapists to practice independently. According to a survey by the American Physical Therapy Association, between 1978 and 1983 the number of self-employed physical therapists increased from 10 percent to 14.6 percent of full-time physical therapists. Since 1983, however, this proportion has increased only to 15.8 percent. Part-time self employment shows a similar pattern, growing from 4.3 to 6.6 percent of employment between 1978 and 1983 and representing 7.7 percent of employment in 1987 (American Physical Therapy Association, 1987a). Whether this reduced growth is the result of a lack of growth in the demand for independent practitioner services or a lack of interest in that form of practice is not known. What is equally likely is that the rate of growth in independent practice will pick up again. Moreover, these self-employment figures do not represent the whole picture of independent practice in the field. Some physical therapists work for the proprietors of independent practices, for example. In 1987, 24.2 percent of respondents to the American Physical Therapy Association's survey said that they worked in a private physical therapy office. This figure probably includes the 17.9 percent who said they were owners, partners, or president of a practice or business (American Physical Therapy Association, 1987a).

Whereas some therapists in private practice have contracted to supply hospital services, others have thriving practices to which physicians refer patients or, in some states, patients refer themselves. Thus, therapists are able to benefit directly from the public's favorable perception of the value of their services. Committee site visits showed that, even in managed care systems in which utilization can be controlled, managers note that patient demand for physical therapy is pushing them to expand services—and in a competitive environment, managers are responsive to patient demand. Last but not least as a factor generating growth in the demand for physical therapists is the aging of the population. Elderly people need a greater volume and intensity of services to treat their multiple problems. Sixty-seven percent of physical therapists report that patients 64 and older are part of their patient population on a typical day (American Physical Therapy Association, 1987a). The demand for services from this important sector can only increase. Some care of the increasing number of elderly patients will take place in their homes. The lower productivity of physical therapists who must travel to their clients, as opposed to providing services in health care facilities, will further stimulate the demand for practitioners.

The current relative availability of financing for physical therapy services should allow these changes to translate into a sharply increased demand for therapists. Insurers and employers have recognized the role of physical therapy in enabling people to return to work or in preventing institutionalization in expensive settings. Consequently, commercial insurers often cover the service. Workmen's Compensation programs cover much of the expense for testing and therapeutic treatments by physical therapists. Increased sensitivity to long-term costs has stimulated employers to cover the rehabilitation of workers and to pay for injury prevention programs in the workplace. Medicare covers home visits by physical therapists and physical therapy services in inpatient and outpatient settings and has not yet placed rehabilitation facilities under any kind of prospective payment restrictions.

In sum, a combination of many factors should generate strong increases in the demand for physical therapists. The only foreseeable major change is the introduction by Medicare of a system of payment for rehabilitation services that contains an incentive to economize or ration services. If the past pattern of hospital staffing in response to DRG recurs, however, even this incentive may not reduce the demand for physical therapy services.

Trends that are important to the future of demand for physical therapists and that should be monitored include the following:

- growth of hospital care;
- physician and public valuation of services;
- changes in rehabilitation reimbursement; and
- perceptions of the effectiveness of physical therapy in facilitating early discharge from hospitals and an early return to work and in preventing injury in the workplace.

The major role of financing in generating a demand for physical therapists is reflected in the response of such demand to the three scenarios described in Chapter 3. A downturn in demand is not foreseen in any scenario.

Scenario 1: The Mixed Model

With a continuation of the several financing systems that currently exist side by side, the demand for physical therapists would be high. Under this scenario, commercial insurers would pay independent practitioners and allow them to serve patients who increasingly want care for sports injuries, lower back pain, and other diagnoses that are treatable on an outpatient basis. Hospital use of physical therapists is stimulated by the admission of older, sicker patients who need services and by facilitating earlier discharges of other patients. Outpatient use also increases as financing continues to be available in all settings. One factor dampening demand, however, is an increasing effort on the part of the Health Care Financing Administration and other third parties to devise more stringent reimbursement screens as a way to constrain the growing utilization of services.

Scenario 2: Prospective Payment

With prospective payment the predominant form of financing, the demand for physical therapists would be somewhat lower than under the mixed payment model. Therapists in independent practice would feel the impact of lower demand as they were forced either to join a managed care system or to rely on patients' willingness to pay for services out-of-pocket. With emphasis on case management, utilization control, and cost-effectiveness the rate of growth in demand for therapy services would be reduced as physicians and case managers became more selective. Proved effectiveness would become increasingly important, and, until a body of research became available to prove effectiveness, the demand for some therapeutic modalities would fall.

Scenario 3: Access

The demand for physical therapists' services would receive added impetus if access to care were increased. Under this scenario, nonacute problems that went untended (e.g., back pain, muscle strain, arthritis, and osteoporosis) and preventive services that were not used in the absence of reimbursement would bring newly financed patients into the medical care system. The diminished need to cross-subsidize services for indigent patients would relieve some of the financial pressures on hospitals, which in turn would allow a lessening of productivity pressures and greater responsiveness to patients' demand for physical therapists.

Supply of Physical Therapists

Graduations from accredited baccalaureate, master's degree, and certificate programs in physical therapy increased by 43 percent between 1979–1980 and 1984–1985 to reach 3,499 in 1985. The increase in that year, however, was only 2 percent (American Physical Therapy Association, personal communication, 1987). This reduced rate of growth should not be interpreted as evidence of a drop in student interest. On the contrary: one dean described physical therapy programs as the "hottest spot on campus." A study conducted for the Health Resources and Services Administration shows that there is pressure on programs to expand their number of students. However, the difficulty of finding clinical sites for training may be slowing expansion (Mathematica Policy Research, Inc., 1987).

Although competition for therapists is encouraging hospitals to continue or start training affiliations to ease their recruitment problems, they are also concerned about the costs of training, preferring more advanced students who require less supervision and are more productive. Partly because hospitals are reluctant to provide training and partly to introduce students to the practice sites in which they are likely to be employed, more non-hospital settings are being used for clinical training (Mathematica Policy Research, Inc., 1987). In the future, the constraints on growth in the supply of physical therapists are more likely to arise from problems in finding qualified faculty and training sites than from a lack of student demand.

Currently, facilities are finding it difficult to hire physical therapists. For the whole period of the study the committee heard more reports of pressure in the labor market for physical therapists than for any other allied health group. Often, it appears that hospital recruitment difficulties are due to the inability of institutions to compete with the earnings available to therapists in other settings or in private practice. A solution is sometimes found in contracting for physical therapy services. In these cases, there is no "shortage," in the sense of therapists not being available at a price the facility is willing to pay, but rather "stress," in the sense of facilities having to alter their way of operating to accommodate the changing market.

The sense of acute shortage reported to the committee from many sources (including representatives of national organizations, which suggests that this was not merely a local phenomenon) is supported by some admittedly limited evidence. Statewide surveys of North Carolina health care facilities reported that the vacancy rate for staff physical therapists almost doubled from 13.8 percent in 1981 to 26.9 percent in 1986. Vacancies for assistants more than doubled from 8 percent to 20 percent (North Carolina Area Health Education Centers Program, 1987a). These 1986 vacancy rates were higher than the rate for five of the six other allied health fields that were surveyed. Only occupational therapy had a higher vacancy rate at 25.1

percent in 1986 (North Carolina Area Health Education Centers Program, 1987a).

Conclusion

If the educational system continues to produce physical therapists at the current rate and the labor force behavior of therapists does not change, some major adjustments must occur to prevent a shortage of physical therapists from now until the year 2000. Shortages affect the various parts of the health care system differently. Sectors that pay workers more or have more attractive working conditions are likely to feel less of an impact. Sectors that are unable to hire a sufficient number of therapists because they cannot outbid the higher payers will be forced to reduce services. These reductions could create an access problem for some patients—probably those in need of long-term rehabilitation services and elderly people.

The necessary market adjustments are likely to be made by both the education and employment sectors, with employers leading the way because they are the first to feel the effects of tight labor markets. Because student interest in a physical therapy career is already greater than current educational capacity can accommodate, salary increases will not be the most effective way of bringing new people into physical therapy. However, more pay should be effective in drawing back into the labor force those who have left and in encouraging practitioners to remain active. Salaries are likely to increase, and hospitals and other employers are expected to seek more productive and effective ways of employing therapists, thus somewhat reducing demand. Extended tenure in the labor market should contribute to the needed adjustment. As salaries rise, and if independent practice and professional growth opportunities increase, practitioners can be expected to remain in the labor force longer and return more readily after leaving. Changes of this sort make major contributions to relieving labor market stresses.

Employers who are concerned about enhancing the supply of physical therapists should begin to understand that the costs of participating in the clinical component of education programs will outweigh the costs of adjusting to both lower levels of physical therapy use and the major salary increases needed to attract therapists. If this and other adjustments occur, graduations will eventually increase, and, as the supply of new therapists responds to demand, the rate of salary increases will abate and a balance between demand and supply will be found.

If, as some desire, a master's degree becomes the entry-level requirement for the field, the supply of new practitioners would be more constrained. Whether raising the entry-level degree would also increase salaries and reduce the demand for therapists is a matter of contention. Some say that higher levels of professional training require greater compensation for the greater educational investment and are thereby linked to higher costs of care—and in times of cost containment, to smaller amounts of care (Havinghurst, 1987). Yet the American Physical Therapy Association believes this argument is wrong for several reasons: more educated practitioners are more likely to work independently with fees that are no higher than the charges assessed by institutions that employ therapists—and even if therapists were more highly paid, the cost of a $3,000 salary increase to full-time, salaried physical therapists in hospitals would represent less than half of 1 percent of the average annual increase in hospital care expenditures (American Physical Therapy Association, 1987b).

RADIOLOGIC TECHNOLOGISTS AND TECHNICIANS

Demand for Radiologic Technologists and Technicians

BLS estimates that between 1986 and the year 2000 the number of jobs for radiologic technologists and technicians will grow by 65 percent, from 115,400 to 190,100. This high rate of growth is similar to that expected for dental hygienists, and it exceeds the expected job growth rates for dietitians, speech–language pathologists and audiologists, and occupational therapists. Jobs for nuclear medicine technologists, who are excluded from the BLS definition of radiologic technologists and technicians, are expected to increase by nearly 23 percent, from 9,700 to 11,900.

To prepare their estimates, BLS analysts evaluate job opportunities in the many different areas radiology encompasses including sonography, fluoroscopy, mammography, computerized tomography, magnetic resonance imaging (MRI), and radiation therapy. Two of the more specialized fields with distinct accreditation for educational programs include radiation therapy and sonography.

In addition to analyzing the prospects for each speciality, BLS analyzes the growth in the number of jobs in different settings—predicting increasing employment opportunities in nonhospital settings such as HMOs, imaging centers, and physician offices (in which 27.4 percent of all radiologic technologists and technicians were employed in 1986 and almost 38 percent are expected to be employed in the year 2000).

Today, hospitals are the major employers of radiologic technologists and technicians, supplying a little more than 60 percent of all available jobs (Table 4-8). BLS predicts that by the year 2000, however, only 48 percent of jobs will be in hospitals. This reduction does not mean that the number of hospital jobs will fall—only that the rate of increase in hospitals will be below the rate of job growth in other settings. Indeed, BLS expects the number of hospital jobs to increase by 21,400—from 70,200 in 1986 to

TABLE 4-8   Major Places of Wage and Salary Employment for
Radiologic Technologists and Technicians, 1986 Actual and Projected
for the Year 2000

Employment Setting	Number of Jobs, 1986	Percentage[a]	Number of Jobs, 2000	Percentage[a]
Total employment[b]	115,400		190,100	
Total wage and salary employment	114,400	100.0	188,200	100.0
Hospitals, public and private	70,200	61.4	91,600	48.7
Outpatient care facilities	2,500	2.2	9,400	5.0
Offices of physicians	31,300	27.4	71,000	37.7
Offices of dentists	1,200	1.0	1,900	1.0
Offices of other health care practitioners	1,500	1.3	4,000	2.1

[a]These percentages were calculated using unrounded figures and therefore will not be identical to percentages that are calculated using the rounded figures provided in the table.

[b]Total employment = wage and salary employment + self-employment. These figures include 1,000 self-employed workers in 1986 and 1,900 in the year 2000 who are not allocated by place of employment.

SOURCE: Bureau of Labor Statistics (1987); moderate alternative.

91,600 in the year 2000. A similar pattern is predicted for nuclear medicine technologists (Table 4-9). The change of inpatient radiology departments from revenue centers to cost centers that has occurred under PPS and the increased use of utilization review were expected to result in the reduced use of ancillary services, especially diagnostic imaging (Steinberg, 1985).

TABLE 4-9   Major Places of Wage and Salary Employment for
Nuclear Medicine Technologists, 1986 Actual and Projected for the
Year 2000

Employment Setting	Number of Jobs, 1986	Percentage[a]	Number of Jobs, 2000	Percentage[a]
Total employment[b]	9,700		11,900	
Total wage and salary employment	9,700	100.0	11,900	100.0
Hospitals, public and private	8,600	88.6	10,000	83.9
Medical and dental labs	500	5.2	700	6.1
Offices of physicians	400	4.1	800	6.6

[a]These percentages were calculated using unrounded figures and therefore will not be identical to percentages that are calculated using the rounded figures provided in the table.

[b]Total employment = wage and salary employment + self-employment. Self-employed persons are not allocated by place of employment.

SOURCE: Bureau of Labor Statistics (1987); moderate alternative.

Pre- and post-PPS employment patterns in hospitals appear to offer equivocal support for this notion.

According to American Hospital Association data, x-ray technologist, radiation therapy technologist, and nuclear medicine technologist employment declined between 1983–1985, compared with 1981–1983, when employment had risen or been close to stable. For other radiologic personnel, employment had been falling before PPS, but the rate slowed after its introduction (Bureau of Health Professions, 1985; American Hospital Association, 1987). It is difficult to ascertain exactly what changes are occurring. In a 1985 survey of nuclear medicine department directors, administrators, or chief technologists, 20 percent of the respondents reported a decline in the number of employed nuclear medicine technologists, 65 percent reported a decrease in inpatient volume, and 58 percent reported an increase in outpatient volume. These data were interpreted as the product of lowered admissions, of physicians ordering fewer tests, and of the shifting of routine testing to the outpatient setting (Crucitti and Pappas, 1986).

A more widely based 1985 survey of hospital radiology by the American Hospital Radiology Administrators (Conway, 1985) asked whether volume had increased, decreased, or remained stable in 33 procedures. More than 40 percent of the respondents reported decreases in three types of procedures including skull and gastrointestinal imaging. By contrast, more than 40 percent of the respondents reported increases in 17 procedures including various fluoroscopy studies, cardiac catheterization, cardiac ultrasound, various computerized tomography (CT) studies, and radiotherapy treatments. The overall findings echoed those of the nuclear medicine survey: 66 percent of the respondents reported a decrease in inpatient workload and 44 and 57 percent of the respondents reported increases in outpatient clinic and private workloads, respectively.

Radiology services appear to reflect a generally observed pattern of post-PPS utilization: services declined dramatically in the 2 years after PPS was introduced and turned up again in 1985 and 1986. Factors that limit further staffing reductions include the increased severity of illness among patients, reduced opportunities to shift the patient to an outpatient setting, and fewer chances to cut unnecessary services (Prospective Payment Assessment Commission, 1987). Looking to the future, the aging population and its need for more intensive care, together with the existing upward trends in radiologic usage, point to continued increases in the demand for radiologic personnel.

The types of personnel likely to be in demand in the future depend to some extent on technological changes; however, it is difficult to estimate the impact and rate of such changes. The emergence of new imaging modalities such as MRI and positron emission tomography or, going back to the 1970s, the new application of computer technology to imaging has generated major improvements in diagnostic capabilities. The new technologies have not always supplanted the old; rather, the new imaging procedures are often used after more customary work is inconclusive. In addition, the new imaging technologies are labor intensive. Scanning procedures are more time-consuming than film x rays. Whether the rate of diffusion of future new imaging modalities will be as great as in the past is an open question. Payers have an interest in controlling the spread of expensive innovations. (Many will remember the attempts that were made to limit the number of CT machines through certificate-of-need reviews.) Today, facilities are more reluctant to buy expensive equipment unless it is believed to be cost-effective or represents a significant improvement in patient care.

Employment outside the hospital is expected to be an increasing source of demand for radiologic technicians and technologists. Freestanding imaging centers, started by physicians to develop a "niche" in the health care market, are already seen as luring technologists away from hospitals. HMOs and group practices are providing onsite radiology; physicians increasingly have x-ray capability in their offices. In some states, unlicensed personnel may operate x-ray equipment in low-volume settings; in others, however, only licensed personnel may do so. Indeed, licensing provisions will be a significant force influencing the demand for radiologic personnel. For example, in some states, ambulatory care centers that hire personnel to carry out two functions must hire licensed x-ray technicians rather than laboratory technicians to provide both x-ray and lab services because the provision of x-ray services requires a licensed technician to operate the equipment. A committee site visit to Boston revealed that newly enacted licensing laws generated a sharp spurt in demand for technicians when licensed personnel had to be hired to replace unlicensed staff. As a result, even an employer who was willing to offer substantially increased pay was unable to attract job applicants.

Another force that could sustain a high level of demand for radiologic personnel is public knowledge about and valuation of x-ray procedures. The media's attention to imaging has developed public consciousness; this, together with physicians' appreciation of the available diagnostic capabilities, should ensure that demand is sustained. Thus, demographic trends, technological trends in hospital care as well as in outpatient care, and other forces will combine to sustain a high level of demand for radiologic occupations. The BLS' estimated 65 percent increase in jobs up to the year 2000 seems reasonable.

Those interested in tracking the future demand for radiologic technicians and technologists should monitor the following factors:

- hospital utilization, especially intensity of care and case mix;
- growth of all types of freestanding facilities;
- licensure changes;
- technological changes that are likely to cause new areas of specialization; and
- results of technology assessment.

Although recent financing changes have had less effect on the radiology field than some had expected, the financing changes envisioned in the three scenarios described in Chapter 3 could have a marked effect.

Scenario 1: The Mixed Model

Under this scenario, overall growth in the health care sector, faster growth in outpatient care, and public and physician appreciation of diagnostic imaging would combine to generate prolonged growth in the demand for radiologic technicians and technologists.

Scenario 2: Prospective Payment

The rate of growth in the demand for radiologic technicians and technologists in hospitals would slow as admissions fell even though the intensity of care increased for an older, sicker patient population. The use of imaging as an aid to speedy diagnosis and discharge would be encouraged. Radiologic technologist and technician demand from outpatient settings would increase, both from a transfer of procedures out of the hospital setting and from an increase in freestanding facilities. In all settings, productivity pressures would also squeeze demand.

Competitive pressures would force managers of managed care systems to seek the most productive sites for radiologic referral. Hospitals and imaging centers would limit staff to price services competitively.

Scenario 3: Access

Because imaging of one sort or another is used in almost all types of health care—primary through tertiary—and by many medical specialities, the increased use of health services that would result from a policy to improve access would inevitably produce the increased utilization of radiology services. Even if such a policy were accompanied by utilization controls, such as case management, it is difficult to believe that anything other than a major increase in demand for radiologic personnel would occur under this scenario.

Supply of Radiologic Technologists and Technicians

In a trend that accompanies a long-term shift from hospital-based to college-based programs, the number of radiography education programs has decreased 23 percent between 1976 and 1986. For several years the changing location of educational programs did not affect the number of graduates substantially. But a sudden decline in graduations of about 15 percent has occurred recently—from 7,393 in 1985 to 6,400 in 1986 (CAHEA, 1987a). This decline may be the result of potential students responding to fears of reduced demand that have been generated by prospective payment.

Two smaller and newer radiologic specialities—nuclear medical technology and radiation therapy technology—each show a different pattern. After rapid growth in the 1970s, nuclear medical technology experienced a 25 percent decline in graduations between 1984 and 1986. By way of contrast, radiation therapy technology graduations show slow but sustained growth over the past 2 decades (CAHEA, 1987a).

There are indications that radiologic technologists, especially those with specialized training, are finding jobs easily. Hospitals are competing with freestanding employers for scarce personnel (Mathematica Policy Research, Inc., 1987), and the committee's site visits found some employers who were unable to hire the staff they were seeking. Other data suggest that, if employers are having a hard time hiring radiologic staff, this may be a phenomenon of quite recent occurrence. A 1986 survey of health care facilities in North Carolina reported that at 8 percent the overall vacancy rate for radiologic personnel was very low compared to other allied health fields—for example, 11.9 percent for medical record administrators and 17.9 percent for respiratory care personnel (North Carolina Area Health Education Centers Program, 1987d).

Finally, adding to the impression of a field in which employers are starting to have difficulties in hiring staff is the result of a survey of education program directors. The percentage who believe that radiography is an attractive opportunity increased from 60 percent in 1981 to 89 percent in 1987 (Parks and Hedrick, 1987).

Conclusion

Even if the decline in graduations from radiologic education programs is halted, strong adjustments in the labor market will be needed to avoid a shortage of practitioners through the year 2000. Salary adjustments are the key in any strategy designed to alleviate labor market stresses. Salary increases can attract new entrants to the field, encourage the return of those who have left, and prolong the attachment to the field of those already in it. Future supply is highly sensitive to even small increments in any or all of these variables. The committee believes that early and significant action in this field is needed to forestall serious problems in the future delivery of health care services.

Focusing on salary increases could be particularly productive in this field. Although starting salaries are competitive, later, radiologic technicians are less well compensated than, for example, computer programmers and operators and engineering technicians—occupations that may be competing for the same students (University of Texas Medical Branch, 1986). Education program directors more often believe that radiographic graduates are more inappropriately compensated than other comparable allied health graduates, except those who work in laboratories (Parks and Hedrick, 1987).

Health care providers play a particularly important role in generating an adequate supply of radiologic personnel. Many education programs are hospital based, and all are heavily dependent on health care facilities to open clinical training opportunities to students. Because of the expense of equipment and the impossibility of simulating patient contact, academic institutions must maintain close ties with clinical sites. Despite such costs as decreased productivity, increases in repeat tests, and faculty salaries, health care providers should not underestimate the importance of offering clinical training opportunities to secure a continuous supply of personnel for themselves as well as for other providers.

RESPIRATORY THERAPISTS

Demand for Respiratory Therapists

BLS predicts that by the year 2000 there will be 75,600 jobs for respiratory therapists—an increase of 34 percent from the 56,300 jobs available in 1986. This level of growth is substantially higher than will occur in total national employment (19 percent) and in some of the allied health occupations (e.g., clinical laboratory technologists or nuclear medicine technologists). Yet such growth appears moderate when compared with that predicted for physical therapist and medical record technician employment (in excess of 70 percent), and occupational therapist and radiologic technician and technologist employment (BLS expects growth in these jobs to the year 2000 to exceed 50 percent).

The BLS estimate of 34 percent growth through the year 2000 is based largely on an assessment of how respiratory therapists will fare in the hospital setting, in which almost 88 percent were employed in 1986. Although BLS predicts only a 12.2 percent increase in overall hospital employment through the year 2000, its analysts expect hospital demand for respiratory therapists to increase by 25 percent because of the increased admissions of older, sicker patients who require more intensive care. BLS also sees some demand for respiratory therapy being generated by improvements in trauma care that allow more accident victims in need of ventilator care to survive. The development of small ventilators for low-birth-weight neonates is a technological factor that will be instrumental in increasing the demand for respiratory services in hospitals. BLS foresees increasing specialization within the profession as therapists become more expert in such areas as neonatal and cardiac care. Simultaneously, BLS expects that respiratory therapists will expand their range of skills, moving into such areas as electrocardiography (EKG). This competency in particular would allow hospitals to curtail the EKG staff employment for 24 hours per day by using respiratory therapists who were already there. Thus, BLS analysts expect that nearly 82 percent of the projected 75,600 respiratory therapist jobs will be in hospitals in the year 2000 (Table 4-10).

The outlook for increased employment of respiratory therapists in home health agencies is not viewed optimistically by BLS analysts who expect reimbursement policies to prevent any significant expansion of home care opportunities for respiratory therapists.

TABLE 4-10   Major Places of Wage and Salary Employment for Respiratory Therapists, 1986 Actual and Projected for the Year 2000

Employment Setting	Number of Jobs, 1986	Percentage[a]	Number of Jobs, 2000	Percentage[a]
Total employment[b]	56,300		75,600	
Total wage and salary employment	56,300	100.0	75,000	100.0
Hospitals, public and private	49,400	87.7	61,900	81.8
Outpatient care facilities	700	1.2	1,500	2.0
Offices of physicians	500	0.9	1,100	1.5
Offices of other health care practitioners[c]	2,000	3.5	3,300	4.3
Other health and allied health care facilities[d]	3,400	6.1	7,300	9.7

[a]These percentages were calculated using unrounded figures and therefore will not be identical to percentages that are calculated using the rounded figures provided in the table.

[b]Total employment = wage and salary employment + self-employment. Self-employed persons are not allocated by place of employment.

[c]Offices of health practitioners other than physicians (including osteopaths) and dentists.

[d]Health care facilities other than the offices of physicians, dentists, and other health care practitioners; nursing and other personal care facilities; hospitals; medical and dental laboratories; and outpatient facilities.

SOURCE: Bureau of Labor Statistics (1987); moderate alternative.

In the current political and financing climate, Medicare reimbursement policies for respiratory therapy in the home support the BLS notion that, by and large, future employment will be generated mainly in hospitals. The services of respiratory therapists are not reimbursable by Medicare on a per-visit basis; rather, the costs must be included in administrative expenses. Thus, employment by home health agencies is low; more often, respiratory therapists are retained as consultants to staff who make home visits. Of 214 home health agencies surveyed, only 12 employed a respiratory therapist either as a staff member or as a contracted consultant (Health Care Financing Administration, 1986b). A recent report to Congress answered in the negative the question of whether Medicare coverage should be expanded to include respiratory therapist visits. The report noted that nurses, who are covered on a per-visit basis, can treat many patients who are in need of respiratory care and can be specially trained, if necessary. Little evidence was found to show that hospital stays would be reduced by expanded payment for home care services, and although many Medicare beneficiaries can be helped by respiratory care, the existing levels of service were deemed sufficient (Health Care Financing Administration, 1986b). Respiratory equipment and supplies for use at home are covered by Medicare under the durable medical equipment benefit. Equipment supply companies support home patients by hiring professional staff (e.g., respiratory therapists) who can supervise the installation of equipment and undertake patient education. (However, the American Association of Respiratory Care reportedly has had difficulty in tracking employment in durable medical equipment companies.) Despite perceptions that increasing numbers of patients could benefit from respiratory therapy services in their homes (see, for example, Gilmartin and Make, 1986), respiratory therapists are unlikely to experience significant increases in home care work unless reimbursement policies change.

A 1986 study by the American Association for Respiratory Care provides tentative support for the BLS view that respiratory therapy employment in hospitals has the potential to grow at a faster rate than overall hospital employment, once productivity gains have reached their limits. The association surveyed hospitals and educators to evaluate the impact of PPS. It found that since 1983 hours of respiratory care services increased in more than half of the surveyed hospitals, and admissions of patients with respiratory-related diagnoses stayed the same or increased in 70 percent of the hospitals. However, in respiratory therapy departments the personnel budgets and level of employment were generally either stable or decreased (American Association for Respiratory Care, 1986b) suggesting that improvements in productivity had occurred.

Other changes that are occurring within hospitals can generate continued steady employment growth for respiratory therapists. As suggested by BLS, respiratory therapists are increasingly being used to provide non-respiratory care services (American Association for Respiratory Care, 1986a). In one hospital visited by the committee, respiratory therapists reported that they had expanded into cardiopulmonary areas such as the cardiac catheterization laboratory, increased their activity in hemodynamic monitoring, and were "filling in" to provide electroencephalography (EEG) and EKG services. The aging population is also likely to increase patient admissions with cardiopulmonary disease and dysfunction. Chronic obstructive pulmonary disease and lung cancer exemplify diseases to which elderly people are particularly prone.

Countering these upward movements in demand are downward pressures that could occur if researchers and managers look more critically at services. A 1986 editorial in the New England Journal of Medicine (Petty, 1986) noted that, in the shift to PPS, respiratory therapy was targeted "as a likely example of undisciplined practices and excesses for reasons that included a dearth of good scientific data on many techniques in common use." Noting studies that showed evidence of the effectiveness of some therapies, as well as one study indicating that sometimes respiratory therapy can be reduced without affecting disease outcome, the editorial concluded with a call for an improved scientific data base to guide practice.

The extent to which respiratory therapy staff are vulnerable to reductions in times of constraint will depend only in part on evidence of the necessity for or effectiveness of services. Other important factors include an absence of patient demand for therapy services and the strength of department managers in each hospital's hierarchy. It was noted on one site visit that, although the volume of respiratory therapy services has diminished outside of intensive care units (ICUs) because of more stringent utilization review and the improved use of medications, simultaneously, ICU activity has shown large increases with sicker patients needing ventilation care.

In sum, the BLS analysis of moderate growth in jobs for respiratory therapists is well substantiated. Hospital employment is the chief source of growth, stimulated by the aging population and the demand generated by new technologies that save extremely sick individuals. Out-of-hospital employment is small and likely to remain so. Even a large increase in non-hospital demand would have only a small effect on total demand for respiratory therapists.

Factors that will have an important effect on respiratory therapy employment include the following:

- hospital admission rates;
- severity of hospital admissions;
- disease patterns, especially cardiopulmonary diseases;
- the outcome of effectiveness studies;

- the expansion of activities of respiratory therapists into new areas;
- Medicare reimbursement of respiratory therapists in home care;
- employment by the durable medical equipment industry; and
- expanded use in nursing homes.

The last three factors can diminish the dependence of the profession on hospital employment. However, because an explosion of out-of-hospital employment is unlikely, growth in the number of jobs will probably continue at the moderate rate forecast by BLS.

In addition to the above factors, which should be tracked to identify trends in demand for respiratory therapists, major financing changes, as outlined in the scenarios in Chapter 3, will also have major impacts.

Scenario 1: The Mixed Model

Growth in hospital employment would continue to be moderate, fueled largely by the aging population. Employment in home care would increase only slightly as reimbursement constrains home visits. Because employment in other settings would continue to be minimal, hospital growth would overwhelm other changes.

Scenario 2: Prospective Payment

Under this scenario, the increased use of prospective payment would force hospital administrators to seek ways to reduce costs as hospital utilization fell. Respiratory therapy would probably be vulnerable unless it could be shown to contribute to early discharges. Hospitals would also seek to increase their stake in nonhospital markets to ensure that, after earlier discharge, patients' continuing care produced revenue for the hospital. Hospitals would become purveyors of more intensive home care, including respiratory therapy in modest amounts. Employment by durable medical equipment companies would increase as they provided more intensive out-of-hospital services. However, if it should occur, the contraction of employment in the hospital sector would overwhelm all other effects.

Scenario 3: Access

The greatest increase in demand for respiratory therapists would occur with this scenario. Hospital use would be stimulated by making financing available to people who today are unable to obtain hospital care. Yet some of the hospital expansion would occur in elective procedures that today are postponed for lack of financing until sickness is acute. These less acutely sick patients are less intense users of respiratory therapy services than are sicker patients, however.

Supply of Respiratory Therapists

The characteristics of today's respiratory therapy work force reflect the multiple routes of entry into the field that have existed until now but that are fast disappearing. Analyses of the 1980 census indicated that a significant proportion of the work force, including credentialed personnel, had only on-the-job training (Health Resources and Services Administration, 1984). Currently, there is a trend toward training in programs that culminate in certification or licensure or both. As a result the shorter programs that provide training for the lower level respiratory technicians are disappearing. The number of accredited technician programs has decreased by 2.3 percent, from 173 in 1980 to 169 in 1986. The number of graduates has decreased by 21 percent, from 3,206 in 1980 to 2,539 in 1986 (CAHEA, 1987a).

Accompanying the move to certified personnel, sponsorship of educational programs has shifted from hospitals to colleges and universities. Community colleges now offer the greatest proportion (66 percent) of programs. The number of accredited therapist programs has increased by 34 percent, from 175 in 1980 to 235 in 1986. Yet the number of graduates has not shown parallel growth. Rather, it has fluctuated from year to year with a high of 3,868 in 1985 followed by a 6-year low of 2,740 in 1986 (CAHEA, 1987a). This fluctuation suggests that during years of low demand there is excess educational capacity. Furthermore, the trend in graduates bears watching to determine whether the 28 percent drop in graduates between 1985 and 1986 is other than an anomaly.

The committee has heard conflicting reports of the availability of respiratory therapists, suggesting that there are substantial differences among local markets. Salary data are equivocal in their support of the notion that the labor market may be very tight. At least two data sets allow comparisons of the rate of salary increases among selected allied health professions: the Bureau of Labor Statistics' (1983–1986) Current Population Survey and the University of Texas's National Survey of Hospital and Medical School Salaries. In the Current Population Survey, the salaries of respiratory therapists showed the greatest rate of increase of the allied health professions under scrutiny. In the University of Texas's survey (University of Texas Medical Branch, 1981, 1986), the rate of salary increase for respiratory therapists fell in the bottom third when compared with rates of increase for 19 other groups of hospital employees (Bureau of Labor Statistics, 1983–1986). These data do not allow any firm conclusion about the present state of the market for respiratory therapists.

Conclusion

If the number of graduates from educational programs can be maintained at approximately today's level, the nation's supply of respiratory therapists should be adequate to the demand for services through the year 2000. This statement implies that significant changes in the rate of salary growth or major improvements in the conditions of employment should not be expected. To maintain this balance, educational capacity and student interest must be sustained. The fluctuations in graduations suggest that students may need encouragement in the form of increased job attractiveness to keep up the necessary level of interest in the field.

Some caveats about the committee's estimate of the balance between demand and supply are in order. In assessing future supply, the committee assumed that respiratory therapy work force behavior would be comparable to the work force behavior of members of other therapy fields. Unlike many allied health fields, men are a substantial proportion (about 40 percent) of the respiratory therapy labor force. The significance of this representation in terms of geographic mobility, labor force attachment, or responsiveness to economic incentives—as compared with fields in which almost all the workers are women—is not fully known. If it is true that men remain in the labor force longer than women, the committee's estimate of future supply may be conservative.

In conclusion, until better information about the long-term labor force behavior of respiratory therapists is available, it is reasonable to believe that labor markets will make necessary adjustments smoothly to maintain a reasonable equilibrium between the demand for and supply of respiratory therapists. The volatility of the number of graduates, however, suggests the need for close monitoring of emerging educational trends.

SPEECH–LANGUAGE PATHOLOGISTS AND AUDIOLOGISTS

Demand for Speech–Language Pathologists and Audiologists

The BLS predictions of an additional 15,500 jobs for speech–language pathologists and audiologists by the year 2000 represents an increase (by 34 percent) to a total of 60,600 jobs. BLS estimates that there were 45,100 jobs in 1986, including jobs in education that were in some cases filled by individuals with baccalaureates rather than the professional entry-level master's degree. The American Speech–Language–Hearing Association (ASHA) has estimated that 42,390 of its members—all of whom hold at least a master's degree—were in the active work force. Non-ASHA members in the active work force, including people with only a bachelor's degree, were estimated to number 41,000 (Shewan, 1987). Thus, the association estimates that there is a total of 83,000 people in speech–language and audiology jobs—a figure vastly larger than the BLS job estimate.

The growth rate predicted by BLS through the year 2000 is similar to that predicted for occupational therapists and stems from a similar factor that is unusual among allied health practitioners—significant employment outside the health care system. In 1986 only 28.6 percent of speech–language pathologist and audiologist jobs were in the health care services industry. Sixty-four percent were in educational services—a sector in which BLS expects demand to be close to stagnant (Table 4-11). Between 1986 and the year 2000, speech–language pathology and audiology jobs in the education sector are expected to increase by only 14 percent. ASHA notes that 13.6 percent of speech–language pathologists and audiologists report that they run their own practices or are independent contractors (American Speech–Language–Hearing Association, 1988).

BLS analysts caution that their classification of speech–language pathologists and audiologists includes those prepared only to the bachelor's degree level. These practitioners are not certified by ASHA, which certifies at the master's degree level and above, and thus cannot work in the 36 states with licensure requirements. BLS analysts believe that most non-ASHA-certified personnel are employed in educational services by state education departments in states that certify individuals who have only a bachelor's degree or who lack other qualifications for ASHA certification.

TABLE 4-11   Major Places of Wage and Salary Employment for Speech–Language Pathologists and Audiologists, 1986 Actual and Projected for the Year 2000

Employment Setting	Number of Jobs, 1986	Percentage[a]	Number of Jobs, 2000	Percentage[a]
Total employment[b]	45,100		60,600	
Total wage and salary employment	42,100	100.0	56,500	100.0
Educational institutions, public and private	27,000	64.0	30,800	54.62
Hospitals, public and private	4,400	10.4	5,600	9.9
Outpatient care facilities	2,700	6.4	4,400	7.7
Nursing and personal care facilities	1,200	2.7	1,900	3.4
Offices of physicians	1,800	3.6	2,900	5.2
Offices of other health care practitioners[c]	1,200	2.7	4,400	7.7

[a]These percentages were calculated using unrounded figures and therefore will not be identical to percentages that are calculated using the rounded figures provided in the table.

[b]Total employment = wage and salary employment + self-employment. These figures include 3,000 self-employed workers in 1986 and 4,096 in the year 2000 who are not allocated by place of employment.

[c]Offices of health care practitioners other than physicians (including osteopaths) and dentists. The figures include offices of speech–language pathologists and audiologists.

SOURCE: Bureau of Labor Statistics (1987); moderate alternative.

There is considerable support for the BLS estimates. Although speech–language pathologists and audiologists may see new opportunities for employment growth under the 1986 Education of the Handicapped Act (which increased the demand for these professionals by funding programs for young children), total employment growth in the education sector will be relatively slow. New employment opportunities will occur in other settings, however. Speech–language pathologists and audiologists are well positioned to benefit from changes occurring in the health care system. Their lesser dependence on hospital employment (which accounted for only 10 percent of jobs in 1986) makes them less vulnerable to any squeeze on employment in that sector. Their reimbursement status positions them to benefit from shifts to care outside of hospitals. Under the Omnibus Budget Reconciliation Act of 1980, a speech–language pathologist may develop a plan of care for patients referred by a physician and be reimbursed by Medicare. Prior to 1980 the amount, duration, and scope of services had to be specified by the physician. Since 1986 speech–language pathology has been included among the therapies that together must be provided for a total of 3 hours per day for a beneficiary to be eligible for Medicare coverage in an inpatient rehabilitation facility. While this could provide an impetus to increased demand for speech–language pathologists, it could also be short-lived as Medicare seeks ways to find an equitable reimbursement system that includes cost-control incentives. Medicare will also reimburse for home care visits, a provision that positions therapists to care for the growing population of patients discharged from hospitals or in need of long-term home care (American Speech–Language–Hearing Association, 1987b). According to the Health Care Financing Administration the estimated number of speech–language pathologists employed by Medicare-certified home care agencies grew from 303 in 1983 to 5,503 in 1985; the figure dropped to 3,113 in 1986 (American Home Care Association, 1987). The extent to which this drop is due to increased contracting for services or other arrangements is not known. Approximately 48 percent of free-standing home health agencies offer speech–language and audiology services (American Speech–Language–Hearing Association, Task Force on Home Care, 1986).

Although only a minority of speech–language pathologists and audiologists are employed in hospitals, their use in that setting has not been constrained by PPS. Indeed, between 1983 and 1985 their FTE employment in hospitals increased by 21 percent from 2,684 to 3,252. Committee site visits uncovered several possible reasons for this increase. One is expanded speech and hearing coverage by HMOs. Audiology personnel working in hospital outpatient areas are finding that HMO patients are covered for the full range of diagnostic testing and hearing aids. (Previously, commercial insurance subscribers were covered for only a narrow range of hearing testing.) Speech–language pathologists also cited a growing demand for services for stroke and head-injured patients whose survival rates have improved with the advent of new knowledge and technology. Audiologists noted a growing incidence of hearing defects in young people who listen to music through headphones. Both occupations cited the growing numbers of elderly patients using their services plus an increasing understanding of their work by physicians that has resulted in more numerous referrals.

In sum, speech–language pathologists and audiologists in their major employment setting—educational institutions—are not likely to experience rapid increases in demand. In health care settings, they are positioned for steady growth. Reimbursement allows them to take advantage of the shift to nonhospital care in many settings. Given the expected slow growth in education and faster growth in health care settings, the overall moderate growth predicted by BLS seems reasonable.

Factors to be monitored by those wishing to track future demand for speech–language pathologists and audiologists include the following:

- Medicare reimbursement of rehabilitation services;
- school system growth and financing;
- patterns of specific diseases and treatment such as stroke, head trauma, and deafness in youth; and
- growth in independent practice opportunities and contractual arrangements with freestanding speech–language pathology and audiology organizations.

The way in which the three scenarios described in Chapter 3 play out for speech–language pathology and audiology is largely determined by the pattern of employment across the various health care settings and outside the health care system.

Scenario 1: The Mixed Model

With this scenario, speech–language pathologists and audiologists would be in steady demand as their services were included in comprehensive HMO benefit packages and increasing numbers were needed to work in the less productive home care environment. The demand for rehabilitation and outpatient services would also show steady growth.

Scenario 2: Prospective Payment

Because only a small proportion of speech–language pathologists and audiologists work in hospitals, the impact of increased prospective payment in this setting would have little impact on total demand. Similarly, bringing rehabilitation services under prospective payment would result in only a small reduction in overall demand. Outpatient care would show overall growth, but speech–language pathology and audiology would not benefit greatly because these services would be seen as less vital than others that related more directly to physical health. Less vital services would be most vulnerable to reduction under prospective payment. Combining the slight growth in outpatient demand with the reduction in inpatient demand would yield stagnant total demand from the health care sector under this scenario.

Scenario 3: Access

Speech and hearing deficits are among the group of health problems that are likely to go unserved if individuals experience financial barriers to health care. Under this scenario, those financial barriers would be lowered and previously ignored communicative deficits would receive attention, stimulating greater demand for speech and hearing services in inpatient and outpatient settings.

Supply of Speech–Language Pathologists and Audiologists

In 1986 304 programs offered degrees in communication sciences and disorders. Of these programs, 21 percent offered only undergraduate degrees. The total number of programs has been quite stable since 1983, ranging between 293 and 304 (Cooper et al., 1987). The number of bachelor's degrees awarded has declined since 1981 by 15 percent to 4,300. The decline was confined to only 2 years, however. The latest figures show an upturn (CAHEA, 1987a).

The picture for master's degrees is a little clearer: the number of degrees awarded since 1982 has remained relatively stable. Yet this trend must be viewed together with that for bachelor's degree graduates (Cooper et al., 1987). Approximately 90 percent of master's degree graduates in speech pathology and audiology have undergraduate degrees in the same disciplines. Furthermore, the number of master's degree graduates closely matches the undergraduate degrees in speech and audiology—with a 2-year time lag (Cooper et al., 1987). It seems reasonable to conclude that most speech–language pathology or audiology undergraduates move on to a speech–language pathology or audiology master's degree and that bachelor's degree graduates are the pool from which therapists are drawn. Consequently, we must consider undergraduate as well as graduate degrees as an indicator of future supply.

The committee is not aware of any evidence that demand and supply are not currently in balance in this field. Although committee members occasionally heard that rehabilitation facilities were experiencing difficulties in filling vacancies for speech–language pathologists, they also heard that some independent practitioners were unable to generate enough business and were returning to employment in other facilities. Such comments were rare, however, and do not disturb the overall picture of an adequate current supply of practitioners. A national survey of starting salaries for speech–language pathologists in hospitals shows an increase of 23 percent between 1981 and 1986. This increase was lower than that for 17 of 19 other types of personnel. The 33 percent increase for audiologists, however, was higher than that of pharmacists and nurses who are thought to be in short supply (University of Texas Medical Branch, 1981, 1986). These data indicate a difference in demand for the two types of practitioners but are not in themselves sufficient evidence on which to base a judgment of the markets.

Conclusion

If baccalaureate graduations remain at approximately the level of the last few years and if most of these graduates go on to master's degrees in speech–language pathology or audiology, there should be a continued balance between demand and supply through the year 2000. This statement implies that significant changes in the rate of salary growth or major improvements in the conditions of employment should not be expected. However, the production of baccalaureate graduates should be carefully monitored. The data to this time do not indicate whether a downward trend is beginning to develop. If a decline does occur, employers who feel the impact of the drop will need such factors as higher salaries to influence people to pursue careers in language and hearing disorders.

CONCLUSION

This chapter applies the best available data to assess how the forces that drive the demand for and supply of allied health personnel will affect allied health labor markets. The committee's intention is to alert decision makers to the kinds and magnitudes of market adjustments that they should expect and encourage to sustain a long-term balance between allied health personnel demand and supply.

For some fields (e.g., physical therapy, radiologic technology, medical record technology and administration, and occupational therapy), we foresee a need for decision makers to use the mechanisms under their control to improve the working of the market so that severe imbalances in demand and supply may be prevented. Employers are already concerned about difficulties in hiring in some of these fields, and there are signs that health care providers are beginning to find some painful as well as some beneficial ways to accommodate new realities. The committee is concerned that inaction may have consequences that would have deleterious effects on the level of health care.

For some other fields (e.g., clinical laboratory technology and dental hygiene), there are factors that could cause instability in both demand and supply. For these fields the market is more likely to make the needed adjustments, and serious disruptions are less likely to occur. Yet there are unresolved issues in both of these fields concerning the match between tasks and levels and types of education. The way these issues are resolved could determine whether major imbalances will occur.

The demand for and supply of speech–language pathologists, audiologists, respiratory therapists, and dietitians are expected to be sufficiently well balanced for the labor market to make smooth adjustments. The kinds of incremental adjustments that make careers attractive and the ways in which personnel are deployed appear likely to remain in a state of equilibrium over time. Nevertheless, changes in the factors the committee has identified as having major effects on demand and supply could cause disequilibrium. These factors should be monitored.

These conclusions about the future outlook refer to the long term. For all fields, there are likely to be periods of greater and lesser imbalance between now and the year 2000.

It is the nature of markets eventually to adjust to change. Projected imbalances in demand and supply do not mean that shortages or surpluses will occur. Rather, they signal that employers and potential employees must and probably will make adjustments. Only rarely are markets unable to accommodate changes in demand and supply through a variety of adjustment mechanisms.

We have identified areas for potential adjustment in both demand and supply, which forms a basis for understanding future policy directions concerning supply and use of allied health personnel. The objective of policy is to make the process of adjustment less painful and less costly. Decrements in quality of care, interruptions or reductions of service, and curtailment of investment in new technologies and organizational forms (such as home care or HMOs) that might improve the efficiency of health care delivery are all possible by-products of personnel shortages. Any decision to intervene in the labor market is made through the political process and reflects society's willingness—or unwillingness—to tolerate painful dislocations. In many industries, such dislocations are viewed as normal and acceptable. Public policy actions have demonstrated that health care is viewed differently. The next three chapters of this report describe what educators, employers, and regulators, together with government, can do to facilitate the smooth working of the market.

REFERENCES

Abramowitz, M. 1987. Blue Cross acts to curb some medical tasks. Washington Post, April 2.

Amatayakul, M. K. 1987. Report from AMRA manpower survey. Journal of the American Medical Record Association 58(3):25–36.

American Association for Respiratory Care. 1986a. AARC Membership Profile and Benefits Survey. Dallas: American Association for Respiratory Care. August 14.

American Association for Respiratory Care. 1986b. Impact of the Prospective Payment on the Respiratory Care Profession. Report of the Task Force on Professional Direction. Dallas: American Association for Respiratory Care.

American Dental Association, Division of Educational Measurements. 1987. Annual Report on Dental Auxiliary Education 1986/87. Chicago: American Dental Association.

American Dietetic Association. 1985. A New Look at the Profession of Dietetics: Report of the 1984 Study Commission on Dietetics. Chicago: American Dietetic Association.

American Dietetic Association. 1987. Unpublished data. American Dietetic Association, Chicago.

American Health Care Association. 1987. Unpublished data. American Health Care Association, Washington, D.C.

American Hospital Association. 1987. Unpublished data from the American Hospital Association annual survey. American Hospital Association, Chicago.

American Occupational Therapy Association. 1985. Occupational Therapy Manpower: A Plan for Progress. Report of the Ad Hoc Commission on Occupational Therapy Manpower. Rockville, Md.: American Occupational Therapy Association. April.

American Occupational Therapy Association, Research Information and Evaluation Division. 1986a. 1986 Education Data Survey. Final Report. Rockville, Md.: American Occupational Therapy Association.

American Occupational Therapy Association. 1986b. President Reagan Signs P.L. 99-457, The Education for Handicapped Amendments of 1986. Government and Legal Affairs Division Bulletin. Rockville, Md.: American Occupational Therapy Association.

American Occupational Therapy Association. 1987. 1986 Member Data Survey. Interim Report No. 1. Rockville, Md.: American Physical Therapy Association.

American Physical Therapy Association. 1987a. Active Membership Profile Study. Alexandria, Va.: American Physical Therapy Association.

American Physical Therapy Association. 1987b. Comments from the American Physical Therapy Association on Preliminary Draft Background Papers for the American Society of Allied Health Professions International Conference, January 15–16, 1987. Alexandria, Va.: American Physical Therapy Association.

American Physical Therapy Association. 1987c. The Impact of the Medicare Prospective Payment System on the Delivery of Physical Therapy Services. Alexandria, Va.: American Physical Therapy Association.

American Society for Medical Technology. 1986. Quality Assurance in Physician Office Laboratories. A White Paper with Recommendations. Bethesda, Md.: American Society for Medical Technology.

American Speech–Language–Hearing Association. 1987a. Demographic Profile of the ASHA Membership, 1987. Rockville, Md.: American Speech–Language–Hearing Association.

American Speech–Language–Hearing Association. 1987b. Health Insurance Manual. Rockville, Md.: American Speech–Language–Hearing Association.

American Speech–Language–Hearing Association. 1988. Demographic Profile of the ASHA Membership. Rockville, Md.: American Speech–Language–Hearing Association. March 9.

American Speech–Language–Hearing Association, Task Force on Home Care. 1986. The Delivery of Speech–Language and Audiology Services in Home Care. May. Rockville, Md.: American Speech–Language–Hearing Association.

Baranowski, J. 1985. Labs in ambulatory care centers: Medicine's growth sector. Medical Laboratory Observer May:27–34.

Bernstein, T. W. 1985. The Impact of PPS on Medical Record Practitioners—Part II. Journal of the American Medical Record Association 56(December):15–19.

Bishop, E. 1983. Dental Insurance: The What, the Why, and the How of Dental Benefits. New York: McGraw-Hill.

Bryk, J. A. 1987. Report of the 1986 census of the American Dietetic Association. Journal of the American Dietetic Association 87(8):1080–1085.

Burda, D. 1984. UB-82 arrives with work for medical records departments. Journal of the American Medical Record Association 55(11):28–31.

Bureau of Health Professions. 1985. Trends in Hospital Personnel 1981–1983. ODAM Report No. 5-85. Washington, D.C.: U.S. Department of Health and Human Services, Health Resources and Services Administration.

Bureau of Health Professions, Division of Associated and Dental Health Professions. 1987. Unpublished data. U.S. Department of Health and Human Services, Washington, D.C.

Bureau of Labor Statistics. 1983–1986. Unpublished data from the Current Population Survey. U.S. Department of Labor. Washington, D.C.

Bureau of Labor Statistics. 1986. Occupational Outlook Handbook. Bulletin 2250. Washington, D.C.: Government Printing Office.

Bureau of Labor Statistics, 1987. Employment by occupation and industry, 1986 and projected 2000 alternatives. Washington, D.C.

CAHEA (Committee on Allied Health Education and Accreditation). 1979. Allied Health Education Directory, 1979, 7th ed. Chicago: American Medical Association.

CAHEA. 1980. Allied Health Education Directory, 1980, 8th ed. Chicago: American Medical Association.

CAHEA. 1981. Allied Health Education Directory, 1981, 9th ed. Chicago: American Medical Association.

CAHEA. 1982. Allied Health Education Directory, 1982, 10th ed. Chicago: American Medical Association.

CAHEA. 1983. Allied Health Education Directory, 1983, 11th ed. Chicago: American Medical Association.

CAHEA. 1984. Allied Health Education Directory, 1984, 12th ed. Chicago: American Medical Association.

CAHEA. 1985a. Allied Health Education Directory, 1985, 13th ed. Chicago: American Medical Association.

CAHEA. 1985b. A Report of a Survey on the Impact of PPS on Clinical Education. Chicago: American Medical Association. December.

CAHEA. 1986. Allied Health Education Directory, 1986, 14th ed. Chicago: American Medical Association.

CAHEA. 1987a. Allied Health Education Directory, 1987, 15th ed. Chicago: American Medical Association.

CAHEA. 1987b. Voluntary Program Withdrawals from CAHEA Accreditation, 1983–87. Chicago: American Medical Association.

Conway, J. B. 1985. Survey results: Programs, services and trends. Radiology Management 7(2):51–71.

Cooper, E. B., J. W. Helmick, and D. N. Ripich. 1987. Council of Graduate Programs in Communication Sciences and Disorders: 1986–87 National Survey. Tuscaloosa, Ala.: Council of Graduate Programs in Communication Sciences and Disorders. October.

Council on Medical Education of the American Medical Association. 1972. Allied Medical Education Directory. Chicago: American Medical Association.

Council on Medical Education of the American Medical Association. 1973. Allied Medical Education Directory. Chicago: American Medical Association.

Council on Medical Education of the American Medical Association. 1974. Allied Medical Education Directory. Chicago: American Medical Association.

Council on Medical Education of the American Medical Association. 1978. Allied Medical Education Directory, 6th ed. Chicago: American Medical Association.

Crucitti, T. W., and V. M. Pappas. 1986. The Impact of the Prospective Payment System on the Delivery of Nuclear Medicine Services. Report to the Bureau of Health Professions, U.S. Public Health Service. Contract No. HRSA 85-351(P). July. New York: The Society of Nuclear Medicine.

Dental Hygiene. 1982. Who we are: A report on the "Survey of Dental Hygiene Issues: Attitudes, Perceptions and Preferences." Dental Hygiene, December:13–18.

Dore, D. 1987. Effect of the Medicare prospective payment system on the utilization of physical therapy. Physical Therapy 67(6):964–966.

Frost and Sullivan, Inc. 1985. Group practice laboratories benefitting from new federal regulations. White paper with recommendations. News of International Research Report for Business. Summer.

Gilmartin, M. E., and B. J. Make. 1986. Mechanical ventilation in the home: A new mandate. Respiratory Care 31(5):406–411.

Gore, M. T. 1987. The impact of DRGs after year 4: A swing to better times. Medical Laboratory Observer, December:27–30.

Grembowski, D., D. Conrad, and P. Milgrom. 1984. Utilization of dental services in the United States and an insured population. Paper presented at the International Association for Dental Research Annual Conferences, Dallas, March. 1984. Washington, D.C.: International Association for Dental Research.

Harper, S. S. 1984. The key to predicting laboratory workload. Medical Laboratory Observer, November:65–67.

Havinghurst, C. C. 1987. Practice opportunities for allied health professionals in a deregulated health care industry. Preliminary draft background paper prepared for the American Society of Allied Health Professions Invitational Conference, Washington, D.C., June 15–16.

Health Care Financing Administration. 1986a. Report to Congress. Study of Registered Dieticians' Services in Home Care. Washington, D.C.: U.S. Department of Health and Human Services, Office of Research and Demonstrations.

Health Care Financing Administration. 1986b. Report to Congress. Study of Respiratory Therapy Services in Home Care. Washington, D.C.: U.S. Department of Health and Human Services, Office of Research and Demonstrations.

Health Resources and Services Administration. 1984. An In-Depth Examination of the 1980 Decennial Census Employment Data for Health Occupations. ODAM Report No. 16-84. Washington, D.C.: U.S. Department of Health and Human Services. July.

Journal of the American Medical Association. 1983. Number of programs, enrollments, and graduates for each allied health occupation. Vol. 250(12):1567.

Journal of the American Medical Association. 1984. Number of programs, enrollments, and graduates for each allied health occupation. Vol. 252(12):1569.

Journal of the American Medical Association. 1985. Number of programs (December 1984), enrollments, and graduates (academic year 1983–84) for each allied health occupation. Vol. 254(12):1606.

Kaufman, M., et al. 1986. Survey of nutritionists in state and local public health agencies. Perspectives in Practice 86(11):1566–1570.

Lucash, P. 1983. EMS volunteers: Facing the challenges of the '80s. Journal of Emergency Medical Services, October:41–45.

Mathematica Policy Research, Inc. 1987. Exploration of Trends and Changes in Clinical Education in the Preparation of Allied Health Professions. Princeton, N.J.: Mathematica Policy Research, Inc. June.

McKay, J. I. 1985. Historical review of emergency medical services, EMT roles, and EMT utilization in emergency departments. Journal of Emergency Nursing 11(1):27–31.

McMahon, E. M. 1986. Approval of a proposal to establish an associate degree in applied science in dental hygiene at the Community College of Rhode Island. Memorandum. State of Rhode Island Office of Higher Education, Providence. December 5.

Medical Laboratory Observer. 1984. The impact of DRGs after year 1: First steps toward greater lab efficiency. December:33–38.

Meyer, D. M. 1988. The president speaks. ASMT Today 3(1):3.

National Association for Home Care. 1987. Unpublished data. National Association for Home Care, Washington, D.C.

National Emergency Medical Services Clearinghouse. 1985. State Emergency Medical Services Personnel Training. The 1985 National EMS Data Summary. Lexington, Ky.: The Council of State Governments.

National Institute on Aging. 1987. Personnel for health needs of the elderly through year 2020. U.S. Department of Health and Human Services, Washington, D.C. September.

North Carolina Area Health Education Centers Program. 1987a. 1986 Allied Health Manpower Surveys: Summary Report. Chapel Hill, N.C.: North Carolina Area Health Education Centers Program. August.

North Carolina Area Health Education Centers Program. 1987b. 1986 Medical Technology Manpower Survey: Final Report. Chapel Hill, N.C.: North Carolina Area Health Education Centers Program. August.

North Carolina Area Health Education Centers Program. 1987c. 1986 Occupational Therapy Manpower Survey: Final Report. Chapel Hill, N.C.: North Carolina Area Health Education Centers Program. August.

North Carolina Area Health Education Centers Program. 1987d. 1986 Radiologic Technology Manpower Survey: Final Report. Chapel Hill, N.C.: North Carolina Area Health Education Centers Program. August.

Packer, C. L. 1985. Automation in the medical records department. Hospitals 59(5):100–104.

Parks, R. B., and H. L. Hedrick. 1987. Program director perspectives on student and employment characteristics. Committee on Allied Health Education Accreditations, American Medical Association, Chicago.

Petty, T. L. 1986. Rational respiratory therapy. New England Journal of Medicine 315(5):317–319.

Price, G. 1988. ASMT Survey II shows strong nonphysician purchasing consulting roles. ASMT Today 3(1):3–4.

Prospective Payment Assessment Commission. 1987. Technical Appendixes to the Report and Recommendations to the Secretary, U.S. Department of Health and Human Services. Washington, D.C.: Prospective Payment Assessment Commission. April 1.

Schraffenberger, L. A. 1987. The Impact of Prospective Payment on Medical Record Practitioners: A Follow-Up Study in 1986. Chicago: American Medical Record Association.

Scott, S. J. 1987. Medicare extends coverage. July 1; HCFA issues interim instructions. OT Week 1(25):1.

Shewan, C. M. 1987. An Update on Supply Estimates for Speech–Language–Hearing Personnel. Unpublished paper, American Speech–Language–Hearing Association. Rockville, Md.

Smith, J. P., and B. I. Bodai. 1985. The urban paramedic's scope of practice. Journal of the American Medical Association 253(4):544–548.

Solomon, E. 1988. Trends in dental education. Paper presented by the American Association of Dental Schools at the IOM meeting, "Roles and Training of Health Professions," Washington, D.C.

Steinberg, E. P. 1985. The impact of regulation and payment innovations on acquisition of new imaging technologies. Radiologic Clinics of North America 23(3):381–389.

University of Texas Medical Branch. 1981. 1981 National Survey of Hospital and Medical School Salaries. Galveston: University of Texas. December.

University of Texas Medical Branch. 1986. 1986 National Survey of Hospital and Medical School Salaries. Galveston: University of Texas. November.

Veterans Administration, Office of Personnel and Labor Relations. 1987. Report of 1986 Survey of Health Occupational Staff. Washington, D.C.: Veterans Administration. March 27.

Whitlock, E., and J. Whitmore. 1987. A report from the American Medical Record Association: Non-management positions. American Medical Record Association, Chicago. June.

5

The Role of Educational Policy in Influencing Supply

IF NO STEPS ARE TAKEN to bolster the future supply of personnel in several allied health fields, health care institutions will be hampered in meeting the public's demand for services. These steps will require coordinated actions by educators and employers, encouraged by modest but strategic federal, state, and private programs. Many of the recommendations in this and the following chapter are directed toward educators, employers, and the allied health professions themselves. Although the committee believes its recommendations will be beneficial to those parties, it looks to public intervention to stimulate and amplify their implementation.

This chapter is divided into three sections. The first deals with policies to influence the decisions of persons choosing careers. The second discusses the role of educational institutions in maintaining or expanding enrollments. The third addresses concerns about the preparedness of the future allied health work force.

THE ALLIED HEALTH STUDENT APPLICANT POOL

For most fields the available trend data on allied health programs and graduations do not signal an imminent crisis requiring dramatic public intervention. Looking to the future, however, the committee is deeply concerned that the weak infrastructure of allied health education may compromise the system's ability to maintain enrollments, let alone increase the supply of personnel in fields in which employment demand is high. A key to the viability of allied health education is its capacity to maintain its share of qualified students from the traditional college-age applicant pool while tapping into less traditional pools of students, particularly minority students.

For a number of years, allied health deans and program directors have expressed concern about the declining number of applicants to their programs and the implications of this decline for the academic quality of the student body. Reportedly, spaces in many programs are going unfilled, and this lack of student interest is jeopardizing the survival of academic programs. Comprehensive data collection concerning applicants to allied health programs is not currently being done. However, CAHEA annually surveys program directors in several allied health fields about whether applications to their programs are increasing, decreasing, or remaining stable. In its 1987 survey, program directors in 13 of 22 fields reported decreases in the number of applicants (CAHEA, 1988).

The clinical laboratory fields in particular were experiencing distress. For example, almost two-thirds of the medical technology program directors reported decreases in applicants in 1987. Of the 116 programs that voluntarily withdrew from CAHEA accreditation between 1983 and 1987, 36 attributed their decisions to a declining applicant pool.

Unpublished survey data from the American Society of Allied Health Professions suggest that only physical therapy has a large applicant pool to draw upon, with about five applicants per academic space. Other fields such as dietetics, medical technology, radiologic technology, and medical record administration average only slightly more applicants than needed to fill their classes.

A recent (1987) survey of the College of Health Deans, an organization composed of allied health administrative units in 20 universities without medical centers from 17 states, revealed that only 3 out of 17 respondents reported that all of their professional classes were filled. Although clinical laboratory programs were those most frequently cited as having excess capacity, many other fields also reported unfilled classes.

Although the current level of applications worries academic administrators, they are even more concerned about the future because of the predicted decline in the college-age cohort of the population, an issue discussed in Chapter 3. This decrease suggests that in the future there may be even greater competition among schools for technically oriented students than there is today. Information from annual surveys of college freshmen on changing occupational preferences shows a slow but steady decline (from 3.3 percent to 1.1 percent) between 1977 and 1985 in women's interest in careers in laboratory technology and dental hygiene, dietetics and home economy (from 1.1 percent to 0.4 percent), and health technology (from 3.7 percent to 1.8 percent). Women's interest in the category headed "therapist" has remained relatively stable over the period; men have exhibited gradually increasing interest over the years (Cooperative Institutional Research Program, 1987).

Academic administrators are also concerned that, with fewer applicants from which to select, the quality of students will decline. Thus far, except for the areas of clinical laboratory sciences and radiography, no decrease in student quality seems to be evident to program directors, as measured by the CAHEA survey. More objective evidence for assessing quality changes, such as grade point averages or test scores during students' first year of professional course work, is not routinely collected. The American College Testing (ACT) Program test scores of high school juniors who intend to major in allied health fields do not bear out a shift in quality (Table 5-1), although the downward trend in dental hygiene may deserve some attention.

Not every allied health field has experienced an applicant deficit, as evidenced by what has occurred in the physical therapy field. Despite a rapid increase in the establishment of physical therapy programs, most directors report that they still have more than an adequate supply of applicants and can limit enrollment to those with high grade point averages. It is not unusual to find physical therapy programs with application-to-acceptance ratios of 10 to 1. In addition to physical therapy, a few of the newer professions such as perfusion and diagnostic medical sonography are also in great demand, with about 60 percent of program directors experiencing application increases (CAHEA, 1988).

Because they are fewer in number and smaller in size, it is difficult to equate the success of programs like perfusion, for example, with programs in physical therapy. Nonetheless, characteristics of perfusion programs are worth noting. Some of the students are often drawn from other disciplines

TABLE 5-1 ACT Test Score Means for Students Specifying Academic Majors

Academic Major	ACT Composite Test Scores				Percentage of Change, 1980–1987
	1980–1981	1983–1984	1985–1986	1986–1987	
Dental assisting	13.3	13.2	13.5	13.3	0
Dental hygiene	16.1	15.5	15.4	15.0	−1.1
Medical technology	18.2	18.2	18.6	18.2	0
Occupational therapy	16.7	16.6	17.5	17.5	−0.8
Physical therapy	17.8	18.0	18.8	18.5	1.0
Radiological technology	14.4	15.4	15.9	15.8	1.4
Nursing (RN)	16.2	15.9	16.3	15.9	−0.3
Pharmacy	20.0	19.8	20.4	20.1	0.1
Overall college-bound population	18.5	18.2	18.3	18.7	1.1

SOURCE: Unpublished data from the American College Testing Program.

(respiratory therapy and critical care nursing, for example) and therefore have had some exposure to the new field. Employment opportunities abound, and not all graduating students enter the clinical field because other attractive opportunities are often available. For example, manufacturers and biomedical engineering laboratories hire some perfusionists; some enter medical school and others choose teaching. Although perfusion is a high-stress profession, it is also a relatively well-paid one. The average salary for a graduating student is $35,000, but highly qualified and experienced perfusionists may earn close to $100,000. Although they are not known to the general public, perfusionists are respected in the allied health world for their success in garnering earnings and their relative independence (Brown, 1987).

Why do some programs fare better than others in attracting students? Some reasons come readily to mind. Undoubtedly, the positive economic outlook for physical therapy—rising salaries, growing autonomy, and high levels of demand for graduates—has affected student thinking. Also, in comparison with such fields as clinical laboratory technology, physical therapy has greater public visibility and more patient contact.

There may be lessons to be learned from schools of social work, which have succeeded in increasing their applicant pool from 2 applicants per opening in 1983 to 3.5 applicants per opening today. Social work is considered to be closely related to (if not directly under the umbrella of) allied health. Deans of schools of social work attribute the revitalization of interest in social work careers to a wide variety of social and economic factors, including the following:

• optimism about the status of social welfare programs in the post-Reagan era;
• a surge (although not as dramatic as during the 1960s) in the sense of social commitment among students;
• occupational outlook projections of higher-than-average growth in demand;
• growth of independent practices and third-party payment;
• adoption by some schools of "business-like" approaches to marketing and recruiting students; and
• salaries that, while not high initially, averaged about $27,800 in 1986–1987 (Health Professions Report, 1988).

Visibility and comparatively high pay are elements that contribute to the attractiveness of a field, and these in turn contribute to the success of schools in obtaining high application rates. Some fields that are viewed by the allied health community as being attractive and offering well-paying careers nonetheless do poorly in attracting students because they lack visibility. For example, occupational therapy shares many of the attributes of physical therapy, but its role in health care is not well known. Medical record administrators can earn over $50,000 per year and advance to hospital executive positions, but that field, too, is little known to the public.

Some allied health occupations (e.g., medical technology and radiography) do not offer particularly good economic rewards but seek to attract scientifically oriented students to work in potentially hazardous environments in which they may be exposed to contaminated body fluids or radiation. Moreover, although laboratory and radiography employment prospects may be rebounding after PPS cutbacks, the atmosphere of job insecurity may still be influencing students' perceptions about those fields.

Student Recruitment

Many of the social factors that influence career choice are beyond the control of health care institutions or academics. The economic attractiveness of careers and their work environments are largely in the hands of employers (a topic that is addressed in Chapter 6) and those who make reimbursement decisions.

There are a number of techniques that schools have used to attract students. Among them are the use of professional recruiters, giving faculty release time to visit high school counselors and students, the distribution of videotapes about the school, and undertaking national promotions (e.g., Lab Week, fostered by the American Society for Medical Technology). Unfortunately, such efforts to influence students' career choices toward an allied health field have not been systematically documented or evaluated.

Many psychological and social theories of career choice and career development have emerged over the years to explain how individual career development unfolds over the life span. These theories suggest the difficulties of intervening in a complex process. Career development is shaped by an interplay of psychological attributes, knowledge about training requirements, educational and occupational opportunities, genetic and childhood influences, evolving personalities, and patterns of traits that individuals express cognitively and psychologically in their choice behavior. Research related to career development finds that, like all human behavior, it is a highly complex process and is part of the total fabric of personality (Lent et al., 1986).

Most of the existing approaches to career development are based on limited samples of relatively privileged persons. The samples typically have been composed of men rather than of women, and the approaches to career development in general have been addressed to persons in the middle range of socioeconomic characteristics. Consequently, these approaches tend to emphasize the continuous and progressive aspects of career development that are possible primarily for persons who are relatively free to choose any career and for whom both psychological and economic resources are available. Such criteria do not necessarily fit women and minorities (Fitzgerald and Crites, 1980).

The impact of several variables (including parental socioeconomic status [SES], academic achievement, and sex) on both selection and persistence in career choice has been investigated in an attempt to determine who is being recruited into professions in general. These variables were used to analyze responses from the U.S. Department of Education's 1972 National Longitudinal Study and recent follow-up surveys. Results showed that children of high-SES parents were four times more likely than children of low-SES parents to engage in professional study at the baccalaureate level and six times more likely to participate in or complete professional training at the graduate level. The SES level of parents did not have as much effect on the aspirations of children, however; children of high-SES families were only twice as likely to wish for a professional career as their contemporaries from low-SES families. Researchers have concluded that the idea of substantial social and economic mobility in the United States has been exaggerated and is difficult to achieve. Only 2 percent of young people from low-SES homes were in graduate-level professional programs 7 years after high school, despite large federal student aid programs and numerous corporate and foundation programs to stimulate opportunities in the professions (Miller, 1986).

In general, the career choice literature does not provide detailed guidance for recruitment efforts. Yet several implications for specific planning interventions can be seen.

• The concepts that people are only economic animals and that work is chosen only for the livelihood it offers are too simplistic. Work also provides a means for meeting the needs of social interaction, dignity, self-esteem, self-identification, and other forms of psychological gratification.

• Personal, educational, occupational, or career maturation comprises complex learning processes that begin in early childhood and continue throughout life.

• Choice occurs not at a point in time but in relation to antecedent experiences and future alternatives.

• Career information must include not only objective factors such as earning possibilities, training requirements, and numbers of positions available but the social and psychological aspects of careers as well.

• Career choice is frequently a compromise between the attractiveness of an alternative, the likelihood of attaining it, and the costs of attaining it (Herr and Cramer, 1984).

In sum, the literature on career choice is suggestive rather than prescriptive for recruitment tactics. Long-range efforts must take into account the need to make individuals aware of careers at an early stage. If women continue to predominate in many of the allied health fields, we must learn more about the dynamics of their career choice behavior.

Successful student recruitment efforts generally depend on positive market signals emanating from the world of work. In the next chapter the committee discusses actions that employers must take to improve the circumstances of allied health personnel in work settings in which the perceptions of unsatisfactory careers accurately reflect reality. However, to the extent that potential students incorrectly believe that a career is unsatisfactory, the problem may require improved communication. Local consortia of professional association members, employer representatives, and educators should be formed to devise recruitment strategies based on community needs, characteristics, and resources. These consortia should target nontraditional audiences, tailoring the message and method of communication to each. A marketing plan geared to attracting newly unemployed workers from a local industry, for example, should not be the same as one that seeks to attract displaced homemakers or handicapped high school students.

The demand for technically oriented people is growing in many sectors of the economy. One study predicts that

The jobs that will be created between 1987 and 2000 will be substantially different from those in existence today. A number of jobs in the least-skilled job classes will disappear, while high-skilled professions will grow rapidly. Overall the skill mix of the economy will be moving rapidly upscale, with most new jobs demanding more education and higher levels of language, math and reasoning skills. (Hudson Institute, 1987)

More specifically, more than half of the new jobs created between 1984 and the year 2000 will need some high school education. Nearly a third will require a college degree; today, only 22 percent of occupations require a college degree (Hudson Institute, 1987). The health care industry is not the only industry that is beginning to understand that one of the challenges of the future will be to position themselves favorably in the competition for the supply of educated, technically able workers. For some allied health fields, there are already indications that potential practitioners are being lost to other professions. It is clear that educators, employers, and the professional associations must act if they want to maintain or increase their share of the work force. The process of change is necessarily interactive. If employers succeed in making allied health employment more attractive, educational institutions will experience increases in the size and quality of the applicant pool. Yet, circularly, the extent to which employers are able to alter the conditions of employment depends in part on the education that workers have received.

The committee recommends that educational institutions, in close collaboration with employers and professional associations, organize for the recruitment of students. They should seek persons from less traditional applicant pools—minorities, older students, career changers, those already employed in health care, men (for fields in which they are underrepresented), and individuals with handicapping conditions.

Minorities

Two major societal problems underlie concerns about minority participation in allied health careers, leading the committee to devote special attention to this issue.

First, as several recent public policy documents have stated, minority populations in the United States have comparatively poor health statuses and use fewer health care resources relative to their needs (U.S. Department of Health and Human Services, 1985). Although a causal relationship between the supply of minority practitioners and improved minority health care and health status is difficult to validate, minority health care workers are more likely to work in geographic areas and at delivery sites that serve minority and other disadvantaged patients. Officials interviewed at three inner-city hospitals, including two public hospitals, said that minorities are at least 50 percent of their total allied health work force. Moreover, data extracted from facility records show that this pattern is relatively uniform across such different fields as clinical laboratory technology, physical and occupational therapy, dietetics, and medical records (Booker, 1987).

Second, there is a lack of parity throughout American society between whites and nonwhites in professional positions. To the extent that the allied health fields can provide improved career opportunities for minorities, a double benefit will occur: education programs will be better able to maintain enrollments, and personnel shortages may be alleviated in underserved geographic areas and institutions that serve poor minority populations.

To supplement a review of the literature on the representation of minorities in allied health fields, the committee conducted extensive interviews with deans and faculty of 10 schools active in the National Society for Allied Health (an organization committed to increasing the participation of black and other disadvantaged minorities in allied health practice, education, and administration). Other schools were added in an attempt to broaden the information base. A school known to have a predominantly Hispanic student body and structured activities to recruit Hispanics to allied health programs was selected, as was a school in an area with a large American Indian population. Finally, a nonminority school in the South was added because it boasts the largest number of allied health programs on a single campus and has been actively involved in minority allied health recruitment and retention efforts for some time (Booker, 1987). Pertinent information from these interviews will be referred to in our discussion of minorities in allied health education.

Table 5-2 presents estimates of racial and ethnic characteristics of allied health personnel based on the results of an analysis of the 1980 census. The data show that minority personnel are underrepresented, relative to their representation in the U.S. labor force, in the 10 allied health fields studied by the committee and particularly in the fields requiring higher education.

CAHEA reports that over the entire range of the fields it accredits the racial mix of students enrolled during 1986–1987 generally mirrored the racial mix of the U.S. population. Blacks represented 11 percent of total enrollments, Hispanics, 6 percent, and American Indians, about 2 percent. What these data fail to reveal is that minorities are overrepresented in fields requiring less education and underrepresented in fields requiring more education. The extent to which minorities have a higher departure rate from programs and careers is not known. Several professional associations in fields requiring baccalaureate and advanced degrees have commented on the need for greater efforts to increase the number of minority students. For example, the 1984 Study Commission of the American Dietetics Association noted:

While no effort has been made in the past to restrict other racial groups, or males, from the profession, little has been done to make the profession more attractive to them, nor has any strong effort been made to recruit them. The 1984 Study Commission believes such an effort is overdue.

TABLE 5-2   Distribution of Personnel (Percentage) in Selected Allied Health Occupations by Race or Ethnic Origin, 1980

		Minority		
Occupation	White (not of Spanish origin)	Black	White (Spanish origin)	Other Minority[a]
Laboratory technician	79.5	11.1	3.3	6.2
Dental hygienist	95.4	1.6	1.6	1.3
Dietitian	84.6	6.7	1.9	8.0
Medical record technician	84.4	9.5	2.2	3.9
Occupational therapist	94.7	2.1	0.9	2.4
Physical therapist	93.4	3.3	1.1	2.0
Radiologic technician	86.2	7.7	3.7	2.4
Respiratory therapist	82.1	10.0	4.9	3.1
Speech and hearing therapist	92.9	4.3	1.5	1.3

[a]These figures include American Indians, Japanese, Chinese, and other Asians or Pacific Islanders.

SOURCE: Health Resources and Services Administration (1984).

Past Efforts to Increase Minority Participation

The Federal Government

The federal government first initiated programs to encourage "culturally or economically disadvantaged individuals" to enter allied health as part of the 1970 health manpower legislation (P.L. 91-519). This statute was extended in 1973 by the Comprehensive Health Manpower Act (P.L. 92-157) and the Health Programs Extension Act (P.L. 93-45) and in 1976 by the Health Professions Educational Assistance Act (P.L. 94-484). Later, an administrative decision was made to provide support for projects that emphasized the recruitment and retention of minorities as well as the disadvantaged (Carpenter, 1982).

Between fiscal years 1972 and 1977 approximately $20 million of a total of nearly $191 million of grants awarded for allied health were allocated for programs targeting minority and disadvantaged populations. Between 1978 and 1981, under P.L. 94-484, a larger share of the total but a smaller amount was awarded for project activities to assist disadvantaged allied health students (Carpenter, 1982).

By fiscal year 1982 the only federal funding of any magnitude that was available for minority recruitment and retention in allied health training was the Health Careers Opportunity Program (HCOP). HCOP has five objectives: (1) recruitment, (2) preliminary education (noncredit), (3) facilitation of entry, (4) retention, and (5) information dissemination. Examples of HCOP activities include career fairs; faculty counseling; tutoring; summer enrichment programs to enhance mathematics, science, and communication skills; and linkage arrangements among undergraduate schools such as historically black colleges and universities (HBCUs), community colleges, and high schools.

Between fiscal years 1982 and 1987 the number of allied health grants under HCOP increased steadily, as did the funds that were awarded. Of the $60 million or more awarded since fiscal year 1985, $5.37 million has gone to allied health programs. The proportion awarded each year to allied health programs rose from 5 percent to nearly 10 percent during this 3-year period (W. Holland, Division of Disadvantaged Assistance, Health Resources and Services Administration, personal communication, 1987).

The Area Health Education Centers (AHEC) Program assists health professions schools in improving the distribution, supply, quality, utilization, and efficiency of health care personnel in the health care service delivery system by encouraging the regionalization of professional education. The program has no legislative mandate to recruit and retain minorities, but it has explicitly encouraged such activities. In fiscal year 1987, AHECs in Arizona, New Mexico, Texas, California, Oklahoma, and at three black medical schools—Drew (Los Angeles), Meharry (Nashville), and

Morehouse (Atlanta)—were cited by AHEC officials as having active commitments to training professionals to serve Hispanic, Indian, and black populations. The AHEC financial investment in the recruitment and retention of minority allied health students and workers was not obtainable from available program data (Area Health Education Centers Program, 1987).

States

The health professions education programmatic resources of most states have been devoted to increasing the supply of minority physicians and dentists, but a few states support initiatives for minorities in allied health training. For example, Connecticut funds the Health Sciences Cluster Program, which exposes high school students to allied health professions; economically disadvantaged students in allied health in Georgia are eligible for a small grant program, the Regents Opportunity Grant Program (Mandex, Inc., 1987). New York State has developed an action plan to improve minority access to the licensed professions (including dental hygiene, speech–language pathology and audiology, physical therapy, and occupational therapy), the core of which is a comprehensive effort to improve curriculum development and teaching in mathematics and science in grades 7 through 12. In addition, the state offers financial assistance to allied health students willing to work in state agencies after graduation (New York State Education Department, Bureau of Higher and Professional Education Testing, 1985).

Allied health is rarely specifically identified in state legislation for targeted funding. Several investigators report being unable to ascertain the amount spent for allied health education because these funds are not distinguished from appropriations for "medical education." Of the 13 allied health program officials interviewed (Mandex, 1987), only one reported that the program received funds for minority recruitment and retention through a line item in the state budget.

Private Foundations

Private organizations also see merit in encouraging minorities to select health care careers. The Josiah Macy, Jr., and Robert Wood Johnson foundations have been quite active in these efforts. However, Robert Wood Johnson Foundation staff report that current activities do not include allied health professions. Macy has sponsored some allied health professions training, but its primary focus, after more than 20 years of involvement in minority health professions education, is still physicians. The Macy experience is worth describing in some detail because of its potential applicability to allied health education. (The following description is taken from Bleich [1986, 1987].)

The basic concept of Macy's high school model is to use foundation funds to supplement tax levy support for participating schools. Strengthening curriculum and premedical advising early in a high school student's education is the centerpiece of this program. Linkages between colleges and universities and the high schools are common and serve as vehicles for faculty development, student exposure to careers, and academic enhancement.

For example, five high schools located in the three poorest (50 percent of all families live below the federal poverty level) counties in rural Alabama have completed a 4-year cycle in the Macy project. Macy reported the following results.

• Of the originally selected 114 students, 79 percent were retained in the honors program.

• All of the honors students scheduled to graduate did so and are going to college; all but two anticipate attending a 4-year school.

• Thirty-three of the 88 graduates specified that they would pursue a health career; 3 specifically cited physical therapy.

• The Macy graduates took the mathematics placement exam given to all University of Alabama incoming freshmen. Of the group, 88 percent placed into calculus or precalculus—55 percent in calculus and 33 percent in precalculus. Macy notes that less than 10 percent of all Alabama freshmen did as well (Bleich, 1986).

The program in these schools, which is called the Biomedical Sciences Preparation (BioPrep) Program and operates in grades 9 through 12, is conducted in conjunction with the University of Alabama School of Community and Allied Health, a school committed to increasing the number of health professionals practicing in rural Alabama. Many of the Macy graduates (57 of 88) were awarded tuition scholarships by the university.

Prior to the BioPrep program, school systems in the three counties (two of them predominantly black with a median of 8.5 completed school years) were unable to identify gifted and talented youth. Initially, there were concerns about the schools' ability to attract sufficient numbers of students for the program; those fears have proved to be unfounded. Macy schools were able to attract more than 100 young people to their rigorous academic programs that emphasized science, mathematics, and language skills. In addition, new classes are being enrolled in several schools, and "in each setting there is growing interest and demand for a more rigorous curriculum" (Bleich, 1986, 1987).

Extensive in-service training has taken place, and curriculum development has been a collaborative activity among high school teachers, BioPrep staff, and selected university faculty. Tutorials, enhanced science laboratories, and independent study have been offered at the schools; bimonthly

Saturday sessions and 6-week summer programs have been held at the University of Alabama.

The Macy Foundation reports that more than 1,200 students have enrolled in their projects. It estimates that more than 4,500 students will be enrolled in grades 9 through 12 when the programs are fully established and that schools will graduate 700 college-prepared minority students each year.

Other high schools in the project report results similar to the Alabama experience, lending credence to the potential of a model that blends public and private resources to produce systemic changes that can be institutionalized for long-lasting benefit.

Lessons That Have Been Learned

More than 20 years of experience in attempting to increase the number of minority allied health professionals suggest four areas that should be targeted for action:

- academic preparation, especially in the sciences and mathematics;
- knowledge of allied health careers and the promotion of minorities;
- financing of institutions and students; and
- linkages and affiliations in training and employment.

Despite efforts of the federal government and individual institutions, the barriers to allied health careers for minorities that were cited in the early 1970s remain serious problems. Can lessons gleaned from past efforts inform policymakers and educators about what kinds of investments need to be made in the future, where they will be most productive, and which stakeholders can lead and contribute to greater success?

Academic Preparation

Astin (1985) notes that minority underrepresentation in engineering, biological sciences, the physical sciences, and mathematics can be linked to low levels of academic preparation in mathematics and science prior to college enrollment. Academic preparation is also the central issue that affects the size and quality of the minority applicant pool for allied health training. Allied health deans and program directors firmly believe that streams of qualified minority applicants cannot be relied upon until academic deficiencies are substantially reduced (Committee/staff interviews, 1987; The Circle, Inc., 1987).

HCOP grantees typically have focused on strengthening the skills of disadvantaged students in communications, mathematics, and the sciences, with 6- to 8-week summer enrichment and tutorial programs the usual interventions. Although there is partial evidence (La Jolla Management Corporation, 1984) that such interventions can work, the conventional wisdom is that the emphasis on mathematics and science should begin as early as possible, starting at or even before junior high school (Bisconti, 1980; National Commission on Allied Health Education, 1980; Flack, 1982; La Jolla, 1984; The Circle, Inc., 1987; Mingle, 1987). Perhaps allied health schools could gain more in the long run by helping to create alliances with others in the community to attack the root causes of poor academic preparedness.

Allied health schools generally draw their students from known "feeder" sources. Strengthening academic preparation at the secondary school level and in other major feeder schools (e.g., community colleges) can contribute to lasting improvements in the quality of their applicant pools; it can also influence curriculum improvement at feeder schools and bring greater visibility to allied health career opportunities. At the same time, early academic and career counseling, a compounding factor (Committee/staff interviews, 1987; La Jolla, 1984; The Circle, Inc., 1986), can be enhanced.

The Josiah Macy, Jr., Foundation provides an excellent example of what can be accomplished if students are introduced to intense academic skills improvement programs early. Macy's success also offers an example of what can be accomplished by approaching problems from a broad perspective. The foundation incorporated a wide variety of resources and addressed areas other than the student's grade point average. It also concentrated on raising school administrators' and teachers' expectations of students, educating parents, acting as a liaison to establish collaborations between colleges and public secondary schools, and raising students' self-esteem.

Knowledge About and the Promotion of Allied Health Professions

Information plays a role both in attracting minority students to careers and in keeping them through training. Informing minorities about the wide range of allied health occupations and promoting these fields as career options are important steps in attracting minority students to these professions.

Educators believe that better information about an occupation's training and practice is crucial to the relatively high attrition rate of minority students in the first year of professional training. Such information is not easily acquired, however. Allied health professions are not widely mentioned in the media, nor are the contributions of allied health occupations to health care delivery explained.

Those interviewed for the study reported that information dissemination through career days, the distribution of brochures, and active recruitment is most effective when coupled with formal and informal linkages with feeder high schools and colleges. One school that recently began recruiting through churches reported that they were a rich and largely untapped source of minority allied health applicants (Booker, 1987).

Research data and the experiences of recruiters suggest that the following factors should be taken into account in shaping effective information dissemination and promotion campaigns (The Circle, Inc., 1987; Mingle, 1987):

- Minority allied health students are likely to be older than liberal arts students; they are also more likely to have children.
- Students who demonstrate potential in high school or community colleges may make up a greater percentage of the applicant pool than high achievers who are already being heavily recruited for medicine, engineering, and other professions.
- Community colleges can become a good source from which to draw students interested in earning a bachelor's degree, especially if linkage arrangements that incorporate approaches to sharpening critical skills and increasing students' awareness of career options are implemented.
- Persons who are disenchanted with their current occupations in other fields may be seeking an opportunity to pursue a new, more challenging and rewarding career.

Financing for Institutions and Students

Deficiencies in academic preparation are fairly widespread among minority allied health students, and deans of allied health schools expect this shortcoming to continue in the near term. They believe that financial support will continue to be needed for activities that help struggling students remain in school. These activities include prematriculation summer programs, faculty and peer tutoring and counseling, computer-aided learning assistance or instruction, and curriculum improvement/faculty development in feeder schools.

Deans of allied health schools have concluded that external support, such as that provided by HCOP, is essential to underwrite some of these institutional expenses (The Circle, Inc., 1987). In general, intensive minority recruitment and retention activities are supported, at least in part and frequently at a substantial level, by external funds. HCOP has been predominant here for all activities except curriculum improvement in allied health training programs. A 1984 assessment of HCOP-supported preparatory activities (i.e., preliminary education, entry facilitation, and retention) concluded: "Since by far the largest expenditures for HCOP are for preparatory activities, it is essential that HRSA [Health Resources and Services Administration] and the grantees focus special attention on providing those preparatory activity services that produce the greatest benefit to the objectives of the HCOP program" (La Jolla Management Corporation, 1984).

Since 1978 funding for allied health under HCOP has increased as a proportion of the total HCOP investment, but total funds for the program as a whole have diminished and authorized purposes have been more narrowly defined. For example, there are currently no federal programs that support minority allied health faculty development or curriculum improvement in minority schools or in nonminority schools that view curriculum changes as one way to recruit and retain more minorities.

The preeminent Minority Access to Research Careers (MARC) and Minority Biomedical Research Support (MBRS) programs, the oldest of the existing minority-oriented programs administered by the National Institutes of Health (NIH), support these kinds of activities, as do other, similar programs. Such programs have been credited with substantial contributions in increasing research, research training, and the number of researchers in institutions that train large numbers of minorities. Included in this cluster are significant numbers of traditionally and predominantly minority schools (Garrison and Brown, 1985; Gonzales, 1987).

Along with a lack of institutional support, insufficient student financial aid is also seen as a deterrent both to minority student recruitment and retention. Allied health deans cited lack of funds as a major reason for student attrition. Many minority allied health students are older and have children; many of them find that school schedules generally do not permit them to continue working. In such circumstances, financial aid is a crucial factor in their persistence in working toward a degree. Bisconti (1981) notes that "a degree in an allied health major frequently is more expensive than a liberal arts degree." Tuition costs may not be higher, but there may be additional costs for clinical education and materials or equipment. Furthermore, the period of training (both preprofessional and professional) may be longer.

Although states are investing in educational support for minority health professionals, the size of these investments varies widely, and most state aid is targeted toward medicine and dentistry. The committees' interview respondents felt that states needed to provide more student financial aid. Models that have successfully contributed to shifting the distribution of medical and dental professionals (e.g., the National Health Service Corps, loan forgiveness, AHEC) offer incentives for minority professionals to work in underserved areas. These are strategies that may be equally effective for allied health practitioners.

Linkages and Affiliations in Training and Employment

Linkages among colleges and high schools are playing an increasingly important role in encouraging the training of minority allied health professionals. Directors of allied health programs with and without HCOP grants acknowledge their value in recruiting students. It appears that linkages with high schools for recruitment purposes are becoming formalized, perhaps in response to HCOP's continued emphasis on such linkages since 1981. Data show that there are more linkages between schools and 4-year historically black colleges and universities than between high schools and community colleges. However, some schools that today lack community college linkages report plans to explore these arrangements. Linkages appear to work well when there is shared commitment and mutual benefit, regardless of whether the arrangement is formal (as in a written agreement that specifies responsibilities and benefits) or informal (a working relationship).

The predominantly minority schools contacted by the committee reported no difficulties in finding adequate clinical placements for their students. These placements were most often in areas with large minority populations. Today, programs are quite dependent on hospitals for placements and have limited experience with other kinds of sites for student clinical training; thus, clinical training may be threatened if hospital revenues are reduced. Yet, several schools reported that clinical sites pay the tuition for students they accept for clinical placements, usually because the hospital is interested in hiring students who train with them. This interest should help sustain affiliation agreements between schools and hospitals, especially if workers are scarce.

No strategy for significant increases in minority participation in the allied health professions will be successful unless it directs resources toward the major barriers to minority participation and involves the complete spectrum of interested parties, both in government and in the private sector. **Minority recruitment efforts must begin before high school. Academic institutions must offer support services for retention and seek to promote educational mobility. To succeed in the long term, these efforts must be made integral to the mission of the educational institutions.**

Ultimately, success will depend on the ability of educational institutions to make a long-term commitment to integrating minority recruitment and retention into the fabric of their allied health programs. The erosion of federal support for this objective would undermine those in the education community who are struggling to gain or maintain such a commitment to minority allied health education. **The committee endorses the objectives of HCOP and believes that funding levels must be maintained at least at current levels.**

MAINTAINING AND EXPANDING
EDUCATIONAL CAPACITY

The future supply of new graduates in allied health fields depends not only on students' careers but also on the maintenance and expansion of educational opportunities.

Hospital-sponsored allied health education programs suffered more closures than any other types of programs. Between 1982 and 1986, 315 hospital-sponsored programs closed, compared with a small number of proprietary school closures. By contrast, there was a net increase in programs at community colleges (100 new programs, or 9.6 percent) and junior colleges (26 new programs, or 4 percent) (CAHEA, 1987a). Table 5-3 shows the net change between 1982 and 1986 in selected CAHEA-accredited allied health programs. Much of the decline in allied health educational capacity can be attributed to the closing of hospital-based training programs—principally programs in laboratory and radiologic technology. Programs that have the largest number of withdrawals from CAHEA accreditation (and that are presumed by CAHEA to have closed) are medical technology (116), radiography (103), and respiratory therapy technology at the certificate level (29) (CAHEA, 1987b).

Among programs that are not accredited by CAHEA, physical therapy grew rapidly—from 84 baccalaureate programs in academic year 1980–1981 to 97 programs in 1985–1986; master's degree programs increased from 9 to 14 during the same period (American Physical Therapy Association, 1987).

TABLE 5-3 Changes in the Number of CAHEA-Accredited Programs in Selected Allied Health Fields Between 1982 and 1986

CAHEA-Accredited Programs	Number of Programs in 1982	Number of Programs in 1986	Percentage of Change
Negative Change			
Medical laboratory technician (certificate)	73	47	−35.6
Medical technologist	639	516	−19.2
Radiographer	790	701	−11.3
Respiratory therapy technician	188	169	−10.1
Nuclear medicine technologist	138	128	−7.2
Medical record administrator	57	53	−7.0
Positive Change			
Medical record technician	85	87	2.4
Occupational therapist	56	63	12.5
Medical laboratory technician (associate degree)	187	214	14.4
Respiratory therapist	204	235	15.2

SOURCE: CAHEA (1987a).

There is no clear evidence that capacity in higher education institutions is in serious jeopardy. Nevertheless, program closings, coupled with fears of a decline in the number of applicants, have heightened allied health program directors' feelings of vulnerability. These feelings, which were expressed by educators to the committee during its deliberations, arise from a threefold concern: (1) allied health education will not be able to maintain its foothold in research universities; (2) clinical education sites will grow scarce; and (3) financially stressed educational institutions of all types, viewing allied health as a costly endeavor, will close allied health programs.

Given the nation's projected need for allied health personnel and their relatively short stay in the allied health work force, any serious erosion of the education sector's capacity to supply the nation with allied health personnel must be avoided. The question for public policy action is whether vulnerability poses a real and present danger that cannot be addressed by market forces alone. If government intervention or private efforts, or both, are required, what actions will offer the greatest return on public and private investments? To answer this question, we must first understand the roles of various important decision makers and how their actions can strengthen or weaken allied health education programs.

Who Influences Educational Capacity Decisions?

The decisions to open or close allied health programs or to expand or contract enrollments are ostensibly in the hands of educational institutions themselves. Typically, a dialogue occurs between a dean or department head and the chief administrator for academic affairs about the desirability of adding programs or the need to close or reduce the enrollment level of a program. The remarks of one university president who was responsible, earlier in his career, for manpower projections at one of the allied health professions associations provide some interesting insights into the context of this dialogue:

It obviously becomes extremely difficult for a university president to justify the continuation of this or any other program when student demand has moved elsewhere, say, to real estate, and when the dean of the school of business is clamoring for those scarce resources to be diverted to their front. Further, since the average age of my faculty is only 49, natural attrition does not facilitate resource shifts.

It would be easier for me to justify maintenance of high cost programs if external support were still flowing to my campus; however, as you are well aware, there has been a steady decline in the amount of federal dollars available for health education. Therefore, academic administrators are on the horns of a dilemma, and now, like health care administrators, we must monitor the environment continuously and respond to changes as never before. Strategic planning is the name of the game. Universities can no longer afford to be all things to all people. (Perrin, 1987)

Decision making does not take place in isolation, and many parties can be involved in precipitating a dialogue and influencing its course. These parties include federal agencies such as the Bureau of Health Professions, state higher education and licensing agencies, state political leaders, accrediting bodies, professional associations, and local health care providers. At times, the pressures exerted by these parties and conversely, the opportunities they have offered schools, through grants, for example, so overwhelm institutional autonomy that it is difficult to discern where control lies.

The issue of control is important: by understanding the distribution of authority over allied health education, we can identify how the forces that shape decisions about educational capacity can be influenced to accomplish public policy goals. These goals encompass not only the size of enrollments but the quality of education, its content, and the ability of the educational system to add to the nation's work force.

The Federal Role

A major, direct influence on the development of allied health manpower training capacity has been the federal Bureau of Health Professions and its predecessor organizations.

In 1966, not long after Congress enacted federal education funding for medicine, osteopathy, dentistry, veterinary medicine, optometry, podiatry, and pharmacy in one law and nursing under another authority, it also provided education funding for 13 allied health fields. The Allied Health Professions Personnel Training Act offered five types of grants:

1. Construction grants for training centers and affiliated hospitals.
2. Basic improvement grants awarded on the following formula: $5,000 times the number of eligible curricula in the center plus $500 times the number of full-time students receiving training.
3. Grants to support traineeships for allied health personnel to become teachers, administrators, or supervisors or to serve in allied health specialities.
4. "New methods" grants to allied health training centers for projects to develop, demonstrate, or evaluate curricula for the training of new types of health technologists (U.S. Department of Health, Education, and Welfare, 1979).
5. Special improvement grants to support projects or centers that would provide no fewer than three curricula with the aid of this funding.

Table 5-4 shows the funding history of this law and its successor pieces of legislation. Although no federal programs have specifically supported allied health training since 1981, allied health students and schools are

TABLE 5-4 Division of Associated and Dental Health Professions[a] Grants, Cooperative Agreements, and Contracts Awarded (in dollars) in the Allied Health Area, Fiscal Years 1967 through 1986

Fiscal Year	Advanced Traineeships	Training Institutes	Special Improvements	Special Projects	Basic Improvements	Other	Total
1967	241,977	0	0	0	3,285,000	0	3,526,977
1968	1,203,648	0	0	799,507	9,750,000	0	11,753,155
1969	1,549,772	0	0	1,225,000	9,750,000	0	12,524,772
1970	1,538,064	0	0	1,231,938	9,701,000	0	12,471,002
1971	2,460,851	482,838	0	4,482,617	9,701,000	0	17,127,306
1972	2,585,936	324,064	10,500,000	7,628,384	0	0	21,038,384
1973	1,951,598	1,139,555	7,000,000	5,639,408	0	0	15,730,561
1973[b]	0	0	10,500,000	0	0	0	15,999,947
1974	2,563,000	999,888	16,000,000	10,126,537	0	0	29,689,425
1975	2,606,713	956,267	10,192,034	6,869,220	0	0	10,624,234
1976	2,563,000	1,000,000	10,499,999	8,197,432	0	0	22,260,431
1977	2,331,580	638,312	8,910,000	8,406,537	0	0	20,286,429
1978	1,443,562	924,070	0	14,345,813	0	0	16,713,445
1979	1,493,949	1,004,907	0	8,151,264	0	0	10,650,120
1980	887,062	0	0	4,251,671	0	738,961[c]	5,877,694
1981	0	0	0	508,143	0	364,516[c]	872,659
1982	0	0	0	0	0	0	0
1983	0	0	0	0	0	0	0
1984	0	0	0	0	0	908,550[d]	908,550
1985	0	0	0	0	0	883,525[d]	883,525
1986	0	0	0	0	0	0	0
Total	25,420,712	7,469,901	73,602,033	87,363,418	42,187,000	38,101,018	274,144,082[e]

[a]Prior to 1983, the agency was known as the Division of Associated Health Professions.
[b]Released impounded funds.
[c]Military Experience Directed Into Health Careers (MEDIHC) cooperative agreement funds.
[d]Grants for allied health personnel in health promotion and disease prevention.
[e]The grand total includes contract award amounts; contract amounts awarded by fiscal year are not available at this time, however.

SOURCE: Bureau of Health Professions Health Resources and Services Administration, unpublished data. 1987. Rockville, Md.

eligible for funds under several general health professions education authorities, including

- the federally-insured HEAL Student Loan Program;
- educational assistance to disadvantaged students; and
- health professions special initiatives (grants for special projects in areas such as health promotion and disease prevention; curriculum development in health policy, clinical nutrition, and the application of social and behavioral services to the study of health care delivery; the development of mechanisms for ensuring the competence of health professions; and the development of instruction, including clinical affiliations, in geriatrics).

Efforts to assess the impact of federal funding have been stymied by a lack of data. A major federal report on allied health concluded the following:

It appears that it [federal funding] added impetus to a trend that was already underway . . . much of the private sector growth in educational programs that occurred between 1966 and 1971 without allied health grant support may have occurred in expectation of federal assistance. Quite apart from the question of the relative importance of federal support in increasing allied health manpower output is the problem of determining what the increase was and where it occurred. Prior to establishment of a federal role in allied health manpower, there was insufficient interest in the problems to allow the collection of data on educational programs. Not until 1972 was reliable information obtained on the type and amount of training offered by colleges and universities. Some collegiate program growth occurred at the expense of hospital-based programs and on-the-job training, another factor for which there are no reliable data. (Bureau of Health Manpower, Health Resources Administration, 1979)

Other segments of the federal government have also played roles. The Health Care Financing Administration, through the Medicare program, has provided support for clinically based education. The Department of Education has helped through its general support of higher education loans and scholarships and in its specific provision of vocational-technical training. The Veterans Administration and the military services have also played a part in civilian training as they train personnel for their own needs. Finally, the Department of Labor has been concerned with entry-level occupations, offering training through the Comprehensive Employment Training Act (CETA) program and later through the Job Partnership and Training Act (JPTA).

The State Role

Through their involvement in higher education financing and regulation, states are a major force in determining the number and distribution of allied health programs. In 1976 (the last year of complete data), 71 percent of public collegiate institutions had at least one allied health program, but only 36 percent of private schools offered allied health education (National Committee on Allied Health Education, 1980).

The propensity to invest in allied health education depends in part on the health of the state's economy. In one of its workshops the committee explored decision making in three states—Texas, Illinois, and New York. Participants included representatives of higher education coordinating authorities, general collegiate administrators, and allied health school deans from different types of institutions. They described decision making and a sense of vulnerability that was related to the economic health of their regions.

Allied health program administrators in Texas, where tax revenues have been falling because of the declining oil industry, felt at greatest risk. The Texas allied health educators believed themselves to be the first line of defense against medical school cutbacks.

The economic situation was somewhat better in Illinois, but overall state higher education cutbacks were forcing state college systems to plan their responses to budget cuts if a pending tax increase did not occur. One school system, having already raised tuition the previous year, had directed its deans to consider the implications of a 5 percent budget reduction. The options available to one allied health dean included the following: (1) not filling vacant faculty positions, (2) offering some courses once instead of twice that year, (3) canceling planned equipment purchases, and (4) closing the school's physical therapy program, which needed more space.

At the time of the workshop, New York State deans and policy officials were focused not on budget cuts forced by the state's economic picture but on the state's responsibility for ensuring an adequate supply of health care personnel. A state health department task force had recently been formed to explore "critical shortages" in nursing, home health care, and physical therapy services. One issue prompting the creation of the task force was the inability of state chronic care facilities to recruit therapists. Deans attending the committee's workshop identified faculty shortages as a major impediment to expanding education programs and enrollments in physical and occupational therapy.

Statewide planning frequently occurs under the auspices of state higher education coordinating bodies, which are responsible for approving new education programs. In evaluating new programs, the coordinating bodies consider such issues as geographic maldistribution of programs and practitioners and the impact of new programs on minority participation. Decision makers who participate in this policy arena often must be reconciled to the fact that the politics of higher education planning (deciding, for example, which among competing institutions should receive the new program) may not lead to the conclusions that make the most sense from a health planning standpoint.

States emphasize different values in their review of criteria for new programs. Missouri notes that its "State-wide review is principally interested in the state's need for programs and services, and resource allocation issues. That is, the statewide need for particular programs and the appropriate means of financing these needs to assure Missouri's citizens financial access to quality educational experience" (Missouri Coordinating Board for Higher Education, 1986). In contrast, Texas has stated that "The expenditure of public tax funds for educational programs in any occupational area is a matter of public policy directed at meeting a public need that cannot or will not be met otherwise. Student interest is not the major concern for expenditure of public tax funds for an occupational training program" (Allied Health Education Advisory Committee, 1980).

The ability of state coordinating bodies to enforce their resource allocation policies varies. Some state authorities may only be able to apply "jawboning" tactics to influence institutional decisions. In some cases, battles are fought during the state legislature's higher education budgeting process—through a specific line-item request for a new program, for example. Depending on state political tradition, legislators may choose to wield influence in favor of constituent educational institutions and in response to lobbying efforts. More often, however, the survival of allied health programs is brought into question when academic institutions find themselves forced to reallocate institutional resources as a result of a budget crisis. In some states, higher education coordinating/governing bodies have statutory review powers for new programs.

The Private Sector Role

The private sector role can be seen in the activities of accrediting bodies, professional associations, and foundations.

Accrediting Bodies   There are a multiplicity of issues surrounding who should control accreditation, how it should be structured, and whether it could be a less costly process. This discussion, however, will focus on accreditation standards, which have a major impact on collegiate decision making about new or expanded programs.

Program administrators must take into account the cost of complying with the standards of accrediting bodies and the recommendations of site review teams. For example, programs sometimes close because they cannot maintain the student–faculty ratios, equipment, or space required by an accrediting body. Often, there is a clash between the accrediting body (which believes its essentials ensure basic minimum standards) and generalist academic administrators (who see site review recommendations as a tool to be used by departmental chairmen to get more support for their programs).

Professional Associations Historically, much of the educational activity of allied health professional associations has been in promoting the shift of educational programs from hospitals to academic institutions. Once this shift was accomplished, an association's interest often centered on raising the entry level of the profession or on creating assistant-level categories of personnel.

Today, associations' educational activities range more widely. They might include consultation to academic institutions contemplating new program offerings, workshops for administrators and faculty, student recruitment programs, and the maintenance of education data bases. Some associations have assumed quasi-regulatory functions in the education accreditation arena. For example, accreditation responsibilities for dietetics, physical therapy, and speech–language pathology and audiology are handled through independent entities operating in conjunction with the professional associations. It should be noted, however, that some of the allied health fields do not have a well-organized professional association that can engage in educational activities.

Supplementing the work of the associations are the American Society of Allied Health Professions and the National Society of Allied Health—two umbrella organizations that cut across disciplinary lines in an effort to help their members address educational issues common to most fields.

Because of an extensive literature and the activities of the Federal Trade Commission in questioning the role of the American Medical Association in limiting the supply of physicians through medical education, it is reasonable to raise the question of whether allied health associations influence the supply of practitioners in their respective fields, restricting entry as a means of enhancing the economic status of their members. An investigation to determine such influence, however, was beyond the scope of this study.

Private Foundations Complementary to the role of federal and state support is the contribution of philanthropy in generating experiments in allied health education. Principal among the foundations is the W. K. Kellogg Foundation, an organization that over many years has spurred institutional development and leadership activities and studies of allied health fields. Currently, the foundation is supporting a clearinghouse at the University of Alabama to clarify and promote the concept of multicompetency in allied health as well as supporting several activities of the American Society of Allied Health Professions.

Why Is Allied Health Education Vulnerable?

As indicated in the previous section's review of federal, state, and private roles, the era of direct efforts to expand the allied health education enterprise has ended. Yet the day-to-day business of federal, state, and private decision makers continues to shape allied health education. Federal Medicare reimbursement policy, state higher education budgeting and regulation, interest groups in pursuit of enhanced professional status, and educational accreditation are all powerful influences on the future of allied health education. How stable educational institutions will be in the future will depend on their ability to compete for higher education resources with other, more entrenched academic programs whose graduates may also be in high demand.

Maintaining Ground in Academia

A number of prestigious institutions—the University of Pennsylvania, University of Michigan, Emory University, and Stanford University, for example—have closed allied health schools and programs. A fundamental component of the rationale for closure appears to have been that the preparation of allied health practitioners did not sufficiently contribute to the aspirations of a research university seeking to concentrate its resources in areas of strength. As allied health deans see some of the most noteworthy programs close, they grow apprehensive about the future of their own programs. They are also concerned about the future of allied health programs because the programs lack the capacity to foster research and produce teachers and academic leaders (Broski et al., 1985; Hedrick, 1985).

Although it is difficult to document the fragile condition of allied health education, the committee believes there is some basis for the deans' apprehension. Furthermore, the committee is concerned that closures have signaled to academic decision makers and public officials alike that allied health education may not be a sound investment for scarce educational dollars.

As Table 5-5 (which is based on 1970s data from the National Commission on Allied Health Education) shows, these programs have long existed in almost every type of collegiate institution. The committee believes that there is no generic or inherent quality that disqualifies allied health education from life on any campus in the nation. The diversity and evolution of the many occupations suggest that some are more suited than others to various academic settings and degree levels. Yet the conclusions that are drawn today about a given field may change tomorrow as knowledge and practice evolve. Each type of collegiate setting has its advantages and disadvantages. Generally speaking, for example, academic health sci-

TABLE 5-5 Percentage of Collegiate Institutions with Allied Health Programs in 1975–1976, by Carnegie Classification of Institutional Type

Type of Institution	Number of Such Institutions in the United States	Number and Percentage with Allied Health Programs		Percentage of All Allied Health Programs in Such Institutions
		Number	Percentage	
Research universities I Leading universities in terms of federal financial support for academic science and award at least 50 Ph.D.s annually (and M.D.s if a medical school is on the same campus).	51	47	92	7.95
Research universities II Among the leading 100 institutions in terms of federal financial support and award at least 50 Ph.D.s (and M.D.s if applicable).	47	41	87	5.36
Doctorate-granting universities I Award 40 or more Ph.D.s (and M.D.s) or received at least $3 million in total federal support in either 1969–1970 or 1970–1971. No institutions are included that grant fewer than 50 Ph.D.s (or (M.D.s).	56	47	84	6.11
Doctorate-granting universities II Institutions awarding at least 10 Ph.D.s.	30	27	90	2.72

Continued

TABLE 5-5 Continued

Type of Institution	Number of Such Institutions in the United States	Number and Percentage with Allied Health Programs		Percentage of All Allied Health Programs in Such Institutions
		Number	Percentage	
Comprehensive universities and colleges I Institutions offering a liberal arts program and several others (e.g., engineering, business administration) that have at least two professional or occupational programs and enroll at least 2,000 students. Many have master's programs and, at most, limited doctoral programs.	380	302	79	22.76
Comprehensive universities and colleges II State colleges and some private colleges that offer a liberal arts program and at least one professional or occupational program (e.g., nursing or teacher training, mainly with a degree in education).	217	135	63	5.25
Liberal arts colleges I Highly selective or among the 200 leading bachelor's-granting institutions in terms of numbers of graduates receiving Ph.D.s at 40 leading doctorate-granting institutions.	126	27	21	0.75
Liberal arts colleges II Other liberal arts colleges, many of which are extensively involved in teacher training, granting degrees in arts and sciences rather than in education.	474	243	51	8.33

Two-year colleges and institutions	1,135	671	59	35.18
Theological seminaries, bible colleges, and other institutions offering degrees in religion	277	5	2	0.07
Medical schools and medical centers Includes only those that are listed as separate campuses in *USOE Opening Fall Enrollment.*	51	35	69	3.95
Other separate health professional schools	29	7	24	0.17
Schools of engineering and technology Technical institutions are included only if they award a bachelor's degree and if their program is limited exclusively or almost exclusively to technical fields of study.	47	10	21	0.5
Schools of business management Included only if they award a bachelor's or higher degree and if their program is limited exclusively or almost exclusively to a business curriculum.	35	13	37	0.3
Schools of art, music, design	58	2	3	0.05
Schools of law	16	2	13	0.05
Teachers colleges	28	5	18	0.32
Other specialized institutions Includes graduate centers, maritime academies, military institutions (lacking a liberal arts program), and miscellaneous others.	35	3	9	0.17

SOURCE: National Commission on Allied Health Education (1980).

ence centers have easier access to clinical resources and a wide range of opportunities for interdisciplinary experiences. However, as reported to the committee, the latitude for decision making and creativity of program design by deans and program directors has traditionally been more limited in academic health science centers than in schools of allied health that are independent of such centers. Community colleges shine in their ability to attract to diverse student populations who are job oriented. Educational programs there are tailored to suit the needs of employers and students in a given local community.

To guide institutions in deciding whether to continue or start allied health education programs, the Southern Regional Education Board (1980) suggests that the following six questions be considered:

1. *Mission*   Is the program consistent with the institution's philosophy and purpose?

2. *Employment*   Will graduates be able to secure employment and will that employment satisfy the local, state, regional, or national mission of the institution?

3. *Accreditation*   Is the institution willing to invest in a program, given the resource consumption implicit in achieving accreditation?

4. *Students*   Will there be sufficient enrollment over a sustained period of time?

5. *Budgetary concerns*   Is the institution prepared to adopt programs in which clinical components may require equipment, supervision, and costs that often exceed those of other types of academic programs?

6. *Faculty*   Is there a sufficient faculty pool on which to draw? What resources will be necessary to attract qualified individuals to teach?

Today, allied health education appears vulnerable on all but the 'employment demand' criterion. The key to improving allied health's bargaining position in academia is to demonstrate value to the parent institution that is striving to fulfill its mission of scholarship or community service. The recommendations that follow are designed to address some of the problems that prevent allied health programs from competing effectively for institutional resources and thus endanger their viability.

Faculty Shortages

Because many allied health fields are relatively new to collegiate environments and have grown rapidly in the past 2 decades, allied health educational programs often face both quantitative and qualitative problems in filling faculty positions. In physical therapy, for example, the number of accredited university programs grew from 48 in 1970 to 113 in 1986. The supply of faculty does not appear to have kept pace. A 1985 survey of academic administrators in these programs reported a need for 152 additional faculty simply to meet current demands (American Physical Therapy Association, 1985). As a result, many programs rely heavily on part-time lecturers without regular faculty appointments, faculty from scientific disciplines who do not hold professional qualifications in the clinical field, and professionals who lack the academic credentials that are traditionally expected of university faculty. For example, in its faculty survey the American Physical Therapy Association reported that only 28.2 percent of full-time faculty in physical therapy programs had doctoral degrees. This proportion was in clear contrast to national data that showed that 54.9 percent of all faculty teaching in institutions of higher education had doctorates (Newman, 1985). The recruitment of qualified new faculty is seriously hampered by the very limited pool of candidates. Even in relatively mature occupations such as occupational and physical therapy, professional associations report that only about 1 percent of all members have doctoral degrees and just over 24 percent have master's degrees (American Physical Therapy Association, 1987; American Occupational Therapy Association, 1987).

In a survey of 124 medical record education programs (which constitute more than 80 percent of all programs), the majority employed only one or two additional faculty members besides the program director; no program had more than four full-time additional faculty. Only five of the directors of these schools had a doctorate. Among the 53 full-time faculty members in university-based programs, only 2 had doctorates, 33 had master's degrees, and 18 had baccalaureates as their highest academic degree (Amatayakul, 1987).

Although some allied health professionals are enrolled in master's and doctoral degree programs, the lack of financial aid and the relatively low earnings of allied health clinicians force most of them to carry out this advanced study on a part-time basis over a long period. Lack of funding has also constrained the development of graduate programs in several allied health disciplines. Although advanced study in such related disciplines as physiology, psychology, or education benefits allied health faculty, the lack of graduate programs in their own disciplines has limited the number of allied health faculty who are active scholars in the field in which they have the greatest teaching responsibility.

The options for producing faculty efficiently should be explored to maximize faculty development resources. The American Occupational Therapy Association has had some success in targeting faculty development efforts toward clinical faculty who might be inclined to pursue full-time teaching appointments (S. Presseller, American Occupational Therapy Association, personal communication, 1987). Another approach would be to focus attention on streamlined allied health certificate programs that give individuals with doctorates in other academic disciplines the opportunity to gain a practice credential for teaching purposes. Holcomb and colleagues (1987) have described a partnership between Baylor College of Medicine, Texas A&M University, and the University of Houston that offers programs in allied health teacher education and administration that have been productive in supplying faculty nationwide.

The rationale for a federal role in faculty development in allied health is similar to the justification for federal support of family practice programs in medicine. From 1972 through 1984, federal grants of more than $200 million fostered the growth of graduate family medicine training activities (Health Resources and Services Administration, 1986). Like allied health, family medicine exists today because the federal government was willing to promote a concept that was designed to address some of the health care system's deficiencies. As a relatively new endeavor, family medicine departments still lack qualified faculty and the ability to garner research funds from traditional sources such as NIH, in part because of noncompetitive research credentials among faculty and in part because of the low funding priority of primary care research. Like allied health, family medicine has yet to prove itself to the academic medical center establishment—a task that is hindered by a reimbursement system that does not generally reward non-procedure-oriented faculty practice.

Federal grants are being used to make the playing field more level for family medicine in the competitive medical school environment. Federal investment in family practice is based on the policy assessment that primary care needs are unmet and that these programs are a cost-effective means of producing and distributing primary care practitioners. Similar national goals relating to issues of rehabilitation, disease prevention, AIDS treatment, and geriatrics can be well served by the support of allied health education.

The committee recommends that federal and state governments fund faculty development grants in allied health fields, especially in areas in which faculty availability and lack of clinical expertise inhibit the production of entry-level practitioners.

Closely tied to the need to improve teaching faculty is the need to advance research in allied health. Research and other forms of scholarly activity are inherent features of academic life. Programs that fail to give sufficient weight to academic research, along with teaching and service to the institutions, are doomed to instability over the long run. In recognition of this fact and with the belief that the practice of any large group of health care professionals ought to be informed by an increasing knowledge base, the 1983 IOM study of nursing recommended that the federal government fund programs to increase the supply of doctorally prepared nurse researchers and support "an organizational entity to place nursing in the mainstream of scientific investigation" (Institute of Medicine, 1983). These recommendations spurred the creation of the NIH Task Force on Nursing Research and, eventually, congressional action that established the Center for Nursing Research at NIH.

In its final report the NIH task force concluded that the extramural and intramural program activities then supported by NIH were consistent with the mission of the institutes and that studies conducted with nurses as principal investigators and studies designed to improve nursing care (but not necessarily directed by nurses) could be fostered through a combination of activities. These activities were intended to help train nurse researchers, encourage greater collaboration by and interest on the part of medical scientists in interdisciplinary work, and enhance the capability of nurses to compete for research support (National Institutes of Health, 1984).

Although there are few data to confirm the impression, it appears that the research capability of most allied health fields is less developed than that of nursing. In part, this increased capability of nursing may be due to the continuing commitment to research provided by the federal Nurse Training Act (Title VIII, Public Health Service Act) and the newly created Center for Nursing Research within NIH. Covey and Burke (1987) offer an additional explanation:

> Because qualified faculty by the traditional standards were not available, selection of our University faculty has often been largely from the practitioner ranks and from those who had perhaps acquired graduate degrees in such unrelated disciplines as education or administration. The focus of their training has been on technological competence and, in some cases, discipline pedagogy but has not always included research. By virtue of their own training, deans and directors themselves are often unable to develop the junior faculty and, in fact, too many deans and program directors either lack an understanding of or simply ignore the tripartite academic mission.

In later chapters of this report that deal with issues of health care management and regulation and with long-term care, the committee notes decisions that administrators, payers, and regulators must make in the absence of an allied health research literature. Medical scientists and other researchers on their own will not and cannot define research priorities from among health care services delivery issues or the clinical applications that typically concern allied health practitioners. Although medical scientists should be encouraged to develop collegial relationships and undertake joint projects with allied health personnel, they are not as likely to be interested in the outcome measurement and cost-effectiveness issues that need to be addressed as are those who deliver the services.

Allied health fields vary in their maturity with respect to a productive research capacity. Some fields such as dental hygiene, in which most practitioners have less than a baccalaureate, are only now beginning to explore the possibilities of a cadre of research leaders to build a body of knowledge linked to a theoretical framework. This research should go beyond simple, unrelated pilot studies. It should define dental hygiene as distinct from dentistry and explore the efficiency of methods and modes of practice (Bowen, 1988). In contrast, other fields like speech–language pathology and audiology have many practitioners with master's degrees and doctorates and a rich history of tapping into a growing knowledge base in human communication services and disorders. Both fields, however, share a concern over the lack of relevant research finding its way to those who provide patient services—whether it be to the communicatively impaired (Ludlow, 1986) or to those seeking preventive services from a dental hygienist.

A cadre of researchers and academic leaders is needed to advance the scientific base of allied health practice. To accomplish this goal, institutions with strong research commitments should consider developing programs that identify and nurture talented individuals. The committee recommends that a federal research fellowship program be instituted to support these activities.

Financing Clinical Education

The closing of hospital education programs discussed earlier in this chapter represents more than a long-term shift from hospital-based to academically based education. Hospitals with limited resources may reduce or eliminate clinical affiliations with education programs in addition to closing their own sponsored programs.

As clinical affiliates attempt to trim their costs in response to reduced revenue, educators fear that hospitals will request remuneration for the supervision of students or seek other means of shifting costs back to the educational institution. As of 1987, it appears that this is not a large problem. When CAHEA (in press) queried education directors about changes over the past 3 years in the costs of the clinical portion of their programs, it received the following responses: 17 percent said they had experienced significant cost increases; 13 percent felt that program viability was threatened; and 15 percent perceived that the program had become a burden to the sponsoring institution. Only 7 percent reported a significant change in curriculum. Allied health educators are also concerned about long-standing proposals to constrain or eliminate Medicare payments for education. Currently, Medicare pays hospitals for the direct educational costs of allied health programs on a reasonable cost basis as an addition to the DRG payment. Payments are intended for provider-operated programs and not for affiliated programs in which the hospital provides part of the clinical training in a university-based program. For the latter, the costs of the training and its benefits to the hospital are presumed to balance one another. Since the passage of PPS, there has been some confusion over whether the costs of jointly sponsored programs are eligible for reimbursement.

Presidential budget proposals to terminate Medicare funding for hospital-based allied health and nursing education programs have added to concerns that hospital financial managers, who are looking for every opportunity to reduce institutional costs, will eliminate clinical affiliations whenever feasible. To those attempting to find ways to reduce the federal budget, the direct support of educational programs represents an open-ended expenditure that is insufficiently targeted to the most important national human resources needs. Most often, these are thought to be the development of greater numbers of primary care physicians and fewer specialists.

Several recent studies sponsored by the Health Resources and Services Administration to assess the impact of proposals to eliminate Medicare's educational support have provided a better understanding of the role played by this source of educational financing. A congressionally mandated study of nursing and nonphysician (i.e., allied health, as defined by the study) costs in educational programs approved for Medicare reimbursement, conducted by Applied Management Services, Inc., revealed that, together, these programs cost Medicare roughly $226 million in the second year of prospective payment. This figure is relatively small compared with the $42.7 billion the government paid to hospitals under Part A Medicare for the same period. The analysis of Medicare cost reports indicates that nonphysician health care education programs cost the 514 providers in the program a total of $167 million. Nursing programs were more expensive, costing 547 providers $533 million (Health Resources and Services Administration, 1987). Medicare pays only for its own share of the allowable direct costs.

Other studies (Lewin and Associates, 1987; Mathematica Policy Research, Inc., 1987) have confirmed the observations of Applied Management Services in interviews with the directors of hospital education programs. Education programs offer numerous benefits to the employer, chief of which is the opportunity to recruit future employees. Additional benefits include motivating existing staff to stay abreast of advances in their fields, and enhancing the reputation of the hospital by providing a community service to local educational institutions.

The committee believes that the federal government should not reduce its support on the presumption that employers—realizing the benefits of education programs—will maintain and even increase their support. Precipitate action to cut Medicare's educational support runs the risk of destabilizing vulnerable allied health education programs. In the committee's view, such destabilization is not worth relatively small, short-term budget savings. In the long run, Medicare beneficiaries would be harmed by limiting clinical experience for students. Moreover, many of these costs are likely to emerge later as potentially more costly recruitment and on-the-job training expenses.

Therefore, **the committee recommends that, until credible alternative approaches are developed, the federal government and other third-party payers maintain current reimbursement levels and mechanisms of support for clinical allied health education**.

The Comparative Cost of Allied Health Education

Allied education programs are perceived by educational planners and administrators to be high-cost programs. As a consequence, they can be prime targets for institutional budget reductions by central administrative staff. Where state higher education funding formulas do not compensate for these higher costs, programs are exceedingly vulnerable to cost-cutting measures when times are hard in higher education.

There has been growing recent interest in constructed cost models to improve the ability of allied health deans and program directors to negotiate with their central administration and explain why their unit costs may be higher than those of other fields. These models focus on key assumptions about faculty contact hours, faculty–student ratios, resource requirements for clinical experiences outside the department, and faculty salaries (Freeland and Gonyea, 1985). Although the models are useful tools for improving efficiency and then demonstrating those improvements to academic administrators, their explanatory power does not change the reality that allied health education is faculty intensive, that it necessitates clinical education experiences requiring coordination and supervision, and that it often has extensive laboratory and space requirements.

The recommendations that have already been made in this chapter will help to address some of the weaknesses allied health programs have in competing for resources. Yet these measures are no substitute for the actions many allied health schools must begin to take to generate the revenue needed to thrive. Medical schools have come to rely increasingly on income generated from faculty practices. Although such activities may not be appropriate or financially advantageous for many allied health fields, they may be so for some if they are established with sufficient forethought and expertise. The notion of generating revenue by providing services needs further exploration, however. For example, the services provided by allied health schools might be educational (extension courses or adult education, for example), or they could involve innovative relationships with industry.

To enhance the stability of allied health education, national organizations such as the American Society of Allied Health Professions should

investigate models in which academic institutions have succeeded in broadening their financial base through such mechanisms as faculty practice plans, extension courses, and industry relationships. The national organizations should also hold workshops to help institutions implement the models and to disseminate information.

In undertaking revenue-generating enterprises, however, allied health deans will confront and possibly exacerbate a problem they have faced before. Faculty resources currently are stretched thin to control costs, and the excessive teaching load leaves little time for faculty to engage in scholarly activity, research, and college committee work. Yet these activities constitute a major portion of the traditional evaluation criteria for faculty promotion and tenure. Consequently, they are the preferred nonteaching activities pursued by faculty wishing to advance their academic careers. Maintaining state-of-the-art clinical competence further adds to the faculty's already excessive work load. Indeed, the committee heard a number of deans complain of the difficulties their faculty members face in maintaining clinical skills and of the concomitant impact of these difficulties on preparing students for the labor market.

To ensure that the clinical competence of allied health faculty is maintained, the institutional award system must accommodate clinical competence because faculty allocate what little nonteaching time they have to those activities that are highly rewarded. The committee recommends that **institutions that offer allied health academic programs reward and encourage faculty clinical competence. Clinical practice that sustains this competence should be made a requirement for promotion.**

It is noteworthy that this concern about the reward system is also one that medical educators have been forced to confront. As the president of the Association of American Medical Colleges has observed, "Despite the realization that teacher–clinicians are essential ingredients of medical facilities, the need is often not recognized by the parent universities whose appointments and promotion policies leave no niche for the clinician–teacher to receive proper recognition" (Petersdorf, 1987).

Preparing Students for Tomorrow's Jobs

In principle, sound educational planning would dictate that academic institutions base their program offerings on an understanding of the knowledge, skills, and socialization required of their graduates—not only for today's health care labor market but for the future as well. By extension, statewide higher education planning should take into account the mix and distribution of personnel at different educational levels that will be needed across the state. Confounding efforts at such rational planning, however, are a lack of clear signals from the labor market about future human resource needs and continuing controversy about matching education to the requirements of the health care delivery system.

Reflecting this controversy, an allied health education advisory committee in Texas highlighted a series of concerns that often surface when such groups view the broad spectrum of allied health fields (Allied Health Education Advisory Committee, 1980):

- the growing amount of narrow specialization at all degree levels;
- the requirements of some professional groups for higher levels of training for professional entry credentials;
- difficulties with the transfer of credits to implement the career ladder concept;
- the most appropriate levels of training for various kinds of allied health personnel; and
- differences in the programs needed to prepare practitioners, master clinicians, teachers, researchers, and managers.

Ironically, these issues are of concern today because, in the past, educational institutions have responded to student and employer demands. Associate degree and certificate programs were developed to provide students who were unwilling or unable to spend 4 years in school before entering the work force an opportunity to enter a field in which those workers with traditional higher credentials were in short supply. Academic health centers and 4-year colleges, in addition to community colleges, sought to meet the needs of their own and local hospitals with 2-year programs. Students with baccalaureates in other than health care fields were accommodated with certificate programs so they could pursue allied health careers. Students who were interested in careers in respiratory therapy, dental hygiene, and radiography, which were principally offered at the associate degree level, found themselves able to enroll in programs that also allowed them to obtain baccalaureate degrees. The result of these developments was the opening of allied health occupations to a wider range of participants.

Having accommodated the needs of different student markets and employers who were either experiencing shortages in some personnel categories or who were attempting to structure their staffing with personnel of different educational levels, the educational system is now faced, not surprisingly, with a state of untidiness that planners find uncomfortable. Further complicating matters is the growing availability of graduate training. Although advanced degrees have long been accepted as appropriate preparation for faculty, administrators, and researchers, there is greater skepticism about graduate work when it comes to the elevation of a field's entry-level qualifications or efforts to develop specialities.

The committee acknowledges this great diversity in educational qualifications but finds that a public policy problem requiring attention may not exist. The diversity in and of itself is not a problem. The test of whether specialization and changing qualifications or standards are dysfunctional is twofold: (1) Is there wastefulness in student educational investments? (2) Is the educational system responsive to society's need for a manpower supply that permits the health care system to function efficiently and provide care of the desired quality?

Educational Investments by Students

To open a new education program and admit a class implies a contract with students that contains certain assurances. No school can guarantee a student a job nor can it guarantee that skills and knowledge acquired in its programs will be marketable in perpetuity. Nevertheless, the committee believes that schools have the responsibility to ensure that (1) professional education is training for a specific, "real" occupation at the end of the line; (2) the program's general education content is sufficiently balanced by occupation-specific skills; (3) if, and when, students wish career advancement through education, there is a relatively efficient pathway to follow; and (4) there is a realistic balance between the role aspirations of professions with the realities of day-to-day work. In fulfilling their responsibilities to students, educational decision makers face a number of dilemmas.

"Real" Jobs   There are numerous job titles under the umbrella of allied health. Not all of them need to have separate, formal academic programs. Yet educators must be sensitive to changing technology and disease patterns that may warrant such recent developments as genetic counselors and MRI technicians.

The Southern Regional Education Board (1980) has recommended— and the committee concurs—that academic institutions contemplating the development of new allied health specialities ask themselves three practice-related questions:

• Are there any legal or professional restrictions on the new practitioners that will tend to inhibit employers from hiring these graduates?
• Is the new speciality sufficiently different from existing specialities to justify the development of a new educational program?
• What degree of liability does the supervisor of the new practitioners assume?

Liberal Education   Faculty in professional or technically oriented programs in higher education face a continuing struggle to reconcile the demands of academia for scholarship and general education with pressures from employers and accrediting bodies to prepare students for technologically demanding jobs. The argument on the side of liberal education is that the educational program ought to be providing preparation for life and not just for a specific job. Graduates must be prepared to respond to the inevitable changes that will occur in society.

Many educators feel the pressure that is exerted by employers (especially employers in fields that require familiarity with instrumentation) to influence programs to produce graduates who do not need extensive orientation. Even at the community college level, which has had a strong tradition of job orientation, there is concern about the appropriate mix of general education and technical/clinical course work. In one small survey, 25 allied health community college deans reported proportions of general education to technical/clinical course work credits that ranged from 8 percent to 35 percent, with an average of 22 percent (Kaminski, 1987). In the name of responsiveness to a changing society, general education courses compete with pressures to incorporate such areas of study as geriatrics, computer applications, multicompetency, and clinical experience in alternative sites of care.

The committee is sympathetic to the dilemmas faced by curriculum planners. Yet it is also concerned that students receive an educational foundation on which they can build a career if they so desire. Part of this foundation entails developing the capacity for and an interest in lifelong learning. A further, important benefit of such a foundation is that, if current skills become obsolete, practitioners have a base on which they can develop an alternative career.

Articulation   Allied health dean Elizabeth King from Eastern Michigan University describes two hypothetical students to illustrate the personal dimensions of the problems of articulation, the process by which students achieve upward educational transitions among academic programs (King, 1985). One student, having worked 7 years as a certified occupational therapy assistant "with a love of the profession and a conscious decision to build upon her current skills," is confused and disillusioned when denied the opportunity to transfer her professionally related course work toward an occupational therapy degree. Meanwhile, another student with an associate degree in general studies, hearing about the good job prospects for occupational therapists but having little knowledge about what occupational therapists do, is advised by the senior college that all of his courses will transfer and he can complete the degree in 2 years.

In general, states have strongly promoted the concept of multiple entry and exit points in health careers to minimize the loss of student time in moving through certificate, associate, and baccalaureate programs. Without strong mandates or incentives, however, such programs have difficulty overcoming some inherent barriers. King discusses a number of them. For example, curricular problems occur in judging the compatibility of didactic and clinical program content, which makes it difficult to assess advanced placement. There is also, at times, a lack of communication between academic affairs and admissions offices to work out problems regarding credit transfer policies. Finally, and perhaps most important, faculty professional biases, in King's view, "the most insidious barrier," create an environment of "undiscussable tension." These biases label community college students as "technically" trained and lacking in problem-solving experiences.

The committee recommends that **alternative pathways to entry-level practice be encouraged when feasible. State higher education coordinating authorities and legislative committees should insist on flexibility in educational mobility between community colleges and baccalaureate programs**.

Role Congruence   There is continuing tension between health care administrators and professional groups over the tendency of a field to assume more sophisticated or broader responsibilities and the perception of employers (or payers) as to the legitimate and valued functions that need to be performed for patients.

Professional associations and program faculty see their responsibilities as the defining and shaping of their discipline. This process is reflected in curriculum content and reinforced by accreditation. Health care administrators become concerned when they believe curriculum is being used as a precursor to expanding the legal scope of practice and reimbursement without recognition of what is possible or likely in practice. They also become concerned when they believe that an occupation is at the same time abandoning "hands-on" patient care for "professional" responsibilities that are not valued highly by those outside the field.

Care must be taken to ensure that students do not become mired in these controversies. Ultimately, these issues are resolved by the market, as shaped by consumer tastes and employer hiring practices, or by public policy, as reflected in reimbursement or licensure decisions. While these issues are being resolved, however, the committee believes that educators have the responsibility to ensure that students have realistic expectations of what their prospective occupation is like today—and not only what it might be in the future.

The Agreement Between Education and Services

Along with the education program's responsibility to students is a responsibility to society to ensure that the health care system has the human resources it needs to function well. Indeed, the rationale for the committee's support of public intervention in allied health supply issues is based on its belief that the link between services and education needs to be strengthened.

In determining their program offerings, allied health educators are cautioned by state higher education leaders and health care administrators to avoid overtraining in both curriculum content and in length and level of preparation. On the other side are the professions who caution against too little training and who strive to elevate educational standards through licensure, program accreditation, and reimbursement standards.

The committee has heard arguments by the first group that raising educational qualifications is not only expensive to the student but to the educational and health care systems as well, both of which are attempting to control costs. Furthermore, proponents of this view contend that "education creep" exacerbates shortages by lengthening the time required to prepare an individual for work. They also contend that there is little evidence to suggest that current levels of education are creating care problems.

Counterarguments are most often based on the expanding knowledge base that practitioners need to master and the limited time available in the curriculum for such mastery. New sites of care, such as in the home or in independent office practice, require a level of judgment that can only be achieved with increased education. Those concerned with an adequate supply of practitioners point to the higher labor force participation rates and longer tenure of those who have already attained the higher credential.

This committee encountered a number of these types of controversies among the allied health fields. Some examples include physical therapists attempting to establish the master's degree as the entry-level standard, role delineation debates among baccalaureate medical technologists and 2-year medical laboratory technicians, proposals to limit the educational routes to entry-level dietetics, and the movement of respiratory therapy to a baccalaureate entry-level standard. The case for promoting a single optimal level of education is an exceedingly difficult one to make on empirical grounds. For example, when an IOM committee explored the controversy over the three educational tracks leading to the registered nurse credential (associate degree, diploma, and baccalaureate), it was unable to find convincing evidence on the difference of performance among the graduates (Institute of Medicine, 1983).

The committee neither endorses nor refutes the position of parties on either side of these debates. In view of the lack of objective empirical evidence and the limited scope of the present study, the committee could not justify offering conclusions that might influence the outcome of these controversies. The committee does suggest, however, that those making decisions ensure that changing existing practice will not limit the supply of practitioners nor make care excessively costly.

From the committee's perspective the only sensible response to the moving targets of health care system change and the lack of certainty about how to match education to future needs is a continuing feedback loop between education and practice. Graduate follow-up studies that incorporate employer perceptions are the most direct measures of how well the curriculum is preparing students. The aim of these studies, however, need not be solely to tailor education to employer perceptions of need. Rather, it should be the start of a dialogue. If students are not applying their educational experiences fully, the problem may at times rest with the work environment. A dialogue could potentially lead to a mutually beneficial set of activities involving more participation from health care managers in curriculum design and greater involvement of educators in health services research with practical application to clinical settings.

Various models are available for institutionalizing such interactions. In some education programs, allied health education and services are jointly administered by the same corporate entity. An example is Rush University in Chicago where education and services are unified. Where this is not feasible, the industry advisory boards common to many community colleges can be used. Faculty practice plans or clinical affiliations may also be a starting point to stimulate collaboration.

In those fields in which instrumentation plays a major role in job functioning, industry/faculty collaboration provides a largely untapped resource. Manufacturers ultimately have a stake in human resources because investments by health facilities in technological innovations may be seriously jeopardized if there is a lack of adequately prepared personnel. Manufacturers should consider collaborating with educational institutions in creative ways—for example, the use of equipment, faculty–industry research projects, short-term employment opportunities—as a means of ensuring an appropriate human resource infrastructure to assist technology transfer.

Yet some stimulus is necessary to overcome the inertia of dealing with these difficult issues of collaboration. The committee sees a role both for states and private foundations in providing that stimulus. **State legislatures should establish special bodies whose primary purpose would be to address state and local issues in the education and employment of allied health personnel. Private foundations should support university-based centers for allied health studies and policy to provide a critical mass of researchers and resources to advance technology assessment, health care services research, and human resource utilization.**

States have a major role in allied health education by virtue of their support of public colleges and universities. In addition to this influence, they are frequently drawn into debates over licensure issues that involve changing scopes of practice and the licensing of new occupations. (These regulatory issues are discussed in Chapter 7.)

Private foundations could have a major impact on the future of allied health education and practice by creating centers of excellence in a few academic institutions. Many advantages might be gained by coalescing a core research faculty that also provides services. These mutually reenforcing activities would enhance the quality of research and patient care. Furthermore, these centers might then be a resource to other allied health education programs regionally or nationally.

The committee believes that the interest of state legislatures and private foundations in the endeavors we describe will be kindled and sustained only by a continuing federal presence in the concerns of allied health education and practice. For this reason, the committee makes the following recommendation about the federal leadership: **The Department of Health and Human Services should maintain an organizational focal point on allied health personnel to implement the grant programs recommended in this report, to coordinate the recommended work of the interagency data task force (recommended in Chapter 2), and to facilitate communication between state legislative committees and the federal government.**

REFERENCES

Allied Health Education Advisory Committee. 1980. Guiding Concepts for the '80s. CB Study Paper 29. Austin: Coordinating Board, Texas College and University System.

Amatayakul, M.K. 1987. Report from the AMRA Manpower Survey. Journal of the American Medical Record Association 58(3):25–36.

American Dietetic Association. 1985. A New Look at the Profession of Dietetics, Report of the 1984 Study Commission on Dietetics. Chicago: American Dietetic Association.

American Occupational Therapy Association. 1987. Member Data Survey. Interim Report No. l. Rockville, Md.: American Occupational Therapy Association.

American Physical Therapy Association. 1985. The Plan to Address the Faculty Shortage in Physical Therapy Education. Final Report of the Task Force on Faculty Shortage in Physical Therapy Education. Alexandria, Va: American Physical Therapy Association. September.

American Physical Therapy Association. 1987. Active Membership Profile Study. Alexandria, Va.: American Physical Therapy Association.

Area Health Education Centers Program. 1987. Health Issues Working Group on Health Professions: Program Inventory. Rockville, Md.: Health Resources and Services Administration. February.

Astin, A. W. 1985. Minorities in American Higher Education. San Francisco: Jossey-Bass.

Bisconti, A. 1981. National and State Profiles of Collegiate Allied Health Education. 1979–80. Hyattsville, Md.: Health Resources Administration.

Bleich, M. 1986. Enhancing Opportunities in Science, Mathematics, and Health Professions: An Invitational Conference. Reno, Nev.: Macy Foundation. July.

Bleich, M. 1987. Strengthening Support Networks for Minorities in Health Science Careers: A National Symposium. New York: Macy Foundation. January.

Booker, N. 1987. Minorities and Allied Health Educaiton. Background paper prepared for the IOM Committee to Study the Role of Allied Health Personnel. Washington, D.C.

Bowen, D. 1988. Dental hygiene: A devloping discipline? Dental Hygiene 62(1):23–24.

Broski, D. C., R. E. Olson, and A. A. Savage. 1985. Increasing research productivity in university-based colleges of allied health. Journal of Allied Health 14(1):160–162.

Brown, R. 1987. Perfusionists: A Case Study. Background paper prepared for the IOM Committee to Study the Role of Allied Health Personnel. Washington, D.C.

Bureau of Health Manpower, Health Resources Administration. 1979. A Report on Allied Health Personnel. November 26. Washington, D.C.: U.S. Government Printing Office.

CAHEA (Committee on Allied Health Education and Accreditation). 1987a. Allied Health Education Directory, 1987, 15th ed. Chicago: American Medical Association.

CAHEA 1987b. Voluntary Program Withdrawals from CAHEA Accreditation, 1983–87. Chicago: American Medical Association.

CAHEA. In press.

Carpenter, H. 1982. Disadvantaged in the Health Resources Administration's allied health training programs: A historical review. Health Resources Administration, Washington, D.C. June.

The Circle, Inc. 1987. Revitalizing Pharmacy and Allied Health Professions Education for Minorities and the Disadvantaged. Rockville, Md.: Health Resources and Services Administration.

College of Health Deans. 1987. Unpublished survey data.

Cooperative Institutional Research Program. 1987. 1987 Freshman Survey Report. Los Angeles: University of California, Los Angeles.

Covey, P., and J. Burke. 1987. Research and the mission of schools of allied health. Journal of Allied Health 16(February):1–5.

Fitzgerald, L. F., and J. O. Crites. 1980. Toward a career psychology of women: What do we know? What do we need to know? Journal of Counseling Psychology 27:44–62.

Flack, H. 1982. Minorities in Allied Health Education. Rockville, Md.: Office of Health Resources Opportunity, Health Resources Administration. August.

Freeland, T. E., and M. A. Gonyea. 1985. Financing Allied Health Clinical Education. Report prepared for the Health Resources and Services Administration, Rockville, Md.

Garrison, H., and P. Brown. 1985. Minority Access to Research Careers: An Evaluation of the Honors Undergraduate Research Training Program. Committee on National Needs for Biomedical and Behavioral Personnel. Washington, D.C.: National Academy Press.

Gonzales, C. 1987. Minority Biomedical Research Program. Bethesda, Md.: Division of Research Resources, National Institutes of Health. March.

Health Professions Report. 1988. Social work schools' enrollment increases, but trend not universal. Whitaker Newsletters, Inc. (New Jersey) 17(2): 2–5.

Health Resources and Services Administration. 1984. An In-Depth Examination of the 1980 Decennial Census Employment Data for Health Occupations: Comprehensive Report. ODAM Report No. 16-84. Washington, D.C.: Government Printing Office. July.

Health Resources and Services Administration. 1986. Report to the President and Congress on the Status of Health Personnel in the United States. Rockville, Md: Health Resources and Services Administration.

Health Resources and Services Administration. 1987. Report to Congress on Nursing and Other Health Professions Educational Programs Reimbursed Under Medicare. Rockville, Md.: Health Resources and Services Administration. December.

Hedrick, H. 1985. Discontinuation of allied health schools and programs. Is there a pattern? Journal of Allied Health 14(1):159–160.

Herr, E. L., and S. Cramer. 1984. Career Guidance and Counseling Through the Life Span. Boston: Little, Brown.

Holcomb, J. D., D. W. Evans, W. P. Buckner, and L. D. Ponder. 1987. A longitudinal evaluation of graduate programs in allied health education and administration. Journal of Allied Health 16(2):119–133.

Hudson Institute. 1987. Workforce 2000: Work and Workers for the 21st Century. Indianapolis, Ind.: Hudson Institute. June.

Institute of Medicine. 1983. Nursing and Nursing Education: Public Policies and Private Actions. Washington, D.C.: National Academy Press.

Kaminski, G. 1987. Allied Health Study: Two Year College Survey. Unpublished paper. Cincinnati Technical College.

King, E. 1985. Articulation of allied health education. Pp. 126–139 in Review of Allied Health Education: 5. J. Hamburg, ed. Lexington, Ky.: University Press of Kentucky.

La Jolla Management Corporation. 1984. An Assessment of Preparatory Activities for the Health Careers Opportunity Program: Final Report. Rockville, Md.: Health Resources and Services Administration.

Lent, R., S. Brown, and K. Lark. 1986. Comparison of three theoretically derived variables in predicting career and academic behavior: self-efficacy, interest congruence, and consequent thinking. Journal of Counseling Psychology 34(3):293–298.

Lewin and Associates. 1987. Hospital Decision-Making About Offering Health Professions Clinical Education Opportunities and the Effects of Payment Policies on These Decisions. Final Report. Rockville, Md.: Health Resources and Services Administration. May.

Ludlow, C. L. 1986. The Research Career Ladder in Human Communication Sciences and Disorders. Bethesda, Md.: National Institutes of Health.

Malone, P. 1979. Creating New Allied Health Programs: Considerations and Constraints. Atlanta: Southern Regional Education Board.

Mandex, Inc. 1987. An Assessment of State Support for Health Professions Education Programs: Final Report. Rockville, Md.: Health Resources and Services Administration. June.

Mathematica Policy Research, Inc. 1987. Draft final report on exploration of trends and changes in clinical education in the preparation of allied health professions. Washington, D.C. June 30.

Miller, J. D. 1986. Multivariate models to predict the selection of and persistence in a career in the professions. Paper presented to the 1986 annual meeting of the American Educational Resource Association, San Francisco, April 17.

Mingle, J. 1987. Trends in Higher Education Participation and Success. Publ. No. MP-87-2. Denver, Colo.: Education Commission of the States and State Higher Education Executive Officers.

Missouri Coordinating Board for Higher Education. 1986. Recommendations to the Committee on Academic Affairs regarding "State-Level Review of Existing Programs in Health Sciences Education." Jefferson City, Mo. April.

National Commission on Allied Health Education. 1980. The Future of Allied Health Education: New Alliances for the 1980s. San Francisco: Jossey-Bass.

New York State Education Department, Bureau of Higher and Professional Education Testing. 1985. Program Guidelines. Albany: New York State Education Department.

Newman, F. 1985. Higher Education and the American Resurgence. Princeton, N.J.: Carnegie Foundation for the Advancement of Teaching.

Parks, R. B., and H. L. Hedrick, 1988. Program directors' perspectives regarding CAHEA-accredited allied health education. Summary of a 1987 survey. Allied Health Education Directory, 16th ed. Chicago: American Medical Association.

Perrin, K. L. 1987. Remarks at the Symposium on the Future of Allied Health Education, Susquehanna University, Selinsgrove, Penn., April.

Petersdorf, R. G. 1987. A report on the establishment. Journal of Medical Education 621 (February):126–132.

Southern Regional Education Board. 1980. Planning and Designing Allied Health Education for Program Review. Atlanta, Ga.

U.S. Department of Health and Human Services. 1985. Report to the Secretary's Task Force on Black and Minority Health. Washington, D.C.: U.S. Government Printing Office. August.

6

The Health Care Employer's Perspective

MANY OF THE THEMES THAT RUN SEPARATELY through this report come together when we begin to view allied health workers from the perspective of health care employers. When the supply of practitioners in an allied health field declines because fewer students choose that career or because schools close, health care administrators who employ allied health personnel are among the first to experience the change. If licensure laws change or a new technology is introduced, employers are among the first to respond to the change. When a glut of workers in an allied health field exists in a locality, employers notice it in the number of responses they get to vacancies they advertise.

Employers are not merely users of a given supply of allied health personnel, however—they are also active participants in the forces that determine the supply of workers. In other words, the quantity of workers demanded and the quantity supplied are not independent. Wage and salary rates and working conditions affect the supply of workers. The supply of workers in turn affects the wages, salaries, and working conditions that they are offered. Yet employers setting wage and salary levels have to balance many considerations other than the amount of money needed to attract the required number of workers. They must consider the payment they can get for services and the bottom-line impact of personnel expenses, the regulatory requirements that constrain work force deployment, and the skills and knowledge demanded by the technologies in use.

In the past, cost-based reimbursement, the absence of competition, and a generally adequate supply of allied health personnel allowed administrators to make the salary adjustments that were needed to maintain their desired staffing levels. They were able to accomplish this without appreciably changing staffing or service levels or the deployment of staff. Yet changes in the health care system and in allied health labor markets may force administrators to rethink their staffing practices. There will be increasing competition for technically oriented workers, who have more employment options than nontechnical workers. In addition, administrators will have strong economic incentives to control personnel costs to compete in terms of price, yet remain financially viable.

These changes have created a new environment with which administrators have little experience. Although some administrators have had to face periodic shortages of nurses, only recently have they faced personnel shortages and price competition simultaneously. There is no historical pattern to indicate how employers will adapt to difficulties in hiring and staffing.

The committee identified some allied health professions in which shortages are likely to occur if changes in the labor market fail to take place. This chapter focuses on forestalling shortages; it emphasizes the importance of planning for the future. Market mechanisms will force adjustments that will eventually decrease stresses in the allied health labor market. Yet markets adjust slowly. For example, there is a considerable lag between educational institutions recognizing and responding to increased student interest in an allied health field and an increased number of graduates in that field. Employers have many reasons to act early to forestall possible personnel shortages. For instance, acute shortages of workers in an allied health field may cause salaries to rise sharply, some services to close, or the initiation of new needed services to be postponed. More subtly, the quality of health care may be eroded if, over extended periods of time, too few existing employees must struggle to maintain services. These and other serious service dislocations could be reduced if administrators were to respond appropriately to early market signals.

In this chapter the committee focuses mainly on what personnel administrators, corporate human resource administrators, and department heads in all types of health care facilities—hospitals, nursing homes, freestanding facilities—might consider doing to help relieve or prevent personnel shortages. It discusses two types of activities that can produce gains in personnel supply: (1) making employment more attractive, and (2) using the available work force more effectively. None of the activities discussed is new; they have been tried in fields other than allied health. There is a need for further investigation, however, to ascertain which activities are best suited to resolve problems with the allied health labor force, taking into account the different characteristics of the work force in each field.

There are other ways in which health care providers can lessen their personnel problems. For instance, hospitals in Texas have responded to shortages by using the state hospital association to mount an elaborate campaign to recruit high school graduates into health careers (Texas Health Careers, 1987). Other mechanisms, such as offering vacationing high school students jobs in health care facilities, are also used to inform and encourage students to select health care careers.

Throughout this chapter, terms such as "human resource administrators" and "facility administrators" are used. These terms are purposefully vague. Health care organizations often have a personnel function to facilitate the details of personnel management, departmental administrators who make decisions about the deployment of staff, and upper level human resource administrators who deal with facility-wide labor force issues. This fragmentation makes it difficult to develop and implement creative staffing arrangements that would likely be part of the solution to allied health staffing problems.

STRATEGIES FOR EMPLOYERS TO ENHANCE THE SUPPLY OF ALLIED HEALTH PRACTITIONERS

Several factors play roles in creating imbalances between the supply of and demand for allied health workers: the diminishing size of the college-age population; students' propensities to choose careers outside of health care; and the decreasing availability of allied health programs on the one hand and the aging of the population, disease patterns, and technological advances in health care on the other. These imbalances will likely remain unless something changes on one or both sides of the equation. However, generalizations of this sort do not apply to all allied health fields or to all parts of the country. Demand and supply vary from place to place, and with varying characteristic circumstances. Individual facilities and areas will in some cases experience an adequate or even excess supply of personnel in fields in which a national shortage is predicted, and the balance between supply and demand will differ among the fields. This is readily apparent today as facility administrators in some parts of the country struggle to hire physical therapists when, for example, respiratory therapists are plentiful.

The expectation is that in many parts of the nation and for many employers of allied health practitioners the labor market will be tight.

To increase the supply of workers, employers can intervene to make education more accessible and employment more attractive. Students may then be more likely to select allied health careers. People who have left the work force to pursue other interests—raising families, new careers, or leisure—may return. In addition, workers may choose to remain in the work force longer or to remain in a particular career longer. Increasing the supply of workers by encouraging greater numbers of students to enter the allied health fields is a strategy that depends both on employers making employment in allied health careers more attractive and on educational institutions expanding programs in response to increased student demand.

The second strategy for coping with shortages, using workers more productively or effectively, in essence reduces the demand for allied health personnel at a given level of output. Yet there are limits to the productivity improvements that can be achieved. These limits can result from regulatory restrictions, the skills of individuals, technological constraints, or the nature of the work. The challenge for administrators in today's competitive health care environment is to try to ensure that productivity improvements are pushed to their limits.

Undertaking one or both of these strategies would require a serious reconsideration of the role of human resource management. For many facility administrators, it would mean giving human resource management a higher priority than in the past. Yet such investments or efforts would be repaid if the service dislocations that could result from tight labor markets were avoided. Moreover, private sector employers must take the initiative in enhancing the supply of allied health personnel. The public policy options, such as programs of grants or scholarships, cannot on their own solve manpower problems. Making education inexpensive and readily available might attract some people into allied health fields, but unless good jobs offering competitive wages are available, too few people will be attracted, and those who choose an allied health occupation will not stay in it long.

Salaries

In a perfectly competitive market, an imbalance between demand and supply would cause prices to change until demand and supply were once again in equilibrium. Thus, if a shortfall of allied health personnel were to occur, wage rates would be expected to rise, demand would fall, and the supply of personnel would increase to match demand. This series of reactions is likely to occur in the allied health personnel market. Yet market forces do not always work freely, and there can be delays before equilibrium is reestablished. If demand increases at a greater rate than supply, wages may rise, but there will be a lag before supply catches up with demand. In addition, wage rates may be slow to respond to supply shortages if employers are unwilling or unable to raise wages. An explanation offered for the slow adjustment of nurses' compensation is that large health care providers, such as hospitals, have often been one of just a few employers of allied health practitioners in a locality. Realizing that these practitioners have few alternative places at which to work, employers have been able to keep wages down (Aiken, 1982). In many local markets, however, the competition for allied health practitioners has been increasing with a proliferation of work sites—freestanding units of numerous types, sometimes independent practice options, and so on. Slow wage adjustments can be expected if employers do not recognize that wage competition is taking place. There are also many reasons why employers may be reluctant to adjust wages.

Sometimes employers recognize that competition for workers is occurring but are unable to compete with the salaries being offered by other organizations. Some types of employers for whom this is likely to be true are discussed at the end of this chapter. During the course of the study the committee often heard of allied health practitioners who left traditional employment settings to establish independent practices or to work for employers paying substantially higher salaries—for example, health spas, food manufacturers, and biotechnology firms. The committee also heard that the traditional service ethic that in the past attracted individuals to relatively low-paying health care jobs is being eroded. Opportunities in alternative places of work or higher paying careers are felt to overwhelm the traditional service satisfaction.

Employers' reluctance to respond to indications of a personnel shortage by raising salaries is due not only to the expense of paying higher wages but also to the fact that the compensation levels of the many types of workers in a hospital are interrelated. An increase in one group's pay is likely to be quickly followed by increases for other workers. Such failures of the market are not unique to health care providers. The *Wall Street Journal* (Mitchell, 1987), noting a serious shortage of skilled blue-collar craftsmen, remarked:

Surprisingly, the labor market has sparked only modest wage gains so far. Although desperate for certain key skills, some employers would rather limp along without a full workforce than raise wages high enough to attract needed workers . . . many companies have chosen to ignore issues of supply and demand for fear that higher labor costs will make it more difficult to compete.

A similar attitude prevails in health care. The *New York Times* (Uchitelle, 1987) cited Jerome Grossman, chairman of the New England Medical Center, where 200 of 2,800 jobs were vacant, as saying "The amounts we can charge patients are capped and so . . . we are forced to make trade-offs." Moreover, there are sometimes alternatives to pay increases. For example, when laboratory technicians are in short supply, chemists and individuals trained in other relevant disciplines can be substituted. When there are alternative sources of workers, such as lower level practitioners or individuals with other training, substitution may be a preferable alternative to raising pay. For example, in one locality in which there is an oversupply of dentists and a shortage of hygienists, an HMO uses dentists to perform the hygienists' tasks. In some allied health fields, however, the freedom to substitute personnel is constrained by regulation.

Alternatively, other ways of dealing with personnel shortages include marginally curtailing services, asking allied health employees to work overtime, or taking measures to increase output.

Other ways of attracting personnel through economic incentives without increasing wages or salaries include paying bonuses for joining and staying on staff, and offering continuing education and day-care subsidies. These methods avoid an upward shift in pay scales; consequently, if utilization or occupancy rates decline the employers are not left with an excessively highly paid staff when the supply of workers is plentiful. Evidently, health care administrators, who are necessarily concerned with their organization's bottom line, have an array of strategies available that can be implemented before wage rates are increased. Thus, a lag in the response of wages to a perceived shortage of personnel is not unexpected.

Although raising salaries has been shown to increase the size of the nursing work force, other economic factors also influence the decision to work. Family income is important. As spouses' incomes rise, nurses tend to reduce their working hours or to stop working altogether. In addition, when nurses' salaries become high enough, some nurses reduce the number of hours they work. Conversely, in times of high unemployment, inactive nurses often return to the work force (Aiken, 1982). These phenomena are likely to occur in some of the allied health fields—in particular, those that are mainly composed of women and that are similar to nursing in education and pay levels.

An analysis of nurses' compensation in relation to changes in the balance of demand and supply notes that sometimes wage increases have lagged behind shortages. The same analysis also notes that wage increases have repeatedly succeeded in reducing shortages (Aiken and Mullinex, 1987).

Pay differentials between various educational levels in the same occupation also have the potential of increasing or decreasing the supply of personnel of a given level. For example, when there was no difference between the earnings of baccalaureate nurses and associate degree nurses, students realized that the economic return to the 2-year education was higher than the return to the 4-year program, and the number of associate degree graduates eventually exceeded the number of baccalaureate graduates (Buerhaus, 1987).

Pay levels affect the supply of allied health practitioners at each point at which an individual makes a career decision. Although economic considerations often are not the sole or primary considerations, earnings potential is one of many factors considered by students who are selecting an educational program. Once started on a career, satisfaction with current earning levels and expected increases in earnings will figure in decisions to continue working; to leave the work force; to pursue child care, leisure, or other unpaid activities; or to change to another occupation with better compensation. Similarly, the return to an occupation will be in part dependent on pay levels—especially when the cost of work includes major expenditures such as child care.

How does allied health compensation compare with that in other occupations? First, compensation for allied health practitioners should be understood in the context of women's earnings, because women dominate many allied health fields. In 1986 women earned on average 69.2 cents for every dollar earned by men (Mellor, 1987). Moreover, occupations in which women represent the majority of workers tend to rank lower in terms of earnings than male-dominated occupations (Rytina, 1982). The American Physical Therapy Association is one group that is trying to address these problems. It recently examined factors contributing to the disparity in professional and economic status between men and women members as indicated by self-employment, administrative responsibility, graduate degrees, and earnings. Full-time salaried female physical therapists had annual salaries that were only 85 percent of those of full-time salaried men. Self-employed physical therapists are more likely to be men (62 percent) and they earn more than self-employed women physical therapists. The annual gross earnings of these women were 71 percent of those of self-employed men. The study concluded that the association should explore approaches for creating career ladders, encourage women to commit themselves to their careers and to the maintenance of their skills, and consider societal barriers that limit women's aspirations and opportunities (Reagan, 1986).

Table 6-1 arrays compensation data for several allied health fields and other selected occupations. These data for allied health occupations were obtained through a national survey of 33 hospitals, 16 medical schools, and 28 medical centers. These institutions were chosen for their similarity in size to the University of Texas Medical Branch at Galveston, which has 1,100 beds and 7,500 employees. Thirteen of the institutions are in Texas, Arkansas, and Louisiana, which represents an oversampling of that region. Thus, these data pertain to large institutions and have a regional bias. The occupational categories are carefully defined and clear, and although the Texas-Arkansas-Louisiana region is oversampled there are no other reasons to believe that the manpower markets of the institutions have any special characteristics. In Table 6-1 the starting rate refers to the rate normally paid to fill a vacancy in the occupation. The maximum rate is the highest rate actually paid to employees in the occupation (University of Texas Medical Branch, 1986).

Data for the other occupations are from a nationwide salary survey of firms with at least 50 employees. Each occupation was divided into levels with detailed job content descriptions for each level. For the non-allied health fields the starting salary in Table 6-1 is for the lowest level, and the maximum is for the highest level (Bureau of Labor Statistics, 1986). Some

TABLE 6-1   Monthly Salary Ranges of Selected Allied Health
Occupations and Other Occupations, 1986

Occupation	Mean Starting Rate	Mean Maximum Rate	Percentage Difference
Audiologist	$1,872	$2,334	25
Dietitian	1,676	2,196	31
Electrocardiograph technician	1,073	1,332	24
Medical lab technician	1,222	1,622	33
Medical record administrator	2,076	2,637	27
Medical record technician	1,272	1,595	25
Medical technologist	1,630	2,174	33
Nuclear magnetic resonance technologist	1,596	2,033	27
Occupational therapist	1,777	2,219	25
Physical therapist	1,845	2,338	27
Radiologic technologist	1,435	1,900	32
Radiation therapy technologist	1,651	2,094	27
Respiratory therapist	1,481	1,855	25
Speech–language pathologist	1,857	2,318	25
Accountant	1,752	5,129	93
Accounting clerk	1,043	1,823	75
Attorney	2,584	8,431	226
Auditor	1,795	3,309	84
Buyer	1,770	3,442	94
Computer operator	1,144	2,416	111
Computer programmer	1,736	3,578	106
Drafter	1,088	2,584	137
Engineering technician	1,407	2,726	94
Engineer	2,322	6,585	183
File clerk	861	1,302	51
Secretary	1,361	2,338	72
Stenographer	1,531	1,812	18
Systems analyst	2,428	5,981	173
Typist	1,049	1,404	34

SOURCES: University of Texas Medical Branch (1986); Bureau of Labor Statistics (1986).

of the occupations selected for inclusion in Table 6-1 were chosen because they require investments in education comparable to those required in the allied health fields. Others were chosen to show how compensation for a lesser educational investment compares with compensation in allied health occupations. The table indicates that starting salaries for allied health fields in some cases do not compare unfavorably with other occupations requiring similar educational investments or that students might consider as alternative careers. For example, auditors and accountants must have bachelor's degrees and receive mean monthly starting salaries of $1,797 and $1,752, respectively; these are similar to or a little below the mean starting salaries for physical and occupational therapists and medical record administrators, occupations that also require bachelor's degrees. In computer fields the starting salaries of systems analysts exceed the starting salaries for speech–language pathologists and audiologists for whom a master's degree is the entry level requirement. Engineering technicians, who are described as "semiprofessional," and computer operators are included in technical support operations and can be considered equivalent to medical laboratory and medical record technicians with associate degrees. Engineering technicians start at salaries roughly $150 per month higher than the equivalent allied health fields; computer operators start at roughly $100 per month lower. It will come as no surprise that attorneys and engineers start at salaries closer to the mean maximum rate than to the starting salary for speech–language pathologists and audiologists.

Increases in earnings over the length of a career are substantially lower in allied health fields than in the other listed occupations. The salary spread for each of the non-allied health fields listed, except typists, is larger than that in any allied health field.

In sum, these data indicate that although allied health practitioners' starting pay is not always competitive with the earnings of workers in alternative fields, the differences are not large. However, the relative lack of a pay ladder puts individuals who stay in allied health fields at a significant economic disadvantage. Although there is no empirical evidence that prospective students turn away from allied health careers because of wage compression, it seems likely that students know of it and react by seeking careers with brighter economic futures.

An important factor for employers who are considering raising pay to alleviate personnel shortages is the value of the job to the institution. This factor is brought out starkly when administrators consider the costs and benefits of expanding the pay ladder—in other words, paying more for experience. In some facilities, and for some allied health fields, experience may be of little value from the employer's perspective. Indeed, recent graduates may be preferable if they bring more up-to-date skills or the enthusiasm of a novice to the job. Why then should an organization reward experience? One answer is the high cost of recruiting and orienting new personnel. In addition, some would say that treating employees like disposable objects by not recognizing loyalty or tenure is simply inhumane management. Furthermore, by combining further education with pay and career progression, the quality of services may be upgraded and advances in knowledge can be incorporated into the facility's practice. This latter point becomes more important when the stream of newly trained practitioners slows. Employers who must substantially increase pay to attract needed personnel may consider examining job content and restricting tasks to ensure that the now more expensive personnel are used effectively. If higher compensation succeeds in increasing by even a small amount the time that individuals remain in the allied health work force (either by continuing to work or by returning to work), the impact on supply can be significant.

Although supply problems may be alleviated by increasing compensation, employers may be reluctant to act. The most fundamental and obvious reason for this reluctance has to do with the facility's bottom line. Higher salaries may not appear justified by the revenue generated for a service. Another possible deterrent for some managers is that pay raises in one occupation may produce similar salary expectations in other hospital occupations.

In the face of price competition and prospective payment, hospital financial administrators feel they have reason to be reluctant to increase salary expenses. At a recent Senate Finance Subcommittee hearing, a spokesman for the American Hospital Association said that the level of Medicare payments constrained hospitals' revenues so that nurses' salaries could not be increased (Health Professions Report, 1987). Yet data indicate that the early 1980s were relatively profitable for hospitals. Hospital operating margins—key indicators of their fiscal health—peaked in 1984 (Table 6-2). By September 1987 total operating margins and patient revenue operating margins in community hospitals were close to the levels of the early 1980s, and there were no signs that the deterioration in financial status had ceased. However, operating margins in the 1960s and 1970s were consistently lower than in the 1980s. Thus, although some hospitals are running in the red and the situation for the average hospital has deteriorated in the past few years, hospital administrators with longer memories may not be feeling so pressured that they will not consider salary increases.

Furthermore, a hospital's financial viability rests to a great extent on its ability to admit and care for patients. If a lack of staff in any allied health field interferes with this ability or slows down discharge rates, then a wage increase is likely to be more than offset by revenue increases or decreases in other costs that result from the return to normal services.

Indeed, employers who need scarce allied health employees may have no choice but to raise wages. As one observer put it,

Gone are the days when doctors and hospitals could look upon America's bright and motivated women as a source of cheap labor denied economic opportunities elsewhere. To attract this pool of talented workers into health care, we must get used to the notion of paying competitive wages. (Reinhardt, 1987)

TABLE 6-2   Operating Margins (percentage) for
U.S. Community Hospitals, 1963–1987

| | Operating Margin | |
Year	Total Revenue	Patient Revenue
1963	2.5	−6.0
1965	2.3	−5.1
1967	2.6	−4.6
1969	2.4	−3.9
1971	2.3	−3.2
1973	1.2	−4.4
1975	2.3	−3.0
1977	3.5	−0.6
1979	3.9	−0.6
1981	4.7	0.2
1983	5.1	1.0
1985	5.2	1.5
1987[a]	4.8	0.3

[a]January through November.

SOURCE: American Hospital Association, Hospital Data Center
(1988).

Other Strategies to Increase Job and
Occupational Tenure

A review of the recent periodical literature of hospital administration reveals scant
coverage of human resource management. Most of that attention is focused on
short-term issues in spite of radical and long-term changes in the hospital's environment as the nation redefines how health care is perceived, delivered and paid
for. (Mansfield, 1987)

So opens the report of a literature review of the nine major hospital
administration and personnel journals for the years 1983 through 1985,
forcing the conclusion that human resource management is not a high
priority for health services researchers or for their audience of health care
corporate executives and hospital administrators. This is a surprising finding when we consider that payroll represents about half of hospital expenses. The review also noted that, of 157 articles related to human resources,
71 percent were published in *Nursing Management*. The committee's own
search of the Cumulative Index of Nursing and Allied Health Literature
(which covers nursing and allied health personnel) and of selected psychological, management, and popular publications was similarly revealing.
Searching literature published since 1983 on such descriptors as the occupational titles of each of the 10 allied health fields covered in this report,
as well as "manpower," "turnover," "retention," and "personnel," 36 articles
were found. Thirty related to nursing.

Human resource administrators are often in a perplexing situation. They manage a resource that is fundamental to ensuring the quantity and quality of care desired by management and whose cost accounts for a major portion of the facility's expenditures. Yet, as the committee heard at one of its workshops, during site visits, and through discussions with knowledgeable observers, human resource managers are not often given the visibility or status they need to do their complex job. Moreover, even large health care corporations have not generally changed the way they manage human resources as they adapt to the changing health care environment.

Human resource administrators are most often expected to respond to and implement the decisions of strategic planners. Yet strategic planners do not always recognize the constraints and changes in labor markets that confront human resource administrators. If, however, strategic management and human resource management were brought together, several benefits could ensue. The importance of human resource management as a vital part of facility management would be confirmed. Plans would be made with cognizance of labor market conditions, and human resource administrators would be in a position to act early to implement plans in whose development they had participated.

However, more often, personnel administrators must assemble a labor force to provide services decided on by other administrators. Experience shows that it is not until labor markets become tight that upper management supports serious efforts to retain and attract allied health practitioners.

The previous section suggested that pay increases would enhance the supply of allied health personnel. But money, although important, is only one of the many factors that make employment in a field an attractive alternative to leisure, home activities, or other types of employment. What makes employment attractive? What nonmonetary aspects of a job produce satisfaction or dissatisfaction? The knowledge base for answering these questions about the allied health fields is sparse. A review of the general job satisfaction literature notes that explanations of differences in satisfaction are usually related either to individual characteristics of workers, including their needs and values, or to the nature of the jobs and the characteristics of employing organizations (Hanson et al., 1987).

Employers should not assume that factors they cannot control, such as family responsibilities, dominate employee decisions. A review of studies of self-reported reasons for resignation of nurses notes that at least one-third of the resignations resulted from job dissatisfaction, and a recent study attributed three-quarters of "contemplated turnover" to job problems (Weisman et al., 1981).

Workers' job requirements are known to vary according to sex, race, age, and so on. The Hudson Institute in its project "Workforce 2000" drew some conclusions about work force problems that employers will have to address if they want to hire the workers of the future. With the increasing age of the work force, they must be concerned about the adaptability of these workers and their willingness to learn. With regard to working women, reform is needed in day care, time off (time off for child care, sick leave, flexible hours, etc.), and policies to assist welfare mothers in entering the labor force. The full utilization of the work force will require integrating blacks and Hispanics into the labor market, but that means overcoming the fact that they are also the least advantaged groups in our society with respect to skill levels and educational backgrounds (Hudson Institute, 1987). Employers using an allied health work force that is largely composed of women will want to pay attention to findings about what makes a job appealing to women. Some results suggest that women's unique work needs stem from their dual responsibilities at home and at work. Studies indicate that factors such as travel time to and from work are more important to women than to men. For those women who are not career motivated and who are more interested in supplementing the household income or getting out of the house, jobs that substitute other rewards for advancement, stability, and high pay may have attractions (Hanson et al., 1987). Some differences in work force behavior between men and women include women being less likely to remain in one occupation and one particular job than men, and women having more frequent career interruptions—although this latter difference may be diminishing. Women who pursue longer term careers are less likely to differ from men in the factors that contribute to job satisfaction.

For many workers, satisfaction, dissatisfaction, and decisions to leave or stay in a job or field are based on factors related to their job tasks, how they fit into the organizational structure, and expectations about their working conditions. The nursing literature is replete with analyses of reasons for dissatisfaction—boredom, limited possibilities for advancement, lack of status, lack of opportunities for full use of their skills, lack of further educational opportunities, lack of autonomy, problems in relationships with physicians, and staffing patterns that do not allow for the provision of high quality care. (See, for example, Price and Mueller, 1981; Weisman et al., 1981 and a literature review that notes that every major study since the 1960s has pointed to the factors of autonomy, interpersonal relations, and job status as critical components of job satisfaction, Institute of Medicine, 1983). Satisfaction often stems from recognition by peers and supervisors, professional growth, perceptions of being important to patient care and to the institution, and involvement in decisions concerning both patient care and institutional policy. An analysis of the importance of these factors in determining turnover found that autonomy is the strongest predictor of job satisfaction, and the supervisor's responsiveness to the nurse's work and communication needs is the best predictor of a sense of autonomy (Weisman et al., 1981).

Findings of this sort have generated numerous strategies (not always adopted) to enrich nurses' working environments in order to extend both job and occupational tenure. Strategies include creating decision-making links among the chief executive officer, nursing service administrator, and staff nurses; introducing primary nursing; and developing patterns of upward mobility. One important difference between nursing and allied health in this regard is that although allied health practitioners hold administrative jobs—managing laboratories, dietary services, radiology departments, and so on—there is usually no umbrella allied health administrator position to promote the interests and raise the level of visibility of the allied health work force. By way of contrast, hospitals commonly have a director or vice-president for nursing, who increasingly is assuming even broader responsibilities such as vice-president for patient services, which sometimes subsumes allied health services. The fragmented, diverse nature of allied health makes the development of a unified power block within institutions difficult. Consequently, these fields have found it difficult to establish the linkages to central administration that have been helpful in addressing work environment issues for nurses.

The nurse–physician relationship is an important factor in the way nurses perceive their roles and in their job satisfaction. For many allied health occupations, physicians also play a major role in shaping an environment that will induce practitioners to extend their tenure. Reporting on a successful effort to lengthen nurses' tenure, one nursing administrator noted:

The physician's role in nurse retention cannot be overstated. When there is close communication between physicians and nurses, an increased level of satisfaction for both parties is evident. Nothing enhances the role of the nurse as much as awareness that a physician is hearing her perspective of a patient care issue. Orthopedic physicians and orthopedic nurses simultaneously requested that nursing practice be expanded to include more activities. Nursing activities then were planned and implemented as a joint venture. (Araujo, 1980)

Reports like these underline the importance of action by facility administrators to encourage physicians to be involved in efforts to extend tenure.

Also of importance is the role of research. Knowledge of the factors that persuade practitioners to leave or remain in their allied health field could be usefully expanded—and what seems obvious is not always the right answer. For example, a small study of burnout among respiratory care personnel (Shelledy and Mikles, 1987) found, to the authors' surprise, that hours worked per shift or per week, shift assignment, frequency of rotation of daily work assignments, variety of procedures performed, and number of treatments per shift did not relate to burnout. Lower burnout rates were found in practitioners with higher educational levels, a greater sense of autonomy, and perceptions that high-quality work was being done in their departments.

Just as with salary decisions, however, it is unreasonable to expect facility administrators to make changes that are not in their institutions' best interests. Although opportunities for upward mobility are generally seen as an important element of job satisfaction, there are clearly limits to the number of higher level practitioners that are needed. In some cases, any sort of upward mobility may be impracticable. As an alternative, employers may find that encouraging an expansion of skills to another area can sustain employee interest and extend tenure in work that could become tedious. Methodist Hospital in Indianapolis, Indiana, sponsors a program called "Add-A-Comp" that enables individuals with health care experience to acquire additional competencies. The program also fulfills employers' needs for cross-trained personnel. Moreover, employees who are more challenged and stimulated are less likely to leave an employer or the work force.

A secondary benefit of improving job satisfaction will accrue to employers interested in avoiding unionization among their employees. Health care union membership, which has been growing despite a national decline in other union membership, stands at about 20 percent. Recent organizing issues have included quality of care, quality of work, stress, job restructuring, and benefits. Because of similar concerns with issues of compensation, job security, and meaningful work involvement, professionals and white-collar workers are identifying with blue-collar workers and with unionized groups (American Hospital Association, Department of Human Resources, 1986). Thus, health care employers cannot rely on their employees' sense of professional status to avoid unionization. By making adaptations to increase job satisfaction, however, employers can attend to issues that might otherwise result in union activity.

Lower level health care practitioners such as orderlies and technicians have negotiated contracts that include retraining programs in case of layoff. As a result, one hospital has started training programs for sterilization technicians and licensed practical nurses (Lunzer, 1987). Organizations with contracts like these have a ready pool of workers whose training can be channeled toward skills needed by the facility. Thus, although unionization can reduce an employer's ability to redesign jobs and may reduce work force flexibility, it can also occasionally increase the options available in uses of manpower.

Job satisfaction also relates to the socialization process that occurs during professional education and through contact with role models. This socialization emphasizes the importance of upward mobility. Studies of nursing indicate that higher levels of education correlate with a greater likelihood of job dissatisfaction (Weisman et al., 1981). Although this correlation could be related to frustrations that occur if practitioners do not fully use their skills, the job dissatisfaction research findings relating to upward mobility, role, use of skills, and autonomy all point to the conclusion that some discrepancy exists between what employers need and the aspirations and needs of graduates from educational programs. More extensive communication among educators, employers, and professional associations might help to improve the fit between the needs of employers and those of their employees, and thus might also help extend job and occupational tenure.

The problem of matching education with workplace needs is also addressed in Chapter 5, in which educational issues are discussed. That chapter contains a recommendation that the groups most influential in developing work site tasks, curricula, and aspirations—educators, employers, and professional associations—should interact more. One special problem they might address is to attempt to ensure that the diversity of employers' needs is matched by a similar diversity in the education of practitioners. Allied health jobs exist in numerous settings—hospitals, nursing homes, primary care practices, and so on. Different settings vary in their need for various ranges of skills and levels of expertise, even in a single field. Reflecting this diversity in the content and level of educational programs would help increase job and occupational tenure by matching practitioners' abilities and aspirations with patient and institutional needs.

Another issue that could usefully be addressed by employers, professional associations, and educators also relates to professional aspirations. Allied health practitioners working in health care facilities of all types become part of a larger group of workers with an organizational structure. The "medical model" of autonomous work, which is pursued by the many physical therapists, speech–language pathologists, and laboratory technologists who become independent consultants, is not always either realistic or attainable in complex medical settings or for most practitioners. These practitioners need goals that provide satisfactory alternatives to independent practice.

A further element, already noted in Chapter 5, is the provision of clinical sites for education. The number of health care facilities providing sites for the clinical component of educational programs is decreasing. Employers should consider that the cost of providing clinical education is often offset in the long run by an increased supply of practitioners and the avoidance of personnel shortages.

ENHANCING THE USE OF THE EXISTING WORK FORCE

Easing scarcities in the supply of allied health practitioners by expanding educational capacity is a strategy that only begins to be effective several years after initiation. Of more immediate effect would be extending the tenure of existing workers and bringing back into the work force individuals who have chosen to leave it. A still different approach is to examine ways of using the existing work force more productively and effectively.

In the early part of this chapter, it was noted that when demand for allied health practitioners exceeds supply, market forces will drive up the wages and salaries employers must pay to hire the needed personnel. This increased compensation will, in the long run, enlarge the supply of workers. It will also diminish the upward thrust of demand as employers, with a more expensive work force, seek ways to contain this expense. An approach that has the potential to provide a dual benefit—increasing job satisfaction as well as using staff more efficiently—is the restructuring of tasks and staff deployment. This approach requires that administrators shed traditional ways of thinking about individual and departmental responsibilities and allow themselves to consider new staff and task configurations. Sometimes expanded roles for lower level staff will permit more flexible staffing of units, to the extent that regulation allows. Occasionally it is possible to combine tasks to form a new, enlarged work module. Using multidisciplinary teams can break down departmental barriers to permit enlarged spheres of responsibility for individual staff. Many new configurations of tasks and staff are possible, but they must be preceded by an investment in human resource management to engage in the necessary fundamental analyses and rethinking of tasks.

A familiar industrial response to manpower shortages or to perceptions of overly high personnel expenses is attempts to improve labor productivity. However, there is a common perception that the service sector of the economy has very low rates of productivity growth (Kutcher and Mark, 1983) and that health care, because it requires a hands-on, one-on-one approach, is not amenable to measures to increase productivity. Certainly, if operating margins continue to deteriorate, it seems reasonable to expect administrators to seek ways of improving productivity. If health care is viewed not as a whole but rather as individual specific services, some areas appear to have some potential for productivity gain. One of the areas often cited is automation in medical laboratories.

Today's financial incentives to reduce costs are expected to encourage the development and adoption of technologies that improve productivity. Some structural changes in the way health care is delivered also have a potential for productivity improvement. For instance, large-scale specialized delivery sites (e.g., special surgery or imaging units) may be able to reap economies of scale in the use of personnel. However, it is unlikely that changes such as these will outweigh other changes—for example, the move to home services and new, complex technologies—that use manpower in a less productive manner.

The advantages and disadvantages of cross-trained or multicompetent allied health personnel have been discussed for many years. In the past the context was their use in solving rural health care staffing problems. Today, they are seen by some as innovative solutions to personnel shortages, especially in small hospitals, physicians' offices, and other small delivery units. Multicompetent personnel are also regarded by some larger hospitals as economical sources of staff who must be available 24 hours a day but whose work time is punctuated by low-use periods. More generally, as revenue restrictions force administrators to examine ways to control labor expenses, employers are becoming interested in increasing labor productivity by decreasing specialization, as evidenced by the American Hospital Association's sponsorship of a number of workshops on the multiskilled concept. A 1986 national survey of medical laboratory managers indicated that 46.3 percent said they could use cross-trained personnel (Watrous, 1987). A survey of hospital administrators, directors of nursing, directors of community health organizations, and physicians in Philadelphia showed that multicompetent practitioners were already employed in approximately a quarter of the hospitals. Sixty percent of the hospital administrators surveyed said they were willing to employ multicompetent practitioners now (Low and Weisbord, 1987), and educators report that their multicompetent graduates generally find jobs that use their training (Blayney, 1982). Using multicompetent practitioners is not an all-purpose solution, but it is the result of an effort to think through the tasks that must be performed and how the educational system can respond to help meet the need.

Productivity improvements, however they are achieved, are defined as decreasing the input per unit of output. Thus, we say that productivity is increased if a laboratory worker, for example, increases the number of tests he or she performs per hour. Another way of thinking about how best to use allied health manpower and thus improve productivity is to redefine output in terms of a contribution to patient care. To make this definition operational, we must evaluate effectiveness. Output can be increased, and pressures on manpower supply relieved, by reducing services that do not contribute to patient welfare.

Suggestions of unnecessary care (or at least a lack of agreement about what is appropriate care) are found in studies that show variations in the amounts of service performed in different countries, in different regions of the same country, and in different types of organizations. But information about the identification of effective and ineffective care by allied health practitioners is not plentiful. Shroeder (1987) reports on studies that have detected patterns of overuse. Overused procedures or technologies, according to these studies, include white blood cell differential counts, measurements of serum lactic dehydrogenase, blood cross matches, barium enema studies, upper gastrointestinal series, nursing service orders, tonsillectomies, chest x rays, prescription drugs, preoperative screening tests, and thyroid function tests. Shroeder adds:

A recent study from our institution estimated the proportion of redundancy among a wide variety of diagnostic and nursing services for patients on a general medical ward. Of the more than 8,000 services ordered for 173 patients during the observation period, 21% were judged to be unnecessary by faculty auditors who reviewed the medical records. The most overused services were partial thromboplastin time (deemed unnecessary in 63% of uses), stat/emergency orders (43%), nuclear medicine studies (26%) and platelet counts (25%).

Another way of assessing overutilization is by determining whether clinical services contribute to patient management. Reports from several teaching institutions and one community hospital show that as few as 3% to 5% of diagnostic tests are actually used in the management of the patients for whom they are ordered. (Shroeder, 1987)

Probably the allied health service most studied for overutilization is the clinical laboratory. Barr (1987) suggests that ensuring effectiveness is in part the responsibility of laboratory scientists, who should ask a number of questions such as "Are the ordered tests appropriate for the patient's clinical condition?" "What level of accuracy and precision is needed for clinical judgment?" Other investigators are working to develop methods for detecting overutilization (see, for example, Eisenberg, 1982; Garg et al., 1985).

Many questions about effectiveness remain unanswered. If cost-containment pressures continue to mount, some employing organizations may initiate their own research. HMOs may shift their focus from a concentration on reducing hospitalization to reducing ineffective care in other areas. Other prospectively paid providers also have reason to try to eliminate excess services.

Finally, some allied health practitioners may want to undertake effectiveness research to justify their place in patient care. Until such research is done, they may be vulnerable to cuts by institutions seeking to reduce personnel expenses.

EMPLOYERS WITH SPECIAL PROBLEMS

Some health care providers are particularly disadvantaged in the competition for allied health practitioners. These employers will find that, for one reason or another, they cannot implement many of the strategies discussed previously in this chapter. In this section the committee discusses the predicaments of two of these employers—rural health care facilities and nursing homes and other long-term care sites. The committee also suggests some strategies they might find useful in trying to cope with their needs for allied health manpower.

Rural Health Care Facilities

According to the Census Bureau, more than a quarter of the population of the United States lives in rural areas. These areas differ from other parts of the nation in many aspects, and often these differences have implications for the delivery of health care.

Rural areas are more sparsely populated than urban localities, and therefore fewer people live in the catchment area of a rural health care provider. In addition, rural populations are more often poor (14 percent below the poverty level, compared with 11 percent in metropolitan areas in 1981) and elderly (13 percent over 65 compared with 10.7 percent in 1980); therefore, they have different health statuses and health care needs. Examples of rural health status differences include higher infant mortality rates; a higher incidence of hypertension, coronary heart disease, emphysema, and some other chronic conditions; but a lower incidence of acute conditions on the whole (Cordes and Wright, 1985).

Some of these differences may be related to differences in the health care services available to rural populations. The hospital-bed-to-population ratio is approximately the same for rural and nonrural areas, thanks to the hospital construction program mandated by the Hill Burton Act of 1946. Yet the number of health professionals in relation to total population is less in rural areas, and the range of services offered by hospitals is narrower (Cordes and Wright, 1985).

That rural hospitals have special problems is well documented. Of the 5,732 community hospitals in the United States in 1986, 47 percent were rural and 17 percent had fewer than 50 beds. Eighty percent of the small hospitals in the United States are rural. Small hospitals anywhere are more likely to close than larger hospitals: of the 214 community hospitals that closed between 1980 and 1985, 75 percent had fewer than 50 beds, 86 were rural, and 128 were urban (Health Resources and Services Administration, Office of the Administrator, 1987).

The reasons for the vulnerability of rural hospitals may relate not only to their rural characteristics but also to their small size. Analyses of American Hospital Association data (Table 6-3) show that, between 1980 and 1986, the smaller the hospital, the greater the deterioration in several key indicators of strength. Operating margins, admissions, and occupancy rates have fallen more and are lower in smaller hospitals. These data show why raising salaries to attract allied health practitioners is not feasible for many small rural hospitals.

It is more difficult to attract practitioners to rural employment than to other settings. Table 6-4 contrasts the ratio of practitioners to population in metropolitan and nonmetropolitan settings for some allied health professions. It is evident that metropolitan areas in 1980 had a more plentiful

TABLE 6-3 Selected Indicators of Hospital Strength

Indicator	Percentage Change, 1980–1986	Actual Percentage, 1986
Operating margin		
All hospitals	1.0	5.4
Hospitals with 25–49 beds	−4.8	1.5
Hospitals with less than 25 beds	−4.5	−6.3
Admissions		
All hospitals	−8.0	
Hospitals with 25–49 beds	−39.8	
Hospitals with less than 25 beds	−44.8	
Occupancy		
All hospitals	−16.1	63.2
Hospitals with 25–49 beds	−36.7	33.2
Hospitals with less than 25 beds	−31.7	27.4

SOURCE: Health Resources and Service Administration, Office of the Administrator (1987).

supply of practitioners in all the listed fields. The lower rural concentration may be due in part to the lower concentration in rural areas of some of the individuals and organizations that usually employ allied health practitioners—dentists, physicians, and so on. But with the hospital-bed-to-population ratio quite similar in rural and nonrural areas, the usual employers of the majority of allied health practitioners would seem to be present.

For rural hospitals, allied health employment problems can be viewed

TABLE 6-4 Geographic Distribution of Selected Allied Health Professions, 1980

Allied Health Profession	Number per 100,000 Population		Nonmetro Ratio as Percentage of Metro Ratio
	Nonmetro	Metro	
Dietitian	26.0	30.9	84
Speech therapist	14.4	19.5	74
Health aide (except nursing)	99.9	138.5	72
Inhalation therapist	16.6	23.1	72
Dental assistant	53.2	75.2	71
Health record technician	5.0	7.2	69
Radiologic technician	31.0	46.3	67
Physical therapist	12.7	21.1	60
Clinical laboratory technician	68.9	120.5	57
Dental hygienist	12.3	23.1	53
Occupational therapist	3.5	9.3	38

SOURCE: Hamburg (1985).

in three ways: (1) the difficulty of attracting practitioners to rural employment, (2) being able to afford the practitioners, and (3) finding practitioners with the type of education and training that suits them for rural employment.

The geographic maldistribution of personnel in some health care fields has been well studied. Less work has focused on the maldistribution of allied health practitioners. Some lessons can be drawn from what is known about other types of health care practitioners. Allied health education, like most health care education, takes place primarily in metropolitan areas. Most often, clinical experience is provided in acute care settings with sufficient patient volumes to support state-of-the-art, high-technology services. Graduates are subsequently drawn to employment in similar settings for several reasons. They perceive these settings as offering high-quality care, personal challenges, full use of their education, and the stimulation of contact with peers and supervisors. By contrast, to city-reared workers, rural facilities are an unknown setting, often perceived as isolated, technologically backward, and with little room for advancement in their field. One lesson from studies of health personnel education and employment decisions is that graduates who grew up in rural areas or whose education included experience in these areas are more likely to choose rural employment.

Individuals whose roots are in rural areas can find the monetary and psychological costs of attending educational programs in metropolitan areas prohibitive. Taking education to rural areas would help bring these individuals into the allied health work force. Such techniques include the use of telecommunications technologies and "circuit riding" faculty. Employers could assist such efforts by encouraging qualified allied health staff to participate in teaching. They could also provide classroom space and clinical experience in their facilities.

The employer's role in increasing the supply of graduates who are familiar with rural settings is thus twofold: first, to work with local high schools and career counsellors to encourage students to pursue allied health careers and second, to work with allied health educators to provide clinical experience in their facilities. In Alabama a group of junior colleges and the University of Alabama formed a consortium in 1969 to enhance the supply of allied health practitioners in underserved areas. As described by Keith Blayney (1981), dean of the School of Community and Allied Health at the University of Alabama:

In 1969, the state's junior college presidents and representatives of the University of Alabama in Birmingham (UAB) met and endorsed the concept of a consortium to link the two-year schools with UAB. The benefits were readily apparent—by sharing students with the Regional Technical Institute (RTI) at UAB, the duplication of specific allied health programs and their high costs could be avoided. Also, students could attend school near their homes for the first year of the program.

After the second year at RTI, graduates were likely to return to their homes, located in the medically underserved areas of the state, and provide ancillary support for medical services there. As the program developed, efforts were made to establish clinical training sites for the students in or near their homes, thus providing an additional impetus to return home.

Before their year of technical training at the RTI ends, the students spend six to eight weeks in on-site clinical training. Although the RTI is located in the heart of UAB's Medical Center, where there is a large volume and variety of clinical materials, it soon became clear that the Medical Center alone would not be sufficient to provide adequate experience for all the allied health students. As a result, linkage students can now complete the last weeks of their clinical training at smaller health care facilities throughout the state. These facilities range from doctors' offices to nursing homes, clinics, and hospitals. This arrangement has other advantages. The students can work close to their homes, in facilities similar in size and scope to those in which they will probably work. Also, upon graduation, the students are often offered positions at the facilities where they did their training.

Since the number of clinical facilities has been expanded, a higher percentage of RTI graudates have returned to rural areas to work. In 1977, 59% of graduates of programs that have clinical training sites outside of Birmingham took jobs outside of the city, while only 34% of the graduates who had no clinical affiliation outside Birmingham left the city.

An evaluation of the linkage program after 11 years found that 66 percent of the graduates who remained in allied health fields returned to their home counties to work (Cooper, 1982). Clearly, this model requires serious commitments by employers and leaders in educational institutions who are concerned with and willing to help resolve some of the problems of rural care.

Another type of linkage would be for rural employers to arrange regular, periodic secondment to an urban facility for their allied health employees. Arrangements with educational programs and leaders in allied health fields to provide lectures or seminars to practitioners in rural areas might also help dispel fears of isolation and ensure that practitioners are kept up to date in their field—generous allowances for continuing education would also help to achieve this goal.

Rural employers who operate low-volume facilities that cannot afford or fully use a full-time staff member can also try to develop linkages. In Wisconsin, 22 small rural hospitals have formed a cooperative that shares services, mobile technologies, and professional staff who travel among the hospitals (Health Resources and Services Administration, Office of the Administrator, 1987). Employer-initiated sharing (as opposed to employees who on their own find several part-time jobs) may also appeal to practitioners because they get full-time employment and benefits that are often not offered to part-time employees.

A further model of cooperation among employers is the regional organization of services with each hospital specializing in certain services. The Robert Wood Johnson Foundation is offering grants for this and other models to help rural health providers with financial problems.

The notion of multicompetent personnel is frequently suggested as a solution for low-volume rural providers. There are currently a small number of programs training multicompetent practitioners. A program providing dual certification at Southern Illinois University at Carbondale, which was started in the 1970s, is popular with rural communities. Recently, however, students have sought certification in only one field, a trend that is thought to be the result of better pay for single-field jobs (Cordes and Wright, 1985). As the committee has noted, the ability to pay competitive salaries is likely to be limited in rural locations and is dependent on reimbursement decisions. Still, without attractive compensation, efforts to ease rural manpower problems will fail in the long run.

Employers who want to hire multicompetent practitioners can help by ensuring that educators know that a demand for them exists and also by making known the mix of competencies they need. If an individual's education is tailored to an employer's requirements, the employer can use the practitioner efficiently, and thus maximize the results from his or her salary.

The third type of problem of rural health providers—finding allied health personnel with the special skills needed for employment in small rural settings—can also be alleviated by linkages with educational programs. Again, providing clinical sites for students ensures that they learn about rural practice. Models for these programs already exist. We have already mentioned the University of Alabama's Linkage Program. Another is the University of Wisconsin Medical Technology Program, which places students in a generalist capacity in small hospital laboratories. This program is said to have contributed significantly to students' interest in clinical laboratories in community and rural hospitals, as the majority of students have been employed in such laboratories after graduation (Bamberg, 1981). Still another model offers students experience on health care teams in rural Kentucky. Students at Kentucky Southern Community College are exposed to rural practice and learn how to function with other members of the health profession team (Bamberg, 1981).

One type of linkage already in place for some rural providers is membership in a multiprovider organization. Regardless of whether this organization is horizontally or vertically integrated, if it includes both rural and urban sites, then an opportunity for innovative solutions to staffing problems exists. Rural members of the organization might negotiate arrangements whereby service at or rotation through a rural location becomes a necessary step for upward mobility in the organization's career ladder.

Long-Term Care Facilities

Long-term care providers (e.g., nursing homes and chronic mental care facilities), like rural health care providers, have special needs and characteristics that make some of the strategies suggested in the earlier part of this chapter inapplicable. For example, it is difficult to increase salaries to attract allied health practitioners when reimbursement is extremely tight. It is also often impossible to provide advancement paths in small facilities, a category into which many nursing homes fall.

Chapter 8 explores some of the reasons long-term care facilities are not seen as attractive work sites. A number of these reasons are subjective and perceptual. Caring for elderly patients and patients with chronic or mental diseases is seen as unsatisfactory in contrast to working with patients in whom real and lasting improvements can be realized. Mental disturbances in patients make practitioners' tasks more difficult and are a condition for which their education often fails to prepare them. In the course of this study the committee uncovered a concern among the providers of long-term care that educators and practitioners in many allied health fields are both unwilling and unprepared for work with elderly patients and patients with chronic conditions. Remarks like the following were often heard: "Physical therapists would rather work in sports medicine and with the acute phase of trauma rehabilitation than with frail, confused, nursing home patients." Long-term care facilities in some regions are not perceived as giving high-quality or sometimes even adequate care. Clearly, a long-term, major effort is needed to change perceptions of work in the chronic care sector. The figures in Table 6-5 suggest that, for dietitians working part-time and for full- and part-time occupational and physical therapists,

TABLE 6-5 Average Hourly Earnings in Hospitals and Nursing and Personal Care Facilities, 1985

Occupation	Hospital	Nursing and Personal Care Facilities	Percentage Difference
Full-time			
Dietitian	$11.52	$10.69	−7.2
Occupational therapist	11.41	11.11	−2.6
Physical therapist	11.98	13.25	10.6
Head nurse	14.37	12.40	−13.7
Part-time			
Dietitian	11.66	11.60	−0.5
Occupational therapist	11.78	11.32	−3.9
Physical therapist	12.71	15.63	23.0
Head nurse	14.84	11.58	−22.0

SOURCE: Bureau of Labor Statistics (1987a,b).

compensation is not likely to be a decisive factor in choosing between employment in a nursing or personal care facility and employment in a hospital. Job satisfaction, however, may be greater in acute care settings.

Lower level personnel—nursing aides and orderlies—have fewer opportunities in the acute care sector. Yet for these individuals the average hourly salary of $5.15 for nursing aides in nursing and personal care facilities might not be competitive with alternative employment in such places as fast-food restaurants, which pay more, require no formal postsecondary education, and in which working conditions are less stressful (Kerschner, 1987).

Long-term care employers can try to use some of the options suggested in the earlier section for rural health employers. Establishing links with allied health education programs to increase curriculum content relating to long-term care could help to deflect some of students' anxieties about serving these special populations. Similarly, providing clinical sites for students can dispel misconceptions about the work, enhance the skills needed to serve in long-term care, and establish ties with an employer.

An Institute of Medicine committee in 1983 recommended that educational programs for nursing should provide more formal instruction and clinical experience in geriatrics. It was believed that this would augment the supply of new nurses interested in caring for the elderly (Institute of Medicine, 1983). This could also be an effective strategy for allied health practitioners, and it is discussed further in Chapter 8.

CONCLUSIONS AND RECOMMENDATIONS

Human resources planning has not been a high priority or an integral part of strategic planning in the health care organization. As a result, there has been little emphasis on or investment in research and experimentation in structuring staffing policies and working environments. Moreover, when there is a plentiful manpower supply, there is little incentive to undertake such an onerous task. The committee foresees, however, that the availability of alternative employment and stable or falling enrollments in allied health education programs will find some employers—particularly hospitals—unprepared to solve staffing difficulties and fulfill service demands. Relying on the government to create incentives, such as educational subsidies for entry into professions that turn out to be poor careers, and complaining about licensing barriers are not likely to be as effective solutions as an investment in improved management capability. Except in the face of appreciably lower operating margins, it will be difficult for administrators to make a convincing case for increased reimbursement (e.g., through the prospective payment system) to help support salary increases without having demonstrated to payers that management solutions have been pursued to their practical limits. To date, employers have relied on new graduates and short-term incentives to offset turnover and prolong tenure in the work force.

The committee recommends that employers strive to increase the supply of allied health practitioners by attracting people into allied health occupations and prolonging their attachment to their fields. Some ways to do this include increasing compensation, developing mechanisms for retention, and establishing flexible schedules and educational opportunities. Employers should also look to new labor pools that include men, minorities, career changers, and individuals with handicapping conditions.

Yet attracting and keeping individuals in allied health fields is only one part of a strategy to relieve pressures. **The committee also recommends that chief executive officers, human resource directors, and other health care administrators develop methods for the effective utilization of the existing supply of allied health personnel. Such methods must grow out of experimentation with new ways of organizing work efficiently and distributing labor among skill levels while ensuring that the quality of care is not compromised.**

As the health industry looks more aggressively beyond cost savings through reduced hospital utilization and toward technology assessment, quality assurance, and nonhospital utilization controls, it is appropriate that allied health services should come under scrutiny. This scrutiny should be viewed by management as an opportunity to work with allied health professionals to use a scarce labor resource effectively. It is also an opportunity for the allied health field to help provide the research underpinning that will be the foundation for decision making.

The committee recommends that health care providers and administrators seek innovative ways to channel limited allied health resources toward activities of proven benefit to consumers. Agencies such as the National Center for Health Services Research and the Health Care Financing Administration should sponsor research and technology assessment to ensure that allied health services are effective and that they are organized efficiently. Associations of employers, unions, accrediting agencies, and professional associations should assist in disseminating research findings and providing technical assistance in their implementation.

If employers are to use limited human resources effectively, personnel must be appropriately educated. In addition, the goals and aspirations of new graduates should accord with the realities of life in the workplace; otherwise, their job satisfaction is likely to be undermined. **The committee therefore strongly recommends that health care administrators and academic administrators engage in constructive exchanges to improve the** congruence of employment and education. **These exchanges, which should take place at the state and local levels, will be enhanced by the participation of educators who are also leaders of the professional associations.** Although the analyses in this study are most often based on national data, the committee emphasizes that conditions differ among states and even among localities. State legislators have a legitimate interest in ensuring an adequate supply of health care personnel, educational opportunities for the states' citizens, and employment opportunities for graduates of state-supported educational programs. **The committee recommends that state legislatures establish special bodies whose primary purpose would be to address state and local issues in the education and employment of allied health personnel.**

REFERENCES

Aiken, L. H. 1982. The nurse labor market. Health Affairs 1(4):30–40. [Cited in Buerhaus, 1987.]

Aiken, L. H., and C. F. Mullinex. 1987. The nurse shortage. Myth or reality? New England Journal of Medicine 317(10):641–645.

American Hospital Association, Department of Human Resources. 1986. Report on Union Activity in the Health Care Industry. Chicago: American Hospital Association. September.

American Hospital Association, Hospital Data Center. 1988. National Hospital Panel Survey. Chicago: American Hospital Association.

Araujo, M. 1980. Creative nursing administration sets climate for retention. Hospitals.

Bamberg, R. 1981. Educating clinical laboratory scientists in the 1980s: Some suggestions. American Journal of Medical Technology 47(4):259–261.

Barr, J. T. 1987. The new age laboratory: There is more to clinical laboratory science than doing the test. College of Pharmacy and Allied Health Professions, Northeastern University.

Blayney, K.D. 1981. The Alabama linkage story. *In* Sharing Resources in Allied Health Education, S. N. Collier, ed. Atlanta, Ga.: Southern Regional Education Board.

Blayney, K. D. 1982. The multiple competency allied health technician. Editorial. Alabama Journal of Medical Sciences 19(1):13–14.

Buerhaus, P. I. 1987. Not just another nursing shortage. Nursing Economics 5(6):267–279.

Bureau of Labor Statistics. 1986. National Survey of Professional, Administrative, Technical, and Clerical Pay. Bulletin 2271. Washington, D.C.: Government Printing Office. March and October.

Cooper, F. R. 1982. A survey of graduates of the University of Alabama in Birmingham School of Community and Allied Health junior college/Regional Technical Institute linkage. School of Public Health, University of Alabama, Birmingham.

Cordes, S. M., and J. S. Wright. 1985. Rural health care: Concerns for present and future. *In* Review of Allied Health Education, 2nd ed., J. Hamburg, ed. Lexington: University Press of Kentucky.

Eisenberg, J. M. 1982. The use of ancillary services: A role for utilization review. Medical Care 20(8):849–860.

Garg, M. L., et al. 1985. A new methodology for ancillary services review. Medical Care 23(6):809–815.

Hamburg, J., ed. 1985. Review of Allied Health Education: 5. Lexington: University Press of Kentucky.

Hanson, S. L., J. K. Martin, and S. A. Tuch. 1987. Economic sector and job satisfaction. Work and Occupation 14(2):286–305.

Health Professions Report. 1987. Federal policy on nursing shortages. Health Professions Report 16(23):2.

Health Resources and Services Administration. Office of the Administrator, Rockville, Md. 1987. Rural hospitals/health services. Executive summary.

Hudson Institute. 1987. Workforce 2000. Indianapolis, Ind.: Hudson Institute Inc. June.

Institute of Medicine. 1983. Nursing and Nursing Education: Public Policies and Private Actions. Washington, D.C.: National Academy Press.

Kerschner, P. 1987. Staffing: Getting the edge on McDonald's and Pizza Hut. Provider April:39.

Kutcher, R. E., and J. A. Mark. 1983. The service-producing sector: Some common perceptions reviewed. Monthly Labor Review 106(4):21–24.

Link, C., and R. Settle. 1980. Wage incentives and married professional nurses: A case of backward-bending supply? Economic Inquiry 19(1):144–156.

Low, G., and A. Weisbord. 1987. The multicompetent practitioner: A needs analysis in an urban area. Journal of Allied Health 16(1):29–39.

Lunzer, F. June 16, 1987. In health care, a move to unions. The Washington Post. Health, Science, and Society: A Weekly Journal of Medicine, pp. 10–11.

Mansfield, C. J. 1987. Human resource management in hospital administration. Journal of Health and Human Resources Administration 9(3):355–368.

Mellor, E. F. 1987. Weekly earnings in 1986: A look at more than 200 occupations. Monthly Labor Review 110(6):41–46.

Mitchell, C. September 14, 1987. A growing shortage of skilled craftsmen troubles some firms. Wall Street Journal.

Price, J. L., and C. W. Mueller. 1981. Professional Turnover: The Case of Nurses. Jamaica, N.Y.: Spectrum Publications.

Reagan, B. B. 1986. Differences in 1982 Income of Female and Male Physical Therapists. Paper prepared for the American Physical Therapy Association. Alexandria, Va.

Reinhardt, U. E. 1987. Somber clouds on the horizon. Health Week 1(10):6.

Rytina, N. F. 1982. Earnings of men and women: A look at specfic occupations. Monthly Labor Review 105(4):25–31.

Shelledy, D. C., and S. P. Mikles. Staff burnout among respiratory care personnel. Respiratory Management (March/April):45–52.

Shroeder, S. A. 1987. Strategies for reducing medical costs by changing physicians' behavior Efficacy and impact on quality of care. International Journal of Technology Assessment in Health Care 3:39–50.

Texas Health Careers. 1987. Publications describing activities from Texas Hospital Association, Austin, Texas.

Uchitelle, L. September 27, 1987. America's invisible army of non-workers. New York Times.

University of Texas Medical Branch. 1986. National Survey of Hospital and Medical School Salaries. Galveston: University of Texas Medical Branch at Galveston. November.

Watrous, M., Jr. 1987. Medical laboratory employer/educator survey. American Medical Technologists Events (May–June):75–78.

Weisman, C. S., et al. 1981. Determinants of hospital staff turnover. Medical Care 19(4):431–443.

7

Licensure and Other Mechanisms for Regulating Allied Health Personnel

THE CONGRESSIONAL CHARGE to this committee directed it to "investigate current practices under which each type of allied health personnel obtains licenses, credentials, and accreditation" (Appendix A, Section 223[b][3]). The committee has taken a rather broad view of this charge, interpreting it to encompass the whole array of mechanisms meant to ensure that allied health personnel are properly trained and competent to practice. These mechanisms, which include licensure and other forms of governmental regulation, voluntary certification, and standards imposed by health care providers and payers, are central to this study in that they interact with and influence virtually all of the other study issues.

For example, the scope of practice for a field that is defined under state licensing statutes and regulations affects the demand for allied health personnel by constraining how they may be used by employers. Certification, if it is accepted as a valid distinction by employers or if it is required by accrediting bodies such as the Joint Commission on Accreditation of Healthcare Organizations, also affects employers' decisions to employ allied health personnel; certified and noncertified members of the same allied health field are then treated as separate labor pools. Regulatory mechanisms also influence supply by defining who may enter and remain in certain allied health fields.

A great deal is at stake here. Health care payers rely on licensure and other credentialing mechanisms to assist them in defining eligibility for coverage and reimbursement for allied health services. The various allied health occupations look to these mechanisms to give them identity and legitimacy by defining the nature and length of training, requirements for entry into the field, and the power to control certain health care practices.

In a time of great ferment in health care, these control mechanisms take on even greater significance. The proliferation of health care occupations, changing models of health care delivery, and new reimbursement methods, along with cost-control efforts by industry and government, place stresses on these controls.

To carry out this part of the congressional charge, the committee held discussions with officials of government agencies and private organizations responsible for the various control mechanisms. It also held a public hearing at which 26 allied health associations and 4 experts presented testimony; two of the experts prepared papers for the committee on state regulation of health occupations. In addition, the committee reviewed the research literature on occupational regulation.

METHODS OF CONTROL

State Regulation

Society applies many quality control methods to health care personnel, including allied health personnel. The states bear the greater responsibility in this control system. Through occupational licensure and other forms of regulation, states exercise their authority to protect the health, safety, and welfare of their citizens. The earliest attempts to regulate health occupations in this country were in colonial Virginia (1639), Massachusetts (1649), and New York (1665), when medical practice acts were enacted. By the beginning of the twentieth century, the Supreme Court had validated this use of the states' police powers, and most states had licensed lawyers, dentists, pharmacists, physicians, and teachers. Between 1900 and 1919, most states also licensed nurses, optometrists, osteopaths, podiatrists, and veterinarians (Carpenter, 1987). Before 1960, this list had expanded to include dental hygienists, practical nurses, and physical therapists. Since 1960, only three health occupations have come to be universally licensed: psychology, nursing home administration, and emergency medical technology. The latter two were licensed as the result of federal legislation.

Table 7-1 shows the licensure status of the 10 allied health fields on which this study concentrates as of June 1987. Among these fields, physical therapists and dental hygienists are licensed in every state. Emergency medical technicians must be certified by some agency in every state. At the other extreme is medical record administration, for which no state requires licensure; this field relies instead on certification (registration) by the American Medical Records Association. All the other fields are licensed in some states: for example, respiratory therapists are licensed in 7 states, audiologists and speech-language pathologists in 37.

TABLE 7-1 Licensure Status of Selected Allied Health Fields

Field	Licensure Status
Clinical laboratory technology	Medical technologists are licensed in 5 states and New York City. Technicians are not licensed in any state.
Dental hygiene	Dental hygienists are licensed in all 50 states and the District of Columbia. Dental assistants are not licensed in any state.
Dietetics	Dieticians are licensed in 14 states, the District of Columbia, and Puerto Rico.
Emergency medical services	Certified in all 50 states.
Medical record services	Neither medical record administrators nor medical record technicians are licensed in any state.
Occupational therapy	Occupational therapists are licensed in 34 states, the District of Columbia, and Puerto Rico. Occupational therapy assistants are not regulated in any state.
Physical therapy	Physical therapists are licensed in all 50 states. Physical therapy assistants are licensed in 18 states.
Radiology	Radiographers are licensed in 17 states and Puerto Rico. Radiation therapy technologists are licensed in 15 states and Puerto Rico. Nuclear medicine technologists are licensed in 10 states and Puerto Rico.
Respiratory therapy	Respiratory therapists are licensed in 7 states.
Speech–language pathology/audiology	Speech–language pathologists and audiologists are licensed in 36 states and Puerto Rico.

SOURCE: Information from professional associations, updated to June 1987.

Licensure is the most restrictive form of state regulation. Carpenter (1987) defines licensure as "a process by which a governmental agency restricts entry into an occupation by defining a set of functions and activities constituting a 'scope of practice,' grants permission to engage in that practice only to persons meeting predetermined qualifications, and establishes structures and procedures for screening applicants and granting licenses to practice." These and other definitions share certain common elements, including:

• licensure is intended to protect the public;
• licensure is exclusionary;
• licensure prescribes the characteristics and qualifications of persons who may be licensed;
• licensure defines a scope of practice for licensees (and therefore licensure laws are often referred to as "practice acts"); and
• licensure prohibits nonlicensed persons from engaging in the defined scope of practice.

Although the standard definitions focus on initial entry, licensure also addresses standards of practice and ethical and business behavior (what it takes to keep a license) and causes for disciplinary action (what it takes to lose a license).

By long tradition, licensure has been, for all practical purposes, a form of state-sponsored self-regulation because it has been carried out by boards composed of members of the regulated occupation empowered to act with a high degree of autonomy. As Shimberg (1984) noted in recounting the history of state licensure:

These boards had broad powers to implement the law by promulgating rules and regulations governing practice standards and professional conduct; establishing minimum education, training, and experience qualifications; examining candidates as to their fitness to practice; investigating complaints against practitioners; and taking appropriate disciplinary action, including suspension or revocation of a practitioner's license where appropriate.

Recent reforms have broadened the membership of licensure boards to include representatives of the public who may or may not have voting privileges. Yet, on the whole, the licensed occupations still are largely self-regulated. This point is elaborated later in this chapter. However, licensure carries with it a whole array of regulations and administrative procedures for implementing the state statutes.

States can and do use a number of modes of occupational regulation other than licensure (Table 7-2). Among the 10 allied health fields covered in this report, title protection through registration or certification by the state is the most frequently used form of regulation other than licensure. This regulatory mechanism is also applied in other fields such as accountancy, in which anyone can practice but only those who have met state standards can use the title "certified public accountant." In one form or another, about 800 occupations are regulated by the states, including architects, real estate brokers, barbers and cosmetologists, electricians, and engineers.

Besides occupational regulation, states also oversee allied health personnel through the regulation of institutions and settings in which they work. Requirements for the licensure of hospitals and nursing homes include personnel standards. In addition, states have other laws and regulations of broad applicability in place, such as those that govern business practices and provide consumer protection, that may be used against incompetent or unscrupulous allied health personnel. The states also define qualifications for civil service positions held by these personnel.

Consumers may use the tort system in any state to file civil suits to seek compensation for malpractice by allied health personnel. Presumably, this mechanism carries some deterrent effect; in the context of quality assurance, however, it must be viewed as a last resort.

TABLE 7-2   Modes of Occupational Regulation

1. PRACTICE STANDARDS
   Without special enforcement
   Through the adoption of statutes and rules, this mode can establish restrictions on the practice of an occupation with civil or criminal penalties enforceable through the courts. This type of regulation requires no inspections, registration, or special enforcement staff. Rather, it relies on action by the harmed parties or by a consumer affairs office.
   With special enforcement
   Through statutes, or rules, or both, this mode can establish restrictions on the practice of an occupation in addition to establishing inspections, enforcement mechanisms, and penalties. However, this mode does not require registration, certification, or any assessment of the practitioner's credentials or competency.

2. REGISTRATION
   Without standards
   Through regulation, a state agency can require persons in an occupation to register and supply certain information without requiring any standards, testing, or enforcement.
   With standards
   It is also possible to have a registration requirement in combination with minimum practice standards that are set by a designated agency. Although registration would not be exclusionary, it would subject registrants to minimum standards and thereby provide some protection to the public.

3. STATUTORY CERTIFICATION
   With state standards and state enforcement
   Through regulation, occupational members can be required to meet certain state standards; only those who meet these predetermined qualifications may legally use the designated title of the occupation. This mode entails standards, testing, codes of practice, possible inspections, and enforcement.
   With private standards and assessment and state enforcement
   Through regulation, an agency of the state may require members of an occupational group to meet certain standards established by a private testing or assessment center or organization (reviewed by the state), with the state handling the certification and any enforcement required. Legally, the state is responsible for the standards set and for monitoring the process.

4. STATUTORY CERTIFICATION AND PRACTICE STANDARDS
   A state may establish, by rule, certification for an occupation and also request the legislature to pass a law that would establish practice standards for that same occupation. This combination would establish a system of title control for those meeting certain required standards of competency, as well as establishing standards of practice for anyone who practices the occupation.

5. REGULATION THROUGH SUPERVISION BY AN ALREADY LICENSED PRACTITIONER
   Certification with standards
   Through statutes and rules, an occupation can be certified and required to work under the supervision of an already licensed occupation; standards for practice can also be established.   Continued

TABLE 7-2   Continued

Through standards of practice but without certification
It is also possible to regulate by providing that the occupation be performed under the supervision of a licensed professional with certain standards set forth but without requiring that the individual be certified.

6. LICENSURE
   Licensure is the most restrictive form of occupational regulation, providing for both title control and an exclusive area of practice. It requires standards of practice, education, knowledge or minimum competency, and inspection and enforcement with civil and criminal penalties.

SOURCE: Goldman and Helms (1983).

Criticisms of State Regulation

Occupational regulation has been in ferment for at least 20 years. Criticisms have come from a number of quarters, and these criticisms have given rise to recommendations for reform. Some changes have occurred as a consequence.

In the 1960s the source of concern was access to health care. With an apparent shortage of physicians, there was concern that restrictive licensing laws were hampering the effective deployment and utilization of physicians' assistants and other physician extenders. This issue was addressed by the National Advisory Commission on Health Manpower in its 1967 report. At the direction of Congress in the Health Training Improvement Act of 1970, the U.S. Department of Health, Education, and Welfare's Office of the Assistant Secretary for Health and Scientific Affairs investigated problems in health care personnel licensure and certification. The department's 1971 Report on Licensure and Related Health Personnel Credentialing contained far-reaching recommendations, including a recommendation to the states for "a two-year moratorium on the enactment of legislation that would establish new categories of health personnel with statutorily-defined scopes of functions." The moratorium was to allow time for further consideration of the tasks and functions of new health care occupations.

Questions about the wisdom of occupational licensure still remain, although the circumstances today are different. The perceived shortage of doctors and dentists has changed to a perceived surplus, and the number of newly emerging health care occupations is increasing. Since the early 1970s the issue of rising health care costs has taken on greater and greater importance. In the context of cost containment, the fact that more and more health occupations have been seeking statutorily protected scopes of practice is worrisome. This proliferation is seen as contributing to inefficiencies in the health care industry, especially in view of the rapidity of technological change.

Allied health personnel are affected by this tension. Many of the allied health fields are new, and, according to the example offered by older, well-established fields such as medicine, nursing, and dentistry, state licensure is crucial to their achieving recognition as professions. Licensure, it is believed, gives legal validation to the field's unique status. It provides a way of excluding unqualified practitioners from providing services; it gives official recognition to the field's scope of practice; and it offers easily verified credentials that can be used by employers and health care payers (McCready, 1982). Licensure is also considered to be necessary to avoid being subject to prosecution. For example, physicians would be vulnerable to prosecution for practicing medicine without a license, since many medical practice acts are so broad that physicians are granted virtually unlimited scopes of practice.

Above all, state regulation is viewed as a means of improving the quality of health care by restricting entry into health care occupations to persons who have proper credentials and by disciplining persons who do not meet standards of professional behavior. Much of the criticism leveled at regulation is based on the lack of evidence on this point.

Criticisms of Structure and Process

The traditional regulatory structures and processes, which were developed in the last century, are criticized as anachronistic and inconsistent with the public policy objective of protection of the public.

By long tradition, the regulation of a health occupation, given a practice statute, is the responsibility of a board. The composition of the board is usually defined in the statute. One of the strongest criticisms of the regulatory structure is that these boards are not sufficiently accountable to the larger public. Until recently, they were composed entirely of members of the regulated occupation, drawn from the membership of their related associations. In many states, they generated their own revenues by charging fees to candidates and licensees; they had their own staffs; they were often located in the home of the board's secretary; and they had considerable rule-making authority with little or no oversight. Their proceedings were closed to the public, as were their records.

By statute, the regulatory boards are charged with setting entry requirements, practice standards, and codes of conduct, and with disciplining licensees who fail to meet those standards and codes. The performance of these functions has also been subject to criticism.

Eligibility standards are defined in terms of education and, in some cases, experience. Boards also require entrants to pass an examination that, in some cases, is devised by the board. In other cases, the board relies on a national examination or commissions a testing organization to develop a state exam. Criticisms that have been leveled at entry requirements are that they are inflexible, offering only one path to entry; that education and experience requirements are unrelated to the demands of practice; that educational requirements rest heavily on accreditation, which in turn is controlled by the professional associations; that examinations are not valid reflections of "real-world" practice requirements; and that the common practice of "grandfathering" current practitioners when licensing a new occupation is inconsistent with the goals of protecting the public health and welfare.

"Standards of practice" are defined in terms of behaviors that are subject to disciplinary action, including fraud and deception in obtaining the license; conviction of a felony; engaging in unacceptable patient care through deliberate or negligent acts; knowing violation of the practice act; continuing to practice although unfit; and lewd or immoral conduct in the delivery of services. "Codes of conduct" most commonly prohibit business practices that are considered unacceptable professional behavior. Traditionally, these have included advertising; practice in chain or department stores, shopping centers, or other commercial environments; and engaging in competitive bidding.

Disciplinary procedures are usually defined in the statute. In some states and for some occupations, revocation of a license is the only sanction provided. In others, the statute defines an array of sanctions of varying degree, including license suspension, censure, and reprimand.

Boards have been criticized for the way they carry out their disciplinary responsibilities: they only investigate complaints of incompetence or impropriety, rather than performing any independent monitoring. Impropriety (i.e., violation of the code of ethics) is more frequently the basis for disciplinary action than is incompetence. The number of disciplinary actions is extremely low in comparison with estimates of the incidence of incompetent practice. The public is not informed of disciplinary actions against licensees. A partial explanation for the historical lack of disciplinary vigor is the inadequacy of the resources available to the task of investigating and "prosecuting" complaints. Without sufficient staff and budget, the regulatory process is more bark than bite.

"Turf" monitoring and turf protection occupy a significant portion of the energies of a state's regulatory apparatus. The various occupations battle among themselves over which parts of health care and which parts of the patient fall under their jurisdiction. These battles are fought by establishing practice acts and by implementing rules and regulations. Yet this is not the only theater of conflict; insurance coverage and reimbursement constitute another. Yet the regulatory arena is where the identity and power of allied health personnel are largely determined.

In carrying out this study the committee encountered many examples of jurisdictional struggles among allied health and other occupations, struggles that caused their roles to be constantly shifting. For instance,

- ophthalmic medical assistants versus optometrists on performing refractions;
- surgical technologists versus nurses on who should perform various tasks in the operating room;
- orthoptists versus physical therapists on fitting braces and other orthotic devices; and
- audiologists versus hearing aid dispensers in hearing testing.

These struggles, in which one occupation seeks to expand its realm of control at the expense of another, are a constant element of regulating health services through licensure. In many cases the issue is which occupation is entitled to perform a specific function. In others, the issue is which occupation or occupations have jurisdiction over some portion of the human anatomy. In still others the issue is under what conditions persons in an occupation perform their functions. For example, in many states, physician referral is required for physical therapy or occupational therapy but not for speech therapy. Another important condition of practice is the level of supervision required. These referral and supervision provisions in licensure statutes define the degree of autonomy of health care workers on the one hand and their degree of availability to consumers on the other. Decisions on these issues by state legislators and regulatory bureaucracies affect the costs, quality, and accessibility of health care services.

The great difficulty facing state decision makers is that the impact on costs, quality, and accessibility of any proposed modification in a health occupation's scope of practice, referral, or supervision is rarely clear. The risks and benefits of change are often hypothetical, difficult to measure, and subject to large differences in judgment. Rhetoric and political power frequently substitute for evidence and rational decision making. Rarely are rigorous studies done.

One of the clearest examples of this problem is the case of dental hygiene services. In the course of testimony by representatives of the American Dental Hygienists' Association (1987a,b) and the American Dental Association (1987) before the committee, committee members learned of the continuing controversy over the required levels of supervision of dental hygienists by dentists.

In general, dental hygienists are only permitted to practice (i.e., perform a variety of chiefly preventive services—e.g., cleaning teeth, taking x rays, applying topical fluorides, and teaching proper dental hygiene) under the supervision of a licensed dentist. The supervision may be "general," which means that a dentist may delegate a given function. The dentist must be responsible for its successful performance but does not have to be physically present while the delegated function is carried out. Alternatively, the supervision may be "direct," meaning that the dentist must be present in the same room as the hygienist, or "indirect," which requires only that the dentist be present in the treatment facility.

Supervision requirements vary among the states. According to the American Dental Hygienists' Association (1987b), 38 states permit dental hygienists to practice at least some preventive oral health services under general supervision. In some states, general supervision is limited to hospitals, nursing homes, adult day care centers, and other institutional settings. In Washington State, dental hygienists have practiced unsupervised in long-term care facilities since 1984.

The American Dental Association is seeking to tighten supervisory requirements for hygienists. In 1986 the association's House of Delegates passed a resolution opposing general supervision and urging state dental societies to eliminate it from state practice acts. The same resolution urged that, in instances in which general supervision could not be removed from the statute, the regulations be changed to require that:

a. any patient treated by a dental hygienist first become a "patient of record" of a licensed dentist;

b. dental hygiene services be given prior authorization by a dentist no more than 45 days before the services are provided; and

c. the dentist examines the patient within a reasonable time after the dental hygiene services are provided.

The justification for this resolution was that general supervision endangers the dental health of the public. Its effect would be to increase dentists' control of dental hygiene services.

Since the resolution was passed, efforts have been made in several states to delete general supervision. A bill to this effect was introduced in Connecticut in 1987. In Texas, where general supervision has been permitted for over 30 years, the Board of Dental Examiners proposed rules that would require direct supervision of all dental hygiene functions (American Dental Hygienists' Association, 1987b). The Virginia Dental Board, which had been on the verge of liberalizing supervision requirements, decided against such action.

Other states are moving to relax their supervision requirements so that dental hygiene services can be provided without the dentist's physical presence. Legislation to this effect has been proposed in Missouri, Ohio, South Carolina, and Wisconsin. At the extreme on this continuum is Colorado, which in 1986 became the first state to allow dental hygienists to provide most of their basic functions without supervision by a dentist. Other functions, which are designated as "supervised dental hygiene," require a dentist's supervision. Diagnosis, treatment planning, and prescription of therapeutic measures continue to be the responsibility of dentists. The statute imposes disciplinary action on dental hygienists who fail to refer patients to a dentist when the treatment needed is beyond their scope of practice. A lawsuit to overturn the statute failed but is under appeal.

In California, 15 dental hygienists are allowed to clean and examine teeth without the supervision of dentists. This demonstration program is one of the state-sponsored Health Manpower Pilot Projects, under which the requirements of state practice acts may be waived for experiments with innovative methods of health care delivery. According to the California Office of Statewide Health Planning and Development (1987), the agency responsible for the program, it "is authorized to approve locally conceived and implemented demonstration projects to prepare and utilize health personnel for new or expanded roles."

To qualify for the program, hygienists needed at least 4 years of clinical experience, certification in cardiopulmonary resuscitation, and special training in instrumentation. They are currently providing services in offices and in other settings such as nursing homes. Some make house calls to people who are bedridden. Their case records are reviewed by a dentist.

The California Dental Association sued to halt the program on the basis that it was a threat to public health and that the procedures followed by the state and by California State University in approving and implementing the program were inadequate. In August 1987 Judge Rothwell B. Mason of the Sacramento County Superior Court ruled against the dental association. His opinion was that the program was consistent with the legislature's intent to enable experimentation with new kinds and combinations of delivery systems and the need for exemptions from the healing arts practice act to permit such experimentation (*California Dental Association* v. *Office of Statewide Health Planning and Development et al.*, Proceedings, August 28, 1987, California Superior Court, County of Sacramento).

In neither the Colorado nor the California cases were the substantive issues resolved; both cases, to date at least, have hinged on procedural matters. In neither case were any data or research findings presented to support arguments about risks or benefits. In addition, no evidence was presented on the issue of what dental hygienists' training includes and what types of responsibilities hygienists are prepared for, on the issue of accessibility of services, or on the costs of services.

In its testimony to this committee the American Dental Association (1987) stated that it "believes that all segments of the public should receive the same high standard of dental care." The association expressed its concerns about the great responsibility placed on dental care providers by the need to diagnose nondental diseases that manifest symptoms in the mouth and the need to provide services to patients who are severely medically compromised (American Dental Association, 1987).

The committee questioned the American Dental Association spokesperson about those circumstances, such as practices in public schools, in which it would be beneficial to allow hygienists to provide prophylactic services to children who had been examined by a dentist but without the dentist being present. The association's official position is that this form of delivery is not acceptable (Institute of Medicine, Committee to Study the Role of Allied Health Personnel, 1987).

The situation in dentistry is not unique. It illustrates issues of cost, quality, and access to health care services that are common to many health care fields. The committee is concerned that such issues are faced by the courts, state legislatures, and regulatory agencies with neither a body of statistical evidence nor the informed judgments of knowledgable, disinterested parties available for guidance. Without such information, there is considerable risk that decisions will be made on purely political and economic grounds.

Criticisms as to Outcome

In addition to criticisms of the structures and processes of state regulation, there have been substantial criticisms of the outcomes of regulation in terms of health care cost, quality, and accessibility. A body of research literature generally calls into question whether state regulation as we know it is serving the public. The literature shows with some consistency that the costs (prices) of health care services and products (e.g., eyeglasses, dentures) are higher in states with more stringent regulation (Begun, 1981; Gaumer, 1984). The incomes of health professionals are also higher in states that restrict the activities of their substitutes and auxiliaries.

Higher consumer prices presumably reduce access to health care by keeping some consumers out of the market entirely. There is also direct evidence that restrictions—for instance, on practice setting—may reduce the quantity of services provided. Begun (1981), for example, found that optometrists practicing in chain outlets conducted more eye examinations in a day than optometrists in private offices. Many states prohibit practice in chain outlets.

The effects of restrictions on quality of care are less clear, largely because of the great difficulty in obtaining data with which to assess quality. This is unfortunate, because quality is central to the policy debate over the extent and nature of occupational regulation. The various health occupations argue for instituting regulations, for changing their scope of practice, and for limiting the scopes of other occupations entirely on the grounds of quality of care.

As Begun (1981) points out, in this context, "quality" is ill-defined: "it may refer to the degree of respect for the professional, the degree of communication or humanism in the professional–client relation, the technical sophistication of the service, or the actual outcome of the service."

Other possibilities include the professional's number of years of training, the degree of trust the client has for the professional, and the degree of client satisfaction.

However quality is measured, its relationship to regulation is equivocal. For example, studies by Maurizi (1974) and by Carroll and Gaston (1977) have suggested that quality is actually lower with greater regulation. On the other hand, Holen's (1977) study of dentistry showed that more stringent state licensing standards reduced the probability of adverse outcomes. Gaumer (1984) concluded from a review of the literature that state regulation could not be shown to reduce the risk of health care personnel making mistakes or errors in judgment, nor in general ensure competence. Begun (1981) showed that restrictions on optometric practice are associated with higher quality, higher cost, and lower accessibility. Yet quality was measured in terms of duration of eye examinations and their complexity, so the result might be attributable to fewer "low-quality" exams being done rather than to more "high-quality" exams.

Criticisms of the outcomes of state regulation are also aimed at its effect on geographic and career mobility. There is considerable research to suggest that state licensure, especially with limited reciprocity, limits the geographic mobility of licensed personnel. It also limits career mobility by prohibiting advancement from one level to another and by prohibiting occupational change without additional education. The difficulty of transferring credits and of obtaining credit for skills acquired on the job means that "initial career choices create a pathway which can be left only by tracing one or more steps backward and essentially starting from an entry level once more" (Carpenter, 1987).

Reforms of State Regulation

Twenty years of criticism have led to a number of recommendations for the reform of state regulation of health occupations, some of which have been implemented.

Criteria for Regulation: "Sunrise" Procedures In the face of a growing number of occupations seeking licensure and a growing concern about the cost-effectiveness of licensure, 13 states have sought to bring a greater degree of reason and due process to what had been largely an ad hoc and political procedure. Minnesota was the first state to enact sunrise legislation in 1973. The Minnesota example, criteria from the Council of State Governments, and principles emanating from the U.S. Department of Health, Education, and Welfare have been used as guidelines in these efforts.

The criteria in general have been similar. Basically, they consist of a set of guidelines to use in deciding whether an occupation should be regulated and another set for deciding on the most appropriate form of regulation.

Criteria for regulating an occupation include evidence of harm from unregulated practice, evidence that the occupation involves specialized skills, and evidence that the public is not protected by any other means. More recently, a criterion of cost-effectiveness has been added by some states. Minnesota's statute and current regulations (see Appendix F) are an example of these criteria. The rules spell out in some detail what constitutes evidence of harm, including the kinds of harm that are recognized and how to assess the potential for harm, and the extent of danger inherent in the occupation's functions.

Minnesota's regulations also appropriately recognize the rather long list of "other means" for protecting the public: supervision by other practitioners, state or federal laws governing devices and substances, employment in licensed facilities, federal licensing or other requirements, civil service procedures, or national certification procedures. A consideration of these other means not only guides the initial decision to regulate at all but can also guide the design of the appropriate regulatory mechanism when one is needed.

The criteria for selecting the mode of regulation follow the principle of using the least restrictive activities consistent with public protection (see Subdivision 3 of the Minnesota statute, Appendix F). The least regulatory mode is the strengthening of the base for civil action or criminal prohibitions, or both. This is essentially a reliance on the deterrent effect of potential civil actions or criminal penalties. The most regulatory mode is occupational licensure, which prohibits persons who do not meet the state standards from engaging in practice. An intermediate mode is the establishment of title protection through registration or certification.

Certification has been used for many years in the field of accountancy. Accountants are certified by the states after meeting certain eligibility criteria. These criteria vary among the states, but all states require passing grades in each of four parts of the uniform national examination given by the American Institute of Certified Public Accountants (CPAs). Some states have education requirements; some also require experience in public accountancy. Certified status allows an accountant to offer independent judgment about an organization's financial records, the value of its assets, and so forth. In general, large organizations have their financial accounts audited and evaluated by CPAs. A lender generally requires an audited statement from a firm seeking a loan. The Securities and Exchange Commission requires an audited statement before approving a stock offering. In these capacities, CPAs wield considerable influence, their expertise is widely understood and respected, and they can command substantial salaries.

On the other hand, a person can prepare a firm's financial statements, complete tax returns, and perform most accounting functions without being certified. Unless a company wants to borrow money or sell shares to the public, it does not have to pay for the services of a CPA. An individual taxpayer is not required to have his or her tax return prepared by a CPA. Thus, there are lower cost options available for a wide variety of accounting services. Using these lower cost and presumably lower quality options is not without risk; an individual might be fined by the Internal Revenue Service or see his or her company fail because of poor accounting services. However, in this field, consumers are able to weigh the risks and benefits and to choose among an array of providers, based on the importance they place on certification and their financial constraints.

The concept of economic impact is relatively new in this arena. It makes explicit a concern that the imposition of regulation, whatever its benefits, carries with it certain costs to society. These include any increases in the cost or price of services, insurance premium costs, the costs of additional training, and the costs of operating the regulatory mechanism itself. In some states, these regulatory operating costs are defrayed wholly or in part through licensing fees and thus do not get charged to the consumer. In evaluating the regulatory burden, however, these costs are significant, irrespective of how they are financed. There is probably merit in having them made public, even if they are paid through licensing fees, as a means of focusing attention on how much regulation costs society.

An economic impact statement requirement is very useful. It could and should be expanded to a broader "environmental impact" statement to incorporate other criteria such as access and quality into the considerations. This broader statement would encourage allied health occupations seeking state regulation, other parties at interest, and the states themselves to make as explicit as possible the nature of the trade-offs under consideration.

Reforms of the Regulatory Structure and Process

The criticisms enumerated above have led to calls that date back to the late 1960s for structural and procedural changes. These recommendations for change have been aimed at increasing the public accountability, efficiency, and effectiveness of state regulatory boards.

Board Composition Widening the membership of regulatory boards has been one of the most consistent recommendations made by critics of state occupational regulation (e.g., Public Health Service, 1977; Begun, 1981; Cohen, 1980; Shimberg, 1982). As stated by Tuohy (1976, cited in Begun, 1981, p. 94), "Governments cannot continue to expect that coherent public policy can be achieved by dealing with professional groups as if they were the 'owners' of their respective technologies." The need for public input has generally been associated with consumer involvement, that is, the inclusion of one or more "lay" members on each licensure board. A number of states have taken this step. These lay members generally are consumers (much of the impetus for having them came from the consumer movement); they may or may not have full membership status—voting privileges, for example.

Although informed consumers have a great deal to offer to the regulatory process, there is some question about whether the addition of 1 or 2 consumers to a board with 8 or 10 members of a regulated field, especially if the consumers cannot vote, will have the desired effect of making the board more accountable to the public. More far-reaching recommendations to this end include:

• Drawing the "public" board members from the appropriate state agency. Bureaucrats would have the advantage of (1) technical knowledge relevant to the task, and (2) a power base from which to exert leverage on other board members. The power would flow from the agency head and, ultimately, the governor (Cohen, 1980).

• Drawing a majority of the board members from outside the regulated occupation. A far cry from one or two "token" consumers, under this proposal boards would be dominated by lay members (Begun, 1981).

• Drawing board members entirely from persons outside the regulated occupation. Board members could be not only consumers but others with relevant expertise in such fields as education, public health, economics, health administration, and health services research (Cohen, 1980).

In the last case, the board could employ as consultants either individuals or a panel of technical advisors drawn from the regulated field. However, because no member of the board would come from the field and because board members would have considerable relevant expertise of their own, they would be likely to avoid "capture" or domination by the field and its association(s).

Location of Boards in the State Administrative Structure   A second major recommendation to improve accountability has been to strengthen the connections between regulatory boards and one or more state agencies. One approach has been to centralize the administrative support, including recordkeeping, the investigative staff, and other common functions of boards in a single state agency, either the health department or a special department established for this function.

Another approach, recommended by Selden (1970), is to have a single board that regulates all health occupations and that is linked to a state agency that provides all administrative, analytical, and investigative support. Subcommittees from each field would develop policies for that field, subject to approval by the full board.

A third approach is to link related health occupations through joint boards. Rather than the single board envisioned by Selden, there would be a number of boards but considerably fewer than the number of regulated occupations. Virginia is moving in this direction with a proposal for a joint board for several allied health occupations.

Structural changes in the direction of greater accountability are highly desirable. To be fully effective, however, they should apply to all health occupations, not just to those that are the newest. States will need to examine and probably revise their practice acts for physicians and other health care professionals and to review the structures of regulation for those fields. A double standard, one applicable to allied health fields and one to medicine, dentistry, and nursing, is not desirable.

Information for the Public   The regulatory process has been criticized for being conducted virtually invisibly. Not only has doing business in a closed fashion been a barrier to public accountability, it has kept the regulatory process from serving an important educational function. Through state regulation the public could become much better informed about the different health care occupations, their credentials, and the services they offer. Public education could also increase state citizens' awareness of the importance of occupational regulation. Such awareness would be likely to elicit greater interest and participation.

No single model for accountability is obviously superior to all others. Each state should use its own mechanisms consistent with the objective of cost-effective public protection.

The Federal Role

The federal government plays a very important role in regulating allied health personnel. Although it does not regulate health occupations directly, it has indirect influence on state regulatory policy by supporting evaluation research, sponsoring policy analyses, and fostering information dissemination. It has direct responsibility for setting standards for eligible providers under Medicare, however, and a shared responsibility with the states for standard setting under the Medicaid program. Medicare conditions of participation, which apply to all institutional providers of health services, are a powerful regulatory tool because providers that do not meet the conditions may not receive payment from the program except in emergency circumstances. These regulations can be used to define the qualifications of allied health personnel working in participating hospitals, nursing homes, and other health care institutions.

The federal influence is also exerted by the actions of the Federal Trade Commission. The commission has conducted and sponsored research on the effects of regulation and has struck down certain anticompetitive practices of regulatory boards such as prohibitions on advertising.

The federal government has taken an important leadership role in health occupations regulation. Reports issued by the U.S. Department of Health, Education, and Welfare in the 1970s were influential in drawing attention to problems in the mechanisms of state regulation. Recommendations from those reports and from studies sponsored by the Labor Department helped shape the new directions in state regulation.

The Bureau of Health Professions has supported studies of occupational roles that are useful in devising entry and practice standards. The bureau has also helped develop and disseminate information on state regulatory activities through its support of the Clearinghouse on Licensure, Enforcement, and Regulation of the Council of State Governments.

In addition, the bureau has supported the National Commission for Health Certifying Agencies (NCHCA), a body that sets standards for organizations that certify allied health personnel. NCHCA sets standards that are designed to ensure that certifying agencies are accountable to individuals seeking certification, to their employers, to health care payers, and to the public. (A copy of their standards is attached as Appendix G.)

The federal Medicare program has a significant impact on allied health personnel through the way it defines covered services. By means of regulation, the secretary of the Department of Health and Human Services can define the qualifications (e.g., licensure) of personnel providing services such as physical therapy, occupational therapy, and speech therapy.

Private Control Mechanisms

Private recognition of competence also offers some assurance to the public; it may take several forms. Membership in an association is an indication that an individual has met certain standards for admission. The standards may include qualifications of education or experience, moral character, and so on. In a number of allied health fields, a basic requirement of membership is graduation from an education program approved by CAHEA. Dental hygiene programs are accredited by the American Dental Association. Physical therapy education programs are accredited by the American Physical Therapy Association.

Certification by a private agency or association generally imposes more rigorous standards than those required for association membership. Certification has been defined as:

... the process by which a nongovernmental agency or association grants recognition to an individual who has met certain predetermined qualifications specified by that agency or association. Such qualifications may include graduation from an accredited or approved training program, acceptable performance on a qualifying examination, and/or completion of some specified amount or type of work experience. (Shimberg, 1984)

In a paper prepared for this committee, Carpenter (1987) notes that certification establishes "standards of competence" and then grants an individual a certificate allowing them to use an occupational title, for example, "registered dietician." ("Registered" is a very confusing term because it may be used to mean licensed, as with registered nurses, or certified, as in this case.) This mechanism is, of course, analogous to certification by a state, except that it does not include legal prohibition against the use of the title by persons not meeting the standards.

Historically, licensure has been concerned with minimum competency, whereas certification has been reserved for those meeting considerably higher standards. In medicine, for example, certification by a speciality board was (and is) viewed as a "badge of excellence" (Shimberg, 1984). This distinction is less clear-cut today, when in some fields certification attests to basic entry standards and in others it attests to special achievement.

Two forms of private accreditation are used as quality assurance mechanisms for allied health personnel. In the context of credentialing allied health personnel, accreditation most commonly refers to a process through which a private association or agency "grants public recognition to a school, institute, college, university, or specialized program of study having met certain established qualifications or standards" (Shimberg, 1984). Educational accreditation is a form of peer review that is meant "to provide a professional judgment of the quality of the educational institution or program" (Committee on Allied Health Education and Accreditation, 1987).

The second form of accreditation that is a quality control mechanism for allied health personnel is the accreditation of hospitals and nursing homes by the Joint Commission on the Accreditation of Health Care Organizations. The joint commission promulgates standards that include qualifications of key hospital personnel. Many of these standards apply to allied health personnel (see Table 7-3).

CONCLUSIONS AND RECOMMENDATIONS

In light of potential future shortages of allied health personnel and the need to find a reasonable balance between health care costs and quality, the committee believes that it is important to maintain flexibility in the use of existing personnel and a variety of routes of entry for new personnel.

It appears that widespread use of licensure carries with it higher costs to consumers, reduced access to health care services, and reduced flexibility for managers. People in health care careers are inhibited from changing fields and from advancing within their fields by rigid requirements imposed by state regulatory mechanisms. Although these control mechanisms are designed and carried out in the stated interest of protecting the health and welfare of the public, their effectiveness in this regard has been mixed at best.

TABLE 7-3 Joint Commission on Accreditation of Healthcare
Organizations' Accreditation Standards for Hospitals

Field	Summary of Relevant Standards (if any)
Clinical laboratory technology	The director is a member of the medical staff and preferably a board-certified pathologist. There are sufficient qualified laboratory technologists and supportive staff to perform the required tests. A qualified technologist is a graduate of an approved medical technology program or has equivalent education, training, and/or experience; meets current legal requirements of licensure/registration; and is currently competent.
Dietetics	A qualified dietitian dispenses the nutritional aspects of patient care and ensures that quality nutritional care is provided to patients.
Medical records	A hospital must employ or have as a consultant a registered record administrator or an accredited record technician. If consultants only are used, medical record supervisors are to demonstrate competence.
Physical therapy	See rehabilitation services.
Occupational therapy	See rehabilitation services.
Radiology	The director of the radiology service is to determine the qualifications and competence of department personnel; at least one qualified radiologic technologist is available; a technologist does not independently perform diagnostic fluoroscopy except under certain circumstances. The director of the nuclear medicine service is to determine the qualifications and competence of department personnel who are not independent practitioners. "When radiation oncology procedures are performed in the hospital, designated qualified technologists are assigned as needed."
Rehabilitation services	Each individual providing physical rehabilitation services must meet relevant licensure, certification, or registration requirements. Separate services are defined, including occupational therapy, physical therapy, prosthetic and orthotic services, psychological services, recreation therapy, social work services, speech–language pathology or audiology services, and vocational rehabilitation services. No specific staffing standards are given beyond the general one. Separate standards require that comprehensive rehabilitation services be provided "in an interdisciplinary manner," and that the quality and appropriateness of these services be monitored and evaluated.

TABLE 7-3 Continued

Field	Summary of Relevant Standards (if any)
Respiratory therapy	Respiratory care services are to be provided by a sufficient number of qualified persons under competent medical direction. If warranted, services are supervised by a technical director registered or certified by the National Board for Respiratory Therapy, Inc. Other qualified personnel may provide services commensurate with their training, experience, and competence; these include registered respiratory therapists or certified technicians; persons with equivalent education or experience; qualified cardiopulmonary technologists; and appropriately trained licensed nurses.

SOURCE: Accreditation Manual for Hospitals (1988).

Statutory certification, which legally reserves the use of a title to persons with specific qualifications, affords most of the benefits of licensure and avoids many of the costs. In conjunction with public education, it gives consumers the opportunity to choose among providers knowledgeably. It does not prevent consumers from choosing lower quality or lower cost alternatives. It permits institutional employers some flexibility in their staffing. It permits innovation—new careers may provide new cost-effective methods of diagnosis and treatment.

The committee recommends statutory certification for fields in which the state determines there is a need for regulation because this form of regulation offers most of the benefits of licensure with fewer of its costs. Medicare and other third-party payers should accept state title certification as a prerequisite for reimbursement eligibility. Such certification can and should be based on examinations and other eligibility criteria the states may establish.

The committee endorses the establishment of sunrise criteria to guide states' decisions about whether to regulate health occupations and, if so, how. These decisions should follow three basic principles:

1. the protection of the public is the sole reason for states to regulate health occupations;

2. the least restrictive regulatory mechanism consistent with public protection should be selected, taking into account other means that are in place; and

3. if, after due deliberation, the decision is made to regulate an occupation, it must be followed by a continuing commitment of resources on the part of the legislature, the governor, and the relevant administrative agencies.

State regulatory structures and procedures must be improved if they are to be effective. In most states the composition of boards, the requirements for entry, and the flow of information to the public are not fully consistent with the public interest.

The committee recommends that states strengthen the accountability and broaden the public base of their regulatory mechanisms. In the near term, the committee suggests the following:

- **Licensing boards should draw at least half of their membership from outside the licensed occupation; members should be drawn from the public as well as from a variety of areas of expertise such as health administration, economics, consumer affairs, education, and health services research.**
- **Flexibility in licensure statutes should be maintained to the greatest extent possible without undue risk of harm to the public. This may mean, for instance, allowing multiple paths to licensure or overlapping scopes of practice for some licensed occupations.**

The regulatory process should be conducted as openly as possible and should produce a flow of information to the public, including:

- the scope of practice of the occupation as defined by state law and regulation;
- the eligibility requirements for entry into the occupation;
- basic information about licensees, including the status of their license and any disciplinary actions taken by the state, as well as basic data such as educational background, which should be collected as part of the licensing process; and
- board membership and procedures, especially procedures for filing complaints against licensed professionals.

Regulatory boards should be well connected to the state bureaucracy.

If a state requires graduation from an accredited educational program for licensure, the state should take an active interest in the accreditation requirements to ensure that they are consistent with the state's interests.

Finally, the committee believes that decisions by states, accrediting bodies, and health care payers regarding scope of practice, referral, and supervision should be better informed. **The Bureau of Health Professions (or another future focal point for allied health personnel in the Department of Health and Human Services) should sponsor a body with members drawn from allied health and other health professions and from the health and social science research communities to assess objectively the evidence bearing on jurisdictional issues. This body, in consultation with other experts and interested parties, should consider issues of risk, cost,**

quality, and access. It should draw on available scientific evidence and identify topics on which research is needed.

Well-designed experiments and demonstrations of innovative roles for allied health personnel will provide valuable evidence to guide regulatory policy.

REFERENCES

Accreditation Manual for Hospitals. 1988. Chicago: Joint Commission on Accreditation of Healthcare Organizations.

American Dental Association. 1987. Testimony before the IOM Committee to Study the Role of Allied Health Personnel's Hearing on Regulation. National Academy of Sciences, Washington, D.C. July.

American Dental Hygienists' Association. 1987a. Paper submitted to the IOM Committee to Study the Role of Allied Health Personnel's Hearing on Regulation. National Academy of Sciences. Washington, D.C. July.

American Dental Hygienists' Association. 1987b. Testimony before the IOM Committee to Study the Role of Allied Health Personnel's Hearing on Regulation. National Academy of Sciences, Washington, D.C. July.

Begun, J. W. 1981. Professionalism and the Public Interest: Price and Quality in Optometry. Cambridge, Mass.: MIT Press.

California Office of Statewide Health Planning and Development. 1987. Health Manpower Pilot Projects Program: Annual Report to the Legislature and the Healing Arts Licensing Boards. Sacramento: State of California Office of Statewide Health Planning and Development.

Carpenter, E. S. 1987. State regulation of allied health personnel trends and emerging issues. Background paper commissioned by the Institute of Medicine Committee to Study the Role of Allied Health Personnel. National Academy of Sciences, Washington, D.C.

Carroll, S. L., and R. J. Gaston. 1977. Occupational Licensing: Final Report. Washington, D.C.: National Science Foundation.

Cohen, H. S. 1980. On professional power and conflict of interest: State licensing boards on trial. Journal of Health Politics, Policy and Law 5(2):291–308.

Committee on Allied Health Education and Accreditation. 1987. Allied Health Education Directory, 1987. 15th ed. Chicago: American Medical Association.

Gaumer, G. L. 1984. Regulating health professionals: A review of the empirical literature. Milbank Memorial Fund Quarterly/Health and Society 62(3):380–416.

Goldman, S. K., and W. D. Helms. 1983. The regulation of the health professions. A policy review prepared for the Commission of Health Regulatory Boards of the Commonwealth of Virginia. Richmond, Va. October.

Holen, A. S. 1977. The Economics of Dental Licensing. Arlington, Va.: Center for Naval Analysis.

Institute of Medicine, Committee to Study the Role of Allied Health Personnel. 1987. Mechanisms for Controlling the Quality of Allied Health Personnel. Public hearing held on July 1 at the National Academy of Sciences, Washington, D.C.

Maurizi, A. 1974. Occupational licensing and the public interest. Journal of Political Economy 82:399–413.

McCready, L. A. 1982. Emerging health care occupations: The system under siege. HCM Review (Fall):71–76.

National Advisory Commission on Health Manpower. 1967. A Report by the Committee on Health Manpower, Vol. 1. Washington, D.C.: Government Printing Office.

Shimberg, B. 1982. Occupational Licensing: A Public Perspective. Princeton, N.J.: Educational Testing Service.

Shimberg, B. 1984. The relationship among accreditation, certification and licensure. Federal Bulletin (April):99–115.

U.S. Department of Health, Education, and Welfare, Office of the Assistant Secretary for Health and Scientific Affairs. 1971. Report on Licensure and Related Health Personnel Credentialing. Washington, D.C.: Government Printing Office.

8

Allied Health Personnel and Long-Term Care

ARLIER CHAPTERS OF THIS REPORT discussed whether the supply of allied health personnel will be sufficient to meet the future demand. This demand has been understood as effective demand, or the number of allied health practitioners for whose services purchasers would be willing to pay, given probable economic constraints. In constrast, this chapter shifts the focus from the number of workers needed to fill jobs to the qualitative improvements that may be necessary if the allied health labor force is to be responsive to the needs of a particular segment of our society—those requiring long-term care. These improvements relate not only to whether care givers have the right technical skills to offer but also to whether services are organized and delivered in a way that enhances the quality of life for long-term care consumers.

Clearly, financing policies are a key to quality care, although the available evidence on nursing homes at least has not shown what the minimum reimbursement, staffing levels, and staff qualifications must be to provide adequate care (Institute of Medicine, 1986a). Resolving these financial issues is beyond the scope of this study. However, the committee believed that it could contribute to policy discussions of long-term care reform by addressing human resource management and educational issues that emerged during the course of its inquiry. As a means of gaining insight into these issues the committee supplemented its review of the literature, discussions with experts, and its own experience with site visits to 11 long-term care facilities in urban and rural areas of California, North Carolina, and Virginia. These site visits guided the committee's selection of the issues it could reasonably address in the context of its overall report. The collaboration of allied health personnel with one another and their interactions with other health care givers was one recurrent issue. The extent to which allied health curricula prepare students for long-term care settings was another.

LONG-TERM CARE AND ITS CONSUMERS

Although long-term care is defined in a number of different ways, for the purposes of this study, it is a broad range of clinical, social, and personal supportive services for people who need assistance over a sustained period of time to maintain or improve their well-being. The goal of long-term care is the maintenance or restoration of the highest possible level of physical, mental, and social functioning of individuals within the constraints of their illnesses, disabilities, and environmental settings (Meltzer et al., 1981; Kane and Kane, 1982).

In emphasizing the many types of services necessary to achieve the highest attainable quality of life and personal autonomy, this definition has two important implications for those who provide care and for how those care givers interrelate. First, care givers of many different professions and disciplines, as well as a patient's family and friends, must be involved. Second, this is a process that relies on a flow of information concerning an individual's needs, required services, and potential for recovery.

Long-term care can be provided in institutional settings such as nursing homes (mostly skilled nursing and intermediate care facilities), institutions for the mentally retarded, residential care facilities (e.g., board and care homes), long-stay hospitals (e.g., psychiatric hospitals), specialized schools, and hospices. It is also provided in ambulatory care settings, in community day care programs, and through home care services. Some rehabilitation facilities provide long-term inpatient care but also offer specialized ambulatory care over an extended period of time.

Although much of this chapter is about the elderly, others need long-term care services, including infants with birth defects, developmentally disabled children, adolescents who have suffered head trauma or spinal cord injury, laborers with emphysema, and elderly people with multiple sensory deficits. Also in need of such services are the chronically mentally ill and the severely retarded. In addition, the AIDS epidemic has focused attention on the long-term care needs of persons with chronic infectious diseases.

Because demographic projections suggest that the largest increase in the need for long-term care will come from the aging population, the service needs of the elderly have received the most attention of late. Indeed, the committee's examination of this topic coincides with the release of two major reports. The first, mandated by Congress, was cochaired by the directors of the National Institute on Aging and the Bureau of Health

Professions in the Health Resources and Services Administration. Their report examines "the adequacy and availability of personnel prepared to meet current and projected needs of elderly Americans through the year 2020" (National Institute on Aging, 1987).

A second study was conducted by the National Task Force on Gerontology and Geriatric Care Education in Allied Health. Established by the American Society of Allied Health Professions, the task force explored the implications of demographic and disease pattern trends for allied health professional education and practice (National Task Force, 1987).

The two studies reinforce some of the themes developed in this chapter. An aging population in need of long-term care will increasingly dominate the practice of most health care workers and will create pressure for greater numbers of personnel in total. Preparation for this future will require significant interventions in the way we educate and "socialize" students to treat patients and work with other health colleagues in the long-term care environment.

DETERMINANTS OF NEED FOR LONG-TERM CARE

A number of factors—health and functional status, income, living arrangements, marital status—influence who among us are likely to become long-term care consumers and the types of services we will receive. A review of these factors reveals why there is concern about the capacity of the health care system to meet these future challenges.

• The need for the formal support of nursing home care increases sharply with age, as do the effects of chronic disabling disease. The nursing home utilization rate is 2 percent for persons 65 to 74 years of age, 6 percent for those 75 to 84; and 23 percent for those 85 and older (Rice, 1985).

• If current morbidity, disability, and functional dependence rates and patterns continue, by the year 2000 about 50 percent more noninstitutional elderly people will require the help of others in daily living activities than required such help in 1980. At the same time, the number needing nursing homes could increase by 77 percent. In addition to the elderly, it is estimated that the number of individuals under 65 years of age who are functionally dependent as a result of chronic disabling disease may well equal that of those over 65 (Institute of Medicine, 1986b).

• Marital status influences the use of long-term care services (especially nursing homes) because people without spouses may not have anyone to provide the personal care that would allow them to stay in the community. In 1985, 84 percent of the elderly in nursing homes were without spouses, compared with 56 percent of functionally impaired people living in the community (Macken, 1986; National Center for Health Statistics, 1987b). If women continue their more rapid (compared with men) mortality improvements (Institute of Medicine, 1986b), there will be more unmarried spouses requiring nursing home care.

• Infectious disease patients are likely to cause a noticeable increase in the demand for long-term care and the services provided by allied health personnel. The number of AIDS patients jumped from 183 in 1981 to more than 49,000 at the end of 1987 (Centers for Disease Control, 1987a). The U.S. Public Health Service estimates that 1.5 million people are already infected with the AIDS virus (Centers for Disease Control, 1987b). Although relatively small proportions of AIDS patients may need long-term institutional care (e.g., those with dementia), there are indications that community care could bring a large demand for home health services (Braun, 1987; R. Widdus, IOM Committee on a National Strategy for AIDS, personal communication, 1987; Long-Term Care Management, 1988).

• More than 250,000 infants are born in the United States each year with physical or mental defects (March of Dimes, 1987). Despite advances in prenatal detection of the diseases that cause disability, data from the Centers for Disease Control show that the incidence of most types of birth defects remained substantially unchanged during the period 1970–1971 to 1981–1983 (Edmonds and James, 1984).

• For the past 15 years, the level of the severely developmentally disabled in the U.S. population has remained steady at approximately 1.6 percent. However, the type of care that they receive has changed dramatically during that time. In 1967, many of these individuals lived in large public or private institutions. Today, there is an increasing demand for relatively small, community-based facilities. The number of such facilities has grown from about 4,400 in 1977 to 20,000 in 1986. With these structural changes, some researchers have detected a substantial increase in staff-to-client ratios that is likely to continue (Braddock, 1988).

Ideally, an assessment of changing demographic and epidemiological patterns, such as those described above, should lead to an understanding of the preventive, curative, and rehabilitative needs of persons who become elderly or ill. Understanding care requirements clarifies the type of education and training programs care givers should have to be able to meet the needs of patients—which should lead to the development of appropriate educational programs.

Unfortunately, this idealized sequence does not occur—for many reasons. Chief among these is the lack of adequate financing, which limits who gets into the formal care system; the amount and quality of services provided; and the attractiveness of long-term care employment to health care workers. The scope of this study did not permit an exploration of the broader financing problems of long-term care; the committee devoted its attention to possible educational strategies and human resource management interventions in nursing homes, home care, and rehabilitation facilities—three settings in which allied health personnel play vital but different roles. The committee also explored the problems of integrating allied health services with those of other care givers in these settings, including aides, who may collaborate with or at times substitute for allied health personnel.

Nursing Homes

The majority of institutional long-term care is provided in nursing homes. In 1985, there were 19,100 nursing homes with 1,624,200 beds. These figures reflect a 22 percent increase in the number of homes and a 38 percent increase in the number of beds since 1974 (National Center for Health Statistics, 1987a).

Despite the demographic and disease pattern changes described earlier, the nation's stock of nursing home beds is not keeping pace with the growth in demand—let alone the probable need. The result is that nursing homes usually have high occupancy rates and long waiting lists, thus allowing operators to select "light" care and private-pay patients. This policy obviously works to the detriment of those who are poor and most in need of care. Efforts to change this situation are constrained by the states, which often seek to limit their Medicaid budgets through certificate-of-need regulations that control the building of new beds (American Health Care Associations, 1985, 1986). Future growth will depend on the federal government increasing its funding of long-term care or helping to create incentives for the small but growing private insurance market.

In 1985 there were approximately 1.2 million FTE nursing home employees. More than 700,000 provided personal care, of which nurse's aides and orderlies were the largest group (71 percent). The number of allied health professionals providing nursing home care on a salaried basis is comparatively small: in 1985 there were approximately 7,000 dietitian/nutritionists, 2,900 registered physical therapists, 2,600 registered medical record administrators, and 1,500 registered occupational therapist FTE employees (National Center for Health Statistics, 1987a; G. Strahan, personal communication, 1987*). Despite efforts to constrain bed growth, BLS projects that nursing home employment will grow through the year 2000 at an annual rate of 3.8 percent, or about three times the projected growth for the overall economy (Personik, 1987).

---

*Personal communication regarding unpublished data from the National Nursing Home Survey, Division of Health Care Statistics, National Center for Health Statistics.

Nursing Home Residents and the Organization of Care

The typical nursing home resident is an 80-year-old white widow who has several chronic medical conditions and was admitted to the nursing home about 1-½ years earlier after being a patient in a hospital or other health care facility. Seventy-five percent of elderly nursing home residents in 1985 were women; only 6 percent were black, and less than 1 percent were of other races. The fact that a higher proportion of the elderly white population (5 percent) receives nursing home care compared with black (4 percent) and other races (2 percent) is probably due to the substitution by nonwhites of informal care in the home for institutionalized care (National Center for Health Statistics, 1987b; Macken, 1986).

A patient enters a nursing home by physician referral or by direct application of the family. All services must be prescribed by a physician and furnished according to a written plan initiated by the physician. The care plan is developed in consultation with the appropriate nursing and allied health personnel. For example, an occupational therapist assists the physician by evaluating the patient's level of functioning, helping to develop the plan, preparing clinical and progress notes, educating and consulting with the family and other agency personnel, and participating in in-service programs. Occupational therapy assistants, under the supervision of a qualified occupational therapist, perform the services that have been planned and delegated by the therapist. They also help to prepare clinical notes and progress reports and help educate the patient and family (American Occupational Therapy Association, 1987).

To be certified under Medicare's conditions of participation, nursing homes must ensure the availability of allied health services. Yet the number of full-time allied health personnel actually employed there is small because most nursing homes find that reimbursements do not cover many of these services. To conserve resources, consulting arrangements and part-time work are the norm for therapists and other allied health workers. When funds are available to hire allied health personnel, many facilities appear to have difficulty in attracting such staff.

Registered nurses supervise or coordinate the direct care of patients in nursing homes, and one tool for enhancing communication among care givers is the team meeting. The regularity of these meetings varies among facilities. Often headed by nurses, the team may not necessarily include allied health personnel. Optimally, the meetings should not only provide an opportunity to exchange information about patients but should also serve as a way to organize the care that best responds to an individual patient's needs.

One approach to incorporating allied health personnel into such a team effort was described to IOM's Committee on Nursing Home Regulation.

In this model, allied health specialists played a strong educational rather than direct patient care role:

Each nursing unit has a primary care team composed of the physician, head nurse and social worker for that unit. The primary care team guides the resident care planning. All members of the team have an equal voice in this planning. Auxiliary staff such as physical therapists, occupational therapists, leisure activity specialists, dietetic technicians, etc., are assigned to each unit and work with the primary care team. In addition to individual relationships, unit team members plan and assess resident care in a variety of organized meetings. These types of meetings may have a different focus. For example, unit clinical meetings focus on residents' psychological problems, rehabilitation rounds focus on physical therapy. These meetings have one thing in common, however; they include all care givers including the nurse aide staff. (Boehner, 1984)

As a practical matter in today's nursing home environment, the rehabilitation services that allied health personnel might be providing directly are either absent or stretched across a large patient base. The linkage of allied health expertise to the activities of nurses and aides becomes a critical element in how well patients can improve their functioning. This linkage is dependent on opportunities for effective communication between allied health personnel and the nursing staff, as well as on the ability of other care givers—aides in particular—to receive and act on the advice of the allied health practitioner.

Nurse's Aides

The quality of life for patients is significantly affected by the quality of care provided by the care givers who have the most frequent contacts with them—the aides. The typical nurse's aide is a woman who is about 35 years old and who has no more than a high school education. She has little or no training in nursing skills. She has been employed in her current job less than 2 years and has less than 5 years' total experience as a paid care giver (National Center for Health Statistics, 1987b; G. Strahan, personal communication, 1987). Most aides are white, but a sizable proportion (32 percent) are black or other minorities, which is higher than their representation in the labor force as a whole (13 percent) (Kahl, 1987).

On an average day, the aide has a wide range of activities. For example:

The aide is expected to do passive range-of-motion exercises for stroke or paralysis patients. If hemorrhaging occurs, she must immediately elevate the body and apply pressure before calling the nurse. She must use correct body mechanics or seek help in moving patients. The aide is expected to reconcile food service deliveries with patient's dietary restrictions. She regularly observes changes in patient status such as whether a patient's toe nails need to be cut and whether decubiti are present. She monitors food and water intake, and emotional states. A capable aide would notice potential circulatory problems, changes in temperature, and paralysis. Aides also provide clean, wrinkle-free bed linens. They receive and return linens to the laundry or food trays to the kitchen. Aides are expected to initiate and facilitate interaction with residents and to assist in and encourage ambulation (Brannon and Bodnar, 1988).

As the foregoing list of duties illustrates, aides have major responsibilities for which they may have little training or experience to prepare them. There is also little status, recognition, or compensation for this key role. While most often viewed as part of the nursing staff, the problems aides encounter are, nonetheless, ones that also concern allied health practitioners or that overlap the responsibilities of allied health assistants. For example, both nurse's aides and occupational therapy assistants play a role in patients' daily hygiene and rehabilitation exercise programs.

The recent IOM report on nursing home regulation, in relating the improved functioning of residents to their sense of well-being, noted how aides shaped the residents' social world:

... 80 to 90 percent of the care is provided by nurse's aides and the quality of their interactions with the residents—how helpful, how friendly, how competent, how cheerful they are and how much they treat each resident as a person worthy of dignity and respects—makes a big difference in the quality of a resident's life. (Institute of Medicine, 1986a)

Because of their importance to the quality of care provided in nursing homes, as well as in home care, the levels and content of aide training have been focuses for reform. It is interesting to note that the recommendation from the IOM Nursing Home Standards Committee to make aide training a regulatory standard was one of the few exceptions to an approach that relied principally on patient outcome measures to ensure quality. Following IOM's recommendation, the Health Care Financing Administration proposed a rule to require that aides receive a minimum of 80 hours of training (Federal Register, 1987). Shortly thereafter, a provision of the Medicare law requiring 75 hours of aide training was enacted through the Omnibus Budget Reconciliation Act of 1987.

In many nursing homes, annual turnover is extremely high for aides, and in some cases, all of the aides may be replaced in the course of a year. High turnover has been linked to several factors, most important of which are employee pay and benefits. Aides generally earn only about $10,000 per year (Kahl, 1987). It is not surprising, then, that during site visits the committee heard reports of aides changing jobs for a 25- to 50-cents per-hour pay increase.

In addition to turnover, earnings play a part in a growing aide recruitment problem. Earlier chapters in this report noted the general tightness of the labor market for technically oriented personnel. Similarly, young, low-wage service workers will also be at a premium. Some employers in the nursing home industry see themselves in direct competition for these employees with the fast-food industry, for instance, which is beginning to offer higher starting salaries and the attraction of greater opportunities to socialize with peer workers in a less onerous atmosphere (Kerschner, 1987). Because of this competition, there is increasing interest in targeting older individuals for recruitment. These older workers (who are also being recruited by McDonald's fast-food restaurants), whose cohort will be expanding in the population in the future, already are a sizable proportion of the aide-level work force: 40 percent of aides are over the age of 35 (Kahl, 1987).

Pay alone, however, will not solve recruitment, retention, and turnover problems. Aides' poor self-perceptions and lack of involvement in the decision-making process regarding their responsibilities will require action by management (Waxman et al., 1984). The lack of career ladders, work scheduling, management attitudes, and understaffing are other common frustrations voiced by the aides themselves.

In light of their critical role in patient well-being and rehabilitation, the questions of how much training aides need to function effectively, how they relate to others who provide nursing and allied health services, and what kinds of pay and careers suit their level of responsibility are issues that nursing home management cannot avoid. If, in the future, there are to be sufficient numbers of people to carry out the responsibilities that aides presently assume, the nursing home industry must not only improve low wages and working conditions but confront the organizational challenge of deploying staff wisely. Allied health care givers in nursing homes will necessarily become involved in these issues. Enhanced pay and responsibility for aides will require that allied health personnel forge new working relationships and increasingly accept pedagogical roles.

HOME CARE

Home health care, which is often viewed as a substitute for nursing home placement or extended hospitalization, shares many of the same generic problems faced by nursing homes. Agencies find it difficult to recruit and retain staff at the aide level, and teamwork is frequently inadequate among nursing and allied health personnel. These problems are exacerbated in home care, which by its very nature requires staff to operate with less direct supervision.

Home Health Care Agencies and Personnel

Although formal community care, such as that provided by home health care agencies, now accounts for only 15 percent of public long-term care expenditures, this area has been one of the fastest growing segments of the health care industry. The number of Medicare-certified agencies nearly tripled from 2,212 in 1972 to 6,007 in 1986; the number dropped slightly to 5,877 in 1987 as agencies reacted to restrictions in Medicare rules. In 1986 there were 105,038 salaried, full-time employees. Registered nurses were the largest category (34 percent) of personnel, followed by aides (25 percent). About 6 percent of home health care employees were physical therapists, 2 percent were occupational therapists, and 3 percent were speech therapists (National Association for Home Care, 1987). Because some therapists operate on a contract basis or work in agencies that are not certified by Medicare, these proportions probably understate the actual number working in home care. For example, about 22 percent of physical therapists work at least part of their week for home health care agencies (American Physical Therapy Association, 1987).

Home health care is not covered by PPS, but since 1985 limitations have been applied to reimbursement for home health care services. As a result, many agencies choose not to participate in Medicare and limit their clientele to private-pay patients. The National Association for Home Care (1987) has estimated that there were an additional 3,700 agencies in 1987 that were not certified for Medicare. Few data are available on recipients or reimbursement under private insurance. Medicaid can also include home health care benefits, but payment levels have fluctuated greatly over the past decade and vary considerably by state. In 1987 New York accounted for 77 percent of all Medicaid home health expenditures, compared with California's 7 percent (Rabin and Stockton, 1987).

Home Health Care Clients and the
Organization of Care

About 80 percent of home health recipients are posthospital referrals. The typical process of referral from physician to nurse to allied health personnel can operate smoothly, but it may also mask a set of uneasy relationships.

The nurse's view of her role has been characterized by Mundinger (1983): "When the referral and physician's plan of care are received by the agency, an initial nurse assessment visit is made within three days. When the nurse's plan is approved, it becomes the operational one for patient care and replaces the original physician order":

The plan devised by the nurse includes all of the care to be given as well as recommendations for referrals. For example, if physiotherapy [sic] is being considered as care needed, it is the nurse who makes the assessment visit to determine whether it is in fact really necessary. The nurse decides on the need for a home health aide. The nurse also can make referrals for other home health services such as occupational therapy, speech therapy, and social worker services. The plan that is submitted to the physician for signature includes all reimbursable care the nurse deems necessary. It also includes illness prevention and health maintenance care required by the patient.

Physicians, as do most professionals, tend to implement the therapies that they know best, value, and use in their own work. Therefore, home care, traditionally a low-technology and low-cost venture, under Medicare has become a service filled with high-cost care. It is not unusual for a physician to order a battery of expensive blood tests rather than make a home visit, or utilize physical therapists for routine range of motion or ambulation of homebound patients. Physicians should be aware that nurses can teach families to carry out these exercises or that a visiting nurse's assessment and history can tell more than blood tests in many cases. (Mundinger, 1983)

The nurse arranges for various services to be delivered separately by therapists or aides, none of whom may meet with each other as a team. Such separation of services means that, although important information can be exchanged through the record, the amount of direct collaboration for patient problem solving among care givers is often minimal.

Because of this pattern of care, growing attention has been paid to the issue of who is the care manager, who controls the mix of services, and how multiple care givers coordinate their services. The care manager (or case manager) is responsible for ensuring the coordination and continuity of services (Levine and Fleming, 1986). As the quotation above illustrates, nurses currently see themselves as fulfilling this function. Physicians and allied health personnel, however, are not necessarily willing to concede this point.

The following represents the viewpoint of the Health and Public Policy Committee of the American College of Physicians, which has argued that physicians ought to be actively involved in assessing the continuing functional as well as medical needs of homebound patients and advising patients on the use of home health care services:

Although Medicare requires the physician to certify a home health treatment plan, typically the physician describes the patient's medical condition to a home health agency, and a registered nurse actually develops and implements the home care plan.

Physicians should play an important role in home health care, not only as providers of medical care, but also as case managers and coordinators of care. Physicians should assure that their patients continue to receive high-quality medical care after discharge from a hospital and while receiving treatment in the home.

Unfortunately, the current reimbursement system does not provide any incentives for physicians to become more involved in home health care. Time spent communicating with home health care personnel, devising home treatment plans, completing certification forms, consulting with the patient and family by telephone, or traveling to a patient's home is not reimbursable. Indeed, HCFA [Health Care Financing Administration] maintains that these costs are subsumed in physicians' payments for office visits and home visits. (American College of Physicians, Health and Public Policy Committee, 1986)

From the perspective of the allied health fields, the interdisciplinary group that constitutes the home health care team "is overly dependent upon a single type of profession, the physician, to write orders." Patient needs should determine whether case management is accomplished by an individual therapist, social worker, nurse, or a team. Yet current reimbursement practices, allied health leaders have argued, do not give the team adequate control over how resources are allocated for the patient's care plan (National Task Force, 1987).

Without a reimbursement mechanism that creates incentives for coordinated and appropriate use of the home care services that are potentially available from a wide array of providers, it will be difficult to overcome problems of fragmentation, duplication of services, and interprofessional competition. Short of such a payment scheme, the solutions commonly cited in the home care and case management literature offer the best hope for improvement. These include greater use of team conferences, more complete documentation of patient records, increased attention to defining the functions of different types of practitioners in home care, more vigorous case management on the part of home health care agencies, and educational experiences that prepare students for interdisciplinary collaboration and case management (Steinhauser, 1984; Trossman, 1984).

REHABILITATION

In moving from a consideration of nursing homes and home care to a discussion of rehabilitation facilities, a major distinction is soon apparent: the team approach to clinical management is a well-recognized fixture in the rehabilitation world. Collaborative behavior among health care practitioners is reinforced by the fact that rehabilitation patients are generally treated for a functional rather than a medical disability. For Medicare reimbursement, regulations mandate that patients must receive a minimum of 3 hours of physical therapy, occupational therapy, speech therapy, or orthotist and prosthetist services per day for 5 days per week (*Medicare Intermediary Manual*, Section 3101.11 (D)(3), Part A). Intermediary Manual). The patient who regresses or no longer improves in function must be discharged into another care environment. The current payment system places a premium on functional assessment and progression toward improved functioning.

There has been significant growth in rehabilitation programs in the last 30 years and a 50 percent growth in the number of rehabilitation beds in the last 5 years. Today, there are 73 rehabilitation hospitals with 6,225 beds in the United States. There are also 512 distinct rehabilitation units with about 13,000 beds in general hospitals. Rehabilitation facilities are currently exempt from the Medicare prospective payment system because an equitable predictor of resource consumption on which to base payment has not yet been found. (Rehabilitation services in intensive care and in medical-surgical units of acute care hospitals, however, are not exempt.) Approximately 32 million people are physically disabled, and 12 million people are severely disabled. The number of severely disabled people has increased and will continue to increase as the population ages and as technological advances improve the prospects of children with birth injuries or congenital defects (England et al., 1987; Lesparre, 1987).

Because patients in rehabilitation settings need specialized and intensive services, the staff typically includes full-time departments of physical, occupational, and speech therapy, radiological and laboratory services, and sometimes respiratory therapy. Social, psychological, and vocational services are also provided but on a consultant basis. Although the staff in rehabilitation hospitals typically work in teams, some experts call for an additional category of case managers to help ensure appropriate and timely referrals, reduce admission delays, and assess insurance gaps (England, 1987; Lesparre, 1987).

By tradition, allied health practitioners, together with nurses, play a central role in the delivery of team health care. For example, the ratio of FTE physical therapists to registered nurses is 1:2 in rehabilitation hospitals, compared with 1:43 in acute care hospitals (American Hospital Association, 1987). A recent survey by the National Association of Rehabilitation Facilities showed that 65 percent of the total costs in rehabilitation hospitals were attributable to staff salaries, wages, and fringe benefits. This percentage compares with an average of about 57 percent for all hospitals. The intensive use of physical therapists, occupational therapists, and specialized nurses results in higher personnel costs in rehabilitation hospitals. Salary increases of 7 percent a year for physical therapists, 6 percent for occupational therapists, and 5 percent for nurses since 1985 reflect the difficulties these hospitals are experiencing in attracting personnel. Competition for these employees has also resulted in growing recruitment costs and the increased use of contract personnel (National Association of Rehabilitation Facilities, 1987).

A survey of 43 rehabilitation facilities in California found vacancy rates of 15.6 percent for physical therapists, 8.6 percent for occupational therapists, and 10.7 percent for speech–language pathologists. Vacancy rates for physical therapy and occupational therapy assistants exceeded 20 percent. Among the consequences of these staffing problems, 24 percent of the respondents experienced admission restrictions, 76 percent showed an impact on outpatient waiting lists, and 58 percent delayed the initiation of new services or curtailed existing ones (California Association of Rehabilitation Facilities, 1987).

Rehabilitation hospitals see themselves as being at a disadvantage in competing for allied health personnel in tight labor markets. They attribute their difficulties to students' lack of exposure to the potential of a career in rehabilitation, which is perceived to be an arduous, unattractive job, bringing little recognition. Rehabilitation administrators fear a continuing diversion of personnel to more attractive practice settings in which patients are less incapacitated and earnings are higher.

A brief examination of the experience of the Veterans Administration (VA), a major provider of rehabilitation services in the nation, offers some insights into the problems often faced by many rehabilitation facilities, especially the public institutions. Although the VA labors under personnel and other constraints peculiar to public facilities in recruiting and compensating its employees, the implications of personnel shortages and coping strategies are an instructive preview of what the future could be for all rehabilitation facilities in the face of widespread shortages.

The VA's Experience

Interviews with central office officials and chiefs of physical therapy and occupational therapy at a number of VA medical centers revealed a consensus on a number of points. Many of the centers' recruitment and retention problems are due to competition for these occupations in the nonfederal sector. The substitution of less qualified care givers was infrequent, although health care delivery services were sometimes curtailed as a result of the shortage. The problem appears to be worsening; patient loads are increasing while physical therapy and occupational therapy staffs continue to decrease.

At one medical center in a mid-Atlantic state, half the physical therapy slots were vacant. Although physical therapy assistants were employed, they were not used in lieu of licensed physical therapists because they are not permitted to evaluate patients. The medical center employed six corrective therapists (a type of rehabilitation personnel used mostly in the VA), but they were also comparatively limited in the type of care they were permitted to provide. A corrective therapist was assigned to the unit to assist patients in walking. In addition, because of a lack of staff, the physical therapy treatment room in a newly built nursing home care unit remained closed. The chief of physical therapy, who carried a full patient load in an effort to offset the shortage, stated that nonfederal employers in the area were paying $24,000–$28,000 for new graduates while the VA started them at $18,000. She added that the presumption among many recent graduates was that, ultimately, they will enter private practice. In her experience, this differed markedly from the goals and assumptions of physical therapists in the past, most of whom spent their entire careers employed by medical facilities.

In another instance, a large medical center in Southern California had a substantial geriatric patient population, a spinal cord injury unit, and an extensive orthopedic caseload. The center also employed a number of well-known specialists in physical therapy. As a result, recent graduates flocked there for the quality of the training they could receive. Recruitment success was high and vacancy rates were relatively low, but physical therapists typically remained there no more than 2 years. Thus, patients were treated for the most part by young, inexperienced personnel.

At a relatively small southern medical center, administrators cited both physical therapist and occupational therapist recruitment problems as limiting the number of bedside treatments provided. There were physical therapy and occupational therapy education programs offered in this city, but the institution had been unable to recruit graduates before they relocated to other geographic areas where the pay was higher. Because the department was too small to require a chief of service, the medical center needed an experienced occupational therapist before it could recruit recent graduates who would need seasoning.

The lack of occupational therapists in another southern medical center resulted in slight modifications of the duties of assistants and such adjustments as program cutbacks and delays in starting new programs. The chief of occupational therapy stated that nonfederal occupational therapy jobs in that city paid $4,000–$5,000 more than what the VA paid, and that it was virtually impossible for the VA to hire experienced therapists. The situation seems unlikely to improve, as a recent survey found that there are 54 job openings in occupational therapy in that city.

At a small rural VA medical center in the Northeast, physical therapy slots have remained vacant for as long as 2 years. In addition to its lack of salary competitiveness in a region with high demand, this hospital also believes that its large geriatric population does not offer the variety that many practitioners seek.

As discussed in Chapter 6 and in the VA case examples, health care administrators who face personnel shortages have relied on several strategies to handle the deficiencies over the short term. These strategies include extensive use of overtime, service targeting to the patients most likely to benefit from them, and downward substitution (or cross-substitution) of allied health personnel to the extent that regulations permit. In the long run, unless rehabilitation facilities are willing to become reconciled to the sort of adaptations described in the VA cases, they will have to improve their capacity to compete for allied health graduates.

The committee believes that the public will neither wish to nor should accept service compromises in the quality and availability of rehabilitative care that are due to major shortages in allied health personnel. Current data and analytic techniques cannot specify the number of personnel needed beyond those who are likely to be demanded under current reimbursement and human resource policies and practices. Yet in the committee's judgment, rehabilitation facilities will not fare well unless the personnel pool grows substantially along with an increase in the share of those choosing to engage in this difficult work.

As we have noted throughout this report, salary adjustments are an inevitable response to this competition. Indeed, the VA has sought exemptions from Congress on salary scales. Along with these adjustments, however, must come a more careful and sustained rethinking of the services that are to be provided and of who provides them. The initiatives to do this will likely come from health care delivery sites that are attempting to cope with service demands and constrained budgets, but educators should not distance themselves from this rethinking process. A new relationship between health care and academic institutions must be forged. Our recommendations in the next section address the nature of this partnership.

CONCLUSIONS AND RECOMMENDATIONS

In this chapter, the committee has concentrated on three generic human resource problems that plague the provision of long-term care.

1. Minimally trained personnel are often the primary patient care givers, especially in nursing homes and home care. As a result, there is too little attention to the linkage between nursing and allied health services in the hands-on care activities of aides.

2. Current efforts to incorporate the care of the aged and chronically disabled into the allied health curriculum are inadequate in view of the important impact these patients will have on the health care delivery system of the future.

3. Collaborative behavior among allied health practitioners, as well as between allied health practitioners and other health care workers, is insufficiently promoted by management in nursing homes and home care agencies and by educational institutions in the educational experiences provided to students.

Education of Nurse's Aides

The passage of the provision in the Omnibus Budget Reconciliation Act of 1987 requiring a minimum of 75 hours of initial aide training should mark the beginning of a long-range educational effort. The act specifies that the content of nurse's aide training is to include basic nursing skills; personal care skills; cognitive, behavioral, and social care; basic restorative services; and residents' rights (U.S. Congress, House of Representatives, 1987).

The committee views this training requirement as a reasonable starting point to raise the skills and knowledge of entry-level workers who provide most of the direct patient care in long-term care facilities. There is also an urgent need, however, for a visible pathway leading to higher levels of education for aides who wish career progression and improved remuneration. Such a pathway into nursing or allied health fields would contribute to raising the morale and self-image of these workers and ultimately reduce the costly turnover of personnel.

In recognition that the greatest amount of direct patient contact and care in long-term care settings and programs is provided by personnel at the nurse's aide level, the federal government and other responsible governmental agencies should require education and training to raise the knowledge and skill levels of these individuals. Demonstration projects should be funded to encourage joint efforts by educators and employers in creating viable career paths for aides.

Tolerance of and empathy with old, chronically ill, disabled, or demented patients is an elusive but critical attribute to be sought among care givers. Without this attribute, individuals are not likely to choose work in long-term settings as a career. Long-term care employers and educators should identify and nurture those with this "people-oriented" attribute. One approach might be for employers and educators to develop local plans in which service in long-term care settings would earn employer-paid educational credits that could be used by personnel to further their educational objectives. Such an investment would yield at least three desirable results: (1) an improved quality of care for patients; (2) the enhanced recruitment of minorities, young people, and minimally educated individuals; and (3) increased stability in the segment of the labor force that provides direct care. This approach would be particularly attractive if educational programs in the established allied health professions would reserve a small proportion of their entry positions (e.g., 10 percent) for applicants from such long-term care settings.

Other innovative programs that could be jointly sponsored by academic institutions (e.g., community colleges) and employers should also be considered in creating a career path. The committee was impressed with the concept of an apprenticeship model, which has had some success in the skilled trades but which has not received the attention it perhaps deserves in the health care fields. The model stresses on-the-job, practical experience combined with formal training. A key element in its success is that the student-worker's prospects for a "good job" in terms of pay and responsibility should be rewarded at the end of the program. These good jobs, while not plentiful in today's long-term care industry, must be developed in the decade ahead if the industry expects to compete in tomorrow's labor market and improve the quality of service it provides.

Enhancing the Curriculum

Although allied health students gain technical expertise in particular areas of concentration during their education, many have only limited exposure to chronically ill and disabled persons. They may therefore have only a superficial understanding of the complexity of the physical, mental, emotional, and social problems of impaired persons and their families. When in training, allied health students may not rotate through long-term care facilities or programs to experience personally the technical difficulties that arise in evaluating and caring for older or chronically disabled persons.

The committee recommends that all allied health education and training programs include substantive content and practical clinical experience in the care of the chronically ill and aged. In general, such curricula should include information on the demographic shifts and changing epidemiological patterns of diseases and disabilities, the biological and psychological aspects of chronic illness and aging, the common medical problems seen in patients, legal and ethical dilemmas, the medical and psychological aspects of death and dying, health promotion and disease and disability prevention, interdisciplinary team participation, the evaluation and assessment of patients' needs, the roles of related health professionals, administrative and management techniques, and communication and supervisory skills.

Among these topics, the committee was particularly impressed during its site visits by the need for assessment, pedagogical, and coping skills. Because of shortages or the uneven distribution of allied health professionals, a member of each allied health speciality may not be available to make an assessment of a patient from his or her own disciplinary perspective. Therefore, it is important that all professional care providers acquire enough knowledge to enable them to make physical, psychological, and environmental assessments of an individual patient and to develop an appropriate care plan. The providers need this broader knowledge even though some of the patient's needs may be outside the narrow area of expertise of a given allied health profession. Because allied health practitioners may be employed as consultants with responsibility for a large number of patients or residents, they must also have the skills to instruct aides and family members in care plan activities and be able to monitor the effectiveness and quality of the assistance given to patients.

A major barrier to curriculum reform is the shortage of faculty who are appropriately trained and experienced in the care of the chronically ill and disabled. In an effort to combat deficiencies in the training of personnel and faculty, the Health Resources and Services Administration established regional resource centers through its Geriatric Education Centers program. The program, which began in 1983, supports the multidisciplinary training of medical, dental, osteopathic, optometric, pharmacy, pediatric, nursing, and allied health students, faculty, and others in geriatric health care. Other governmental programs that have provided multidisciplinary training include special project grants and the Area Health Education Centers (also sponsored by HRSA), Long-Term Care Gerontology Centers (sponsored by the Administration on Aging), and VA's Geriatric Research, Education, and Clinical Centers. Despite these programs the National Institute on Aging task force estimates that the current number of faculty members specializing in aging and geriatric care ranges from 5 to 25 percent of the total number needed (National Institute on Aging, 1987). A major focus for the faculty development grants recommended in Chapter 5 should be the encouragement of more faculty specializing in geriatric care.

Orienting allied health education toward geriatric care will not make salaries more competitive or improve working conditions; neither will it change the fact that such patient care is physically and emotionally difficult. The committee believes, however, that education in geriatric care will help those who do choose work in these settings to remain longer by giving them the necessary knowledge and coping skills. It will also allow more students the opportunity to consider the possible rewards of such a career and will encourage more faculty to engage in health services and clinical research that is relevant to the problems faced by long-term care providers.

Improved Teamwork

The committee noted that the collaborative behavior seen among rehabilitation hospital staff is frequently absent in nursing homes and home care. In the absence of financing incentives that encourage teamwork, the responsibility rests with managers to organize their personnel in ways that maximize interaction among allied health practitioners and other care givers. The committee therefore recommends that **because the problems associated with chronic illness do not fall within the boundaries of any single discipline, administrators and care coordinators in long-term care settings should develop effective means for ensuring that all personnel involved in patient care work closely together to meet patient needs.**

Health care managers would be greatly helped in these endeavors if educators provided the foundation on which to build collaborative behavior in later practice. Allied health practitioners need to understand and appreciate the special skills and roles that their fellow allied health workers play, together with the assets and limitations of others on the long-term care team.

The issues of recruitment, education, personnel utilization, and regulation that have been raised throughout this report take on a special significance in the nation's struggle to achieve humane care for its growing numbers of elderly and chronically ill patients. Society will be under great pressure to accommodate larger numbers of patients in the settings discussed here. It will also be under at least as great a pressure to limit the resources that may be necessary to raise the standard of care. Allied health practitioners who are caught up in this struggle will be challenged to use their ingenuity—both on a personal level, as care providers, and collectively, as an important force for reshaping the care system.

The remedies suggested in this chapter are not new: they can be found in the work of current committees and task forces and even in past Institute of Medicine studies on nursing and health care teams (Institute of Medicine, 1972, 1983). But the time to move teamwork and geriatric education ahead is long past due.

No single recommendation the committee can devise will accomplish this movement. It must come from leaders in the health professions who are willing to concede a measure of control and autonomy in favor of the common goal of collaborative patient care. It will require the ingenuity of educators in seeking additional resources for curriculum reform. It will also demand the resolve to initiate a painful process of resource allocation that places a higher value on care giver collaboration and preparation for the demands of long-term care.

REFERENCES

American College of Physicians, Health and Public Policy Committee. 1986. Home health care. Annals of Internal Medicine 105(3):454–460.

American Health Care Association. 1985. Trends and Strategies of Long-Term Care. Washington, D.C.: American Health Care Association.

American Health Care Association. 1986. Nursing Homes, A Sourcebook. Washington, D.C.: American Health Care Association.

American Hospital Association. 1987. Unpublished data from the Annual Hospital Survey and Survey of Rehabilitation Hospitals and Units. American Hospital Association, Chicago.

American Occupational Therapy Association. 1987. American Occupational Therapy. Rockville, Md.: American Occupational Therapy Association.

American Physical Therapy Association. 1987. Active Membership Profile Study. Alexandria, Va.: American Physical Therapy Association.

Boehner, E. M. 1984. Managing to achieve quality of life. Background paper prepared for the Institute of Medicine Committee on Improving Quality in Nursing Homes. Washington, D.C. October.

Braddock, D. 1988. Challenges in community integration. *In* Integration of Developmentally Disabled Individuals into the Community, 2nd ed., L. Healy, J. Harvey, and S. R. Novak, eds. Baltimore, Md.: Brookes Publishing Co.

Brannon, D., and J. Bodner, 1988. The Primary Care Givers: Aides and LPNs. Mental Health Consultation in Nursing Homes. New York: New York University Press.

Braun, S. April 1, 1987. Hospices for AIDS cases: A beginning. The Los Angeles Times, p. 1.

California Association of Rehabilitation Facilities. 1987. Survey on rehabilitation manpower. Unpublished data. California Association of Rehabilitation Facilities, Sacramento. December.

Centers for Disease Control. 1987a. AIDS Weekly Surveillance Report—United States, December 29, 1987. Atlanta, Ga.: CDC.

Centers for Disease Control. 1987b. Human Immunodeficiency Virus Infections in the U.S.: A Review of Current Knowledge and Plans for Expansion of HIV Surveillance Activities. Special report. Atlanta, Ga.: U.S. Department of Health and Human Services. November 30.

Edmonds, L., and L. James. 1984. Temporal trends in the incidence of malformation in the United States, 1970–71, 1982–83. Morbidity and Mortality Weekly Review 34:255.

England, B., C. Armkraut, and M. Lesparre. 1987. An agenda for medical rehabilitation, 1987 and into the 21st century. American Hospital Association, Chicago.

Federal Register. October 16, 1987. Medicare and Medicaid, Conditions of Participation for Long Term Care Facilities. Vol. 52(200):38582–38606.

Institute of Medicine. 1972. Education for the Health Team. Washington, D.C.: National Academy of Sciences.

Institute of Medicine. 1983. Nursing and Nursing Education: Public Policies and Private Actions. Washington, D.C.: National Academy Press.

Institute of Medicine. 1986a. Improving the Quality of Care in Nursing Homes. Washington, D.C.: National Academy Press.

Institute of Medicine. 1986b. A Study Plan "Toward a National Strategy for Long-Term Care of the Elderly." Institute of Medicine Committee to Plan a Major Study of National Long-Term Care Policies and the National Academy of Sciences. Pub. No. IOM-85-05. Washington, D.C.: National Academy Press. April.

Kahl, A. (Bureau of Labor Statistics). 1987. Remarks at a symposium on nurses' aide training. Sponsored by the National Citizens Coalition on Nursing Home Reform, Washington, D.C. November.

Kane, R. L., and Kane, R. A. 1982. Values and Long-Term Care. Lexington, Mass.: Lexington Books.

Kerschner, P. 1987. Staffing: Getting the edge on McDonald's and Pizza Hut. Provider 13(4):39.

Lesparre, M. 1987. Paradoxes of medical rehabilitation. *in* Perspectives, a supplement to Medicine and Health. New York: McGraw-Hill. November 16.

Levine, I., and M. Fleming. 1986. Human Resources Development: Issues in Care Management. Rockville, Md.: National Institute of Mental Health. May.

Long Term Care Management. 1988. AIDS: What role for nursing homes? Long Term Care Management (Newsletter). February 4. New York: McGraw-Hill.

Macken, C. 1986. A profile of functionally impaired elderly persons living in the community. Health Care Financing Review 7(4):33–49.

March of Dimes. 1987. Birth Defects, Tragedy and Hope. White Plains, N.Y.: March of Dimes Birth Defects Foundation.

Meltzer, J., F. Farrow, and H. Richman. 1981. Policy Options in Long-Term Care. Chicago: The University of Chicago Press.

Mundinger, M. 1983. Home Care Controversy. Rockville, Md.: Aspen Publishers, Inc.

National Association for Home Care. 1987. Home health agency statistics. Unpublished data. National Association for Home Care, Washington, D.C. August.

National Association of Rehabilitation Facilities. 1987. Letter of August 7, 1987, to the U.S. Department of Health and Human Services Health Care Financing Administration from Carolyn C. Zollar, General Counsel. Washington, D.C.

National Center for Health Statistics. G. Strahan. 1987a. Nursing Home Characteristics: Preliminary Data from the 1985 National Nursing Home Survey. Advanced Data From Vital and Health Statistics No. 131. DHHS Pub. No. (PHS) 87-1250. Hyattsville, Md.: Public Health Service.

National Center for Health Statistics. E. Hing. 1987b. Use of Nursing Homes by the Elderly: Preliminary Data from the 1985 National Nursing Home Survey. Advanced Data From Vital and Health Statistics No. 135. DHHS Pub. No. (PHS) 87-1250. Hyattsville, Md.: Public Health Service.

National Institute on Aging. 1987. Personnel for Health Needs of the Elderly Through the Year 2020. Washington, D.C.: U.S. Department of Health and Human Services. September.

National Task Force on Gerontology and Geriatric Care Education in Allied Health. 1987. An aging society: Implications for health care needs, impacts on allied health practice and education. Journal of Allied Health (Special Issue) 16(4).

Personik, V. A. 1987. Projections 2000: Industry Output and Employment Through the End of the Century. Monthly Labor Review 110(9):45.

Rabin, D. L., and P. Stockton. 1987. Long-Term Care for the Elderly: A Factbook. New York: Oxford University Press.

Rice, D. 1985. Health care needs of the elderly. *In* Long Term Care of the Elderly, C. Harrington, R. Newcomer, and C. Estes and Associates, eds. Beverly Hills, Calif.: Sage Publications, Inc.

Steinhauser, M. 1984. Occupational therapy and home health care. American Journal of Occupational Therapy 38(11):715–716.

Trossman, P. 1984. Administrative and professional issues for the occupational therapist in home health care. American Journal of Occupational Therapy 38(11):726–733.

U.S. Congress, House of Representatives. 1987. Omnibus Budget Reconciliation Act of 1987. Conference Report, H.R. 3545, Report No. 100-495. 100th Cong., 1st sess.

Waxman, H., M. Carner, and G. Berkenstock. 1984. Job turnover and job satisfaction among nursing home aides. The Gerontologist 24(5):503–509.

APPENDIXES

A

Congressional Mandate: Study of the Role of Allied Health Personnel in Health Care Delivery*

Sec. 223

(a) (1) The Secretary of Health and Human Services shall arrange for the conduct of a study concerning the role of allied health personnel in health care delivery. The Secretary shall request the National Academy of Sciences to conduct the study under an arrangement under which the actual expenses incurred by the Academy in conducting such study will be paid by the Secretary and the Academy will prepare the report required by subsection (c). If the National Academy of Sciences is willing to do so, the Secretary shall enter into such an arrangement with the Academy for the conduct of the study.

(2) If the National Academy of Sciences is unwilling to conduct the study required by paragraph (1) under the type of arrangement described in such paragraph, the Secretary shall enter into a similar arrangement with one or more appropriate nonprofit private entities.

(b) The study required by subsection (a) shall:

(1) assess the role of allied health personnel in health care delivery;

(2) identify projected needs, availability, and requirements of various types of health care delivery systems for each type of allied health personnel;

(3) investigate current practices under which each type of allied health personnel obtain licenses, credentials and accreditation;

---

*Public Law 99-129, signed October 22, 1985.

(4) assess changes in programs and curricula for the education of allied health personnel and in the delivery of services by such personnel which are necessary to meet the needs and requirements identified pursuant to paragraph (2); and

(5) assess the role of the Federal, State, and local governments, educational institutions and health care facilities in meeting the needs and requirements identified pursuant to paragraph (2).

(c) By October 1, 1987, the Secretary of Health and Human Services shall transmit to the Committee on Labor and Human Resources of the Senate and the Committee on Energy and Commerce of the House of Representatives, and make available to the public, a report:

(1) describing the study conducted under this section;

(2) containing a statement of the data obtained under such study; and,

(3) specifying such recommendations for legislation and administrative action as the Secretary considers appropriate.

B

Participants in Workshops and Public Meetings

COMMITTEE PUBLIC MEETING HELD JULY 1, 1987

American Association for Marriage and Family Therapy
MICHAEL BOWERS
American Association for Respiratory Care
MEL MARTIN, *President*
American Association of Bioanalysts
DON LAVANTY, Government Relations
American Association of Certified Allied Health Personnel in Ophthalmology
NORMA GARBER
ELLA ROSAMONT-MORGAN
American Association of Certified Orthoptists
BARBARA CHASSIN
RANDY GOUTERMAN
American Association of Medical Assistants, Inc.
DON BALASA, *Assistant Director*
American Cardiology Technologists Association
STEPHEN KANIECKI, *President*
LINDA HUMSTON
American College of Cardiology
FRANCIS J. MENAPACE, JR.
American College of Nurse-Midwives
KAREN BODENHORN

American College of Radiology
ROBERT BRADEN
MARK MISHKIN, Committee on Human Relations
MARIE ZINNINGER
American College of Surgeons
CINDY BROWN, *Washington Associate*
American Dental Association
BRENDA HARRISON, *Director*, State Government Affairs
J. O'DONNELL, *Director*, Legislative Policy
L. P. WHEAT, *Director*, Government Relations
LOUIS SCHUHRKE, Council on Dental Education
American Dental Hygienists Association
DIANE DE ROOS BASSAGE, *Second Vice-President*
WILLIAM SCHMIDT
American Dietetic Association
PATTI BLUMER
BOB EARL, *Manager*, Government Affairs
JEAN MINSKOFF
American Hospital Association
BARBARA KREML, *Director*, Human Relations
American Medical Record Association
RITA FINNEGAN, *Executive Director*
American Medical Technologists
ELEANOR BORS, *Executive Director*
WILLIAM ROBBINS, *Member*, Board of Directors
American Occupational Therapy Association
JEANETTE BAIR, *Director*, Practice
STEPHANIE HOOVER
SUSAN SCOTT, *Director of Government and Legal Affairs*
American Orthotic and Prosthetic Association
WILSON LATKOVIC, *Assistant Director*
GEN. WILLIAM MCCULLOCH, *President*
CHARLES UNGER
American Physical Therapy Association
FRANK MALLON, *Associate Executive Vice-President*, Professional
Relations
TOM WELSH, *Chief, Physical Therapy*
American Society for Medical Technology
SIDNEY OLIVER
LYNN PODELL, *Executive Director*
GLENDA PRICE
American Society for Parenteral and Enteral Nutrition
JANET GANNON, *Director of Professional Development*

American Society of Allied Health Professions
  DAVID BROSKI
  PAT GILLESPIE
American Society of Clinical Pathologists
  BARBARA CASTLEBERRY, *Vice-President*
  PAUL CHERNEY, *Chairman*, ASCP Board of Registry
  CATHY COHEN
  BOBBI-LYNN WATNIK, *Legislative Assistant*
American Society of Cytology
  SALLY-BETH BUCKNER
  ANN H. CLARK
American Society of Electroneurodiagnostic Technologists
  LEIGH O'NEAL, *Member*, Board of Trustees
American Society of Microbiology
  DIETER GROESCHEL, *Chairman*, Committee on Laboratory Practices
    for Microbiology
American Speech–Language–Hearing Association
  MORGAN DOWNEY
  JAMES LINGWALL
Association of Surgical Technologists, Inc.
  BARBARA GAY
  WILLIAM TEUTSCH
Bureau of Labor Statistics, U.S. Department of Labor
  ANN KAHL, *Economist*
Congressional Research Service
  JANET KLINE, *Chief*, Health Section
Gini Associates
  EUGENIA CARPENTER, *President*
Greater Southeast Community Hospital
  THOMAS CHAPMAN, *President*
  MICHELE JOHNSON, *Administrative Fellow*
Health Care Financing Administration, U.S. Department of Health
  and Human Services
  STANLEY E. EDINGER, *Science Director*
Health Resources and Services Administration, U.S. Department of
  Health and Human Services
  JERRY MCCLENDON
National Board of Cardiovascular Testing, Inc.
  DIANA GUNTHER
  CAROL ROBBINS
National Coalition for Arts Therapy Associations
  JAMES MITCHELL, *Director*

National Commission for Health Certification Agencies
  BARBARA HICKEY
National Hearing Aid Society
  TIMOTHY WATERS, *Attorney*
National Society for Cardiopulmonary Technology
  MICHAEL R. BOIVIN
National Society of Allied Health
  HARLEY FLACK, *President*
Office of the Assistant Secretary for Health, U.S. Department of
  Health and Human Services
  CAROL ZUCKET, *Senior Program Analyst*
Office of the Assistant Secretary for Planning and Evaluation, U.S.
  Department of Health and Human Services
  HERBERT C. HAMMOND, *Policy Analyst*
Society of Nuclear Medicine, Technologist Section
  MARCIA BOYD, *President*
  PAUL COLE
  VIRGINIA PAPPAS, *Deputy Executive Director*
Virginia Citizens Consumer Council
  HELEN SAVAGE
Virginia Department of Health Regulatory Boards
  RICHARD MORRISON

WORKSHOP ON FACTORS THAT AFFECT THE DEMAND FOR ALLIED HEALTH PERSONNEL HELD APRIL 26–27, 1987

RONNI CHERNOFF, *Associate Director of Geriatric Research*, Education and
  Clinical Center for Education and Evaluation, Veterans
  Administration Medical Center, Little Rock, Arkansas
BRENT ENGLAND, *Director*, Section for Rehabilitation Hospitals and
  Programs, American Hospital Association
NORMAN F. ESTRIN, *Vice President*, Science and Technology, Health
  Industry Manufacturers Association
CHERLYN S. GRANROSE, *Assistant Professor*, Department of Human
  Resources Administration, Temple University
MARTHA HOPLER, *Director of Human Resources*, Medlantic Health Care
  Group
CHARLES HOSTETTER, *Deputy Director*, AIDS Services Program, Health
  Resources and Services Administration
DONALD JACKSON, *President*, Rehabilitation Systems of Illinois
STANLEY B. JONES, *Vice President*, Consolidated Health Care, Inc.

LAIRD MILLER, Health Systems Management

SEYMOUR PERRY, *Professor of Medicine and Deputy Director*, The Institute for Health Policy Analysis, Georgetown University Medical Center

RICHARD SCHMIDT, Scanlon, Hastings and Schmidt

DENNIS J. TREAT, *Director*, Washington, D.C., Group Operations, The Prudential Life Insurance Company of America

KEITH WEIKEL, *Executive Vice President*, Health Care and Retirement Corporation of America

COMMITTEE MEETING OF AUGUST 31–SEPTEMBER 2, 1987

List of Participants

TEXAS

JOHN BRUHN, *Dean*, School of Allied Health, University of Texas Medical Branch, Galveston

YVONNE NEWMAN, *Director*, Health Affairs Division, Texas Higher Education Coordinating Board

PAUL RAMIREZ, *Dean*, Health and Public Services Occupations, El Paso Community College

LEO SELKER, *Assistant to President*, Texas Women's University

ILLINOIS

DAVID BROSKI, *Dean*, College of Associated Health Professions

RODERICK T. GROVES, *Chancellor*, Illinois Board of Regents

ARCH LUGENBEEL, *Dean*, Trident Technical College, Charleston, South Carolina (formerly at Southern Illinois University)

RICHARD TWOREK, *Dean*, Health Services Institute, City Colleges of Chicago

ROBERT A. WALLHAUS, *Deputy Director for Academic Affairs*, Board of Higher Education

NEW YORK

RUTH BAINES, State University of New York, Albany

EDMUND MCTERNAN, *Dean*, State University of New York, Stony Brook

EDWARD SALSBERG, *Director*, Bureau of Health Resources Development, New York State Health Department

LEROY SPARKS, New York City Technical College, Brooklyn

Additional Participants

TULLIO ALBERTINI, Health Resources and Services Administration,
U.S. Department of Health and Human Services
CATHERINE B. JUNGE, U.S. Department of Education
GERRY KAMINSKI, *Dean*, Health Technologies Division, Cincinnati
Technical College

A Sample of Allied Health Job Titles and a Classification of Instructional Programs in Allied Health

ALLIED HEALTH JOB TITLES*

Clinical Laboratory Technology

Associate Laboratory
  Microbiologist
Chemist (Biochemistry)
Laboratory Associate

Laboratory Microbiologist
Laboratory Technician
Principal Microbiologist

Dental Services

Dental Assistant

Dental Hygienist

Dietetic Services

Assistant Director of Food
  Service
Associate Supervising Dietitian

Chief Dietitian
Dietary Aide
Dietitian

Emergency Medical Services

Ambulance Technician
Ambulatory Care Technician

Emergency Medical Service
  Specialist

---

*The job titles were taken from the New York City Health and Hospital Corporation.

Medical Record Services

Assistant Director of Medical
  Record
Assistant Director, Medical
  Record Service
Associate Medical Record
  Specialist

Medical Record Specialist
Senior Medical Record Systems
  Analyst

Occupational Therapy—Occupational Therapist

Physical Therapy—Physical Therapist

Radiological Services

Nuclear Medicine Technician

Radiation Technician

Respiratory Therapy

Respiratory Therapist

Respiratory Therapy Technician

Speech–Language Pathology/Audiology

Audiology Clinician
Speech Clinician

Staff Audiologist
Staff Speech Pathologist

Other

Addiction Counselor
Addiction Specialist
Assistant Addiction Counselor
Assistant Bio-Medical Equipment
  Technician
Assistant Community Liaison
  Worker
Assistant Supervisor of
  Recreation
Bio-Medical Equipment
  Technician
Electrocardiograph Technician

Electroencephalograph
  Technician
Medical Equipment Specialist
Operating Room Technician
Orthoptist
Physician Assistant
Psychiatric Social Health
  Technician
Rehabilitation Counselor
Rehabilitation Technician
Senior Electrocardiograph
  Technician

A CLASSIFICATION OF INSTRUCTIONAL PROGRAMS
IN ALLIED HEALTH

The Classification of Instructional Programs (CIP), developed by the U.S. Department of Education's Center for Educational Statistics (CES) in 1979–1980, was updated for the first time in 1985. CIP is a taxonomy for instructional programs at all levels. It is used in all CES surveys and is the accepted government standard for education information surveys.

17. Allied Health

17.01 Dental Services

>   17.0101 Dental Assisting
>   17.0102 Dental Hygiene
>   17.0103 Dental Laboratory Technology
>   17.0199 Dental Services, Other

17.02 Diagnostic and Treatment Services

>   17.0201 Cardiovascular Technology
>   17.0202 Dialysis Technology
>   17.0203 Electrocardiograph Technology
>   17.0204 Electroencephalograph Technology
>   17.0205 Emergency Medical Technology—Ambulance
>   17.0206 Emergency Medical Technology—Paramedic
>   17.0207 Medical Radiation Dosimetry
>   17.0208 Nuclear Medical Technology
>   17.0209 Radiologic (Medical) Technology
>   17.0210 Respiratory Therapy Technology
>   17.0211 Surgical Technology
>   17.0212 Diagnostic Medical Sonography
>   17.0299 Diagnostic and Treatment Services, Other

17.03 Medical Laboratory Technologies

>   17.0301 Blood Bank Technology
>   17.0302 Chemistry Technology
>   17.0303 Clinical Animal Technology
>   17.0304 Clinical Laboratory Aide
>   17.0305 Clinical Laboratory Assisting
>   17.0306 Cytotechnology
>   17.0307 Hematology Technology
>   17.0308 Histologic Technology

17.0309 Medical Laboratory Technology
17.0310 Medical Technology
17.0311 Microbiology Technology
17.0399 Medical Laboratory Technologies, Other

17.04 Mental Health/Human Services

17.0401 Alcohol/Drug Abuse Specialty
17.0402 Community Health Work
17.0404 Home Health Aide
17.0405 Mental Health/Human Services Assisting
17.0406 Mental Health/Human Services Technology
17.0407 Rehabilitation Counseling
17.0408 Therapeutic Child Care Work
17.0409 Population and Family Planning
17.0410 Sign Language Interpreting
17.0499 Mental Health/Human Services, Other

17.05 Miscellaneous Allied Health Services

17.0502 Central Supply Technology
17.0503 Medical Assisting
17.0504 Medical Illustrating
17.0505 Medical Office Management
17.0506 Medical Records Technology
17.0507 Pharmacy Assisting
17.0508 Physician Assisting
17.0510 Podiatric Assisting
17.0512 Veterinarian Assisting
17.0513 Health Unit Coordinating
17.0514 Chiropractic Assisting
17.0599 Miscellaneous Allied Health Services, Other

17.06 Nursing-Related Services

17.0601 Geriatric Aide
17.0602 Nursing Assisting
17.0605 Practical Nursing
17.0606 Health Unit Management
17.0699 Nursing-Related Services, Other

17.07 Ophthalmic Services

17.0701 Ophthalmic Dispensing
17.0705 Optometric Technology
17.0799 Ophthalmic Services, Other

17.08 Rehabilitation Services

17.0801 Art Therapy
17.0802 Corrective Therapy
17.0803 Dance Therapy
17.0804 Exercise Physiology
17.0806 Music Therapy
17.0807 Occupational Therapy
17.0808 Occupational Therapy Assisting
17.0809 Occupational Therapy Aide
17.0811 Orthotics/Prosthetics
17.0812 Orthopedic Assisting
17.0813 Physical Therapy
17.0814 Physical Therapy Aide
17.0815 Physical Therapy Assisting
17.0816 Recreational Therapy
17.0817 Recreation Therapy Assisting
17.0818 Respiratory Therapy
17.0819 Respiratory Therapy Assisting
17.0820 Speech/Hearing Therapy Aide
17.0822 Recreational Therapy Aide
17.0899 Rehabilitation Services, Other

17.99 Allied Health, Other

17.9999 Allied Health, Other

D

Estimates of the Current Supply of Personnel in 10 Allied Health Fields

Making an accurate assessment of the supply of allied health practitioners in each of the various fields is not easy. For many occupations, there is no reliable data source for either the total number of qualified people, the number working, or the number not working but available if the right market conditions were to occur. BLS uses the Occupational Employment Survey (OES) to collect data on the number of filled jobs. In fields with a high incidence of persons holding multiple jobs, however, BLS data are an inaccurate reflection of the labor force. Another major source of data is the decennial census of the United States, which was last conducted in 1980. These data are now dated, and their definitions of allied health fields often do not match the professions' definitions. A third source of data, memberships of the allied health professional associations, may provide information from only a small fraction of the supply of practitioners. Because not all practitioners in a field are listed as certificate, license, or registration holders and not all listed practitioners are in the active labor force, using these categories as a data source does not always offer accurate representations of the labor force.

Despite these data limitations, some estimates of the supply of practitioners can be made. For example, in fields in which holding multiple jobs is not common, the BLS data closely approximate the number of people working in the field. In addition, professional associations collect data on both the number of qualified practitioners and the number of practitioners active in the field. This appendix presents supply estimates that have been derived from various sources of data. Although it is difficult to pinpoint a "best figure," the estimates can be used to map a reasonable range of the number of people working in each of the 10 fields highlighted in this report.

Dietitians

BLS estimated total dietitian employment in 1986 to be 40,201 positions (38,201 people held wage and salary jobs, and 2,000 people were self-employed dietitians). BLS defines dietitians as people who "organize, plan, and conduct food service or nutritional programs to assist in [the] promotion of health and control of disease." Dietitians "may administer activities of a department providing quantity food service" and "may plan, organize, and conduct programs in nutritional research."

The American Hospital Association's 1985 annual survey indicated that there were 14,993 full- and part-time dietitians employed in U.S. registered hospitals that year. BLS estimates that 37 percent of all dietitians were employed in hospitals in 1986. Assuming that the number of dietitians working in hospitals did not change significantly between 1985 and 1986, and that the number in 1986 was roughly equal to the association's 1985 survey figure, we can then extrapolate from the American Hospital Association data (14,933 dietitians employed/37 percent of dietitians) and estimate that there were about 40,100 dietitians employed in 1986—a figure that confirms the BLS estimate.

The American Dietetic Association reported 44,570 registered active dietitians on its rolls at the end of 1987.

Dental Hygienists

The Occupational Employment Survey defines dental hygienists as people who "perform dental prophylactic treatments and instruct groups and individuals in the care of the teeth and mouth." BLS estimated that dental hygienists filled 86,676 jobs in 1987—none was self-employed. As mentioned earlier, the BLS data pertain to jobs. People who hold more than one job are counted at each job site. Because the practice of holding multiple jobs is common among dental hygienists, the number of dental hygienist jobs that are filled greatly exceeds the number of working dental hygienists.

The Bureau of Health Professions of the Health Resources and Services Administration estimate that there were 45,800 dental hygienists in 1984 filling an estimated 76,000 jobs. Thus, each working hygienist filled an average of 1.66 jobs. Assuming the job-to-hygienist ratio was about the same in 1986 as in 1984, the committee estimates that there were about 52,200 working hygienists in 1986.

Dental hygienists are licensed in every state and the District of Columbia. To obtain a license, a candidate must graduate from a dental hygiene school accredited by the Commission on Dental Accreditation and pass both written and clinical examinations. According to the commission's 1986/1987 annual report, a total of 51,713 students graduated from accredited schools between 1976 and 1986.

Emergency Medical Technicians

BLS estimates that there were 65,229 paid emergency medical technicians (EMTs) in 1986. According to the OES instrument, EMTs "administer first aid treatment and transport sick or injured persons to medical facilities, working as a member of an emergency medical team." EMTs are not ambulance attendants and drivers.

Because there are many volunteer EMTs, the number of paid EMTs understates the true supply of practitioners. The 1985 National Emergency Medical Services Clearinghouse survey indicated that approximately 95,000 EMTs are certified annually in 42 states. However, New York, Texas, and California, three of the most populous states, were not among those reporting. Certification is generally valid for 2 years; the committee therefore estimates that there are at least 200,000 certified EMTs in the United States in any given year.

Medical Laboratory Technologists and Technicians

According to BLS estimates, there were 239,350 jobs for medical laboratory technologists and technicians in 1986 (this figure includes 1,000 self-employed persons). The OES defines medical and clinical laboratory technologists as people who "perform a wide range of complex procedures in the general areas of the clinical laboratory or [who] perform specialized procedures in such areas as cytology, histology, and microbiology." Their "duties may include supervising and coordinating activities of workers engaged in laboratory testing and include workers who teach medical technology when teaching is not their primary activity." Medical and clinical laboratory technicians are defined as persons who "perform routine tests in medical laboratories for use in treatment and diagnosis of disease." They "prepare vaccines, biologicals, and serums for prevention of disease" and "prepare tissue samples for pathologists, take blood samples, and execute such laboratory tests as urinalysis and blood counts." Laboratory technicians "may work under the general supervision of a medical laboratory technologist." Although BLS collects separate data for the two categories of laboratory personnel, the data are combined for reporting purposes.

It is difficult to estimate the ratio of technologists to technicians. Of the 209,000 registrants of the American Society of Clinical Pathologists in 1987, 82 percent were medical technologists. In September 1987 the registry of the National Certification Agency for Medical Laboratory Personnel was composed of 83 percent technologists and 17 percent technicians. If the above ratios are applied to the BLS estimate of total employment of medical laboratory technologists and technicians, the numbers of technologists and technicians in the work force in 1986 would have been about 196,267 and 43,083, respectively. A word of caution is in order, however. Technicians may be less likely than technologists to be certified; thus, our estimate may underrepresent technicians and overrepresent technologists. Unfortunately, there is no easy way to verify the ratio of technicians to technologists.

Medical Record Administrators and Technicians

BLS does not estimate total employment for medical record administrators.

The American Hospital Association's 1985 annual survey shows 7,639 full- and part-time medical record administrators employed in U.S. registered hospitals in that year. If, as indicated by the American Medical Record Association 1986 membership survey, approximately 73 percent of all medical record administrators work in acute care facilities, we can extrapolate from the American Hospital Association data to determine the total number of persons employed as medical record administrators: 10,464. If this is the case, more than 20 percent of people filling medical record administrator jobs must be unregistered because the American Medical Record Association reported only 8,240 registered medical record administators in 1987.

Medical record technician employment was estimated by BLS to be 39,888 in 1986. The OES defines medical record technicians as persons who "compile and maintain medical records of hospital and clinic patients." The American Medical Record Association reported 14,690 accredited record technicians in 1987.

The American Hospital Association's 1985 annual survey shows 43,383 full- and part-time medical record technicians employed in U.S. registered hospitals. This figure is not only substantially higher than the BLS estimate of 24,500 jobs in hospitals, but it is also higher than the BLS estimate of total technicians' jobs in all settings. The reasons for this difference are not known, but they may be sought in an examination of the ways in which job definitions are developed and then interpreted by survey respondents.

Occupational Therapists

BLS estimates that there were 29,355 jobs for occupational therapists in 1985. The OES defines occupational therapists as persons who "plan, organize, and participate in medically oriented occupational programs in hospitals or similar institutions to rehabilitate patients who are physically or mentally ill."

The American Hospital Association 1985 annual survey shows 10,595 full- and part-time occupational therapists employed in U.S. registered hospitals. The American Occupational Therapy Association reports that about 28 percent of its members worked in general and pediatric hospitals in 1986. BLS estimates that 32.5 percent of total occupational therapy employment is in hospitals.

The total active membership of registered occupational therapists in the American Occupational Therapy Association at the end of 1987 was about 27,300. Until mid-1987, registered occupational therapists automatically became members of the association, and the tally of active members represented about 99 percent of the professional work force. Membership in the association is now voluntary.

Physical Therapists

Total 1986 employment of physical therapists was estimated by BLS to be about 61,168 positions, including 5,000 self-employed persons. The OES defines physical therapists as persons who "apply techniques and treatments that help relieve pain, increase the patient's strength, and decrease or prevent deformity and crippling."

The American Physical Therapy Association estimated the number of licensed physical therapists to be 65,890 as of June 1986. All states require practicing professional physical therapists to be licensed.

Radiologic Technologists and Technicians

According to BLS estimates, there were 115,429 jobs for radiologic technologists and technicians in 1986. The OES defines radiologic technologists as persons who "take x-rays, CAT scans, or administer non-radioactive materials into [a] patient's blood stream for diagnostic and therapeutic purposes." Hospitals were asked to include in the category of radiologic technologist all workers whose primary duties were to demonstrate portions of the human body on x-ray film or fluoroscopic screens. Radiologic technicians were defined as persons who "maintain and safely use equipment and supplies necessary to demonstrate portions of the human body on x-ray film or a fluoroscopic screen for diagnostic purposes." Included in the BLS "radiologic technologists and technicians" category are radiation therapists and sonographers. Nuclear medicine technicians are not included.

The Bureau of Health Professions estimates that there were 143,000 radiologic health service workers of all types in 1986, including nuclear medicine technologists.

Nuclear Medicine Technologists

Nuclear medicine technologists "prepare, administer, and measure radioactive isotopes in therapeutic, diagnostic, and tracer studies utilizing a variety of radioisotope equipment." They "prepare stock solutions of radioactive materials and calculate doses to be administered by radiologists." They "subject patients to radiation [and] execute blood volume, red cell survival and fat absorption studies following standard laboratory techniques."

BLS estimates that there were 9,677 nuclear medicine technologist jobs in 1986, of which 89 percent were in hospitals. Over 88 percent of the respondents to a 1987 survey conducted by the Nuclear Medicine Technology Certification Board indicated that they worked in hospitals.

The 1985 American Hospital Association survey of U.S. hospitals indicated that there were 7,972 full- and part-time nuclear medicine technologists employed in U.S. registered hospitals in that year. If approximately 89 percent of all nuclear medicine technologists work in hospitals, the American Hospital Association data suggest that the total number of nuclear medicine technologists employed in 1985 was about 9,000, which is in close agreement with the BLS estimate. The Nuclear Medicine Technology Certification Board reported 10,298 certified technologists in August 1987.

Respiratory Therapists

BLS estimated that there were 56,333 jobs for respiratory therapists in 1986—there were no self-employed respiratory therapists. The OES defines respiratory therapists as persons who "set up and operate various types of equipment, such as iron lungs, oxygen tents, resuscitators, and incubators, to administer oxygen and other gases to patients."

The 1985 American Hospital Association survey indicated that there were 32,623 respiratory therapists employed in U.S. registered hospitals in that year. The American Association for Respiratory Care states that the majority of respiratory care practitioners work in hospitals. BLS estimates that 88 percent of such jobs are to be found in hospitals.

Speech Pathologists and Audiologists

BLS estimates that jobs for speech pathologists and audiologists numbered 45,129 positions in 1986, including 3,000 self-employed practitioners. The OES defines speech pathologists and audiologists as health care practitioners who "examine and provide remedial services for persons with speech and hearing disorders and perform research related to speech and language problems."

The 1985 American Hospital Association survey identified 5,354 speech pathologists and audiologists who were employed in U.S. registered hospitals in that year. If, as BLS states, hospitals provide only about 10 percent of total employment for speech pathologists and audiologists, the total number of speech pathologists and audiologists employed in 1985 would have been about 53,540—substantially higher than the BLS estimate.

There are 56,287 speech pathologists and audiologists who are certified by the American Speech–Language–Hearing Association. Ninety-two percent of certified practitioners are members of the association. Although basic occupational preparation is at the master's level, persons holding only a bachelor's degree in speech pathology and audiology are employed in some settings and may be considered a part of the labor supply. There is no estimate of the number of bachelor's-level practitioners.

E

Projections of Demand and Supply in Occupations

This appendix describes the purposes to which projections of worker demand and supply are put and the characteristics these projections must have if they are to serve these purposes. The various methods that have been used for making projections are summarized, and the limitations of each are discussed. The accuracy and limitations of the methods used by BLS are also considered. A final section points to needed research and suggests how the projections can best be understood and used.

PURPOSES OF PROJECTIONS

Economic history amply demonstrates the rise and fall of industries and of occupations. Fluctuations in supply are most likely in those occupations that require long training periods; this pattern occurs because the supply of workers in a particular field that develops in response to market signals may take years to get through the educational pipeline. Workers investing time and money in education, employers concerned about the availability of skilled workers, and a public interested in stability of wages and prices and in getting services when they need them all have an interest in our ability to anticipate changes in employment at least a few years in the future.

Projections may be made for a variety of purposes, among which are the following:

• evaluating the adequacy of training or education programs in light of the potential need for workers;

- estimating the feasibility of major proposed programs for government expenditure (such as defense, public works, or facilities) in terms of the availability of skilled workers to accomplish or staff them; and
- providing information on future employment opportunities for the guidance of individuals choosing courses of education or training.

Examples of the first of these purposes include the insistence of Congress that federally supported programs of vocational education and training of the unemployed or the disadvantaged be planned with future employment opportunities in mind. Similarly, the congressional consideration of such programs as highway construction, community mental health facilities, and the Strategic Defense Initiative ("Star Wars") programs—to name a few—included an inquiry into the availability of the highly skilled personnel that are required for these projects. BLS launched its occupational outlook research program in 1940 in response to the concern of guidance professionals that young people have adequate information with which to choose among careers. The same motivation lies behind the efforts of state governments to provide local projections of employment growth by occupation.

The rationale and assumptions underlying the projections may differ depending on the purposes these projections must serve. Both vocational guidance and evaluations of the adequacy of training programs to meet future needs for skilled workers call for a realistic estimate of future economic demand in the occupation. Estimating the feasibility of proposed human resources programs, on the other hand, calls for the translation of program goals—whether or not they are realistic—into personnel, and adding to these requirements a realistic estimate of the demand for the same types of workers in the rest of the economy.

On the supply side, vocational guidance purposes require projections of the most probable worker supply in comparison with the economic demand. These types of projections give the best picture of future employment opportunities and the competitive situation in each field. For evaluating the feasibility of a proposed program a forecast of the most probable supply is also desirable; such a forecast would show whether the program can be accomplished without special measures to attract more workers to the field. For appraisals of the adequacy of present training programs, however, a major element of the estimate of future supply—the number of trainees— is the quantity for which the exercise is undertaken, the unknown in the equation, and there is no need to estimate it independently. One way to look at the supply is to treat the losses to the occupation resulting from death, retirements, and net mobility to other occupations as components of "replacement needs." These replacement needs should be added to the estimated growth of the occupation to get the total demand that has to be satisfied by the flow of trainees.

In all of the above, we have discussed demand and supply as though they were independent of each other; in fact, they are interdependent. An increase in demand, by raising wage rates, elicits an increase in supply, and supply also affects demand through its effects on wages and costs. Only when there are constraints on demand, such as those imposed by the technology of an industry (a steel mill cannot employ pastry cooks to roll steel), or constraints on supply, such as limited educational facilities or licensure, is the adjustment of worker demand and supply impeded.

Yet in those occupations that require long periods of education or training, it may take several years for the signal of an increase in demand to fill the educational pipeline and produce an increase in graduates; it is for these occupations that projections are particularly useful in facilitating the adjustment of demand and supply. In the absence of projections, young people have only the current market situation to guide them. If they react strongly to a current shortage of graduates and high salary offers, they may find that when they graduate, 4 years later, the field has become overcrowded and salaries are dropping, conditions that may cause the current year's entrants to avoid the field and precipitate a shortage 4 years later. (The operation of "cobweb" patterns in the labor markets for highly trained workers is demonstrated in a number of papers by Richard Freeman.)

Projection Methods

A variety of methods have been used to project demand and supply. The simplest has been to ask employers how many workers they expect to employ in the future. This method appeals to many people as a straightforward way to tap the expert knowledge of the people who will make the decisions. Yet it has produced such poor results that, after years of use, it was abandoned early in the 1970s. Researchers found that few employers could make the necessary projections of their sales and of technological changes in their industries to develop good estimates of their future occupational requirements. (Indeed, most employers do not reply to the surveys or give casual, off-the-cuff answers.) There is some tendency for each firm to assume it will gain a larger market share; and an offsetting tendency for companies to report that their personnel requirements 5 years in the future will be the same as they are now. Finally, this method makes no allowance for employment in new firms, which, according to some research, are and will be a major provider of additional employment.

A second method that has been used to project demand and supply is to extrapolate past employment trends in the occupation. This method is based on the assumption that, whatever factors have operated in the past will continue to operate. Unfortunately, history is full of instances in which the employment situation changed radically—as any buggy whip manufacturer will attest. Another deficiency of this method is its tendency to treat the occupation as if it were in a vacuum and unrelated to other events in the economy and in society. This limitation is illustrated by the attempt in the early 1950s to extrapolate the growth of the engineering profession by assuming that the exponential growth it had shown would continue. With such growth, engineers would have exceeded the total labor force in a short time, leaving no draftsmen to prepare drawings, no bookkeepers to pay salaries, and no trash collectors to haul away their refuse.

A more sophisticated approach of late has been to associate the growth of an occupation with causative variables that can themselves be projected independently. For example, projections of the population by age have been used to project the demand for teachers: the pupils in elementary grades 6 years hence have already been born, as have those who will be high school students 14 years hence. Changes in pupil–teacher ratios or other strategic variables can be used to modify the results of these projections. Similar methods have been used to project the demand for physicians (Graduate Medical Education National Advisory Committee) and nurses (Western Interstate Committee on Higher Education). In some cases, regression analysis has been used to measure the relative effects of the variables on the result: the projection of employment.

This method may be used to yield estimates of the *need* for workers in the occupation rather than estimates of the economic demand. If the relevant ratios (e.g., the pupil–teacher ratio in the projection of employment for teachers) are set at an ideal level that is nevertheless in line with what experts in the field consider optimum, the resultant projections can be viewed as projections of need. To the extent that they are based on current ratios, which in turn reflect the current market situation, or are adjusted for the future to reflect expected changes in the market situation, the resultant estimate will be closer to an estimate of demand. Each approach serves a different purpose.

The advantages of this approach over the simple extrapolation of past trends are obvious. This method attempts to take into account some of the strategic factors affecting employment. This is not an easy task, however; demand in an occupation may be affected by technological changes; market changes; the way consumers spend their money and the amount of income they have to spend; government expenditures on education, health, highways, and military material; and the capital expenditures of industry. Even more important than these factors are the context of the growth of related occupations and industries and the entire interwoven structure of the economy and of society. When we consider the combination of factors that affect employment in health occupations—for example, the importance of population trends, social trends, income and expenditure patterns, the science and technology of medical practice, the financing of medical care, training and licensure, and the growth and attractiveness of alternative occupations—it becomes apparent that a comprehensive approach is called for.

BLS, which began its research in this area in 1940 and issued its first occupational projection 5 years later, at first tried the approach of studying individual occupations but concluded that a comprehensive analysis was needed. With support from the Veterans Administration (which wanted information to help in the vocational choices of the millions who studied under the World War I G.I. Bill), BLS published outlook information on hundreds of occupations beginning with the first *Occupational Outlook Handbook* in 1949. The handbook has been a biennial publication since the mid-1950s.

The broad occupational coverage, frequent publication, and wide use of the projections (150,000 copies of each edition of the handbook are bought by high schools, colleges, libraries, and community agencies) have had important implications for the research program. Spreading research costs over so many occupations has allowed a more comprehensive approach than could be supported if interest were focused only on a few occupations. The continuing research effort has led to accumulating experience, deepening knowledge of each occupation, and ongoing contacts with industry, professional organizations, unions, and research institutes that are familiar with each field. It has also permitted regular appraisals of the accuracy of the projections and analyses of the possible reasons for errors. As a result of this experience, new research programs and data collection systems have been instituted, an example of which is the occupational employment statistics program begun in the early 1970s. Research is also being conducted on tables of working life and on how people move from one occupation to another, one purpose of which is to develop insight into some of the elements of supply. Over nearly five decades of experience, occupational research methods have changed and improved. The wide publication of the results of such research has ensured that industry and professional groups in each occupation have cooperated with the bureau in giving information and carefully reviewing drafts. The use of research results in schools and in vocational guidance undoubtedly influences the perceptions of students about employment opportunities and the occupational choices they make.

The basic approach followed by BLS is to estimate the employment in each occupation that will be generated by economic demand. This estimate is based on the demand for the goods or services the occupation provides, which in turn is affected by the total spendable income available to consumers and governments and by the changing patterns of what they spend it on. These patterns are influenced by a wide variety of social and economic factors, including changing tastes and styles, scientific discoveries and tech-nological change affecting both what is produced and how it is produced, the growth and changing composition of the population, taxation and government expenditure policies ("guns or butter"), and what other countries are buying from and selling to us.

Producing such estimates is a formidable task, and predicting what will happen in the future on so many different fronts is hazardous. Natural disasters, social cataclysms, and business cycles are hard to predict. Yet some of the changing factors move relatively slowly: there are lags between scientific discoveries and the commercial exploitation of new technology, between the initiation of a new style and its widespread adoption, between the first Japanese automobile sold in the United States and Japan's subsequent market success. These lags mean that useful projections can be produced, provided certain conditions are met: (1) projections are confined to a relatively short time horizon (about 10 years is enough to guide educational policy and the career choices of individuals); (2) sets of alternative projections are made to show the effect, for example, of alternative assumptions as to the state of the economy or the business cycle; (3) events are constantly monitored; (4) the projections are revised at frequent intervals; and (5) continuous research is carried out on the accuracy of the projections and on the adequacy of the methods.

BLS projections begin with the population projections made by Census Bureau demographers. The census data give the number of consumers and are a basis for BLS's projections of the labor force, which are based on the trends in labor force participation by each age, sex, and race group. From the total human resources thus projected, BLS estimates the gross national product (GNP) that will be generated by making assumptions about the growth of output per worker, changing hours of work, and the level of unemployment that must be taken into account. To provide for the uncertainties of the business cycle and to suggest the range of error to users of the projections, three sets of projections are usually made: a "high," "moderate," and "low" forecast. The BLS assumptions about productivity, hours, and unemployment are adjusted to yield an estimate of GNP growth under these three conditions.

This somewhat simplified recital of an elaborate process may give the impression of a mechanical juggernaut that rides roughshod over the entire economy of 110 million people with all its complexity, nuances, and infinite variety, mashing up the professions in which we are interested with masses of coal miners, factory workers, and fast-food slingers. What has not been said is that, at each step of the BLS process, special knowledge is introduced whenever it is available, and the factors that enter into the calculations are adjusted on the basis of information on developing and newly emerging trends in the industry. In the most recent projections, for example, forecasts for the mining industries took into account the latest petroleum import analyses for the target year from the Department of Energy. Projections for the machinery and computer manufacturing industries incorporated analyses of the market situation and foreign competition. Projections for health services considered such developments as cost containment policies, the shift of many surgical procedures to physicians' offices and outpatient facilities, the growth of new group practices and nursing and personal care facilities, and the aging of the population. The bureau's extensive research program on productivity and technological development yields insights about the growth of overall productivity and of productivity in each industry, and the technological developments that affect the numbers and kinds of occupations that are employed. The advantage of the comprehensive interactive approach is that special information or analyses on any aspect of our complex economy can be inserted and implications drawn—not only for a particular occupation or industry but for all of the others as well.

In contrast, there is no unifying and systematic method for projections on the supply side. The supply of workers in an occupation is affected by two factors: (1) the inflow of trainees and of persons who acquire the necessary skills by experience or work in related occupations or by the study of related subjects and (2) the outflow of persons retiring, dropping out of the labor force temporarily, dying, or transferring to other occupations. Supply, of course, is also affected by the relative wages in this and other occupations available to workers.

Projections of the number of college graduates in each field have been published by the Department of Education; they were based on the projected population of the appropriate age and on mathematical extrapolation of trends in the proportion of the population completing college. The total degrees awarded were distributed by field (college majors) using mathematical extrapolation of past trends. Because there was no attempt to take into account the effects of social and market factors on the decisions of young people (except insofar as these factors were embodied in projected past trends), these projections cannot be considered realistic. They do, however, serve a useful purpose: they can be used to illustrate what would happen to the outflow of graduates, an important component of the supply of workers, if nothing happened to change the choices people make about future careers. If such estimates are compared to independent estimates of future demand or the requirements for attaining some national goal such as a proposed community mental health program, a disparity between the projected demand and the projected supply could point to policy measures that might be required to attain the goals (e.g., scholarships or other inducements to undertake training for the occupations).

To determine the outflows and inflows that affect occupational supply, BLS has pursued a number of avenues of research. For example, the bureau has developed tables of working life (similar to life tables), showing the annual attrition to a population at each age, to estimate losses resulting from deaths and retirements. These age-specific rates were then applied to the age composition of each occupation to estimate annual losses. The tables take no account of differences in work life patterns among occupations, however, nor of losses resulting from transfers to other occupations. More recently, studies have been made of transfers into and out of occupations (Eck, 1984), and more complete attrition rates for each occupation have been estimated, including shifts into unemployment and withdrawal from the labor force (either retirement or temporary withdrawal).

BLS does not make projections of worker supply in occupations. It does publish estimates of annual attrition or replacement rates. This information is offered, together with the projected rate of growth in each occupation and information on the unemployment rate, as clues to the employment opportunities in the occupation. The inclusion of information on replacement rates makes clear the point that projected growth alone does not tell the whole story about employment opportunities.

Projections of employment demand for more than 300 occupations are published in technical articles and bulletins. (The most recent projections of general economic growth, industrial growth, and occupations were published in the September 1987 issue of *Monthly Labor Review*). Brief articles on each of about 200 occupations involving relatively long periods of training are published in the *Occupational Outlook Handbook*; profiles of the basic numbers—employment, projected employment growth, unemployment rates, replacement rates, and number of people completing training in a recent year—for about the same number of occupations are published in a series of bulletins called *Occupational Projections and Training Data*, of which the most recent (BLS Bulletin 2206) was issued in 1984.

State and Local Projections

In most states, employment projections for the state and major geographic areas within the state are made by state agencies, most commonly employment security agencies, but sometimes universities or other economic analysis organizations. Until a few years ago, there was a cooperative federal–state relationship in this work, with BLS providing technical consulting and sometimes tabulation work, but this cooperation has been discontinued as a result of budget cuts. The states are continuing their work, however. The National Occupational Information Coordinating Committee, which is composed of representatives of the Departments of Labor and Education, and its affiliated state occupational information coordinating committees give leadership to these efforts.

The states use varying methods, but they all have a few elements in common. The national projections of the growth of industries are generally taken as a framework, and past changes in each state's share of national employment in the industry, together with projections of the state's population and any available input from the economic development agency of the state, are used to project the industry's growth locally. Industry occupational composition data from the Occupational Employment Survey (which is conducted by the state agencies in cooperation with BLS) are used to project employment by occupation. Replacement rates provided by BLS are also published.

Evaluation of BLS Projections and Methods

Any evaluation of BLS's projection methods should begin with a look at the scorecard—that is, at how accurate the projections have been. The bureau has published a number of evaluations of the accuracy of its projections, comparing them to actual employment in each industry and occupation when the target year's statistics become available. The two most recent evaluations will be analyzed here: those for the 1960–1975 projections (Carey, 1980) and the 1970–1980 projections (Carey and Kasunic, 1982). (No more recent evaluations have been published, in part because changes in the classification system for occupations have made it difficult to compare earlier projections with employment data gathered since 1983.)

Comparing a projection that purports to reflect demand, without regard to supply, with the actual employment in the target year is not entirely logical. It is justified only if one can assume that the supply will adjust itself to match the demand, which does not always happen.

There are a number of ways to consider the accuracy of projections. One is to compare the number of workers employed in the target year with the number projected. The purpose of the projections, however, is to anticipate change, to distinguish occupations that are growing rapidly or slowly, and, especially, to perform the more difficult task of identifying occupations that shrink while the economy as a whole is growing. Our evaluation will therefore concentrate on how well the *rate and direction of change* in employment was projected.

To begin with, we must look at the degree of variabilty in growth rates among occupations. If growth rates vary in a narrow range around the average, we would expect projections to be fairly accurate; if growth rates are widely dispersed, the projections may be judged by more lenient standards. Table E-1 arrays the actual changes in employment in occupations included in the two BLS evaluation studies referred to above according to broad groupings of their rates and directions of change as compared to the average change for all occupations.

This little table could well have been made the preface of this paper: it powerfully demonstrates the variability of occupational change, the risk undertaken by anyone who invests in long and expensive training for an occupation, and the difficulties of the forecaster. In a 10- or 15-year period when the average occupation grew by about 30 percent, between one-fifth and one-third of the occupations under study actually experienced declines in employment. The number of occupations that grew at a rate triple the average was about the same as the number that grew at a rate less than the average. There was virtually no clustering around the average. Obviously, occupations are highly volatile in their rates of employment and subject to diverse economic forces.

An evaluation (Goldstein, 1983) of how well the BLS projections for these occupations succeeded in predicting the actual changes shown above concluded that, first, users of the projections had some warning of the declines: 5 of the 16 occupations that declined from 1960 to 1975 had been predicted to decline, and small increases of less than the average had been predicted for the other 11. In the 1970–1980 period, 6 of the 20 occupations that declined had been projected to decline, and small increases of less than the average had been projected for 7 more.

Second, did the projections identify the occupations that were growing rapidly and that needed special attention in planning training programs? In the first period, 21 occupations grew at more than twice the average rate; 15 of them had been projected to grow that fast. In the second period, 14 occupations grew at more than twice the average rate, but in only 2 of them had such growth been projected.

Taking all of the projections together, how close did they come to the actual employment changes that occurred? Going back to the class intervals shown in Table E-1, we might say that if the predicted change was in the

TABLE E-1 Growth Rates in Employment in Occupations with Increases and Decreases in Employment, 1960–1975 and 1970–1985

Item	1960–1975	1970–1985
Average (weighted) change (in percentage) for all occupations	32.6	28.9
Total number of occupations compared	76	64
Occupations with declines in employment	16	20
Occupations with increases in employment	60	44
Below average (more than 10 percent below the average)	11	10
About average (within 10 percent above or below the average)	17	9
Somewhat above the average (between 10 percent above the average and twice the average)	11	11
Twice to triple the average	11	5
More than triple the average	10	9

SOURCE: Carey (1980); Carey and Kasunic (1982).

TABLE E-2 Projected and Actual Employment Changes (percentage) for Six Health Occupations, 1960–1975

Occupation	Projected	Actual
Nurses, professional	73.5	68.5
Dietitians and nutritionists	35.1	44.6
Optometrists	17.6	10.0
Attendants, hospital and other institutions	140.7	122.4
Dentists	43.8	23.1
Physicians, medical and osteopathic	66.7	40.2

SOURCE: Carey (1980); Carey and Kasunic (1982).

same interval as the actual change, it was on target. For the first period, 40 percent of the predictions were on target; for the second, 33 percent were on target. If we consider as reasonably close those predictions that were in the class intervals adjacent to the actual change, we find that 40 percent of the predictions in the first period and 27 percent of those in the second period were reasonably close. By these standards, which are perhaps somewhat lenient but whose leniency is justified by the variability of economic employment changes, we would consider 80 percent of the projections in the first period and 60 percent in the second to be either on target or reasonably close.

Another question that must be answered is: Were the errors biased so that projections were consistently too high or too low? Of all the projections in the first period that were not on target, one-third were too low; in the second period, roughly half were too low. Thus, there is some evidence of a pessimistic bias in the second period.

Our concern in this report is somewhat more narrow, however. We must thus consider how well the method predicts the growth of the the allied health occupations. It is a reasonable hypothesis that the economic, technological, social, and institutional factors that are peculiar to the health industry and its occupations may make the general projection method used by BLS inappropriate for use in these fields.

The evaluation studies we have cited do not include many of the allied health professions, largely because they included only occupations for which the statistics were comparable over the 10- or 15-year spans between the original projections and the target years. The comparison data needed for the allied health professions, with their dynamic changes over recent decades, are not available. Yet we can still test the hypothesis of peculiarity with evaluations of the accuracy of the projections for other health occupations (Tables E-2 and E-3).

It appears that the projections captured the general magnitude of the employment changes in these fields rather better than they did for all of the occupations evaluated earlier in this section, although one could wish

TABLE E-3   Projected and Actual Employment Changes (percentage) for Five Health Occupations, 1970–1980

Occupation	Projected	Actual
Optometrists	20.0	19.4
Osteopaths	43.7	39.3
Physicians and surgeons	48.5	43.3
Registered nurses	42.7	59.9
Dentists	32.0	22.3

SOURCE: Carey (1980); Carey and Kasunic (1982).

for more accurate projections for dentists and physicians in the first period and for nurses in the second. From these data, the hypothesis of peculiarity of the health fields is not supported. Let us turn, however, to some of the aspects of the projection method that raise questions or present problems.

Demand or Requirements?

In traditional economic analysis, demand and supply are equated at a price or wage. Yet there is no explicit evidence of this process in the BLS projection methods. Instead, the employment estimates for future years may be seen as requirements generated by the levels of production or services that the projected economic changes will engender. Indeed, changing relative prices throughout the system could change the projected economic relationship—for example, in tracing the demand for raw materials generated by the production of finished goods. However, the adjustments made at various steps in the projection process to introduce technological change and changes in markets and foreign trade have the effect of inserting price and market changes into the system.

At the end of the process, it is true that there is no systematic attempt to modify the employment estimates for each occupation by a consideration of supply. Indeed, as the forecasters lack projections of supply, this cannot be done. The projections of occupational employment will be consistent with actual employment in the target year only if the supply of trained workers (perhaps forewarned by publication of the estimates or, in the 1960s, responding to policy measures that were designed to raise supply to meet increased demand resulting from new entitlement programs) adjusts to the employer's requirements. Although the projections are not true estimates of demand in the sense of traditional economic concepts, they do come close to the goal of a realistic estimate of the number of jobs that will be offered, as distinct, for example, from an estimate of ideal needs.

Occupational Composition of Industries

Evaluations of the accuracy of the projections made by BLS staff have concluded that the subject industries' total employment was more accurately projected than was employment by occupation. From the foregoing discussion, we might suspect that the lower accuracy of occupational projections may have resulted from the fact that demand had not yet been confronted with supply. If it had, a different level of employment would have emerged.

Less accuracy could also have been the result of the quality of the occupational data; until recently the only reasonably complete source of data on the occupational composition of each industry was the decennial population census. In household surveys such as censuses, people report their occupation by whatever name they have to describe it, telling the census enumerator briefly what activities they perform. These reports are classified by census clerks into the approximately 400 occupations the census tabulates. There is potential error first in the respondent's report: some people overstate their occupational status, as is evident from independent data. Second, the census clerks do not always have enough information to classify the occupations correctly; terminology varies across the country. (The same comments apply to another source of occupational employment data, the Current Population Survey, which is conducted by the Census Bureau. The occupational estimates of this survey are based on a smaller sample than those in the population census and thus have larger sampling errors and somewhat less occupational detail; however, they are available annually.)

To improve the accuracy of occupational composition data, BLS initiated an Occupational Employment Statistics (OES) survey, early in the 1970s in cooperation with state agencies. Employment by occupation is collected from employers by means of a separate questionnaire for each industry that lists the occupations found in that industry. The questionnaire contains brief definitions of the occupations that have been worked out in consultation with employers to ensure understanding and accurate reporting. The sample plants in the survey are chosen to represent all size classes in the industry and to yield accurate estimates.

The survey is limited to wage and salary workers in each industry; BLS adds the self-employed in each occupation using data from the Current Population Survey.

Because it is based on reports from employers, the OES counts each worker more than once if he or she has more than one job at a time. This practice introduces a small inaccuracy in the occupation employment estimates; in the series of surveys of dual job-holding that was made from 1958 to 1980, the number of persons with more than one job averaged about 5 percent of the total employed—the exact figures were 6 percent for men and 3 percent for women.

The BLS estimates count workers whether they work full-time or part-time and do not distinguish between these two categories. Thus, in any occupation, there could be many part-time workers in the figures. In 1986, 18.7 percent of all persons at work were working part-time—5.3 percent for economic reasons (no full-time work was available or they had been temporarily assigned to part-time work) and 13.4 percent because they preferred part-time work. There was more part-time work among women— 27.5 percent of women worked part-time, 6.5 percent for economic reasons and 21 percent voluntarily. The incidence of part-time work varies among occupations, in the occupation group "technicians and related support personnel," in which many allied health professions are included, 12.9 percent of workers were part-time (2.2 percent for economic reasons): among women technicians, 20 percent were on part-time (3.4 percent for economic reasons). (All data in this paragraph are from the Current Population Survey.) There are therefore fewer FTE (full-time equivalent) jobs than the number of people employed in an occupation implies.

The definitions of each occupation worked out for the OES were, as noted above, designed in cooperation with employers to facilitate reporting. The definitions must be understood within the culture of each industry and must be consistent across industries so that the employment estimates for each occupation are additive. This qualification, however, may not always provide the nuances in definition that professional societies—concerned about qualifications, licensure, and similar matters—would like to have. Appendix C lists allied health occupations and related occupation definitions.

We have suggested two reasons for the lower degree of accuracy of the occupational employment projections compared with those for industry employment: (1) the demand projections are not tested against occupational supply and (2) the basic data on the occupational composition of industries used in past projections were inaccurate. We should consider a third reason: the way in which occupational composition is changing is not well understood, and the adjustments inserted into the system to allow for the effects of technological and other changes thus are not adequate.

The theory underlying the use of occupational composition data in forecasts is that the technology of each industry and the way it does its business calls for a unique mix of occupations. In a gross sense, this is certainly true: pastry cooks are not employed in steel-rolling mills. But there could be differences among plants in the same industry that result from differences in processes, in equipment, in the way the work is organized, and in the local supply of trained workers and the extent to which less-trained workers are substituted for them. For those familiar with hospitals and other health service institutions, there is no need to belabor the point that occupational composition may differ from one to another for many reasons.

When the acting commissioner of the Bureau of Labor Statistics first testified before Congress on the request for funds to conduct occupational outlook research, he stated that the research would consider the occupational composition of the most technologically advanced plants in each industry for clues as to the way composition would be changing. Now, nearly half a century later, this kind of analysis is made possible for the first time by the OES. Not only are the occupational statistics better but the collection of reports from individual plants offers a potential that has never before been available except from a few industry wage surveys: The chance to analyze why the occupational composition differs among plants in the same industry and how it is affected by the size of the plant and by new technology—analyses that may lead to better projections of occupational employment.

Staffing of the Projections Research

The number of BLS occupational outlook research staff has been reduced over the past few years as a result of budget cuts, and the burden on individual staff members has therefore increased. With some 200 occupations to cover with articles in the *Occupational Outlook Handbook*, staff are spread thin. Nevertheless, when the National Academy of Sciences staff visited them to discuss their projections, it was found that no fewer than four economists were working on health occupations. They were in touch with developments in their fields and in the health care industry generally and were familiar with the issues and findings of recent studies.

Use of the Projections and Further Research Needs

It should be apparent that forecasting for years in advance is always hazardous and that this truism applies particularly to employment by occupation. While there is always hope that the data and methods will improve in the future, the best we can realistically expect is that the degree of error will be somewhat reduced. The user of projections must bear this in mind and take them as only rough indications of the direction and general magnitude of changes.

Of the projection methods we have reviewed, that of the Bureau of Labor Statistics appears to be the best in its ability to take into account multiple factors. BLS staff have been doing such projections continuously for a long time; they have accumulated experience, knowledge, and contacts in each field; and they check their errors and are innovative in improving data collection and analysis methods.

For any projections of employment in the allied health professions the Institute of Medicine committee would be well advised to build on the work BLS has done—not necessarily to accept the projections without question but to take advantage of the analysis of the framework of the U.S. economy within which the health industry operates, and to examine the assumptions and judgments made by BLS staff in the health fields, modifying them if necessary. Our discussions with BLS staff made it clear that they are earnestly searching for understanding and would welcome any insights that would improve their projections.

Before we can have any assurance that occupational supply can be understood or projected, more research needs to be done on occupational mobility and the factors that determine how people shift employment among occupations. The same may be said about the factors affecting occupational choice.

On the demand side, the weakest link has been in converting projections of employment by industry, which have a fair degree of accuracy, into projections by occupation. Now, however, analysis of the factors that affect the occupational composition patterns of industries can be performed because for the first time we have occupational data for individual plants.

BLS practice in publishing its projections has been to issue only 10-year or longer projections (without the intermediate years). Yet intermediate-year projections are likely to be more accurate because they are closer to what we now know; in addition, they are useful for many purposes. They also lend themselves to more frequent evaluations of accuracy, a practice that, if adopted, would enable BLS to correct its more distant projections.

REFERENCES

Carey, M. L. 1980. Evaluating the 1975 projections of occupational employment. Monthly Labor Review 103(June):10–20.

Carey, M. L., and K. Kasunic. 1982. Evaluating the 1980 projections of occupational employment. Monthly Labor Review 105(July):22–30.

Eck, A. 1984. New occupational separation data improve estimates of job replacement needs. Monthly Labor Review 107(March):3–10.

Goldstein, H. 1983. The accuracy and utilization of occupational forecasting. *In* Responsiveness of Training Institutions to Changing Labor Market Demands, R. E. Taylor, H. Rosen, and F. C. Pratzner, eds. Columbus, Ohio: The National Center for Research in Vocational Education.

Minnesota Sunrise Provisions

MINNESOTA STATUTE 214 (ENACTED 1976), SECTION 214.001

Subdivision 1. The legislature finds that the interests of the people of the state are served by the regulation of certain occupations. The legislature further finds: (1) that it is desirable for boards composed primarily of members of the occupations so regulated to be charged with formulating the policies and standards governing the occupation; (2) that economical and efficient administration of the regulation activities can be achieved through the provision of administrative services by departments of state government; and (3) that procedural fairness in the disciplining of persons regulated by the boards requires a separation of the investigative and prosecutorial functions from the board's judicial responsibility.

Subdivision 2. Criteria for regulation. The legislature declares that no regulation shall be imposed upon any occupation unless required for the safety and well being of the citizens of the state. In evaluating whether an occupation shall be regulated, the following factors shall be considered:

(a) Whether the unregulated practice of an occupation may harm or endanger the health, safety and welfare of citizens of the state and whether the potential for harm is recognizable and not remote;

(b) Whether the practice of an occupation requires specialized skill or training and whether the public needs and will benefit by assurances of initial and continuing occupational ability;

(c) Whether the citizens of this state are or may be effectively protected by other means;

319

(d) Whether the overall cost effectiveness and economic impact would be positive for citizens of the state.

Subdivision 3. If the legislature finds after evaluation of the factors identified in subdivision 2 that it is necessary to regulate an occupation not heretofore credentialed or regulated, then regulation should be implemented consistent with the policy of this section, in modes in the following order:

(a) Creation or extension of common law or statutory causes of civil action, and the creation or extension of criminal prohibitions;

(b) Imposition of inspection requirements and the ability to enforce violations by injunctive relief in the courts;

(c) Implementation of a system of registration whereby practitioners who will be the only persons permitted to use a designated title are listed on an official roster after having met predetermined qualifications [note that legislative action is not required here]; or

(d) Implementation of a system of licensing whereby a practitioner must receive recognition by the state that he has met predetermined qualifications, and persons not so licensed are prohibited from practicing.

MINNESOTA RULES 4695.0800: FACTORS FOR DETERMINING THE NECESSITY OF REGULATION

Subpart 1. Consideration of factors. In the review of an applicant group questionnaire, the subcommittee, council, and commissioner shall base their recommendation or decision as to whether or not the applicant group shall be regulated upon the factors contained in Minnesota Statutes, section 214.001, subdivision 2.

Subpart 2. Factor of unregulated practice. In applying the factor of whether the unregulated practice of an occupation may harm or endanger the health, safety, and welfare of citizens of the state and whether the potential for harm is recognizable and not remote, at minimum the relevance of the following shall be considered:

A. harm shall be construed to be a condition representative of physical, emotional, mental, social, financial, or intellectual impairment resulting from the functions rendered or failed to be rendered by the applicant group;

B. potential for harm may be recognizable when evidenced by at least one or more of the following: expert testimony; client, consumer, or patient testimony; research findings; legal precedents, financial awards, or judicial rulings;

C. potential for harm may be recognizable when evidenced by at least one or more of the following characteristics of the applicant group;

(1) inherently dangerous nature of the applicant group's functions;

(2) dangerous nature of devices or substances used in performing applicant group's functions;

(3) exercise by practitioners of the applicant groups of an observable degree of independent judgment when: identifying or evaluating a consumer's or client's symptoms; formulating a plan for consumer or client care, service delivery or treatment; and/or providing consumer or client care, delivering service, or implementing a plan of treatment;

D. potential for harm may be remote when evidenced by at least one or more of the following: infrequent or rare instances of impairment; impairment which is minor in nature; or secondary or tertiary effects of the applicant group's function.

Subpart 3. Occupation requiring special skill factor. In applying the factor of whether the practice of an occupation requires specialized skill or training and whether the public needs and will benefit by assurances of initial and continuing occupational ability, the existence of the following items shall be considered as indicating that specialized skill or training or their continuation is required:

A. that the functions performed by the practitioner are several and their performance necessitates a thorough understanding of the complex relationship between those functions;

B. that the one or more functions performed by the practitioner requires a detailed understanding of the specific components of the function and the relationship between the functions and the symptoms, problem, or condition that function is intended to address or ameliorate;

C. that the absence of specialized skill or training is likely to increase the incidence and/or degree of harm as defined in subpart 2 to the consumer as client; and

D. that there occur frequent or major changes in areas of skilled knowledge and technique of which the practitioner must keep informed in order to meet current standards.

Subpart 4. Factor of more effective means. In applying the factor of whether the citizens of this state may be effectively protected by other means, at a minimum the relevance of the following shall be considered:

A. Indicators of protection by other means shall include but not be limited to:

(1) supervision by practitioners in a regulated occupation;

(2) existence of laws governing devices and substances used in the occupation;

(3) existence of laws governing the standard of practice;

(4) existence of standards for professional performance;

(5) employment in licensed human service facilities which are required to employ competent staff;

(6) existence of federal licensing as credentialing mechanism;

(7) existence of civil service procedures which effectively screen potential employees for competence;

(8) graduation of members of the applicant group from an accredited educational institution or training program;

(9) mandatory participation in on-the-job training programs which are required by law or by professional organization of the occupation;

(10) existence of professional credentials and standards of performance which effectively sanction malpractice; and

(11) existence of a national certification process which effectively attests to the competency of recognized professionals.

B. Indicators of protection by other means shall be assessed and evaluated at least in view of the extent to which they:

(1) address all practitioners within an occupational group;

(2) appear sufficient to protect the general public from harm caused by the practice of the occupation in question; and

(3) appear to be permanent and ongoing mechanisms.

Subpart 5. Overall cost effectiveness and economic impact. In determining whether the overall cost effectiveness and economic impact would be positive for citizens of the state, the following shall be considered:

A. Positive cost effectiveness and economic impact results where the benefits expected to accrue to the public from a decision to regulate an occupation are greater than the costs resulting from that decision.

(1) Cost effectiveness means the relationship of the benefits anticipated from a decision to regulate an occupation to the overall costs to the public resulting from that decision.

(2) Economic impact means the direct and indirect effects on the price and supply of services provided by the occupation under consideration for regulation. Direct effects include impacts on the cost and supply of practitioners who would be regulated. Indirect effects include: the degree to which the existing practitioners will be precluded from practice because of regulation; the degree to which persons aspiring to practice the occupation, who if not for regulation could practice the occupation successfully, but will be prohibited because of inability to meet entry requirements; impact on ability of minorities or protected classes to enter occupation; or impact on innovations in the delivery of care or services as a result of regulation.

(3) Costs of a decision to regulate include the estimated costs to state and local governments of administering the proposed regulatory program; educational requirements and training costs including costs

associated with experiential requirements of the proposed mode of regulation; and costs to the public such as reduced or increased access by potential or existing providers to labor markets.

(4) Benefits of a decision to regulate an occupation include access to less expensive but similar providers; measurable improvements in quality of care; reductions in costs of services; process for seeking redress for injury from malpractice, or other unprofessional conduct; and reduction in the potential for public harm from unregulated practice.

B. Cost effectiveness and economic impact can be evaluated through consideration of the following factors:

(1) degree to which regulation directly or indirectly impacts the costs and prices of goods or services provided by applicant group;

(2) impact upon the current and future supply of practitioners of the regulated occupation;

(3) degree to which existing practitioners will be precluded from practice because of regulation;

(4) impact, if any, on innovations in delivery of care or services as a result of regulation;

(5) costs of additional education and training required as a result of the regulation of the occupation;

(6) manner in which and degree to which regulation will result in improvement in the quality of care;

(7) degree to which services of the applicant group substitute for currently regulated occupations and estimated comparative cost of applicant group and currently regulated practitioners;

(8) degree to which services of the applicant group supplement currently regulated occupations;

(9) whether regulation confers or facilitates access to reimbursement for government assistance programs such as Medicare and Medicaid; estimated impact on programs and budgets; and

(10) impact on expenditures by government and private third party payors, if any, resulting from regulation of the occupation.

APPENDIX
G

National Commission for Health Certifying Agencies' Criteria for Approval of Certifying Agencies

A certifying agency responsible for attesting to the competency of health care practitioners has a responsibility to the individuals desiring certification, to the employers of those individuals, to those agencies that reimburse for the services, and to the public. The National Commission for Health Certifying Agencies was formed to identify how those varying responsibilities can be met and to determine if a certifying agency meets those responsibilities. Membership of a certifying agency in the Commission indicates that the certifying agency has been evaluated by the Commission and deemed to meet all of the established criteria. In order to be "approved" for membership in the commission, a certifying agency* shall meet the following criteria:

1. Purpose of Certifying Agency
   a. shall have as a primary purpose the evaluation of those individuals who wish to enter, continue and/or advance in the health professions, through the certification process, and the issuance of credentials to those individuals who meet the required level of competence.

2. Structure
   a. shall be non-governmental;
   b. shall conduct certification activities which are national in scope;

---

*Amended December 1984. The term *certifying agency* as used in this document means an independent, not-for-profit certifying agency or a not-for-profit association with a certifying component.

    c. shall be administratively independent* in matters pertaining to certification, except appointment of members of the governing body of the certifying agency. A certifying agency which is not a legal entity in and of itself shall provide proof that the agency's governing body is administratively independent in certification matters from the organization of which it is a part;

    d. shall have a governing body which includes individuals from the discipline being certified. A certifying agency which certifies more than one discipline or more than one level within a discipline shall have representation of each on the governing body;

    e. shall require that members of the governing body who represent the certified profession shall be selected by the certified profession or by an association of the certified profession and such selection shall not be subject to approval by any other individual or organization;

    f. shall have formal procedures for the selection of members of the governing body which shall prohibit the governing body from selecting its successors;

    g. shall provide evidence that the public consumer and the supervising professional and/or employers of the health professionals have input into the policies and decisions of the agency, either through membership on the governing body or through formalized procedures as advisors to the governing body. This criterion is effective January 1, 1981; and

    h. the certifying body of a professional organization shall be separate from the accrediting body of the professional association.

3. Resources of Certifying Agencies
    a. shall provide evidence that the agency has the financial resources to properly conduct the certification activities;
    b. shall provide evidence that the staff possesses the knowledge and skill necessary to conduct the certification program or has available and makes use of non-staff consultants and professionals to sufficiently supplement staff knowledge and skill.

4. Evaluation Mechanism
    a. shall provide evidence that the mechanism used to evaluate individual competence is objective, fair and based on the knowledge and skills needed to function in the health profession;

Administratively independent means that all policy decisions relating to certification matters are the sole decision of the certifying body and not subject to approval by any other body and that all financial matters related to the operation of the certifying component are segregated from those of the professional association.

b. shall have a formal policy of periodic review of evaluation mechanisms and shall provide evidence that the policy is implemented to insure relevance of the mechanism to knowledge and skills needed in the profession;

c. shall provide evidence that appropriate measures are taken to protect the security of all examinations;

d. shall provide evidence that pass/fail levels are established in a manner that is generally accepted in the psychometric community as being fair and reasonable. This criteria is effective January 1, 1981, after standards are established; and

e. shall provide evidence that the evaluation used evidence of attempts to establish both reliability and validity for each form of the examination.

5. Public Information
   a. shall publish a document which clearly defines the certification responsibilities of the agency and outlines any other activities of the agency which are not related to certification;
   b. shall make available general descriptive materials on the procedures used in test construction and validation and the procedures of administration and reporting of results;
   c. shall publish a comprehensive summary or outline of the information, knowledge, or functions covered by the test; and
   d. shall publish at least annually, a summary of certification activities, including number tested, number passing, number failing, number certified and number recertified (if agency conducts a recertification program).

6. Responsibility on Applicants for Certification or Recertification
   a. shall not discriminate among applicants as to age, sex, race, religion, national origin, handicap or marital status and shall include a statement of non-discrimination in announcement of the certification program;
   b. shall provide all applicants with copies of formalized procedures for application for, and attainment of, certification and shall provide evidence to the Commission that such procedures are uniformly followed and enforced for applicants;
   c. shall have a formal policy for the periodic review of application and testing procedures to insure that they are fair and equitable and shall give evidence to the Commission of the implementation of the policy;
   d. shall publicize nationally appropriate data concerning certification program including eligibility requirements for certification, basis of examination, dates and places of examinations;

e. shall provide evidence that competently proctored testing sites are readily accessible in all areas of the nation at least once annually;

f. shall publicize nationally the specific education background or employment backgound required for certification;

g. shall give evidence that a means exists for individuals who have obtained a skill or knowledge outside the formal educational setting to be evaluated and obtain certification or in the absence of such means, provide reasonable justification for exclusion. These means employed should be consistent with the evaluation standards. The criterion is effective January 1, 1982;

h. shall provide evidence of uniformly prompt reporting of test results to applicants;

i. shall provide evidence that applicants failing the examination are given information on general areas of deficiency;

j. shall provide evidence that each applicant's test results are held confidential;

k. shall have a formal policy on appeal procedures for applicants questioning examination results and shall publish this information in examination announcements; and

l. shall have a formal policy, acceptable to the Commission, delineating grounds, based on applicants prior or current conduct, for refusing applicants eligibility to take the certification examination and shall provide applicants the opportunity to present their cases to an impartial decisionmaker in the event of denial of eligibility or denial of certification. (Effective January 1, 1987)

7. Responsibilities to the Public and to Employers of Certified Personnel

a. shall drive to insure that the examination adequately measures the knowledge and skill required for entry, maintenance and/or advancement into the profession;

b. shall provide evidence that the agency awards certification only after the skill and knowledge of the individual has been evaluated and determined to be acceptable;

c. shall periodically publish a list of those persons certified by the agency;

d. shall have a formal policy and procedure for discipline of certificants, including the sanction of revocation of the certificate, for conduct which clearly indicates incompetence, unethical behavior and physical or mental impairment affecting performance that is acceptable to the Commission. These procedures shall incorporate due process (effective January 1, 1987);

e. any title or credential awarded by the credentialing body shall appropriately reflect the practitioner's daily occupational duties

and shall not be confusing to employers, consumers, health professionals and/or other interested parties (effective January 1, 1985);
The membership committee may consider the following factors
in determining whether practitioner's titles or credentials comply
with this criterion:

(i) educational background;

(ii) function of profession;

(iii) occupational duties and breadth of these activities;

(iv) level of supervision by other practitioners, or of any other
practitioners; and

(v) various titles already in the field, other titles considered,
and a justification of why these titles were not utilized or
why they were changed.

8. Recertification*

a. shall have in existence or shall be in the process of developing a
plan for periodic recertification:

b. shall provide evidence that any recertification program is designed
to measure continued competence or to enhance the continued
competence of the individual.

9. Responsibilities to Commission

a. shall provide the Commission on a regular basis with copies of all
publications related to the certifying process;

b. shall advise the Commission of any change in purpose, structure
or activities of the certifying agency;

c. shall advise the Commission of substantive change in test administration procedures;

d. shall advise the Commission of any major changes in testing techniques or in the scope or objectives of the test; and

e. shall undergo re-evaluation by the Commission at five year intervals.

---

*In this document the term *recertification* includes periodic renewal or revalidation of
certification based on reexamination, continuing education, or other methods developed by
the certifying agency. This criterion is effective January 1, 1982.

Source Material

American Dietetic Association. 1972. The Profession of Dietetics: Report of the Study Commission on Dietetics. Chicago: American Dietetic Association.

American Dietetic Association. 1985. A New Look at the Profession of Dietetics: Report of the 1984 Study Commission on Dietetics. Chicago: American Dietetic Association.

American Medical Association. 1987. Allied Health Education Directory—1987. Chicago: American Medical Association.

American Physical Therapy Association. 1979. The beginnings of "modern physiotherapy." *In* The Beginnings: Physical Therapy and APTA. Washington, D.C.: American Physical Therapy Association.

American Physical Therapy Association. Undated (ca. 1980). A Decision for Change. Alexandria, Va.: American Physical Therapy Association.

American Society of Clinical Pathologists. 1987. Board of Registry Newsletter. March.

Biglow, L. A. 1982. Medical records education: An historical perspective. Journal of American Medical Records Association, August.

Burton, G. G., and J. E Hodgkin. 1984. Respiratory Care, 2nd ed. Philadelphia: J. B. Lippincott.

Coltey, R. W. 1978. Survey of Medical Technology, Chap. 1. St. Louis, Mo.: C. V. Mosby.

Corbett, F. R. 1909. The training of dietitians for hospitals. Journal of Home Economics, 1(62). Cited in American Dietetic Association. 1985. A New Look at the Profession of Dietetics: Report of the 1984 Study Commission on Dietetics. Chicago: American Dietetic Association.

Fay, M. 1979. Changing radiologic technology education: Evolution or revolution? Part I. Radiologic Technology 50(6):667–673.

Fay, M. 1979. Changing radiologic technology education: Evolution or revolution? Part II. Radiologic Technology 51(1).

Firestone, D. T., and C. Lehmann. In press. Changing roles for changing times. Journal of Medical Technology.

Grunewald, L. R. 1928. The study of physiotherapy as a vocation. Part IV. The Physiotherapy Review 8(5).

Hardwick, D. F., J. I. Morrison, and P. A. Cassidy. 1985 Perspectives in pathology: Clinical laboratory—past, present, and future. An opinion. Human Pathology 16(3):206–211.

Hazenhyer, I. M. 1946. A history of the American physiotherapy association. The Physiotherapy Review 26(1). Reprinted in American Physical Therapy Association. The Beginnings: Physical Therapy and the APTA. Washington, D.C.: American Physical Therapy Association.

Hopkins, H. L. 1983. An historical perspective on occupational therapy. *In* Willard and Spackman's Occupational Therapy, 6th ed., H. L. Hopkins and H. D. Smith, eds. Philadelphia: J. B. Lippincott.

Ikeda, K. 1971. Twelve years of the registry. Cited in R. M. Williams. 1971. An Introduction to the Profession of Medical Technology. Philadelphia: Lea & Febiger.

Journal of the American Medical Association. 1929/1971. Vol. 92:1052. Cited in R. M. Williams. 1971. An Introduction to the Profession of Medical Technology. Philadelphia: Lea & Febiger.

Karni, K. R., G. D. Price, and E. C. St. John. 1986. Perspectives in clinical laboratory education. Journal of Medical Technology 3(2).

Laboratory Medicine. 1982. Professionals levels definition.Vol. 13(5):312–313.

Lanrose, N. 1983. Assessment and Intervention in Emergency Nursing. Bowie, Md.: R. J. Brady. Cited in J. I. McKay. 1985. Historical review of emergency medical service, EMT roles, and EMT utilization in emergency departments. Journal of Emergency Nursing 11(1):27–32.

Lunz, M. E. 1987. The impact of the quality of laboratory staff on the accuracy of laboratory results. Journal of the American Medical Association 258(3):361–363.

Medical Record News. 1978. AMRA: The first 20 years. August.

Motley, W. E. 1983. History of the American Dental Hygienists' Associations. 1923–1982. Chicago: American Dental Hygienists' Association.

Paden, E. P. 1970. A History of the American Speech and Hearing Association. Washington, D.C.: American Speech and Hearing Association.

Pennell, M. Y., and D. B. Hoover. 1970. Health Manpower Source Book—Section 21, Allied Health Manpower, 1950–1980. Bethesda, Md.: National Institutes of Health.

Rockwood, C. A., C. M. Mann, J. D. Farrington, O. P. Hampton, and R. E. Motley. 1976. History of emergency medical services in the United States. Journal of Trauma 16(4):299–308.

Spahr, F. T. 1985. 1985 ASHA Directory Supplement. Rockville, Md.: American Speech–Language–Hearing Association.

Torres, H. O., and A. Ehrlich. 1976. Modern Dental Assisting, Chap. 1. Philadelphia: W. B. Saunders.

U. S. Department of Commerce, Bureau of the Census. Statistical Abstracts of the United States. 1987. Washington, D.C.: Government Printing Office.

U. S. Department of Health, Education, and Welfare. 1979. A Report on Allied Health Personnel. Washington, D.C.: Government Printing Office.

Williams, R. M. 1971. An Introduction to the Profession of Medical Technology. Philadelphia: Lea & Febiger.

Index